CYNTHIA OZICK'S
FICTION

Jewish Literature and Culture
Series editor, Alvin H. Rosenfeld

CYNTHIA OZICK'S FICTION

Tradition & Invention

ELAINE M. KAUVAR

Indiana University Press
Bloomington and Indianapolis

The paper used in this publication meets the minimum requirements of American
National Standard for Information Sciences—Permanence of Paper for Printed
Library Materials, ANSI Z39.48-1984.

(∞)™

Manufactured in the United States of America

Library of Congress Cataloging-in-Publication Data
Kauvar, Elaine M. (Elaine Mozer), date.
  Cynthia Ozick's fiction: tradition and invention / Elaine M.
Kauvar.
      p.   cm.—(Jewish literature and culture)
  Includes bibliographical references and index.
  ISBN 0-253-33129-3 (cloth)
  1. Ozick, Cynthia—Criticism and interpretation. 2. Jews in
literature. I. Title. II. Series.
PS3565.Z5Z67 1993   92–19603
813'.54—dc20

      1   2   3   4   5   97   96   95   94   93

For Erwin and Evelyn

For within all human groups tradition demands an absolutely central position, even as the creative impulse, which insinuates itself into every tradition, calls our attention to the living relationship of giving and receiving. We desire to understand how the given and the spontaneous—that which newly flows into the stream of tradition—are combined in passing on the patrimony of each generation to the next.

—Gershom Scholem

Your pier-glass or extensive surface of polished steel made to be rubbed by a housemaid, will be minutely and multitudinously scratched in all directions; but place now against it a lighted candle as a centre of illumination, and lo! the scratches will seem to arrange themselves in a fine series of concentric circles round that little sun. It is demonstrable that the scratches are going everywhere impartially, and it is only your candle which produces the flattering illusion of a concentric arrangement, its light falling with an exclusive optical selection. These things are a parable.

—George Eliot

Contents

Preface

Her apprehension of the perilousness of idolatry, her allegiance to the judgments of history, her concept of tradition as itself innovation—these convictions have increasingly occasioned the speculation that Cynthia Ozick may eventually be judged our T. S. Eliot. Like Eliot, she urges a return to tradition, a celebration of the "singularity of culture"; she shares his historical sense, and there is ample evidence she shares as well his obeisance to high art. In her essay "T. S. Eliot at 101," published in 1989, she announces her unwillingness to renounce the legacy of the Eliot era: "I admit in some respects, to being arrested in the Age of Eliot, a permanent member of it, unregenerate. The etiolation of high art seems to me to be a major loss. I continue to suppose that some texts are worthier than other texts. The same holds for the diminishment of history and tradition: not to incorporate into an educable mind the origins and unifying principles of one's own civilization strikes me as a kind of cultural autolobotomy" (124). For Cynthia Ozick as for T. S. Eliot, high art is defined by its permanent receptiveness to history and by the complexity a historical consciousness imparts. To countenance novelty over history or to prize invention over tradition is to have relinquished the exhilaration and nobility of high art and to belong instead to an age for which history has lost its authority, an age that spurns belief in art's redemptive power; it is to be consigned to the fate of our times.

Ceding to Eliot's poetic powers and according him the influence he once commanded, Ozick nonetheless seizes the facts of the poet's life and employs them in the service of literary interpretation, thus breaching the wall surrounding that celebrated formulation—the objective correlative. And she pierces through to the reasons the author of the objective correlative espoused an exclusionary conception of civilization. In fact, she accomplishes exactly what Eliot's formulation was designed to prevent: the exposure of the personal, but that is precisely where the storyteller finds the secrets that animate the poet's metaphors. Perhaps hers is an unfashionable position; it is certainly one Eliot reviled. What he sought to mask, Ozick seeks to unmask. Their views are instructively divergent: for Eliot the mind that creates was separate from the man who suffered; for Ozick they are inseparable and their union exhibits itself in the forms she declares twins, the biography and the novel. Her conviction amounts to a revision of an idea once so revered and so influential as to be embraced as a given. More importantly, Ozick's new formulation intimates the necessity for literary critics to be awakened to the fact of an "inexorable and undivorceable" marriage between biography and art.[1] Lamenting the loss of knowledge "saturated in historical memory," the "passion for inheritance," the "sense of connecting the present with the past"—the chief tenets of the Eliot epoch—Ozick gives every sign of wanting to reclaim the power high art possessed while disclaiming the reactionary views of its leader. Her inspired

linkage of art and biography, her persistence in writing lives or imagining biographies—these may well be among the elements of a new age, one that
harks back to tradition as the source for invention. But precisely how those
convictions shape her imaginative processes has yet to be fully explored. It
seems more essential than ever to reassess her fiction, to provide a reading that
exposes the substructure of her texts, examines the themes that obsess her
tales, reveals their shifting perspectives and competing ideas, and conse-
quently, establishes Cynthia Ozick's place in contemporary American letters.

That is the aim of *Cynthia Ozick's Fiction: Tradition and Invention,* a
chronological reading which traces the development of the storyteller's
thought and art, illuminates their intricacies, elucidates patterns, and detects
interconnections that have eluded attention. Emphasizing the themes that obsess Ozick's fiction—the battle between Hebraism and Hellenism, the lure of
paganism and the dangers of idolatry, the implications and consequences of
assimilation, the perplexities of the artist and the besetting dangers of art—I
demonstrate the dialectic existing between the tales, the storyteller's habit of
doubling both within tales and between them.

Of crucial importance to understanding Ozick's oeuvre, *Trust,* the subject
of chapter 1, has been mainly misunderstood or entirely neglected for over
twenty-five years. It reveals that from the very beginning of her career Cynthia
Ozick has engaged with what many postmodern writers have largely repudiated; for her the principle of continuity overwhelmingly takes precedence over
the desire to create new forms and the decision to use the self as the source for
fiction. Moreover, *Trust* makes the storyteller's passionate commitment to
high art abundantly clear, calling into question the prevailing assumption that
Ozick's is a "religious point of view."[2] *Trust,* I maintain, belongs not to religion but to the tradition of the great nineteenth-century novels. Reflecting the
historical presence common to fiction of that century—its concern for an informing moral imagination, its belief in human volition—Ozick's first novel is
imbued with values which, for the most part, have all but disappeared, so
meaningless have they become to writers at the end of the twentieth century.

Never a writer interested in rupture or "the new," Cynthia Ozick recounts
in *Trust* a tale that grows out of a long tradition—the son's quest for a father.
But she revises that tradition when she places at the heart of her novel a
daughter's effort to find a father and when she adds to the search for identity
an exploration of the three cultural forces in western history. Central to the
novel is a conundrum, the identity of the nameless narrator's father, the mystery the narrator seeks to unravel. To decipher it is to recover her own history.
For Ozick, however, history is necessary but insufficient: to own a future is
not only to redeem the past, it is to judge its meaning. Her conviction—"history as a judgment on events"—along with the importance she ascribes to
memory, informs all of Cynthia Ozick's art. To appreciate it, to begin to
fathom its depths, we must realize that its predominating themes originate in
Trust, for as I apprehend it and as I show through the seven chapters of *Cynthia Ozick's Fiction,* that novel is one to which we much continually return if

we are to understand fully the storyteller's cognition of history and memory, not to mention the various meanings Ozick attaches to the father, to whom she attributes a significance that transcends the personal.

Just as for Ozick it is not enough to regain one's history, it is not adequate merely to discover the self, for the self, as she perceives it, is inextricably tied to the apprehension of culture. For that reason, she includes three fathers, embodiments of three cultures, in *Trust;* for that reason, her narrator must distinguish among their beliefs. Dismissed by her "not father," a Christian, at the end of part 3, the narrator is left with her stepfather, Enoch Vand, a Jew, and her real father, Gustave Nicholas Tilbeck, a pagan. They epitomize the conflict central to Ozick's work—the battle between Hebraism and Hellenism—whose terms Enoch Vand sets forth in his essay, "Pan Versus Moses," and whose modalities I chart in my first chapter. Although the narrator undergoes an initiation rite under her father's tutelage and obtains an answer to the enigma at the core of her existence, allowing her to achieve independence, at the end of the novel she remains caught between two world views and, as I argue, she does not attain a resolution. Out of her "struggle for exactitude" come Cynthia Ozick's portrait of the artist as a young woman, the convictions crucial to her art, the path the storyteller's own fiction follows. And the matrix for its ideas, I insist, resides in *Trust*.

Her next two volumes of fiction, *The Pagan Rabbi* and *Bloodshed,* are the concern of my second and third chapters. How Ozick develops the ideas appearing first in *Trust,* often turning them inside out to consider them from another perspective, constitutes the focus of my discussion; for I see the existence of opposing ideas in *The Pagan Rabbi* and *Bloodshed* as manifestations of the dialectical strategies characteristic of an Ozick text. If, for example, *The Pagan Rabbi* limns the strife over an inherited tradition, *Bloodshed* portrays the betrayal of that tradition. Faced with competing traditions at the end of *Trust,* the narrator chooses neither her father's paganism nor her stepfather's Judaism; however, I show the generations at war in *The Pagan Rabbi* and Ozick widening the dichotomy between Judaism and paganism into an expression of art's predicaments.

Juxtaposing the father, from whom the son inherits a tradition, and the son, who is vital to her principle of continuity, the storyteller depicts the fundamental ambivalence a father's transmission provokes and the dissension existing between the artist and tradition. Doubling and dividing, a pattern whose prominence I divulge in my chapter on *Trust,* mark that ambivalence, demonstrate the contrary attitudes Cynthia Ozick entertains simultaneously, and accentuate the doubleness she perceives clinging to all existence. The ways in which her vision informs the structure of *The Pagan Rabbi* and *Bloodshed* shape my discussions of those volumes, for I argue she pairs tales in order to scrutinize ideas from disparate angles. And they form the poles of her ongoing dialectic. Of paramount importance to my exegeses of Ozick's second and third collections of tales are the conclusions that in *Trust* the search for a father and a tradition becomes in *The Pagan Rabbi* and *Bloodshed* an exploration of

tradition and its discontents and that from her third volume of tales emerge
Cynthia Ozick's meditations on tradition, the storyteller's apprehension of the
Second Commandment, a nuanced perception of idolatry.

But if, as Ozick proclaims in the preface, the tales in *Bloodshed* move
steadily to a resolution—that the "story-making faculty itself can be a corridor
to the corruptions and abominations of idol-worship, of the adoration of
magical-event"—I demonstrate in my fourth chapter, "The Uses of Fantasy,"
how in *Levitation* she challenges the implications of the very resolution she
reaches at the end of *Bloodshed*. Emphasizing the tribal in her second volume
of tales, Ozick adduces the nature of the artistic imagination in her third volume. The themes reverberating throughout *Levitation* affirm the principle of
continuity and uphold the father as the agent of transmission. What *Levitation*
ultimately furnishes, I believe, are portraits of artists which render conflicting
ideas toward the idea of tradition and its value to the writer. Of the necessity
for maintaining tradition Cynthia Ozick is certain; about its meaning to the
writer, I establish her as less decisive, for I constantly call attention to the dynamics of her dialectic, her habit of juxtaposing competing ideas. In fact, my
chapter on *Levitation* begins with a discussion of its title story that stresses
how in pairing it with "Usurpation," the last tale in *Bloodshed*, the storyteller
advances that dialectic, trains her lens on writers' lives, and ends her third collection of stories with a novella that integrates all of the tales' concerns in a
full-fledged biography of an artist.

If *Trust* depicts the artist as a young woman, the concluding fiction in *Levitation* unfolds the tale of a middle-aged attorney who initially represses her
creative urges by proclaiming the primacy of her reason. In fervently restrain-
ing them, the attorney seeks on the one hand to obey the laws of her tradition—hence her denial of imagination; and on the other hand she aspires to a
forbidden competition with the Creator—hence her unconscious fabrication
of a golem. The clash between the law and the imagination, a resounding one
in *Trust*, predominates in "Puttermesser and Xanthippe." But the narrator's
quest for a self in *Trust* becomes in "Puttermesser and Xanthippe" the effort
to conquer the self; for unlike the girl in *Trust*, Ruth Puttermesser knows the
identity of both her parents and embraces the values of her tradition until her
desire to create ultimately escalates into a fight against veneration, a transgression of the Second Commandment. The age-old debate between Hebraism
and Hellenism in Cynthia Ozick's first novel develops, I point out, into a conflict which must perforce confront the artist as she endeavors to accommodate
the passion for creativity with the demands of responsibility.

In my fifth chapter, "The High Muse of Fusion," I ascertain that the novelist undertakes to resolve that conflict in her second novel, *The Cannibal Galaxy*. Choosing a failed astronomer as her main character, Ozick recounts his
history. After escaping the Holocaust, Joseph Brill turns his energies toward
founding a school with a Dual Curriculum. Beleaguered by his lifelong divided
sensibility, Brill tries to unify it by linking Scripture and art so that art and
Judaism can coexist peacefully. Fundamental to that desire, I aver, are Ozick's

attempts to bring together the artistic imagination and moral responsibility, for the storyteller extends the split between the Jewish and the gentile civilizations into a metaphor for art itself. Furthermore, the intense ambivalence between the generations in *The Cannibal Galaxy*, the travails of which I delineate in my chapter on *The Pagan Rabbi*, becomes, from my point of view, the artist's confrontation with her forefathers, a problem with which Ruth Puttermesser wrestles and which, I demonstrate, thrives in all of Ozick's work. Both the strategy of dialectical thinking and the problems raised by forefathers exemplify the novelist's dialogical relationships with other writers' texts. If Ozick sets out to reconcile the Hebraism and Hellenism controversy in *The Cannibal Galaxy*, she ends by rekindling the dispute at the same time that she imparts her fresh cognition of the imagination.

And the imagination is the hub of *The Shawl*, the volume containing "The Shawl" and its sequel "Rosa," which I discuss in my sixth chapter. Though they were published three years apart, the stories are thematically joined and together they reverse the situation Ozick develops in *The Cannibal Galaxy*; for in *The Shawl* she follows the life of a woman victimized by the Holocaust. Unlike Joseph Brill, Rosa Lublin was imprisoned in a concentration camp and forced to witness the murder of her infant. That is the tragic event we learn of in "The Shawl"; its sequel takes place over thirty years later in Florida where Rosa Lublin finds herself after having destroyed her store in New York. Unable to rescue her infant Magda from the Nazis, Rosa Lublin kept herself alive but at a terrible cost. That Ozick has "Rosa" begin not with her character's liberation from the death camps and their unspeakable horrors but with her life after three decades have passed evinces, I conclude, the storyteller's apprehension of how Rosa Lublin's tormentors continued to torment their victim. And although "The Shawl" ultimately celebrates the human will to survive, "Rosa" portrays the abiding anguish of the survivor.

In addition, my exposition of *The Shawl* takes into its purview Ozick's exploration of the psychological consequences unleashed by intense rage, for I do not believe that "Rosa" is confined thematically solely to the Holocaust. Indeed, I see in *The Shawl* two tales mirroring the themes that obsess *The Cannibal Galaxy*, to which I determine the tales are wed. The idea of hell, for example, haunts all three stories; moreover, the relationship between mother and daughter in *The Shawl*—a prominent one in *Trust* as well—recalls Hester Lilt and her daughter Beulah in *The Cannibal Galaxy*. But as I observe throughout my book, Ozick's work obeys its own laws and *The Shawl* is no exception: its concerns are the obverse of those found in *The Cannibal Galaxy*. Common to both the novel and the novella, however, is Ozick's vision of the artist, for what first seizes the storyteller's imagination proves to be the complex enterprise of art. In Rosa Lublin's ruminations are the disquieting travails of the artist and the dangerous underside of the imagination.

"Rosa," I believe, is a novella of psychological implications, and they govern Ozick's fiction from *Trust* onward. In that novel, Ozick stresses the need to know one's father; "Rosa" chronicles the necessity for separating oneself from him. The narrator of *Trust* gains self-knowledge when she discovers her origins; but in "Rosa" Ozick inverts and augments the themes of her first novel by unveiling Rosa Lublin's painfully acquired understanding that the identity her father disavowed is one she must acknowledge. A figure to whom Cynthia Ozick accords monumental significance, the father continues to incite ambivalent feelings in *The Shawl*, where the storyteller deepens his meaning rather than quiet the turmoil he occasions. Exposed to the blaze of her imagination, that recurrent figure becomes multidimensional; and he has yet to recede from Cynthia Ozick's texts, as her third novel, the subject of my last chapter, "The Pulse of Ancestry," makes abundantly clear.

Related to *The Shawl*, *The Messiah of Stockholm* is most closely linked to *Trust*, but Ozick, as I explain, reverses its principal theme: the narrator of *Trust* unearths what is irrevocable in *The Messiah of Stockholm*—the past— and discovers what the main character of *The Messiah of Stockholm* invents. Envisaging Lars Andemening as bereft of a father and driven to determine the "pulse of ancestry," Ozick enlarges the import of the patriarch to encompass his role as literary predecessor. The reviewer Lars Andemening fancies himself Bruno Schulz's son, the Polish writer's doppelgänger. In Lars's ruling obsession, Ozick records her commentary on the Polish writer's life: Schulz's obsession with his father, with supra-reality, assimilation, and paganism. Interwoven into her own novel are elements from Bruno Schulz's art, which she reinterprets to explore the perplexities of art itself and the fate of writers whose interests lie outside the mainstream.

And Lars Andemening bears significant resemblances to many of her characters: akin to Rosa Lublin, he worships his imagined dead father in whom he finds a source of inspiration, which, in turn, recalls Puttermesser's way of creating a golem. The opposition between fantasy and reality, the clash of imagination and reason, the idolatry which writers risk—these iterative themes lie at the nub of *The Messiah of Stockholm*. A reviewer, Lars Andemening is one of Cynthia Ozick's artists, and her witty portrait of the literary world unmasks its workings, its frustrations, its injustices. Beyond that, *The Messiah of Stockholm* is a discourse on literary predecessors, a meditation on writing itself; and, I think, the novel ultimately shows the storyteller at a turning point, to have arrived at a new level of her powers.

And they are nourished by tradition, for out of it, Cynthia Ozick insists, arise not only the innovative but the redemptive. In *Cynthia Ozick's Fiction* I probe the dynamics of the storyteller's imagination, affirm how springing from the depths of a rich heritage, Ozick ascends to entirely new heights, to unexpected realms. If tale by tale her fiction defies predictability and incorporates diverse viewpoints, collectively it reflects a writer whose passion is knowing the different dimensions of existence, those lying outside the self-referential. Her disavowal of that as material for fiction accounts, I am convinced, for her acute knowledge of psychological motivation, her ability to penetrate into the fate of fury long submerged and unravel the intricacies of human guilt; it accounts for her mastery of psychological enigmas. Hers is not a parochial art:

her fiction resists narrow categories and defies rigid ideologies. To experience its splendor is to attend to its ambiguity and complexity.

Thus far, however, critics have continued to focus on the novelist's Jewish roots, her Jewishness.[3] Whatever useful points Ozick's contemporary critics have made, they cannot illuminate any of the intricacies of Ozick's fiction by viewing it solely as a product of American Jewish writing. That conviction not only restricts Ozick's art severely, but it also erects rigid criteria by which art is to be judged. Unfortunately, too many critics have taken as a statement of Ozick's credo an essay she published in 1970, "Toward a New Yiddish." Arguing against the desire of American Jewish writers to blur the uniqueness of their tradition by seeking universalism, Ozick enjoined them to maintain the distinction of their tradition and asserted that "Literature does not spring from the urge to Esperanto but from the tribe." Such a statement counsels attention to a writer's individuality; it does not seek to perpetuate unalterable and parochial expectations.

That her heritage has quickened in her a conflict over the act of artistic creation and has given rise to a theme that obsesses her writing should not be surprising; that critics have been content either to label her work the product of American Jewish writing or to declare the appeal of her fiction limited because she draws on her tradition is quite another matter. On the one hand, some have questioned whether the "Jewish materials used in [Ozick's] stories are sometimes inaccessible or maybe even alienating to many potential readers"; on the other hand, the storyteller has been held responsible for not employing those materials in recognizably Jewish ways. The competing judgments, both critical of the meaning of Judaism to her fiction, have created a peculiar situation: either Cynthia Ozick is too Jewish or else she is not Jewish enough. Neither view avails. Both preclude understanding. To consign her art to the interests of a special audience, to declare her fiction beyond the comprehension of those unfamiliar with Judaism is to gainsay her capaciousness; it is to regard her heritage as a terminus instead of what it is—a threshold. Worse: the attempt to confine Cynthia Ozick's imagination to the "tribe," which is its provenance, denies the "hugeness of vision," which is its power (Ozick, A&A 168). Ozick's tales and novels are most profitably read and discussed for what they are: tales and novels.

The clash of embattled issues that reverberates in her texts, that smashes certitude and resolution, thickens them with ambiguity; yet the irrepressibly froward side of her genius remains unacknowledged, indeed unrecognized. However accommodating it is to see her only as the eloquent and pious champion of Judaism who, as Joseph Lowin concludes, contains her contradictions in a "Jewish way of writing fiction," there is reason to be skeptical (78). That she draws sustenance from the "momentous standards" of the "Jewish Idea" and that she does not "deign to begin with a consciousness of rupture between normative Hebraism and her own vision" are, as Harold Bloom observes, the "given of her fiction," and it "must be honored" (CO 1). To honor that given is not to stop at it. "The source of fiction," she writes, "*is* chaos. Call it imagination; call it, the Keatsian way, negative capability; or Freudian-style, the Unconscious" ("Young Self" 166). Whatever the imaginations of great writers are called, they are frequently unruly—even wildly so—and paradoxical; for the imagination is free to obey its own dictates, to wrestle, to wrestle boldly and magnificently, with any established authority it chooses. Surely a writer whose texts are as antithetical as Ozick's are, surely a writer who recurs, again and again, to the battle to attain artistic freedom from patriarchal restraint, who admits in one sentence to dreading the imagination and in another asks, "Why do I, who dread the cannibal touch of story-making, lust after stories more and more and more"—surely that writer is not as resolutely pious or as monolithic as her critics have claimed (*Bloodshed* 12). And that is why to limit any of her work to being a "Jewish text, a Jewish representation of reality" is to diminish Ozick's perception of Judaism, to divest her minute particulars of their concrete and universal power, the power of a redemptive literature (Lowin 88).

We have been asked to believe, however, that her fiction belongs to uniquely Jewish forms, a judgment which violates her autonomy and which denies her originality. To say of *The Messiah of Stockholm*, for example, that "Although her imposter constructions lend intrigue to the literary mystery, they compromise the Holocaust import of the work" is to demand that an American Jewish writer be aware of her Jewish identity while she writes. No imaginative writer commences with a purposeful thesis, is guided by a definite direction; a Jewish writer cannot consciously or intentionally fashion a Jewish literature. That Jewish history, Jewish values, and Jewish sources permeate and enrich Ozick's art is undeniable. That the novelist has begun any tale with a consciousness of her Jewishness or with a plan to write about the Holocaust is another matter. Her position on that point is germane:

> Finally, about writing fiction. In theory, I'm with Theodor Adorno's famous dictum: after Auschwitz, no more poetry. And yet, my writing has touched on the Holocaust again and again. I cannot *not* write about it. It rises up and claims my furies. . . . I am not in favor of making fiction of the data, or of mythologizing or poeticizing it. . . . I constantly violate this tenet; my brother's blood cries out from the ground, and I am drawn and driven. ("Roundtable" 284)

Cynthia Ozick does not choose deliberately to write on the Holocaust; rather, the subject of the Holocaust arises "unbidden, unsummoned," like the process of art itself.[4] In a talk, she described that process: "The writer must put herself aside as a Jew while in the act of writing, or the writing will turn out prescriptive, tendentious, conscientious. And imagination cannot sustain, imagination will die under the ministrations of, conscience, prescription, persuasion."[5] Because imaginative writing cannot have a goal or a program, the critic must cease requiring them lest she fault the art for failing to conform to aims which by its very nature art cannot maintain.[6]

Keenly aware of the laws that govern the complexities of Ozick's fiction, I have been sparing of the voguish theoretical approaches, which prize such issues as ethnicity and gender, and have chosen instead a close engagement with Ozick's texts. What has prompted that choice comes neither from indifference to previously unrecognized literature from other cultures, nor from a lack of sympathy for the goals of the women's movement. Rather my decision results from the failure of previous critics to assess the importance of Cynthia Ozick's art to a realm broader than that of American Jewish literature. To subject her fiction to a feminist theoretical examination without illuminating the ways her imagination works and what it does is to station her art behind another fence; or, as Robert Alter has rightly observed of some contemporary theorists, it is to use the literary work "as a prooftext for preconceived, and all too general views (*Pleasures* 19)."

And specificity is what ethnic studies and feminist criticism frequently lack. I decline an ethnic designation for Cynthia Ozick because it smacks of marginality both for the Jew as writer and for the writer who is a Jew; and marginality is precisely the issue against which Ozick inveighs and the state over which her work triumphs. It is worth hearkening to some observations Ozick made on the subject of Jewish identity:

> But even after you have made it plain that it is illogic if not insolence to label a Jew an "ethnic"; even after you have made it plain that to say you are a Jew is a conceptual act, a labor of the intellect, a clarifying insight in the midst of babble and misperception and confusion—after all this, how is it possible to declare that the toil of writing fiction is unrelated to one's self-understanding as a Jew?
>
> The answer is contained precisely in the question. To be a Jew is an act of the strenuous mind as it stands before the fakeries and lying seductions of the world, saying no and no again as they parade by in all their allure. And to be a writer is to plunge into the parade and become one of the delirious marchers. (Farewell Tribute)

For many of the same reasons, I find a relentlessly feminist approach to Cynthia Ozick inappropriate and uninstructive. Notwithstanding the fact that she has steadfastly declared herself a "classical" feminist, one who adamantly opposes the "idea of literature-as-physiology," who resists attributing to the body what the mind toils to achieve, her texts will not submit to readings that search for social justice, the woman as hero, or the like. Her fiction, like that of all great writers, whatever their genders, arises from the welter of experience, the idea of human possibility; that dark repository approached in dreams, the contours of which become visible when the lamp of art is made to shine through. Of overarching concern to *Cynthia Ozick's Fiction: Tradition and Invention,* therefore, is attentiveness to Ozick's own universe and that, I am convinced, demands not a predetermined mode of reading but a kind of archaeological enterprise, a stripping away of layers, scrutiny of the texts themselves. Without denying the relevance of Ozick's polemics, without ignoring the potential revelations other approaches might provide, theoretical or not, I would argue that the task confronting the critic of Ozick's fiction at the present moment is to eschew the ideological for the text, to realize that for

Cynthia Ozick there is never an "only." Hers is a force of almost unprece-
dented modulation.

It is time to regard Cynthia Ozick not as a spokeswoman for normative
Judaism, not as a redeemer of its literary efforts, not even as something of a
feminist, but as the writer who dreamt a dryad, envisioned fashioning a golem,
and whose idea of paradise once was to recline under a tree flanked by a bottomless supply of fudge and an unending stack of library books, minus their
reminders of the date due and their threats of the fines to be assessed. It is
time, in other words, to arrive at the mainspring of her art, and that, I submit,
will establish Cynthia Ozick's centrality in contemporary American letters, a
recognition long overdue.

Acknowledgments

My first debt in writing this book is to my mentor and friend Jean Hagstrum. His example has always inspired and inspirited. I am grateful to L. S. Dembo who, as editor of *Contemporary Literature,* first encouraged me to write this book and later made valuable suggestions about my manuscript.

Grateful acknowledgment is also due to Alvin Rosenfeld, whose sensitive reading of my manuscript greatly improved it. Maier Deshell, the editor of *Congress Monthly,* helped me considerably with archival and bibliographical matters; and Rochelle Mancini, *Congress Monthly*'s assistant editor, was especially helpful in locating material about Jacob Glatstein.

Thanks are due to Martin Stevens, former dean of the School of Liberal Arts and Sciences of Baruch College, for making it possible for me to receive a Research Fellowship from Baruch College (CUNY) from September 1986–January 1987.

Parts of this book reflect earlier efforts. I wish to thank the University of Wisconsin Press for allowing me to quote from my article, "Cynthia Ozick's Book of Creation: *Puttermesser and Xanthippe*" (*Contemporary Literature,* Spring 1985, pp. 40–54) and from my interview with Cynthia Ozick (*Contemporary Literature,* Winter 1985, pp. 375–401). I also wish to thank Kent State University Press for allowing me to quote from my articles, "The Dread of Moloch: Idolatry as Metaphor" and "Courier for the Past: Cynthia Ozick and Photography" (*Studies in American Jewish Literature,* Fall 1987, pp. 111–146).

Several friends deserve special acknowledgment. I thank Robert Spector for his unfailing advice and support. My conversations with my friend and colleague Philip Cavanaugh throughout the writing of this book were of inestimable value: his intellect is an ideal one against which to test ideas. I want to thank Michael Fleisher for a host of reasons: he will know how deeply grateful I am to him. To Edward Alexander, let me add in profoundest gratitude, my indebtedness is of such variety and such depth as to beggar the formal limits of an acknowledgment page.

Finally, to my brother and my sister, to whom this book is dedicated, I owe particular thanks. I am grateful to my brother for his support but especially for dragging his sister kicking and screaming into the twentieth century and insisting that she purchase the computer, with his generous assistance, on which this book was completed. My sister is my dearest reader: I cannot adequately thank her for her painstaking reading of my manuscript.

CYNTHIA OZICK'S
FICTION

ONE

The Struggle for Exactitude

When in November of 1963 Cynthia Ozick completed *Trust,* she had actually finished her third novel, the first having been worked on over a period of seven years before *Trust* and abandoned, the second having been completed in six weeks but never published.[1] For Ozick, those years constitute a "kind of apprenticeship." For the reader of her fiction, however, her first novel, to which she gave the Blakean title *Mercy, Pity, Peace, and Love*—she abbreviated that to *Mippel* and then jokingly referred to it as the Mippel on which she "had sucked for so long"—reveals the matrix of Ozick's characteristic novel of ideas.[2] Conceiving *Mippel* as a "philosophical" novel in which she would "pit the Liberal-Modernists against the Neo-Thomists," Ozick revealed herself to be a novelist concerned not only with ideas but with manners, a novelist in the tradition of George Eliot, Henry James, and Joseph Conrad.

Those ideas are of predominant importance to her first published novel, *Trust.* But they are broadened into a novel whose scope is Tolstoyan, whose subject is "History as a judgment on events" (Ozick, "We Are the Crazy Lady" 681). Yet that novel still has not been accorded the attention it so clearly merits. Its neglect has a history. At first *Trust* was received favorably if uncomprehendingly. When he reviewed it for the *New York Times* in 1966, for example, David L. Stevenson placed the novel in the "tradition of narrative . . . of James, Conrad and Lawrence. . . . the tradition that explores and reveals the inward man." Having attributed to Ozick's novel a largeness of scope, Stevenson then diminished the novel's value when he consigned *Trust* to a recognizable type—a woman's novel. Here are his comments on the narrator, a young woman: "She longs to play some simple, easy feminine role herself. . . . She has cultivated her wit, but has been unable to define her role as a woman. . . . Thus the daughter, at the age of twenty-two, is eager for the prerequisites that should be hers as a woman, but is floundering badly in their pursuit" (Stevenson 9, 10). A year later Eugene Goodheart acknowledged *Trust*'s "psychological drama" in one paragraph of his essay and then in the next paragraph discounted the novelist's capacity to tell a clear tale: "Yet it is hard to say what the novel is *really* about. The massive accumulation of detail, the constant nuancing of every situation obfuscates the fable" (12). If one critic judged the narrator of *Trust* unable to define her role as a woman, the other critic objected to the heroine because she lacks "every grace a woman can have. . . . her ungraced condition . . . compromises the gift of perception and expression that she must possess as a narrator" (Goodheart 14).

What accounts for these views? Certainly they have something to do with the critical climate during which the novel appeared, as Stevenson's and Goodheart's comments on women reveal. To write a novel twenty-five years ago with a woman as the narrator was to risk exclusion from the ranks of serious writing. More precisely, it often meant being regarded as the author of a woman's novel; which is to say, a romance, pulp, trivia. In her witty essay "We Are the Crazy Lady and Other Feisty Feminist Fables," Ozick describes her efforts to rescue *Trust* from such a fate:

> Everything I was reading in reviews of other people's books made me fearful: I would have to be very, very cautious, I would have to drain my narrator of emotive value of any kind. I was afraid to be pegged as having written a "women's" novel, and nothing was more certain to lead to that than a point-of-view seemingly lodged in a woman; no one takes a woman's novel seriously. I was in terror, above all, of sentiment and feeling, those telltale taints. I kept the fury and the passion for other, safer, characters. . . .
>
> My machine-narrator was there for efficiency only, for flexibility, for craftiness, for subtlety, but never, never, as a "woman." I wiped the "woman" out of her. . . . I meant my novel to be taken for what it really was. I meant to make it impossible for it to be mistaken for something else. (682)

We live in an era of theory in which gender studies flourish, making it unfashionable to apply the label "women's novel" as a critical or derisive judgment. Still, with the exception of Victor Strandberg's rich essay which surveys Ozick's oeuvre from her first published novel to *Levitation,* no critic has given *Trust* the recognition it both demands and deserves.[3] Critical reactions to the novel in the eighties have either breezily dismissed it, merely summarized its plot, or unfortunately assigned it another label.[4] Whatever useful points Ozick's contemporary critics have made, they cannot illuminate a novel as multilayered as *Trust* is, or any of the intricacies of Ozick's fiction for that matter, by viewing it solely as a product of American Jewish writing. Nor can the key to those intricacies be found in Ozick's essays. In an intriguing "Forewarning" to her second collection of essays, *Metaphor & Memory,* Ozick admonishes: "In other words, if a writer of stories is also a writer of essays, the essays ought not to be seized as a rod to beat the writer's stories with; or as a frame into which to squeeze the writer's stories; or, collectively, as a 'philosophy' into which to pen the writer's outlook" (xi). Indeed, Cynthia Ozick's essays and stories are frequently irreconcilable; both are more profitably read by acknowledging their conflicting viewpoints and competing ideas. To search for clues to the meaning of *Trust* in "The Lesson of the Master," therefore, is to distort Ozick's artistic relationship to James entirely.

When she wrote "The Lesson of the Master" and divulged her mistaken apprehension of his advice—how as a young woman she chose art over life—Cynthia Ozick did not claim Henry James as the artistic model whose path she followed in writing *Trust*. Instead her essay laments an idealization common to the young, an identification with an older artist, a young writer's desire to achieve what an elderly writer had attained over a lifetime. To this misunderstanding Ozick imputes the sacrifice of her youth. But her essay, like many of the essays which have been used against her stories, has been "seized as a rod to beat" *Trust* with, as the means to disregard it as a Jamesian exercise, evidence of homage and influence—a lengthy, nuanced, complicated, and inaccessible first novel. Ozick has written much about Henry James—a master's thesis entitled "Parable in Henry James," an essay on *The Sacred Fount*, another essay on his unfinished tale "Hugh Merrow." She admired, and continues to admire, his art, the Master's moral imagination. In James's novel she discerned the fusion of ethics and tale, the emphasis on the relationship between realization and action. An adumbration of her later convictions, her master's thesis affords the unique opportunity to witness the genesis of her mature perceptions.

James, she wrote in her analysis of *The Golden Bowl*, held that the "essence of all ethical values is consistency." Later, her sense of James as a moralist who held the conviction that revelation must be an amalgam of action and interpretation was to evolve into her concept of the "Judaized novel." Of that novel she writes in "Toward a New Yiddish": "The novel at its nineteenth-century pinnacle was a Judaized novel: George Eliot and Dickens and Tolstoy were all touched by the Jewish covenant: they wrote of conduct and of the consequences of conduct: they were concerned with a society of will and commandment" (A&A 164). What she apprehended as James's "skill of duplicate vision" emerges in the structure and imagery of *Trust*, as does her distinction between myth and fairy tale, her observation of the evils often consonant with great wealth. Recognizing in *The Golden Bowl* the "sense that money, a neuter, can attain a negative ethical significance, a depth of evil association, and can become morally corrupting," as it does for James's Amerigo and Charlott Stant, Ozick envisioned an analogous situation in *Trust* when she created Allegra Vand's trust fund and unfolded its corrupting effects. Akin to the "moral imperative" she discovered in James is her repudiation of myth at the end of *Trust* because myth traffics in the super-human and lacks the moral. Early in her career she discovered that "James, although a recorder of internal scriptures, was no Blake, and never fashioned gods and demigods"; her observation grew into a firm conviction about the perilousness of idolatry. Of central significance to *Trust* and of abiding importance throughout Ozick's fiction and essays is history; of James's *The Sense of the Past* she wrote, "Thus it may be inferred from *The Sense of the Past* that, for James, history was moral or was (at least) a record of certain ethical realities, a declaration of an 'ought.' "

But we ought not take this thesis as evidence of Ozick's priesthood at James's altar. Though many of the values she embraced when she wrote her thesis may be discerned in her work, they have altered in form and depth; for as great artists progress, they transform their youthful convictions into cognitions bearing the stamp of maturity. Those are evident in "Henry James's Unborn Child," an essay she published in 1986. She brings to James's fragment "Hugh Merrow" the ability, as the Master himself might have observed, to commune with the unseen. And she unearths the explanation for Henry James's puzzling—he completed one hundred twelve stories—inability to finish "Hugh Merrow." Foreshadowings in the Master's notebooks, her commanding knowledge of his work, her acute understanding of his life, the "figurations of the text"—these Ozick employs to solve the mystery of James's fragment. In the process, she demonstrates not an intractable idealization of James but her powerful imagination at work: "In 'Hugh Merrow' . . . James was flinging himself past the threshold of the erotic into the very birth canal itself. In the face of psychological pressure so plainly unsupportable, he withdrew" (M&M 63).

To gainsay the importance of James to Cynthia Ozick is to deny fact; to claim that he is the inspiriting god hovering over *Trust* is to turn fact into exaggeration. Certainly her use of the name Isabel in *Mippel,* the abundant allusions to *The Portrait of a Lady* in *Trust*—a chapter in part four quotes the first line of James's novel—establish his presence in her creative consciousness. But the charge that Ozick has not brought to *Trust* the considerable force of her intellect and a different originality is quite another matter. Ironically enough the supposition that *Trust* is overwhelmingly Jamesian resembles the charge F. R. Leavis leveled against *The Portrait:* "Henry James wouldn't have written *The Portrait* if he hadn't read *Daniel Deronda.* . . . The fact, once asserted, can hardly be questioned."[5] Leon Edel's response to Leavis's proclamation is as true of Cynthia Ozick as it is of Henry James: "Writers as creative as Henry James do not write wholly out of their reading of other books, and *Daniel Deronda* fell on ground already fertile" (Edel in James, PL xviii). The assumption that Ozick's reading of James produced *Trust* is just that, an assumption.

In fact, the question of James's influence on Ozick is rather more complex, for throughout her oeuvre, Ozick engages in what certain contemporary theorists might call a dialogue with the Master, or to purloin Harold Bloom's more precise formulation, her reading of James is that of a "revisionary agonist," and the relation between their texts is "agonistic," Ozick's reading of him revisionistic (*Agon* 50). In tale after tale beginning with *Trust,* Ozick alludes to James only to revise, for her own original purposes, what she has beheld in his work. Though we cannot trust the teller, we must at least listen to her, for her warning about the differences between her tales and her essays suggests the agon between them and urges us to attend to that as an artistic practice, to regard her as a strong reader and a strong novelist, and to approach her texts without predetermined judgments. Those distinctions still escape readers of *Trust.*

The history of certain masterworks abounds in attitudes comparable to the ones that have plagued *Trust,* and they help account for the reasons some works of art—*Moby Dick* springs immediately to mind—fail to capture the attention of their time, but later, in a different literary clime, achieve the recognition denied them and ultimately command the admiration once refused them. Over two decades have elapsed since *Trust* was published; Ozick's stories and novels have earned critical acclaim. Surely that acclaim warrants a fresh evaluation of *Trust*. Imbricated, nuanced, and exquisitely wrought, it introduces a unique power, an originating one. Ozick's integrating vision recalls the great novels of the nineteenth century which refracted a vast historical presence, functioned as beneficial agents of the moral imagination, were unswervingly concerned with human volition, and so fashioned literature into an instrument for self-examination. The fashionable disavowal of historical relevance and the passionate attempt to create new forms have been adamantly rejected by Cynthia Ozick from the beginning of her career:

> Inventing a secret, then revealing it in the drama of entanglement—this is what ignites the will to write stories. The creation of forms has no part in this; I have no interest in "the new." Rupture doesn't attract me: I would rather inherit coherence than smash and start over again with enigma. The secrets that engage me—that sweep me away—are generally secrets of inheritance. . . . (M&M 111)

Her convictions that history is judgment, that continuity is essential, penetrate to the very vitals of her work and are a corridor of access to her fiction. For Ozick history and memory are the desiderata of true innovative literature, the literature that redeems.[6]

In *Trust,* therefore, Ozick undertakes to depict not only a quest for self-knowledge but an exploration of the three cultural forces in history. And in their attitudes, which range from "historical abominations" to utter indifference, the characters in *Trust* provide the evidence by which they are to be judged (18). The novel's four parts reflect the writer's concern for history: the first and fourth parts, which take place in 1957, frame the second and third parts which return to 1946 and 1935 and illuminate the puzzling events of the novel's present. The time of the novel, the world after the unimaginable abattoir in Europe, explains and sustains the manifold ironies of the title, for *Trust* is about betrayals in every conceivable form—the failure of trust in love, sex, politics, law, art, marriage, motherhood, fatherhood.

The absence of the nameless narrator's father constitutes the conundrum central to the novel, the enigma around which the four parts of *Trust* are structured, the mystery the narrator determines to solve. This subject, the search for a father, itself has a rich tradition: in America William Faulkner, Robert Penn Warren, and Thomas Wolfe have all built novels around a man's search to find a father; the theme has appealed to the English writers George Eliot and Charles Dickens and the Irish writer James Joyce. Rarely have women written about a daughter's efforts to discover a father; the relationship between fathers and daughters itself has been a long neglected field of study until very recently.[7] From the beginning of her career, however, Cynthia Ozick has written about this crucial relationship. The various meanings attached to the father pulse through her fiction, accruing multiple significations, and the father constitutes a prevailing presence, becomes a momentous figure. In *Trust* the conventional reunion with a father is lent new vigor and concrete power, as Ozick deepens and extends this traditional theme beyond the confines of a personal discovery into a universally important apprehension of culture. "This ostensible father's tale" affirms Ozick's belief "that stories ought to judge and interpret the world" (*Trust* 550; *Bloodshed* 4).

I

To establish the importance of memory and history to human experience, Ozick has named the four parts of *Trust* "America," "Europe," "Brighton," and "Duneacres," the locations of her narrator's revelations.[8] Part 1 begins in New York with the narrator's graduation and unfolds the present situation, the plans the graduate has for traveling in Europe, which are suddenly interrupted by a perplexing summons from her father. Absent from her life for twenty-two years, Gustave Nicholas Tilbeck has been almost obliterated from his daughter's life. In fact, the girl possesses only a childhood memory of him. In part 2 the narrative returns to Europe where she was taken at age ten and where in Paris she unknowingly glimpsed Gustave Nicholas Tilbeck when he came to extort money from her mother Allegra Vand, an heiress to a considerable trust fund. How she acquired it and what she did with it is the subject of "Brighton." Learning the tale of her mother's youth, the daughter recovers her own history and at last owns the prerequisites for judging the present. "Duneacres" reflects the results of her discoveries; for in part 4 the narrative returns to the present in New York and culminates in the two days the narrator spends with her father on Town Island where the mystery of paternity is finally unraveled. The architecture of the novel dramatizes the process Ozick deems essential to gaining a future. The disclosures of memory and history enable the narrator to judge the meaning of the past, to decode the present; they prepare her to embark on a future.[9]

Not to know the identity of one's father is to lack the facts crucial to an individual's history; it is to belong nowhere. That "no aunt, cousin, mother, sister, father had come to see" the graduation ceremony accents the narrator's alienation and rootlessness (15). And the graduate experiences on that momentous occasion not the hopeful expectations of the young but the disillusionment common "to the very old" (15). In the opening scene she stands by herself in a muddy field empty of celebrants, and as she watches a man spearing make-believe diplomas, temporary substitutes for the real thing, she apprehends a principle of Time:

> When first Time makes himself known to us, it is not as that ancient progenitor who comes to announce that we are mortal, but inadvertently, accidentally, in a moment unforetold especially by himself; and we see him then in his everyday dis-

guise, that of a young bridegroom, and he brings us then not death but recognition, and not the end of knowledge but its beginning. (15)

The last random call of a bugle announces the beginning of her knowledge, but she realizes the bugle's note cannot be sustained, and as a tiny worm devours the center of the browning flower that has fallen on the sleeve of her graduation gown, the graduate muses on the surfeit of deceit and fraud that fills an alluring world. More an observer than a participant at her own graduation, she envies those about to be married; and seized with "greed for the world," the graduate longs to believe "in the future, most of all in some impermeable lacquer to enamel an endless youth." Instead she regards her graduation as the dawning of a "strange diaspora," the "exile" she must enter alone (14, 14, 15).

The scene reveals the essence of the mind that suffuses the novel with its illumination. It is a mind at once aware of the significance of a formal occasion yet attentive to the undercurrents rising in its aftermath. This ability to view one side of an event and then to turn it inside out and examine it from another angle, a watermark of Cynthia Ozick's fiction, reveals the novelist's duplicate vision. The narrator of *Trust* confronts the event, records it, and recounts it coolly and impartially; but Ozick matches her narrator's objectivity with psychological complexity. Having been denied knowledge of her real father by Allegra Vand, who has successfully attempted to re-father her daughter—first with Allegra's former husband William, whom Allegra retains as an attorney, and then with her second husband Enoch Vand—the narrator is adrift in a world to which she does not belong. Unaware that William has betrayed the terms of the trust, she believes his recoil from her is evidence of a "Calvinist probity"; William is "all [her] Protestantism," a "monument" commanding respect and admiration (76, 22). If William is all her Christianity, Enoch, a Jew whom Allegra calls "Disraeli in the mornings and in the evenings Moses," is all her Judaism (69). Father-surrogates, William and Enoch also have philosophical significance: they represent two pillars of Western Civilization—Christianity and Judaism. Although Enoch refuses to re-father Allegra's daughter, he nonetheless occupies a central place in the narrator's consciousness, for it is with his ideas that she scrutinizes and assesses the world.

Enoch Vand's namesake, the scribe of righteousness in the Book of Enoch, is described in Genesis: "Enoch walked with God; then he was no more, for God took him" (5:24). In the pseudepigrapha Enoch is the prophet to whom God reveals the secrets of the universe, the predetermined course of human history, and the future of the world. The possessor of such knowledge, the prophet Enoch was revered for his wisdom, for providing an account of creation, for announcing a vision of the apocalypse. From the very beginning of *Trust*, Enoch Vand's influence on the narrator is apparent. Wishing for the bugle's sound to return, she thinks immediately of Enoch in words alluding to his namesake: "Only the year before Enoch had told me that the sign of understanding would be the absence of any sign, that revelation came unproclaimed, that messiahship was secret" (13). That she remembers Enoch's insight at her graduation; that Enoch foretells the meaning of her visit to Duneacres—he calls it a "voyage"—foreshadow his role in the novel (63).

The revealer of Tilbeck's summons, Enoch is not the guide to her father's life. Of Tilbeck she knows very little, having only accidentally seen his name on an envelope in Enoch's desk drawer. Struck by his "educated but wild" handwriting and deprived of any concrete information about him, the daughter devises an adventurous but discreditable life for the father whom she imagines variously as a sailor, a voyager, an artist, and above all, a shameful embarrassment (21). Oblique remarks from Allegra and Enoch, the omission of her father's name from the daughter's school applications, and the dark secrecy that surround Tilbeck's doings incite ambivalence. On the one hand, the narrator conjectures her father might be a genius, singular and unorthodox. On the other hand, she thinks of him "as dun and dank and indecent and somewhat yellowish . . . moist and dirty, quartered in a moist and dirty cellar, in the manner of geniuses," or she fancies him an "indolent mariner," even a "terrible Nile-god," who "lay on the beach of his island, nude to the waist" (22, 24). That Tilbeck continually succeeds in extorting money from Allegra leads her daughter to surmise the money must be forthcoming from an allegiance and to conclude that "some issue turned mysteriously in the sand" at Duneacres. Secretly and intuitively, she essays retrieval of the history attached to "that languid merchant of the past" (25).

Barring her access to the past, Allegra urges her daughter to remember Europe as her birthplace, her "lost continent," the country where her gold and silver dress, redolent of money, has been purchased (75). When she wears the dress, her daughter reminds Allegra of Tilbeck. And her mother's observation makes the daughter think of her father: the "dress she had brought for me singed my skin with a blaze of gold and silver, the hot gold of my father's beach and the burning silver of his sea" (36). The *bon voyage* party, which Allegra Vand has arranged to celebrate her daughter's trip to Europe and which is attended by the attorneys she has asked William's son to bring and the poets she has invited herself, impresses the narrator as "counterfeit and sad." She judges the guests "rank phonies" and finds their separate versions of the world equally tiresome (53, 41). Wherever she is—at her own commencement or at the party given in her honor—the girl feels like an "attendant more bereft than curious," an outsider who belongs nowhere (55). The high note from a brass horn, one of the instruments in the little orchestra Allegra has provided, breaks off and the narrator recalls the bugle at her graduation. That bugle had promised something, a sign perhaps. The horn portends nothing, but it signals another of her recognitions:

> Nothing in the world can be sustained, neither bugles nor hope nor woe nor desire nor common well-being nor horns, and even redemption, that suspect covenant, can be revised by the bitter and loveless Christ to whom alone nothing, not even

life is irretrievable. Relief is our reward for recognizing this truth, that the note cannot be sustained forever and the irretrievable can never be returned to us; and there is no alternative but to go on with the facts exactly as they are (53).

But facts can be incomplete, as she learns when William's son divulges the terms of the trust fund. His father has told him Allegra's father destined his money for the upkeep of a "marine museum" on Town Island; but the narrator knows Allegra sends checks drawn on the trust to maintain not a museum but Tilbeck's existence at Duneacres. Tilbeck is, however, a "sort of museum," housing "matters which had to be dug after, collected bit by bit, and reconstructed" (73). To describe Tilbeck as a museum is to suggest that he lodges not only the historical relics of an ancient civilization but also its artifacts. The "admission price" to that museum, the narrator concludes, is fierce: "What you paid was yourself. In order to get in you had to join the bad and dirty things on display: you had to change and be one of them" (74). Allegra has tried to prevent her daughter from entering that museum by bringing her closer either to the world or to a temple—to Enoch's worldliness or to William's holiness. The metaphors Ozick attaches to Enoch, William, and Tilbeck mark the civilizations they represent, the cultures the narrator explores in her relationships with the men. William's Christianity is contrasted to Enoch's secular brand of Judaism, and both religions are distinguished from Tilbeck's paganism. Shut out by William, even though her mother has given her his surname, the narrator is yoked to Tilbeck; but she sees the world through Enoch's eyes.

And the world she observes is Allegra's. Peopled by attorneys and poets and saturated with wealth, her mother's milieu acquaints the narrator with the vacuum at the core of American acquisitive culture. Her fortune enabling her to do whatever she pleases, Allegra is immured in money-sickness, in the "complications of wealth," its capacity to buy men and to engender labyrinthine mysteries (57). To secure a future and to attain a name, her daughter must penetrate the secret of the trust fund's labyrinth. In part 1 the narrator evinces her lust for the world by reading everything in the newspapers and by attending to all that passes before her; but she possesses only fragments of her history, partial truths. Ozick renders this state in the pervasive imagery of halves: appearing first in "America" and then reappearing throughout *Trust*, this imagery accretes significance. Toward the end of part 1 the narrator reflects on a childhood experience in Europe that half captures her likeness to her father and half allies her to her stepfather. Fed the shellfish *oursin* by her governess in France, the child became ill: "To be sick at my stomach was to take after my father" (58). But to be sick from a fish forbidden to Jews, a fish whose name signals the effects of the war, is to resemble Enoch. Linking "America" to "Europe," the girl's memory of this event exemplifies the way Ozick's art works: perceiving the doubleness inherent in every situation, the storyteller renders the modulations of reality by doubling and dividing. Each event, each object, each image takes on dual significance. Voices compete, views clash, experiences conflict. Such an art is protean; such a vision encompasses the breadth of human experience that for Cynthia Ozick never remains monolithic.

To delineate the gulf separating Enoch's and Tilbeck's worlds, part 2 is divided into the narrator's memories of her stepfather's activities in Europe, where as a ten-year-old the child was taken just three months after the war, and her recollection of her mother's "private visitor," the child's unknown father (130). The narrator's remembrances mark the first appearance of a theme predominant in Ozick's fiction—the necessary recovery of childhood. For that reason the narrator recalls vomiting a map on the border of Germany: a "Mediterranean of bad milk in the heart of this known and yellowish world—not simply known but precisely known, exactly and profoundly known . . . known, memorized, and understood, unmistakably and perilously known by its terrific stink" (83). The incident epitomizes her feelings about Europe and associates the color yellow, which was attached to Tilbeck in "America," with Europe. Afterwards, the child has a nightmare in which "a thing with ochre eyes and a brass tail which ended in a dagger" leaps through the window of her room, clanging its metal forelock on the metal bedpost" (91). The dream elements gather together her early experiences in Europe and symbolize her impressions of it. Prompted by her witnessing, "as in a dream," a "one-legged giant"—a soldier—shoot himself, the terrifying dream transforms her horror of the soldier's death into an image of the monster that for her represents Europe (82). The nightmare reverberates the war—its yellow armbands, its metal weapons—and along with Enoch's "cadenced psalming of the deathcamps," remains a "hieroglyph of Europe" (111).

Her association of Europe and Egypt is not fortuitous. Enoch has come to Europe as a "liaison among the dead of all nations," as the man appointed to sort out and count the corpses from the death camps. Reversing Isaiah's prediction, Enoch aims "to have the murderer lie down with the murdered" (85, 88). His lists of foreign names, his marks on the yellow form-sheets, his apocalyptic statements—these the narrator remembers as idolatry, Enoch's thralldom to the cult of a single idea. A worshiper of Baal, he is devoted not to the sacred or the holy but to the profane. To stress his secularism and the ambition that allows Enoch to enter Europe immediately after the war, Ozick employs Greek allusions. Always addressing a "muse, perhaps Clio," he regards the dead as the slaughtered, for he "was past Lethe, and well past Nepenthe, and far past the Styx or Paradise" (96, 97). He curses the "grim-faced nymph Geopolitica" and pleas for the "Evil Inclination"—the *yetzer ha-ra* in the Talmud—and the "Angel of death jointly to carry her off" (97).

That desire and his pursuits, which conjure in the narrator the "Argonauts after golden fleece, Israelites after Zion," suggest the meaning of his cosmopolitanism. Enoch is a Jew divided from Judaism. In effect, he incarnates his own aphorism with which "Europe" begins: "And upon what Holiness cannot build, Worldliness is founded. Now when Holiness essays introspection and ends with self-deception, it gives birth to Worldliness" (81). Allegra's attempt to re-father her daughter with Enoch is tantamount to providing her with "Secular Man" rather than "homo Puritanus," the disaffected William who has denied the narrator his paternity (100). To give her daughter Secular Man is to convert her to Europe, for Allegra regards Enoch and Europe as one— "all spectacle, dominion, energy, and honor" (98). Instead of the scorched plain, the smoke and cinders, that Enoch beholds, Allegra gazes at Europe's "spires . . . and the domes, windows, and pillars of those exhausted groves; also icons rubbed beyond belief." Instead of the death camp gas that chokes Enoch, Allegra quenches her thirst from the "fountain of the world" and never detects Europe's stench (98).

In these opposing views, Ozick reformulates the Jamesian idea of Europe. Dying in 1916, James never lived to inhale the deadly gas that continually plagues Enoch.[10] James could surrender himself to the tutelage of an older civilization, the Europe of memory and history, a museum wealthy Americans might enter to acquire aesthetic and intellectual refinement. Saturated with such culture, the Master was to proclaim Europe the prime source of civilization and an inspiration for his art. His view affronted by an endless spreading field of ash, the inhuman scene of postwar Europe, Enoch Vand sees not the million windows in the house of fiction, but rather the "many mansions" in the "house of death" (100).[11] For that reason, Ozick has given him as a last name the Yiddish word for wall, a reference to the destruction of the Temple and its remaining Western Wall and to the Holocaust and the wall of the Warsaw Ghetto.[12] And the child, who amuses herself by searching for the empty cartridge shells that have supplanted the seashells on the beach and who hears Enoch brooding over the "paper remnants of the damned," comes to think of Europe as a "gassed and blighted continent" with a god she hopes differs from America's (98, 99).

The blight is invisible on the lawn where in the rain—the rain that in *Trust* always accompanies revelation—the child has a transcendental experience. As the rain droplets fall "through the thinly purple beam of sun as through a slung net," the color of the grass alters. Sensing "influences," she stands in the "awesome light" stirring a "puddle" with her "shining stick" and feels "purified and simplified, and transmuted, like the grass, less by a force than by an illusion" (113). Her apprehension of nature's beauty precedes Tilbeck's arrival in "Europe" just as in chapter 4 of "Duneacres" the girl is aware of nature's power before meeting with her father. In Europe, she knows nothing about her mother's visitor; to prevent her discovery of Tilbeck's real identity, her mother locks the child in her room.

But one of its windows provides a view of the visitor's dilapidated blue bicycle and a tiny American flag protruding next to the bicycle's rear reflector. The flag, she fancies, is a "declaration, a trimming, a boast even," but the sound of the bicycle's rattling metal parts reminds her of the brass demon who invaded her sleep (138). Expecting the formidable and dire enemy her mother fears, the daughter is puzzled by the flag which seems to project its owner's anticipation of a favorable outcome, to represent a "sort of glorious and healthful omen of America, of everything that was not Europe" (194). On the visitor's cablegram she had glimpsed the "uninteresting" word "child" and the name "Nick," a name that "goes too quick." That Allegra has stuffed the letter into her pocket "as though it were an invidious apple from the Tree of Knowledge" arouses the child's curiosity and hints at the narrator's meeting with her father in part 4 (134). Lying on the bed, the child imagines the mattress as a human map, like the vomited one of nations and continents, containing the "essential blotches, blights, and streams of humanity" (163). Eager to hear the adults' conversation, she creeps out the window onto a ledge where, drenched by the rain, she eavesdrops. The mirror on the bureau in her mother's room yields "up its witness" and rewards the narrator with the knowledge she must always accumulate alone and unseen. In a gesture symbolic of her effort to shroud everything in secrecy, Allegra pulls the curtain across the window, shutting off the mirror, sealing in time, severing her daughter from her history (154).

However, the intoning of the rolls of the death camps never leaves her ears and their names connect her to the world's history, making her aware that one's name must be spoken. The ledgered names Enoch calls out are doubled by the barcarolle of the names the honeymooners sing to each other in the house where Allegra and her daughter spend their last night in Paris. There she wonders if a "storage house of names" exists "designed to nurture and preserve . . . the names . . . of the living and the dead together: so that immortality might consist merely in one's name having been uttered even a single time, by anyone at all"; there the narrator understands that to be called by one's name is to attain an "assurance of one's doubtful existence" (177).[13] Until she can recover her past, she will remain like the nameless cartographers of the human map, stripped of "identity or talisman" (177).

Her recognition that one's existence is predicated upon possessing a name concludes the section of "Europe" in which Enoch is a dominating presence and begins the part which is given over to Tilbeck. He has left behind ENCHIRIDION OF WOODLAND FLOWERS, a handbook his daughter discovers in the garden. Rain-soaked, the pages of the little guidebook are fused, and as she turns it over, the book splits in half revealing two illustrations, minutely and literally drawn. The two woodland flowers, which bloom near water, recall her divided attitude toward her father in "America." The first flower, the false hellebore, has stout and erect stems; extremely poisonous, its rootstalks are utilized to prepare emetics and its seeds can "kill [the] small creatures" who "are sometimes fatally lured" to the plant's beauty (179). The second flower, the jewelweed, has seed-pods "shaped like horns-of-plenty" which, when ripe, expel their seeds everywhere (180). Unmarred even by a bug, the guidebook's two perfect pictures declare the innocence of the manual's owner, even his whimsy. Nick's blue bicycle and the handbook convince his daughter that the Beelzebub Allegra expected has "turned out to be nothing more pernicious than the jewelweed's habits and the hellebore's way," innocent but suspect protocols (181).

The remembered halves of ENCHIRIDION, remnants of Nick, are probed by "ozymandian ideas," inheritances from Enoch (181). In this way, Ozick connects her narrator to Nick and to Enoch. Thinking of Nick as Titus, who destroyed the Temple, the narrator alludes to Tilbeck's pagan and destructive lawlessness, for she is "influenced by [Enoch] more than he or his wife guessed." Her attraction to her stepfather's agile intellect, to Enoch's desire "to contend with the facts," is reflected in her avid reading of newspapers. Again and again, the narrator recurs to Enoch's authority to decode the meaning of her own experiences (181, 171). This situation, the narrator's interest in Nick tempered by her attention to Enoch, is heightened by the pairs and halves that pervade the novel. The two couples who are honeymooners want two rooms side by side. As Allegra is explaining that she originally bought ENCHIRIDION for the flower scene in her novel *Marianna Harlow,* in which two girls tease a single hero into eating two different plants, the two couples race barefoot "across the dewy grass like Greek runners, chasing one another in an impromptu game that half resembled tag, and half something Biblical: the honeymooners cast out from Paradise by two croaking angels, more or less toothless, beating staffs of broken bread upon the lintel of Eden" (192–93). The wedding party is pagan; theirs is an activity that resembles the eruption of the jewelweed's spasmodic seed-pods. But the honeymooners play a game that unites them with Enoch, the "Adam of Europe fallen into Paradise" (192, 100). Objects from Enoch's and Nick's worlds are brought together in a final hieroglyph of Europe, an overturned rain-barrel. Before coming to rest on the ground, the rain-barrel "rocked twice"; then "like a toppled urn," it conjures up "an idol thrown down." In the iron barrel images of fertility—the fish and the water—mingle with images of death—the cartridge shells and the drawing of the poisonous hellebore (193).

At the end of "Europe," the doubling and dividing reach a crescendo. "Halfway along" the hill the narrator spies Nick's flag. Two taxis wait to take her and Allegra to the ship where a colonel expresses his disapproval of bringing a child to Europe "in the middle of everything" (194, 201). His legs "stiff half from habit, half from some perhaps secret ailment," the colonel declares the voyagers "halfway to America," a statement which displeases the young girl (202). If they are at the mid-point in their journey, she muses, they can either be halfway to America or halfway to Europe, a "question" only "of point of view" (204). It is a point of view that clarifies the significance of halves: they augment the competing perspectives confronting someone in the middle of everything.

The imagery of halves, the color yellow, and the labyrinthine trust fund form a cluster of images alluding to the mystery located at the core of *Trust*— the identity of Gustave Nicholas Tilbeck. What the discovery of that hinges on is glimpsed in a baby's plaything—a spool of yellow thread. At first yellow characterizes Tilbeck's beach; then as the principal color of part 2, yellow yokes Tilbeck to Europe, and finally the color takes on mythological overtones. A symbol of the future, the baby aboard the ship is a metaphoric possessor of Ariadne's golden thread, the thread given to Theseus to ensure his safe exit from the labyrinth after slaying the Minotaur. As if to foreshadow the significance of the events on Tilbeck's yellow beach at Duneacres, Ozick concludes part 2 with a metaphor in which yellow predominates: "a dozen years later . . . Enoch stood at the doorway of his ambassadorship and . . . as its price, I was sent to my father's unknown doorway, the yellow, dank, and unknown doorway" (205). The two doorways, concrete representations of the structure of "Europe," summarize the doubleness peculiar to the narrator's world. It is a world divided between Enoch Vand and Gustave Nicholas Tilbeck.

Before she can reach Tilbeck's doorway, however, she must uncover the path that leads to it—the history of her mother and father. But the "long conspiratorial drone" behind the closed door of her mother's room renders that tale inaccessible. Ozick transforms the significance that James's "metaphor of opening doors" has in *The Portrait of a Lady*. There, as Dorothy Van Ghent points out, they are combined with the "theme of 'seeing' (the theme of the developing consciousness)" (700, 695). In *Trust* doors are mainly closed and are barriers not so much to increasing perception but to facts, to what Isabel Archer owns: the "heritage of the past." To prevent her daughter from meeting her unknown father in Europe, Allegra locked the child in its room; to exclude her daughter from the discussion of Tilbeck's letter at the beginning of part 3, Allegra shuts the door to her room. If closed doors obstruct the truth, they fire the narrator's fancy just as the "condemned" door in *The Portrait* becomes "to the child's imagination, according to its different moods, a region of delight or of terror" (33). About the "paternal command" the narrator conjectures: "I was not to be chauffeured or chaperoned into my father's mysteriously tardy jurisdiction: quite the opposite, he meant me to deliver myself up to him unaccompanied and free of home-snares, in the manner of Beauty returning, unguided and unguarded, to the terrible Beast" (210). Facts are obtained either forthrightly as James's Isabel Archer acquires them or, as the girl must procure them, furtively. Standing on the terrace of her mother's house in New York where she has been banished for hovering, she remembers "that long-ago ledge in Europe." It and the terrace are places of her "unredeemed childhood, a natural platform for one who is part of the scene and is at the same time outside the scene—the habitat, in short, of an eavesdropper" (219). Not to be an eavesdropper is to be an "intruder," in front of whom Allegra and her husband invest "every conversation with a Doppelgänger" and force the narrator to retreat to that "wafer in the air on which one accumulates reality" (219, 220).

But what is real must be judged, not merely accumulated. Manifesting the importance of yoking memory, history, and judgment, the structure of *Trust* corresponds to the Jewish idea of history, which accords it a dominant place and which maintains that the past has meaning.[14] It is this conception of history that Enoch expounds in "Brighton":

You think history is a sort of bundle one generation hauls off its back to launch onto the next. Every twenty-five years or so the bundle gets heavier and heavier. Nobody dares to throw it off and walk away and leave it behind. . . . But those are not the facts. Those are not the facts. . . . That isn't what history is. It doesn't keep on accumulating without conscience forever and forever. . . .

It's history that's the force! It's history that avenges and repays! It's history that raises the dead! And when we talk of redemption it's history we mean! (230–31)

Of decisive importance to the organization and the resolution of *Trust*, Enoch's proclamation, indeed his precise words, reappear in "On Living in the Gentile World," an essay Ozick published in 1972 and in which she proclaims, "The Jew chooses against nature and in behalf of the clarifying impulse. He chooses in behalf of history."[15] That such an explanation of history occurs near the beginning of part 3 implies that its revelations are necessary but insufficient: the narrator must assess the meaning of the events she has ascertained from her mother's letters in Brighton.

Awaiting the tenth of September, the date planned for her visit with Tilbeck, the narrator wants to hear not about the world but about her father, not of the "extraordinary sign," but of the ordinary fact (236). For that she must see William. Her "not-father" abounds in actuality and rectitude and is a perfect source for the uncompromising reply (239). To receive it she must travel from Main Street in New Rochelle, where "no one stood in doorways," to the door of William's office on Wall Street. She means to learn her father's tale before she arrives at Duneacres: "it was an island I was headed for; they would have me be Robinson Crusoe without any of the skills or imaginings of civilization, and worse, without a memory of how I came to be swept to that shore" (245). The allusion to Robinson Crusoe's island foreshadows the enlightenment and transformation to be obtained on Tilbeck's island. Before beginning her trip to William's office, she buys an aluminum dipper "to remind [herself] of the heavens—of the North star," of Enoch Vand, whose namesake guided Rabbi Ishmael through the upper world (246). Her earthly guide, however, turns out to be an albino cabdriver, a cultist of experience, a "philosopher for whom the world is cleft, like the devil's hoof, in two" (250). A fit escort for the "devil's own seed," whose guidebook is split in half, the driver has as an emblem of his divided world a rear-view mirror. It reflects his image the way the flag on the blue bicycle gave notice of the private visitor's identity.

The narrator's expedition, which takes place two days before the trip to Duneacres and which commences outside of Manhattan in New Rochelle and culminates in lower Manhattan on Wall Street, constitutes another instance of doubling and represents a journey to the underworld. Its gates are guarded just as access to William's office, where the narrator "entered hell," is barred by guests attending an engagement party for the attorney's son (316). A mere attendant at her own celebration, she is a "violator" at William's son's (254). The carnivorous would-be poet Euphoria Karp recalls the "parasite poets" at the *bon voyage* party, but Euphoria Karp's propensity to pun—she has written "Operation Cyst, A Gynecological Garland of Visceral Verses" and "Owed to the Placebo"—resembles Enoch's retreat into a "bramble of word-manipulation." Resenting her stepfather's "intricacies," the narrator disdains the would-be poet's doggerel. Enoch's glibness, Euphoria's gabble, the cab-driver's malapropisms and neologisms—these exemplify the word-manipulation forsworn by the narrator, for whom language is the means to divine reality, not obscure it. Attentive to the import of words, attorneys are no better than word-manipulators, for they tamper with facts, as the narrator discovers in the story of William's fraudulence. From William's son the narrator learns that her grandfather Huntingdon appointed William as the trustee responsible for the construction of a marine museum on his estate at Duneacres. It was a mandate William never carried out, nor did he keep up Huntingdon's place. Imparting to the girl the actuality of what she always regarded as a "familiar marble certainty . . . reliable and unchanging," William's son razes the narrator's monument, reduces William to a "trampled grotto, violated shrine," a heap of rubble (309, 310). But William's office, an "unlucky labyrinth," is a place to learn the truth (311). Determined like Enoch to see "consequences *as* possibilities," the narrator barters her freedom for truth, and in that transaction she discovers the fact of her illegitimacy and enters the doorway to hell (311).

William's chronicle of the particulars surrounding her birth differs significantly from Enoch's view of history; Supplanting history with destiny, which the girl deems irrelevant, William rearranges facts so as to invest them with morality. "In court, about to be sentenced," she stares out the window where she fancies she sees the "god Pan . . . clutching a bunch of wild flowers, hellebore and jewelweed, and laughing a long and careless jingle of a laugh, like bicycle bells" (317). The fantasy recalls her first glimpse of her unknown father through a window in Europe and identifies the narrator with the Pan-like Tilbeck. But Enoch's influence informs her alteration of William's tale: "He did not tell it as I shall tell it, with the crowding of chronology" (322).

The history of her mother's youth includes the story of William and Allegra's relationship. Religious, dutiful, and scornful of the symbolic and the intangible, William was drawn first to paleontology and then to law. Exactly the opposite of William, the reckless and wild Allegra had written a poem affirming her allegiance to Shelley, a champion of Greece. Despite their conflicting attitudes, Allegra and William married, but on their honeymoon in Cape Ann during September, Allegra threw her Shelley into the water. William mistook her gesture: to drown Shelley was not to accept William, and Allegra turned her back on William to have intercourse with him. When they returned from their honeymoon, Allegra made plans to assemble a camp at Duneacres to discuss a classless society and to prepare for a "Moscow March for a Better Future," a proletarian youth movement. Though he disapprovingly compared the camp to Brook Farm, William wanted Allegra's loyalty so he disobeyed the terms of the trust, financed the camp, and reneged on a promise to the Armenian boy John Vermoulian. He responded to the loss of his job by cutting his throat with a fish-cleaning knife. In turn Allegra betrayed her husband. She went to Moscow with Enoch Vand and Nick Tilbeck on a ship Ozick ironically names the *Croesus,* and finally after more than a year of traveling, Allegra took a cottage in Brighton, England, with Nick. There William was cuckolded by Tilbeck and Allegra gave birth to his daughter.

The walls of the cottage at Brighton, their "color . . . the inside of an eggshell," suggest birth, the birth of the narrator and the creation of *Marianna Harlow.* Inspired by Nick, who claimed it was "Walter Pater crossed with George Eliot," the novel is itself a reflection of *Trust's* duality. If halves and doubles pervade *Trust, Marianna Harlow,* whose chief influence is *The Bobbsey Twins,* concerns the conflict between twins, is about "passion and death" (379, 28). Ozick's allusion to Richardson's voluminous novel is not fortuitous, for like *Clarissa, Marianna Harlow* raises the issue of filial disobedience, and its author was addicted to the epistolary form, as evidenced by the "Long, long letters" Allegra wrote William from Brighton, the letters Enoch claims comprise "a little history of abandonment" (473). Allegra's "Genre writing," a dominant form in Cynthia Ozick's own fiction, enables the narrator to reconstruct her mother's story, and judge the three fathers.

It was Nick, the narrator learns, who ascertained that Allegra was a pagan and who "called [her] an ancient Greek"; it was Nick who devised the dart game without a target, and it was with Nick that Allegra heard the dryad shriek, heralding her daughter's birth and warning of her lover's disappearance. The lover who vanished, not the husband who misunderstood, embittered Allegra: she signed William's divorce papers, but grieved over the loss of Nick's Sacred Beauty and ancient Greece. In a letter to William about the "sort of thin and holy-looking" tree outside her window, Allegra explained the distinction between her paganism and William's Christianity: "If you want to know what I mean by Sacred I mean anything that's alive, and Beauty is anything that makes you want to *be* alive and alive forever, with a sort of shining feeling" (385). Her image connects the child's "shining stick" and the "sheeny heads" of the wild wedding party to the Sacred Beauty revered by pagans and anticipates the girl's experience in front of a tree on Town Island.

The dichotomy between the two world views begins to tell again in Brighton as Ozick juxtaposes Enoch, who practices the "cult of a single idea," against Nick, who represents the "cult of art . . . the cult of experience" (372, 69). Enoch's ideas of Social Justice clashed with Nick's feelings about Sacred Beauty and ancient Greece, as a conversation recorded by Allegra makes clear. To Nick's assertion that man's birthright is personal Enoch responded: "it belongs to him personally, he personally must act on it, but in itself it's an abstraction. His birthright is a message against killing; against killing as a theory and a methodology." The message, Enoch had argued, is like God, "an abstraction that can't be proved." It was an abstraction Nick rejected. Because he wanted a tangible God whom he could "touch with a clang," Nick "had to settle for gods" (398–99). Because only personal values mattered to him, he abandoned Allegra and their daughter in Brighton, leaving Enoch to quit the Party and marry the new mother.

Her daughter's illegitimacy, William explains, motivated Allegra to remarry and to submit to Tilbeck's demands, to agree to her daughter's visit to Duneacres in exchange for Tilbeck's promise not to reveal the circumstances of the girl's birth. In effect the mother has traded the daughter for Enoch's ambassadorship. Recognizing Allegra has paid for the one man the girl thought was untouched by her mother's money, she moves closer to Tilbeck, the only free man, the "only one who seems to value her" (437). But William disdains Enoch, who could have salvaged a name for the illegitimate child through adoption, and Nick, to whom she feels a new allegiance. Her "not-father" strips her of any relationship to him whatsoever, despoils her of respect for him, and removes himself from her world. Her interest in the Christian civilization he represents crumbles with him. Never accepting Christ, whom she calls bitter and loveless, and once mistaking the Holy Ghost for a candy bar, she identifies with Enoch, for whom Christ was a "great villain." However, the narrator's "plain pagan philosophy" allies her to Nick and not Enoch, who "insisted God ought to stay what he is, a principle which it is blasphemy to visualize" (321, 427). For the first time in the novel, she stands in the doorway looking out on an open horizon. Where she will arrive when she walks from that doorway is intimated in the finality of her departure from William and in the tension between Enoch's power and Tilbeck's magnetism, the competing forces of part 4.

II

"Duneacres," like "America," begins with the narrator's reflections on marriage, an important and recurrent motif in *Trust*. Although William insisted Allegra agreed to marry Enoch for respectability, her daughter knows that "it is only the secret reasons which really account for a marriage." All that was irretrievable—Nick, Brighton, time—convinced Allegra to marry Enoch, to "invent his future," to "succumb to the ordinary" (447, 454, 448). But Enoch's future and her father's summons have provided the narrator with the opportunity to redeem her past and have compelled her to confront the extraordinary fact of her illegitimacy. On that fact rests the issue of the girl's freedom, which Allegra hoped to give her daughter by hiding from her the existence of Gustave Nicholas Tilbeck. To answer Allegra's tearful question about the timing of her daughter's discovery, Enoch repeats an aphorism from the talmudic tractate *Pirke Avot* (Ethics of the Fathers)—"If not now, when?" (468). That the girl believes the present propitious emerges in her decision never to enter Enoch's house, "that Embassy, bought for him by my mother, paid for by my surrender to my father. . . . Did they pity me, those counterfeit fathers, false Enoch, false William, who gave me for hostage so that my mother in her appetite might take an Embassy . . . ?" (476).

Made immediately before her departure, this resolution underscores the necessity for her trip to Town Island, where enlightened by the history Enoch has provided her, she can judge her father and attain true freedom—liberation from the bondage of not knowing. The ultimate self-comprehension the narrator attains must also encompass apprehension of her place in the universe: for Ozick full consciousness entails not only self-knowledge but knowledge of civilization as well. Anticipated in each part of the novel, the issue of Hebraism-versus-Hellenism animates part 4, in which Ozick doubles images, motifs, and allusions appearing throughout *Trust* and then weaves them together into a tapestry of exquisite beauty. Each episode in "Duneacres," from the initial experience the narrator has in front of the tree to the final revelation she gains in Huntingdon's house, brings her progressively closer to the truth, to full understanding.

To reach the first stage of her quest, the narrator is transported by her mother's chauffeur, another of the escorts who accompany her on her pursuit for information, to a swamp near Duneacres where Tilbeck has directed her to wait for him. There the narrator becomes aware, as she had in Europe ten years earlier, of Sacred Beauty in a tree "with a full misty mane like a bush" standing near the remains of a dock. As she awaits Tilbeck's arrival, she experiences nature's power in an Emersonian vision of the tree:

> In the middle of this the tree blazed. Lens upon lens burned in the leaves with a luminosity just short of glass and nearer to vapor; the veins were isinglass ducts swarming with light, running knife-bright into stems, and the stems pursuing twigs, and the twigs branches, and the branches hurtling into the bole like rays recaptured, undoing refraction: the whole short powerful trunk a prism in remorse gathering in its tribes of beams, all imaginable exiled light flowing and flowing home to the mother-light. (480)

At first, the tree is an "eye," then a "mind," living because she lived and "had made it." Her wonder quickens as she gazes at the tree's incandescence: "I came to the wooden lily-leaf to sit upon it and stare, as once the Buddha sat and stared, and, seeing, showed himself divine; I was nymph, naiad, sprite, goddess; I had gifts, powers; and the tree worshipped, because I could conjure flame in it." Then the sun slides away, taking its light from the tree, and she knows herself to be "profane"—profane because irreligious, because uninitiated (481).

But the tree's light transforms. Fusing numerous allusions, Ozick multiplies the significance of the tree. Each of her allusions anticipates the events about to transpire at Duneacres; each possesses profound implications for the last part of *Trust* and for the vision it affords. The Swedish Tilbeck's "whitewatery hair" connects him to Yggdrasil, whose uppermost branches were thought to be "bathed in watery white vapours," and suggests him as a source of cosmic knowledge (Eliade, *Patterns* 265, 276, 277). Like the burning bush in Exodus, the tree constitutes a revelation of God and a promise of liberation. Refracting and reflecting the sunlight, the tree resembles the Inverted Tree in the *Zohar,* which illuminates the secret relationship of God, human beings, and the universe.[16] The Bodhi, the tree of Buddha's awakening, was the agent that freed him from bondage, and Buddha, the "Awakened One," was identified with light (Eliade, *History* 2:217). Garnering those associations and adding to them the trees present at initiation ceremonies in ancient Greece, the divine life inhabiting Zeus's sacred oak, and the tree in the Book of Enoch which was an emblem of the great judgment, Ozick fashions the tree in the swamp into a multifaceted symbol of the rites about to be performed at Duneacres. The scene in the swamp, richly imbricated, is a hieroglyph of "Duneacres"; such a scene begins each part of *Trust,* itself a series of recognitions.[17]

The narrator's vision fades: the "sun had carried off its consecrations." Left alone in the swamp all afternoon, the girl speaks "to the tree (which out of convenience represented Tilbeck)." Imagining herself as a dryad who has "given life . . . to a tree," the narrator identifies with Tilbeck, who in Brighton declared a dryad the presider over his daughter's birth (482). However, the similarities the tree bears to biblical trees and to the tree in the Book of Enoch make the tree in the swamp an emblem of Enoch Vand, an embodiment of both Hebraism and Hellenism. That the narrator calls the tree a "recently looking-glass tree . . . in which [she] nearly saw [herself]" and that the tree then becomes "perfectly opaque" recall and double the experience the ten-year-old child had on the grass in France (482). The twenty-two-year-old feels similarly transmuted, but clarity wanes and she mistakes the boy, who finally arrives to cross her over to Duneacres, for Tilbeck.

Naked to his waist, the boatman conjures up the narrator's image of her unknown father as an indolent mariner lying half-nude on his beach. Increasing the imagery of halves, Ozick reinforces the conflict central to part 4. The boy moves in his craft "like a sort of Norse centaur, the top half human, the lower half presumably the parts of a boat." When she hears her father's name, the narrator wonders whether the voice calling Tilbeck belongs to a boy or to the water. Another dimension to her voyage is signaled by the "primordial glance" the boatman gives her, his glasses that twinkle "light like semaphores," the question he asks her about the *Odyssey* (483, 487). The question recalls Tilbeck's allusion to Homer's epic in part 3, links the boy to the girl's father, and suggests a double significance to the structure of *Trust.*

On one level, the four-part structure of Ozick's novel dramatizes the meaning of memory and history in the Jewish experience, the sustaining and enduring conviction that history judges humanity, that humanity's awareness of the past presses humanity toward a more searching consciousness of the moral life, a more exigent conception of the self as a part of the universe. Recovery of the father entails perforce comprehension of the shaping cultural forces of humanity. The narrator's rejection of William at the end of part 3 severs her from Christianity and affirms Hebraism and Hellenism as the forces in part 4.

Explicitly connecting her novel to the *Odyssey,* to the journey undertaken by Telemachos and to the adventures encountered by his father, Ozick intimates the importance Homer's epic possesses for *Trust.* Into the narrator's final recognition, the novelist interweaves allusions to the Telemachy and the Wanderings of Odysseus, fusing Telemachos's quest with Odysseus's homecoming. To gain illumination and all that it implies, the narrator must seek a reunion with the father who disappeared into Europe during the war just as Telemachos must discover whether his father survived the battle in Troy. Neither the girl nor Telemachos can be certain of their fathers, for as Telemachos tells Athene, "nobody really knows his own father," the father whom the son, like the girl, envisages in doorways.[18] Anxieties about the present and the future beset Telemachos and the narrator. Their connection between past and present lost, their identities and egos weakened, both children must search for and find their fathers. For those reasons, Telemachos journeys to Pylos and Sparta; for those reasons the narrator questions Enoch and William. Knowledge of Odysseus and Tilbeck will assure their children that theirs are not births "that will go nameless" (1.222). Along with his hosts' knowledge of Odysseus, Telemachos receives gold and silver gifts. Reviving in part 1 the Greek custom of gift-giving, Ozick transforms the narrator's gold and silver dress into an emblem of Tilbeck, alludes to the purpose of Telemachos's voyage, and identifies it with her narrator's.

As the boatman, "Charon the ferryman," who is "part of every story," steers the girl closer and closer to Duneacres, the mythic significance of the place deepens; for she learns that Tilbeck is thought to have an "island right off Greece," an island she names Crete (550, 492). The alliance she envisions between Tilbeck and Crete and the presence of nine members of the Purse family on Town Island suggest a likeness between them and the nine Curetes who originated in Crete and protected the infant Zeus. The mention of Crete, the number nine, the water that "blossomed like . . . the labyrinths of the human ear"—these refer to the tribute paid to Crete every nine years when youths and maidens were thrown to the Minotaur (501). Forging a link between Charon and the boatman, whom she names Henry David Thoreau Purse, Ozick intimates that her narrator's voyage is one bound for the core of the universe.

As they approach the beach, "that sliver of . . . initiation into daughterness," the girl glimpses Mrs. Purse kneeling on the sand: "Objects littered the sand, some mobile, some not. From afar, it was a view of the pristine and the not-yet-corrupted: Eve in Paradise on the world's sixth day, surrounded by the forms of nature" (504, 499). But proximity converts the narrator's image: "Mrs. Purse was Circe modernized, extemporized, and finally mechanized" (505). The two portraits of Mrs. Purse represent the contrast between "Eve, who produced self-conscious lust" and "Circe, who rewarded it," distinguish the Bible from the *Odyssey,* and set forth the conflict between Hebraism and Hellenism (504). Ozick implies that Town Island, like the Garden of Eden and Circe's island, will not only initiate but will transform. That she chooses the name Purse, a reference to Circe's brother in book 10 of the *Odyssey,* recalls

Odysseus's plans to remain on Circe's island two days, the length of time the narrator spends on Town Island.

The Purse family, whom Tilbeck has invited to stay at Duneacres, is awaiting a flight to Pakistan where, aided by a grant from the Ford Foundation, Mr. Purse, a paleontologist, plans to pursue his research. Endowing the Purses with "representative American characteristics" and naming four of the children after the Transcendentalist writers Whitman, Emerson, Thoreau, and Bronson Alcott and the other three after the religious leaders Mohandas K. Gandhi and George Fox and the advocate of abolition Harriet Beecher Stowe, Ozick conjures up Allegra's attempt to resurrect Brook Farm on Town Island. A "compendium of both the strengths and petty vices of middle America," the Purses "step into the role of ambassadors from America that Enoch and Allegra fail to fulfill" (Strandberg 96).

Mr. Purse's interest in paleontology, the tangible, and Mrs. Purse's addiction to puns and extravagant language, revive in Duneacres the two world views represented throughout the other parts of *Trust* by attorneys and poets. If the Purses embody a contest central to the novel, that between reason and the imagination, their camp embodies the American ideals Allegra's camp sought to escape. Resourceful and inventive, Mrs. Purse cannibalizes the beach and transforms its detritus into objects that function. Though the Purses claim to be Quakers, followers of the doctrine of inner light taught by George Fox, that light radiates their paganism. Adopting the "stance Emerson calls for in his essay 'Circles' "—his belief in the newness of each moment in nature—the Purses exhibit their reverence for the pagan gods of nature and "become part of the Dionysian procession on Tilbeck's magic island" (Strandberg 97). The Purses participate in the idyll into which Tilbeck has transformed Town Island, it is true; but the duplicate view the girl initially has of Mrs. Purse suggests that like Tilbeck's Hellenism, the Purses' Americanism is not unalloyed. If the family members are ingenious, their last name registers their acquisitiveness; if Mrs. Purse is bound by marriage vows, she feels free to break them. Her "nightly trysts with Tilbeck" may, as Victor Strandberg argues, "signify her larger importance as a sort of love goddess," but they also testify to her lawlessness, to the possibility of her having an illegitimate child like the narrator (Strandberg 97).

Together the nine Purses are yoked to Tilbeck as a symbol of cosmic knowledge, for Odin hung on Yggdrasil nine days in order to conquer death and gain wisdom. A source of such wisdom, Tilbeck also has the capacity to conduct the initiation rites on Town Island, and in that connection, the nine members of the Purse family conjure up the nine days Demeter wandered upon the earth looking for her daughter. Multiplying associations, Ozick also alludes to *Navapatrika* (the nine leaves), the Indian rite of fertility and regeneration. Town Island may be a place for initiation rites and rites of regeneration—a place which "harbors nature's deeply immanent Life Force"—but it is also a location haunted by the death of John Vermoulian (Strandberg 95).[19] Unlike her mother, the daughter will participate in these rites on Town Island; she will confront her destiny in America, not in Europe.

This inversion of James's sense of Europe as the place for a young woman to affront her destiny instances once again the way in which Ozick reverses, for her own artistic purposes, convictions important to the Master's art. That the narrator quotes the first sentence of *The Portrait of a Lady* when she first sees Tilbeck and the table under the trees signals a comparison of Duneacres and Gardencourt. That the narrator observes Tilbeck before he notices her recalls the second chapter of the *Portrait* when Isabel Archer makes her appearance in the doorway before Ralph Touchett sees her. Like the house at Gardencourt, Duneacres "had a name and a history" (James, PL 18). If the English manor house is haunted by a family ghost, Huntingdon's estate has been the site of a suicide. Placing Isabel Archer on the threshold of the doorway, James implied his heroine's potential for life and freedom; Ozick's narrator stands outside the house, aware of where freedom is to be found. Their lives stretching before them, the two heroines follow divergent paths, arrive at diverse destinations.

The scene witnessed by the narrator marks the disparity between hers and Isabel Archer's destinies. Before her, on a patch of ground lacking court lines and missing a net, Tilbeck plays tennis with Mr. Purse. Devoid of rules and boundaries—the essence of Tilbeck's life—the game, reminiscent of the dart game Tilbeck invented in Brighton, demands imagination, something wanting in Purse, for whom the palpable is an absolute necessity. Governed by opposite forces, Tilbeck and Purse appear to be divided by attitude, separated by age. Abandoning himself to play, Tilbeck laughs, misses serves, pants "recklessly," stamps youthfully "through fierceness of weed-growth like a clever circus horse" (511). Concentrating on work, Purse seems old as he dashes after the ball, breathes vigorously, and "looked like what he was, a father" (512). As "perfect as the rich yolk of an egg," the late sun makes the players seem closer than they are, and as the narrator walks toward them through what once might have been a "formal garden," she sees

> decayed trellises and dead thorns all over . . . and in the center of a sort of grove an astonishing stone ruin, broken like a Greek shrine. It was the remains of a fountain. A hollow finger of pipe protruded from the ground; and a long thick ugly serpent-like chain meandered near it. The chain led to rubble—a stump with kicked-away points at either end: it was an anchor of stone. (510)

Tilbeck's domain is a fallen paradise, a blasted Garden of Eden, a dilapidated Arcady. The "rot of disappointment" seizes the narrator, for the recognition that her father cares for nothing save pleasure, that she was made by a "boy of seventeen" out of the "merest merest whim," dashes her dreams (512).

Calling her "Tourist," Tilbeck functions like the girl's cicerone the way Ralph Touchett and Gilbert Osmond function as Isabel's. But Tilbeck guides his daughter through the filth, the mouse feces, the rotting walls of the "ruined abbey" Huntingdon called Duneacres (519). Now a tourist, the narrator remains, as she has throughout *Trust,* an attendant, an eavesdropper, an interloper. And Tilbeck annihilates her imaginings of him when he reveals his father to have been a Swedish longshoreman who died drunk in the gutters of Seattle and then avows, much to the "disinterested observer's" dismay, that truth can only be "partisan" and is never "seen from the center." Every crevice in Duneacres, he repeatedly points out, is filled with "filth" (516, 515). His constant emphasis on dirt recalls Allegra's admonishing her small child not to be "always fooling with something filthy" (186). Her mother's remark joins the girl to her father, but her answer to Tilbeck's question about what she judges allies her to Enoch. Only "History" and "records," she replies, can distinguish "what's real" from "what isn't" (515, 518). Of her first day at Duneacres, she concludes: "It was an idyll" (520).

Toward evening, as their conversation continues, she thinks of Tilbeck as a "centrality of light . . . that issues . . . that receives," a the tree in the swamp (526). Declaring himself a Greek who dreamt up the Parthenon—that memorial to artistic grandeur—he reminds her that she, too, is part Greek. But she corrects her father's misapprehension by echoing her stepfather, from whom she learned that slaves built the Parthenon. When Tilbeck invites her to take his side against Allegra, the girl's perception of him is telling: "His eyes seemed silver, rooted deeply into his face like a startling pair of flowers: the thick lids an inch of leaf" (530). Invoking the two flowers in ENCHIRIDION and alluding to the tree in the swamp, the narrator reveals her impression of her father. It recalls her apprehension of the private visitor: "Expecting the infernal Dante, I had found the Virgil of the Eclogues—a green land with a shepherd in it . . . a factor of the earth," a factor linking her to nature (531).

That identification of Tilbeck and Virgil establishes Town Island as Arcady, the domain of Pan, the realm Virgil idealized and transformed into a Utopia. But Duneacres is haunted by betrayal and death.[20] Allegra remembered her experience with Nick in Brighton as a Golden Age; her daughter considers her father the fabricator of an idyll, a romance remote from the realities of everyday existence. And her sense of an idyll is Enoch's: "An idyll twists nature, and spins us lawns and pipers where life delivers a marsh and toilers, and, ignoring a rapacious commerce in slaves testifying to other things, gilds us a Greece of athletes, leaf-crowned, beautiful" (422).[21] Because she knows the difference between reality and "hoaxing Romance," the daughter scorns her father's "Vikings and his Greeks"; they inhabit the myth Tilbeck has fashioned for himself, a myth Enoch has told her cannot own the "reality of the possible." But she values Nick's walk: it "was as real as his hand" (422, 533, 421, 533).

Proclaiming the word "now" as the one "to live by" and announcing the time ripe "to look into the mirror of the future," Tilbeck invites her on a boat ride. On the beach she finds a pocket mirror, Nick's mirror of the future. In its reflection, she sees her face and her shining lips; but the mirror cracks "like the two remembered halves of the vernal ENCHIRIDION," like Tilbeck, who looked "like a faun—half man, half motor" (535, 534). Half man Tilbeck thinks of himself as part god: "Why not Thor? Why not Loki? Why not Apollo. . . . I was named all wrong. More's the pity. Well, in my time they didn't call babies

Zeus" (535). To his list the girl adds Pan. Like ENCHIRIDION and the mirror, the list is constructed of halves, of gods who are half fertile, half deadly. Sky gods and storm gods, Zeus and Thor are "fecundators." However, Loki, often a malevolent imposter, consorted with the gods and possessed a demonic side not unlike the "terror-awakening" characteristics ascribed to Pan (Kerényi 174). Alluding to these gods, Ozick implies that the girl's initiation into daughterness is doubly significant; it is a fertility rite, but one with certain destructive elements.[22]

They are suggested by the mirror, which gives back a new reflection but which cuts the girl's finger and by Nick, who licks it the way the country people do "in Sicily . . . to stop a virgin's bleeding." Elsewhere in *Trust* the tongue occurs in connection with Tilbeck, but in conflicting contexts. Thinking of how lust for money breeds deceit, the daughter imagines her father "owning some iron god or demon nourished by the taste of purity and panting after innocents with his long iron tongue, licking them to rust and corrosion at last" (74). But one of his emblems, the fertile jewelweed, has blossoms "culminating in short spurs the hue of a kitten's tongue" (180). Ambivalence also inheres in the image for Nick's eye—a "great lily" (535). Clutching the false hellebore, a poisonous flower belonging to the lily family, Tilbeck can arrest. But he is also the Buddha who awakens:

> Another wetness wet my finger. Instantly the air dried it. The same wetness came on my lip. I tasted his saliva on my lip. The taste of the blood from my finger mingled faintly on the inner skin of my lip. Carelessly and silently he entered my mouth. . . . His hand massing at my ankle was a tower. The faculty of taste altered and became skill. Carelessly and silently an evanescent tissue of the wine's floweriness opened a deep secret room. Unseeingness unlocks. Strange and new, I breathed the minotaur.
>   Then ran. (535)

Replete with incestuous overtones and suffused with images from initiation myths, the scene garners significance from each of them and intimates the narrator's experience is a night journey—an exploration of the underworld of the psyche, an event symbolic of the new birth that bestows spiritual regeneration. That they are connected to the Curetes in their function of initiators makes the Purses part of the rite of passage. It and their name add another dimension to the experience, for the name Perses is relevant to Persephone and the Eleusinian Mysteries.[23] The Mysteries in which Demeter, to whom Nick refers in part 3, participated were celebrated in the month of Boedromian (September–October), the same month Allegra and William went to Cape Ann for their honeymoon, the same month Crusoe embarked on his voyage.[24] Foreshadowed by the primordial look the girl recognizes on her boatman's face, the Eleusinian initiation was thought to reveal, among other things, the nature of sexuality and procreation. A mirror and blood were part of the Mystery religions: one suggested self-knowledge and the other was dripped onto the initiates as part of the rituals.[25] To those allusions Ozick adds Gnostic implications which she intimates in the pervasive filth at Duneacres. The Gnostic initiation, in which the initiate "puts on 'filthy garb' " or "the 'fleshly envelope,' " signified an "act of 'awakening' " in which the novice attained knowledge of self and an identity (Eliade, *History* 2:381–83). Yoking elements from the Gnostic tradition to other initiation myths, she affirms the scene on the beach as an introduction to sexuality, an immersion in matter.[26]

To gather metaphors, images, and motifs from various initiation rites is to dramatize the universality of the girl's psychic experience, the erotic and incestuous attachment to the father. The same capriciousness and carelessness Tilbeck displayed when he left his illegitimate daughter in Brighton affords him license to excite in her the very desires which she must tame in order to mature. Superimposing mythic elements from the world's sacred history onto psychic truths, Ozick affirms a conviction crucial not only for *Trust* but for all of her fiction: an individual's self-knowledge is inextricable from knowledge of civilization's history.[27] That the narrator glimpses herself in half of the mirror recalls the looking-glass tree in which she nearly saw herself and suggests that her self-knowledge is incomplete, that her identification with Tilbeck is partial. She has breathed the Minotaur, not seen him. The initiation rites are unfinished.

Throughout the four parts of *Trust* and at each step of the girl's discoveries, references to labyrinths are prominent. Early in "America," the trust fund is recognized by the narrator to be "labyrinthine as a cave, and as difficult to comprehend"; before she is aware of her illegitimacy, she compares William's office to an "unlucky labyrinth"; and as Thoreau Purse steers her closer and closer to Tilbeck, the water reminds her of a labyrinth (58, 311). Running from Tilbeck, "from the faun, head of a family," she hears his Pan-like laughter just as she enters the house (535). To complete the initiation, she must penetrate to the heart of the labyrinth and slay the Minotaur. That entry into the center of the labyrinth has resonances for initiation rites and for achieving total reality is made clear by the symbolic power accorded to centers by all religious traditions: "Since the creation of the world began in a given centre, the creation of man could only take place on that same spot, *real* and *living* in the highest degree" (Eliade, *Patterns* 378).[28] The source of all reality, the center is crucial to initiation myths and to Theseus's ordeals in the labyrinth at Crete: "To reach the 'centre' is to achieve a consecration, an initiation. To the profane and illusory existence of yesterday, there succeeds a new existence, real, lasting and powerful" (Eliade, *Patterns* 382).[29] Until the narrator returns from the labyrinth at Duneacres, the estate Huntingdon planned as a museum in which the history of the origin of life could be learned, it cannot be said that she has ended her journey.

Her second day at Duneacres brings her progressively closer to the labyrinth's center. In the morning Mrs. Purse asks the narrator why Tilbeck lured her to the beach "in the dead of night" (537). Aware that her answer has "some fantastic element" in it, she tells Mrs. Purse the boat ride her father proposed did not occur, but the narrator stiffens with shock when she learns Tilbeck has lied and told the Purses that her mother is dead (539). And she joins to Tilbeck's lie the fantastic element in the walk on the beach: "Tilbeck dared anything. He dared the lie that plays with life and death. He trusted . . . in a God like a man—interested more in the phantasmal re-arrangement of justice than in justice" (539). The bloody underside of nature, its "tragic grain," begins to show when the girl's cut finger reminds Mrs. Purse of the young Armenian's suicide, an event that has made Mr. Purse call Town Island a "cemetery" (425, 543). Suspicious of Tilbeck's involvement in John Vermoulian's death, Mr. Purse doubts the truth of Tilbeck's claim—that he and the girl are father and daughter, like Prospero and Miranda.

The allusion to Shakespeare's *The Tempest* augments the significance of the unusual events on Town Island. A day spent there with Tilbeck is idyllic. The "idyll" begins "to pall" on the second day when the narrator recognizes, the way Enoch had in Brighton, "that there is no Eden without its secret coil of treachery," that within magic lurks the perilous power to distort truth (549, 428). For the narrator of *Trust*, "Magic is inanity, is imbecile, and exists for its own sake"; like "stasis" and "monomania," magic impedes progress and "leads nowhere" (551). To watch the Purses, the narrator concludes, is to witness monomania; to listen to the Purses' children is to understand that words can be adored as "magic-in-themselves" rather than valued "for their uses" (551). The narrator's rejection of magic allies her to Prospero who, like Tilbeck, enlightens his daughter and awakens her. But the narrator of *Trust* is also related to Ariel, for the two days she spends on Town Island is exactly the length of time Ariel must remain on Prospero's island. Connecting her narrator to Ariel, Ozick stresses the girl's capacity for change; nicknaming one of the Purse children Caliban, she severs the girl from the Purses' stasis. If Caliban, the "thing of darkness," confounds Prospero's powers and remains "A devil, a born devil, on whose nature / Nurture can never stick," Ariel symbolizes change (IV.1.188).[30] Their incapacity for change, their willed apartness from the process of "becoming," their "terrifying chatter (word-love)"—these make the narrator repudiate the "Purselets out of the tale" and align her with Prospero. When she eschews the magical process that renders "lyre" and "lute" indistinguishable from "liar" and "loot," she echoes Prospero's abjuration of magic and illusion in the famous epilogue to *The Tempest;* and in her choice of the words lyre and lute, emblems of art, Ozick indicates from what direction her narrator's destiny beckons (551).

That destiny is shaped by the transformations on Town Island, which approximate the changes that occur on Prospero's island after new visitors arrive by boat. Approaching the shore of Tilbeck's island, the boat resembles a horse that "cantered on the water"; then the boat "came like the dolphin" whom Huntingdon "revered as the equal of humankind," and finally the boat is associated with Tilbeck when the girl, remembering that her father "sings Robert Frost," thinks, "In the sea there is no road not taken" (521, 548). The boat, the horse, and the dolphin—attributes of Poseidon—align Tilbeck to the

Greek god of the trackless sea and anticipate the meaning of the subsequent events. At first the narrator envisions the visitors, Stephanie Pettigrew and William's son, the way Allegra and Nick must have looked when they came to the island. The narrator's "movie-sense" of the boat's movement augurs the history the narrator will recover from the visitors to Town Island, the island which, unlike Circe's, "turned men from what they seemed to what they were" (548, 561).

Further knowledge of what Tilbeck is becomes clearer at the "Last Supper" which he arranges and at which he disparages Christianity.[31] At the piano, his head "reared wonderfully back, like some sky-white horse," Tilbeck declares himself "Thor at the clavier." Ozick establishes his unmistakable identification with water gods and paganism when the rain begins. The storm gods Zeus and Poseidon are as irresponsible as Tilbeck, who "sticks to himself" (569). Unlike Enoch Vand who believes in "wedding-glue" and remains "engaged and engrossed in the world" and unlike his stepdaughter who devours newspapers because she is eager to learn about the world, Gustave Nicholas Tilbeck burns newspapers out of indifference to facts about others, "just to show 'em what it is to own yourself. Show who you belong to" (543, 570). His laughter mounting as he plays the piano, he conjures up the narrator's vision of him at the window of William's office, the sight of Pan laughing his musical laugh and clutching his woodland flowers. A woodland god, Pan was born laughing and passed his days idly playing his pipes. Tilbeck has dwelt in the Arcady Allegra's money has provided, staying the same, never changing. But knowledge, the "only real event in the world," turns in the narrator. What the mother knew once the daughter knows now. Adding another dimension to the tongue imagery, her father says she has come to Duneacres "to get the taste of things," to get the taste of him (530).

Hunger for a taste of his life has the narrator wandering with Stephanie and William's son through her grandfather's house to retrace Tilbeck's path, to penetrate the secret in the center of the deep room. Their "slow voyagings through those ruin-laden upper rooms," which seem to the narrator "mazily interconnected," link labyrinth to water (586, 584). And the narrator's "underwater sense," the "viscous floating memory" of "that birth fluid . . . [that] vast amniotic pool" reveal that the secret the labyrinth harbors is knowledge of the narrator's own creation—the "thing or spirit, whatever it might be, that connects us to the certainty of life" (581, 582). The three wanderers penetrate to "the egg's center, a crucial pith, an innermost room" where they are awash "in a yellow sea," the water near the indolent mariner's beach (584). Anticipated by the color of the walls in the cottage at Brighton, the sun behind Tilbeck's tennis game, and the moon after the initiation scene on the beach, the egg imagery recalls the color of the tree in the swamp, the tree the narrator designated Tilbeck. Identifying him with Zeus, the sky-god, Ozick joins Tilbeck to the primordial egg from which Eros sprang and to the cosmic egg common to creation myths. Whatever myth the egg belongs to, its symbolic value "is not that of ordinary birth, but rather the *repeating of the archetypal birth* of the cosmos, the imitation of the cosmogony . . . the resurrection which . . . is not a birth, but a 'return,' a 'repetition.' " The egg's ritual significance is that it "guarantees the possibility of *repeating the primeval act,* the act of creation" (Eliade, *Patterns* 414–15, 416).[32]

On a "quest for consequence" because she, like Isabel Archer, likes "places in which things have happened," the narrator watches the lovers kiss and feels what her mother felt: the "flick of a tongue" has established her daughter as initiate, has given her "knowledge of the private thing," the principle of generation (585, 586; PL 35). But she is not Stephanie and William's son's witness:

> I did not see them. I saw Nick. I saw myself. We lay crouching in one another's mind: private. In me private knowledge grew like a worm. . . .
>
> Yet something had happened—not in them. In me the private thing turned: knowledge turned, love turned, what my mother knew I knew. (586–87)

The girl knows the "privacy of complicity" has "failed" the lovers, just as the absence of accord had stymied Allegra and William. If a volume of Shelley's poetry came between Allegra and William on their honeymoon in Cape Ann, *"The Law of the Sea* separated" the lovers' "torsos like a grid" in Huntingdon's mansion (585). Observing Stephanie Pettigrew and William's son, the girl conjures up his father and her mother. The present, the time the girl's father lives by, occasions in his daughter memories of the past. They attach to the events the narrator perceives now meaning they would not otherwise have had and transform them into the powerful agents that usher unremembered thoughts into consciousness. Recovery of them yields self-knowledge, the insight the narrator must attain to lift the embargo on her future. Ozick renders that intricate psychological process with consummate narrative skill. Recounting the lovers' sexual activities, the narrator blurs identities, brings her own recollections into sharp relief, and apprehends in Stephanie and William's son's experience her mother's with William. With her understanding of Allegra comes the daughter's alliance with her mother. When the daughter returns to her father, however, she discovers he "had all the while been waiting" for Stephanie (588). Astonished and dismayed, the narrator revives Tilbeck's interest in her with the announcement, "The same for my mother and the same for me" (590). And her mother's lover argues with his daughter the way he had with his lover long ago in Brighton: "For a moment," his daughter thinks, "we seemed to echo the flirting lovers in the wood" (590). The moment is ephemeral, for the reappearance of Stephanie and William's son diverts Tilbeck's attention and provokes the narrator's jealousy.

As the rain, Ozick's constant signal of approaching clarity, steadily grows more abundant, the narrator witnesses the "instant of love's consummation," but the union is not between the lovers she had expected. A re-enactment of the intercourse between her mother and her father, the sex act engaged in by Nick and Stephanie symbolically recreates the coupling of the mythological deities, Poseidon and Demeter. In her treatment of that myth, Ozick moves from the intensely erotic to the profoundly psychological, and the coital scene eventuates in a dramatic psychic recognition and a twofold perspective of civilization. The lovers lie on the floor where a brown blanket "lay in furrows like a brown sea," its wool the "color of earth" (587, 593). An emblem of Poseidon and Demeter's mating, the blanket recalls the browning edges of the blossom the graduate brushed off her gown. As once she huddled on the window ledge and hovered on the terrace, the narrator crouches "on the ledge of the world"—to accumulate reality (593). From that vantage point, she views the union from which her life began. An earlier version of Allegra, Stephanie Pettigrew, an "artist's poor copy of the hanging masterpiece, daringly embellished with up-to-date technique," recapitulates Allegra's experience with Gustave Nicholas Tilbeck.

The description of his member, the position he assumes with Stephanie during intercourse, the rainstorm accompanying the lovemaking—these details link Tilbeck to Poseidon. His copulation with Demeter is evoked in the imagery that suffuses the lovemaking scene between Tilbeck and Stephanie:

> his steed hardens its headless neck, all sinew and maneless muscle, all sudden brutishness and power . . . it bears him up on the crest of its canter, he climbs sideways to her side and still that stallion stays high in an arrested leap between his thighs, it strains outward as though it would shoot free, a slow wax tear glistens in its blind cup. . . . and encumbered by the life that prances out of his fork he falls to his knees astride her haunch. . . . then reaches a single vast hand curved and spread to contain her and takes the swell of her crotch and fast and brutally, before she can sprawl, he flips her over. And penetrates. (596–97)

Imparting to the girl knowledge of her engendering, the scene doubles as a revelation of the mythic union of the sea and the earth, of Poseidon and Demeter; for when Poseidon began to pursue Demeter, she turned herself into a mare and he transformed himself into a stallion and coupled with her. From their act came a daughter whose name was never spoken outside the mysteries.[33] A rendering of that mythic event, the scene at Duneacres invokes an episode in Brighton and the narrator's experience in the swamp. Imagining Tilbeck the lover "is like some woodcutter with a great bole before him" which he must fell before dark, his daughter recollects the darts Tilbeck and Allegra threw at the tree near their cottage to make the dryad cry out. An image of Sacred Beauty for the mother in England, the tree in the swamp in America becomes a harbinger of enlightenment for the daughter, and together with the saw the woodcutter thrusts into its center, the tree at Duneacres becomes in her mind part of a metaphor for the couples' lovemaking.

And it rekindles the illumination that went out of the tree in the swamp, the light cast back by history. The brutish sensuality of the lovers' primitive and pagan act—"Nature, red in tooth and claw"—evokes the idea children often have of the primal scene, the fantasies of savage carnality they must master to achieve mature sexuality. In resplendent language and with acute sensitivity, Ozick recounts one of the sexual theories common to children, the fantasies, Freud reported, in which the "individual reaches beyond his own experiences into primaeval experience" to fill "in the gaps in individual truth with prehistoric truth" (371). That time, Enoch claims, excludes "moral man" who "has no prehistory, because before history there was no man, there were only beasts" (398). Suffused with psychic truths, the scene makes clear a distinction between Hebraism and Hellenism. They are symbolized in the narrator's description of Tilbeck's genitals and the memory of Enoch's:

> I see the neck of the animal he rides kneeling . . . its long straight neck yearns from its ruff and collar, it is a thick-flanked headless beast and new to me. —I think of Enoch and the door always open to insult my mother's delicacy, and I coming by one day and seeing how his stream falls from a tender fat creature with a short neck scalloped out of the head, and in the head a pouring cyclops-eye—the Jews are different. (595)

Uncircumcised, Tilbeck's member is a "steed. . . . huge, taut, distended . . . untender, cunning yet blunt"; her father and Stephanie's sexuality is primitive, untamed, loveless—an expression of the carnal lust that befits the coupling of Poseidon and Demeter in their animal guises (596, 597). Circumcised, Enoch's penis, a tender creature, is observed by the girl when he urinates, and his flaccid member makes her think of the blinding of the Cyclops, a kind of castration, a reminder of Tilbeck's skepticism about Enoch's potency. But the reference to one-eyed Polyphemus evokes the meaning of the covenantal circumcision, a penance imposed by God's law, a ritual that reinforces the difference between nature's lawlessness and human civilization; the opposition between paganism and Judaism. Further ambivalence inheres in that antithesis, however; for bestial and lawless as Tilbeck's sensuality is, it results in the fertility that Allegra and Enoch Vand's childless marriage lacks. The observer rather than the arbiter in *Trust*, the narrator reports these dissimilar historical values without comment. Instead, imbued with the "sense that a mirror has peered into a mirror and viewed infinity," she starts after the light that leads from the lovers (598). And Ozick confers new meaning on that light, which at first irradiates the tree in the swamp, by transmuting it into the metaphoric equivalent of Ariadne's golden thread, the means to the narrator's exit from the labyrinth.

The harbinger of autonomy is the empty wine bottle that has washed up overnight after Tilbeck drowned. Having discovered Tilbeck's existence from the name scrawled inside an envelope, his daughter learns of her father's death from the scrap of paper in the bottle and at last understands him: "The mind that set the letters down loved no one. . . . There was no signature. When you write to the ocean you do not leave your name. Gustave Nicholas Tilbeck does not leave his name for the ocean or for me" (603). Neither Tilbeck nor Poseidon, to whom the note is addressed, cares for anything save the law of his own existence.[34] The note from Harriet Beecher Stowe Purse "to Poseidon M. D. (Master of the Deep) By an Amanuensis" proclaims, "The god of love is always a baby. Cupid! Christ!" (603). Written in the "unmistakable voice of *Marianna Harlow,*" the message yokes Nick to the creation of Allegra's novel as well as to the Master of the sea. Replicating her mother's experience, the daughter has encountered the same source of inspiration. The presence of a muse on Town Island is augured by the nine members of the Purse family who allude to the Ninefold Muse or the White Goddess, Graves's notion of the patroness of poetry. But the narrator renounces the Purses' addiction to language for its own sake and evinces instead her love for language in its capacity to make real and moral distinctions. In recounting her quest for self-knowledge and in telling the tale of her discovery of language's uses, the narrator of *Trust* paints her own portrait. If the discovery of art and culture in Europe leads finally to imprisonment and renders Isabel Archer's a portrait of a lady, of the "*artiste manquée,*" the recognition of the purpose and value of language releases the narrator of *Trust* from slavery and makes her portrait one not of a lady but of an artist as a young woman (Sabiston 30).[35] One of Tilbeck's roles is that of male muse.

In the guise of the water divinity Poseidon, Tilbeck was "untamed . . . faithless" and possessed "no moral qualities," but the sea with which he is bound up annihilates and recreates—"at once purifying and giving new life" (Eliade, *Patterns* 206–7). As Master of the Deep, Tilbeck provides the answer to the enigma whose existence precluded his daughter from liberation and independence, the attainments vital to a regenerated existence. For this gift, his daughter feels gratitude: "Love broke in me: infatuation" (603). Ozick, however, qualifies the word "love" with the word "infatuation," a state the narrator of a later tale "Shots" explains is "unilateral," is like being under a "special spell . . . in thrall to a cult" (*Levitation* 53). But Tilbeck is not one-sided. A water god, he is a life-giver and a destroyer; Pan-like, he has such emblems as the fertile jewelweed and the poisonous hellebore. John Vermoulian's suicide, the ruined garden, the fountain "broken like a Greek shrine," the decaying house filled with "feces of mice," purple mold, and fly-like insects—all symbols of "decay and all-devouring time"—affirm Tilbeck's island as a realm whose bliss is sullied by death. The girl apprehends at Dune-acres the truth Enoch Vand discovered in Brighton—"Death is even in Arcadia."[36] A place destined to house a fleeting and irretrievable dream, Duneacres was secretly called "Doomacres" by Huntingdon, who built his sand-castle on silt. It is pronounced unfit by the country men who come to investigate the circumstances of Tilbeck's death: "They said the place would never have stood up as a museum—the foundations were no good. . . . The floor wouldn't hold" (604). An "issue of the floor," the daughter has not inherited her father's name; though she claims Tilbeck was her father, the Purses gainsay it and are believed. Nonetheless, she finds him splendid: "My father devised and invented himself, and chose to stay at the crest: the same for my mother, the same for me" (609).

For that reason, she is prepared to believe anything about Tilbeck, to welcome him even as a "tawdry muse," to accept that to remain the same, her father had to "dip his whole head into a vat of fake youth" (609). A male muse, a collector of Greek jars, Gustave Nicholas Tilbeck hoped to breathe life into "one of those boys on an amphora, bright-haired, goat-legged, with a little tibia-pipe poised and halted for laughter, among those love-exalted girls" (609). Ozick's allusion to the stilled time on Keats's urn underscores the ambivalent rewards represented in Tilbeck's example, for even as the changeless and perfect figures on the urn are protected from the ravages of time, they remain unfulfilled precisely because they are suspended in time. The idyllic and distorted notion of nature possessed by Nick severs him from Enoch and distinguishes the experience the mother has with her muse from her daughter's. Allegra, as Tilbeck said, "mistook an episode for a principle," but his daughter knows the "Muse is in charge of artifice," that time and decay are ineluctable (590, 608). That awareness elicits her envy of Stephanie's last moments with Tilbeck: "she gave out a sense of . . . totality: she had had her life, now it was over, she needed no more, the rest was commentary" (610). In this allusion to *Avot*, Ozick summarizes the essence of Stephanie's (and Allegra's) encounter with Tilbeck's paganism in words which, in the Talmud, constitute the essence of Judaism.[37] The girl's conclusion bears Enoch's mark. The narrator's cognizance of the powerful but ephemeral experience at Duneacres is her own: "What has happened and will not come again is easily recognized by everyone, but the moment of recognition itself is unique and terrible, like birth and disclosure, and like these cannot be re-experienced. Once is all" (610).

The death of the Pan-like Tilbeck, like the legend behind the cry, "The great god Pan is dead," signals the inevitable end of the old religions at the birth of Jesus and Christianity, but the great god Christ has already died in the form of William and so the narrator returns home to Enoch and Allegra. There the narrator learns her stepfather was an ambassador for only two hours; there Allegra accuses her daughter of having been won over to Tilbeck's side and denounces her for talking "like a Goddamn little Jew"(623). The girl rejoins by reminding her mother that she "can't be an ancient Greek" and by correcting her idea of Enoch's need for "something to do in the world" with one of Nick's opinions: "Needing isn't wanting" (625, 627). Now both Enoch Vand and Gustave Nicholas Tilbeck inform the narrator's consciousness.

The inadvertent glimpse of one of Enoch's typed notes discloses the word "sinner," a word distinctly different from Tilbeck's "child": "It [the word] was Enoch's and a private one and was not 'child'—how near now the private visitor's first note reverberated! how distantly his briny last! Babies did not inhabit Enoch's vows and views. He would never have smelled divinity through the diaper" (622). In their words, child and sinner, lies the divergence between Enoch's and Tilbeck's beliefs, the antithesis between monotheism and polytheism, the subject for Enoch's essay, "Pan Versus Moses." Thought up on the eve of Enoch's departure for Washington, the essay is summarized by Allegra:

It's Moses making the Children of Israel destroy all the grotto shrines and green-wood places and things. It's about how Moses hates Nature. Enoch said the Jewish God is the Lord of Hosts but it's the Lord of Guests who really keeps the world. The Lord of Hosts lives in his house and calls 'Come in, Come in,' but the Lord of Guests lives anywhere at all and says "You're already here." (626–27)

Enoch's essay echoes Deuteronomy (7:5 and 12:2) and posits two of its fundamental tenets: the worship of one God in a sanctified central sanctuary and the destruction of pagan images in their diversiform sites.

"Pan Versus Moses," a case stated in legal terms, and "Vand's Halforisms," so called to indicate "he believed in them only half his life," recount a journey and a return that parallel the narrator's. The halforisms, which the narrator spreads on the floor where she sits, are the record of an individual's ethics. One of five children born to an immigrant tailor, Enoch became the Marxist youth leader of Allegra's socialist camp at Duneacres. The invention of Adam Gruenhorn—the name that Enoch assumed at Brighton and that caused Allegra to say two births had occurred there—the maxims summarize the beliefs that inspired Enoch's Marxism and led to a political career. Richly evocative, the adopted name imputes to Enoch's role in *Trust* a double significance. Comparable to the biblical Adam, Adam Gruenhorn lost his innocence: in Brighton his discovery of the Party's forfeiture of the Ideal drove him out of paradise and "he was left like Adam to know his shame" (427). The tale Ozick tells of Enoch's life invites comparison with the decisive events animating the Pentateuch.

A book that traces humanity's creation, its primeval history, its enslavement and liberation, its belief and apostasy, its acceptance of and adherence to God's commandments, its education in the wilderness, and its acquirement of a second corpus of law, the Torah may be said to concern Israel's search for God, the people's experience with Him and its understanding of Him.[38] For each stage of his life, from the advent of Adam Gruenhorn to the collapse of Enoch's two-hour ambassadorship, Ozick offers a parallel to Israel's history as it is recorded in the Pentateuch. His innocence gone, Enoch married Allegra and despite the Holocaust went to Europe to pursue his career, to enslave himself to numbering corpses, to fall prey to idolatry. Intoning the census of the dead in Europe, he engrossed himself in the contents of a black-covered ledger which he clutched to his heart "like a tablet of the Law: not God's but Europe's." His "baal, the Lady Moloch," the ledger replaced the Torah and allowed the Canaanite storm god hegemony (125).

Pervasive during this period of Enoch's life are lists and numbers. Feelings, ideas, events, directions—these Ozick characterizes by halves, and they recall Numbers, whose Hebrew title means "in the desert" and whose text is dominated and structured by lists.[39] The Hebrew term *midbār*, or wilderness, serves as a "designation of the clearly circumscribed period which followed upon the Exodus and preceded the Conquest of Canaan," and that period "falls into two unequal stretches of time," revealing Numbers to be, as Shemaryahu Talmon explains, "The Book of Israel's Failings" (39, 46). Its subject is Israel's transgression and God's punishment, and the book chronicles the journey through the desert—"a passage to [the] goal" of re-establishing "the supreme sanctuary of Israel . . . not the goal itself" (Talmon 63). Talmon's commentary on Numbers sheds light on the meaning of Europe to *Trust,* for when Enoch entered it, Europe was similar to the wilderness of biblical literature: desolate, chaotic, cruel, inhuman. Afterwards Enoch undergoes a rite of passage toward a different end which he only completes after his two-hour ambassadorship when, as he remarks, he is "freed" (635). His recovery of Covenant is augured in "Pan Versus Moses," which takes as its text two doctrines from Deuteronomy, and occurs at the end of the novel. Enoch begins to learn Hebrew from a refugee under whose tutelage he reads the Hebrew Bible and studies the Talmud, beginning with the Ethics of the Fathers. *Avot* resembles the form of "Vand's Halforisms," but differs from them in scope. Concerned with moral behavior, which the tractate derives from the teachings of the Torah, *Avot,* a "whole body of moral dicta—each one summing up with remarkable conciseness a life's experience and philosophy," makes Enoch's halforisms whole.[40]

Enoch Vand's transformation and the relationship Enoch has with the narrator of *Trust* recall his namesake's career. Enoch the son of Jared, a cobbler, was translated from the earth to heaven where he became the archangel Metatron, "God's vice-regent," the "lesser YHWH." Metatron disclosed the entire history of humanity to Rabbi Ishmael, the reporter of the prophecies.[41] In *Trust* Enoch Vand, a tailor's son, provides the narrator with Allegra's letters, the history of her world and the basis for the chronicle of her discoveries. Unlike Rabbi Ishmael, the girl's tale culminates in a homecoming, in the return that is also a commencement. The two homecomings—Enoch's from Washington and the girl's from Town Island—have double significance, for in them Ozick juxtaposes two traditional ideas of the Return, the Hebraic and the Hellenic. In her version of the *nostos,* Ozick fuses Telemachos's return with Odysseus's, and in the girl's encounter with Tilbeck, the storyteller reconceives the significance Homer attaches to Telemachos's and Odysseus's experiences. His reunion with his father brings Telemachos not independence but renewed dependence, and the landing at Ithaca proves to be the signal discovery of Odysseus's voyage.[42] The journey to Town Island is brief and ends with Tilbeck's drowning, the event which permanently separates the narrator from her father and heralds her independence from him. When the narrator attributes to the experience a change in her life, her mother barks, "Don't tell me in two measly days you found yourself a father." To which the daughter responds, "Not a father" (619). What she will find is alluded to in one of the novel's epigraphs, an aphorism by Enoch Vand: "Offer the resourceful man one of two legacies: a mammoth trust fund by inheritance of wealth, or a minuscule fund of trust by inheritance of nature; and he will choose the one which least inhibits venturesomeness."[43] What the narrator has found emerges in the interpenetrating allusions Ozick employs to depict Town Island.

All of those allusions refer to islands of transformation, to which the number two is important. Odysseus plans to spend two days on Circe's island, the length of time it takes Ariel to achieve his freedom and the number of years for Robinson Crusoe to escape slavery. Although Tilbeck claims he and his daughter are Prospero and Miranda, Ozick intimates that once Tilbeck apprises the narrator of himself, he ceases to resemble Prospero and bears instead a likeness to Ferdinand's father, for the imagery which limns the dead Tilbeck derives from Ariel's song in the first act of *The Tempest*. News of her former lover's death elicits from Allegra the remark, "Full fathom five," and her daughter sees the "sea-change" at her father's scalp, Nick's "agate" eyes (616, 609, 610). The lover who inspired *Marianna Harlow* suffers the fate of Allegra's copy of Shelley whose own epitaph comes from Ariel's song. The father, however, alters his daughter's future. But in allying her narrator to Prospero and her father to Ferdinand's father, Ozick sunders the girl from Tilbeck. His island offers her temporary enchantment from which she must be released to attain full consciousness. That Emerson, Thoreau, and Harriet Beecher Stowe haunt Town Island in the form of the Purses suggests the island's capacity to provide self-discovery, self-reliance, and freedom—the achievements vital to the American way of life.[44]

The kinship Ozick secures among Enoch, the narrator, and Prospero not only reveals her destiny as an artist but indicates she will concern herself with a "society of will and commandment" and will write about "conduct and the consequences of conduct" (A&A 164). To link the narrator to Prospero is to affirm reality as the proper provenance of art. To yoke her to Enoch is to connect art to moral seriousness; for Enoch Vand, whose namesake was a scribe, the "writer of all the signs of wisdom among all the people," is a writer himself, one who upholds Mosaic law and one who declared Moses a "writer, after all—he wrote the tablets" (Charlesworth 73 [1 Enoch]; *Trust* 363). Prospero and Enoch exemplify the two groups who people *Trust*—the poets and the lawyers—and who represent the competing versions of the world involved in the debate between Pan and Moses, or the dichotomy between Tilbeck's way of life and Enoch's. The conflict between Pan and Moses originates in two contrasting world views, the Greek and the biblical. Of decisive importance to the way in which Ozick conceives of their divergence are the essays on Judaism by the German rabbi Leo Baeck.

Especially important to her work is Baeck's "Romantic Religion," an essay Ozick declared "in some way broke open the conceptual egg of [her] life."[45] In an interview with Bill Moyers in 1986, she said of Baeck's essay: "I was immensely influenced by an essay called 'Romantic Religion,' which I read at the age of 25, by Leo Baeck, which seemed to decode the universe for me—or at least decode our planet in the universe. And that particular essay altered my life forever, I believe. It helped me understand all societies."[46]

That she read "Romantic Religion" seven years before she began writing *Trust,* that the essay is strikingly similar to another of Baeck's essays, "Two World Views Compared," suggest their importance to Enoch Vand's future, to

Gustave Nicholas Tilbeck's fate, and to her own literary convictions. At the end of "Two World Views Compared," Baeck concludes that "there are two ideational forces opposed to one another, a dual type of discovering and knowing that is given to the human spirit" (143). One of those forces originates in Greek thought and conceives of "existence as a work of art," an idea that enables humanity to transcend mutability and to consummate its being, but not to behave ethically. A world in which humanity feels the drive toward God, toward the infinite, struggles with His commandment, and is "perpetually renewed" and reborn—that is the biblical world of "sacred unrest," the "world as the great and revelatory drama of creation" (145, 143, 144).[47]

From these world views, Baeck postulates two kinds of religions, classical and romantic. Of romantic religion he writes: "Tense feelings supply its content, and it seeks its goals in the now mythical, now mystical visions of the imagination. Its world is the realm in which all rules are suspended; it is the world of the irregular, the extraordinary and the miraculous, that world which lies beyond all reality, the remote which transcends all things" (J&C 189–90). Faith in romantic religion means an acceptance of one's predetermined fate, a cessation of "all wrestling and striving"; belief in such a religion produces the "finished man" who knows "only dead history" and so forfeits the future (J&C 206, 218). But classical religion possesses "living history" (J&C 218). Because classical religion belongs to an "ethical idea of history," fosters Commandment and the imperative to deed, classical religion affirms the "idea of becoming, of the never-quite finished, of the directed ascent" whose "goal lies ever again in the distance" (J&C 217). The exemplar of stasis and myth, Gustave Nicholas Tilbeck epitomizes Baeck's idea of the Greek world view and romantic religion; whereas Enoch Vand, the model of change and growth, exemplifies Baeck's conception of Judaism, a classical religion. And Enoch's Return is a *t'shuva* (a turning) as Baeck defines it—the ability always to return to God, to "freedom and purity," the assurance of an "ever fresh beginning" (EJ 163, 206).

That regeneration is resounding at the end of *Trust*, which concludes as it begins, with commencements and weddings: "Where I was and what I did during that period I will not tell; I went to weddings" (639). Still an observer and not yet a participant, the narrator knows the significance of "wedding-glue," as Enoch calls it, but like Nick she "sticks to [herself]." Ceremonies expressive of human attachment and its potential generative powers within the constructs of civilization, weddings and marriages play a major part in *Trust*. Yearning to be wed "to the world," the narrator discovers Allegra's first marriage, a barren and failed one, led to another childless marriage (14). The sterile marriages are countered by pagan coupling: the episode at Brighton, the honeymooners in Europe, the intercourse at Duneacres. A reflection of nature's untamed fecundity, the pagan scenes are depicted in imagery associated with Aphrodite, whom Poseidon loved and whom Theseus took as his escort. The goddess of the physical love that unites men and women, Aphrodite rose from sea foam, was borne to land on a seashell, and transformed herself into a fish, a symbol of the sea's fertility—the events informing the prevailing imagery of *Trust*. But Ozick attaches to the divinity of love Shelley's celebration of her as the supreme inspiration of sublime poetry, the guide of his highest poetic aspirations.[48] Confounded by the "tethered imagination" of her husband, the young Allegra, the "skylark-emulator," envisions the pages of her drowned Shelley metamorphosed into an "undersea anemone," a reminder of "Adonais" wherein Keats is transfigured into Urania's "nursling" (335, 327, 336). Away from the man who reproved fantasy, the Allegra of Brighton wrote *Marianna Harlow* and "crammed all the chinks of Chapter Twelve with arrowheads and goat-hooves of Venus and Pan" (382). If Venus is the source of divine inspiration, she is also a Greek goddess who signals the deepest conflict in *Trust*.

The narrator's attendance at weddings underscores the complexity Ozick attaches to the divinity of love, for adverting to the wedding masque in *The Tempest* and the metaphor of marriage in "Epipsychidion," Ozick intimates the narrator's desire to join nature to morality, to plight the future to Shelley's supernal power. But attendance at weddings does not necessarily testify to union. Instead, the girl's presence at the ceremonies embodies the ambiguity with which the novel concludes: Cynthia Ozick's "sense of an ending" reopens the question that remains significant because no answer can fully silence it. However much the narrator is influenced by Enoch, her return is not a *t'shuva*, nor is her homecoming precisely a *nostos*. Tilbeck, the presider at her initiation ceremonies, has not conferred on her life a principle by which to live. Caught between two worlds, she is, as she tells her mother, at a turning-point. Although the Purses call her Miss Tilbeck, it is without conviction; neither she nor William's son is ever addressed by a first name and that absence is conspicuous. Failing to achieve his own identity, William's son abides merely as a son. Not nobody, the narrator is not yet somebody. To attain that status she must possess her own name. She must recognize her face in an undivided mirror. Despite Enoch's influence, despite Tilbeck's drowning, despite her homecoming, it cannot be said that she has chosen Hebraism over Hellenism, though in William's office she has thought, "Godlessness inevitably produces vulgarity. Civilization is the product of belief" (322). Nonetheless, her elliptical report in the last paragraph of the novel acknowledges neither Pan nor Moses as the victor in their debate.

That contest, as Ozick has written, is the "central quarrel of the West" (A&A 181). It is also the provenance of her own "unholy conflict," the one "between moral seriousness and its clash with aestheticism" (Interview with Kauvar 381). Jewish thinkers have been engaged in the battle between Hebraism and Hellenism since the first century of the common era. Behind the perduring Judaic polemic against the ideals of Greek civilization is the informing ethos of the Bible, its conception of history as a realm of meaning and purpose. From the biblical heritage came the undeviating demand on the human will and the resistance to a fixed and unalterable fate. The biblical world view permeated and penetrated Jewish thought in the Middle Ages and inspired and animated the thinking of succeeding generations. Sometimes Hellenism appeared as a threat, at other times a reconcilable force; sometimes as an abyss into which one might stumble and again as a summit to be surmounted, but always as a culture whose intellectual and artistic achievements were subordinate to Judaic moral belief and ethical behavior.[49]

Such convictions pose a special predicament for a writer with a deep Jewish consciousness: to arrogate to art saving power is to abrogate a "heritage that stressed . . . moral wisdom grounded in belief" and to raise the disquieting question of whether the whole artistic enterprise is finally not only factitious but heretical (Alter, *Defenses* 15). A writer contrives a separate realm wherein she directs the outcome of human events. As if she were the Supreme Being, the Jewish writer rivals Him when she constructs her fictional world, which is her own creation, a product of her fantasy, her own image. For this reason, "The Jews have had no tradition of aesthetics as an autonomous realm, no historically rooted notions of the poet as hero and guide" (Alter, *Defenses* 15). The heritage that has imbued Cynthia Ozick's art with moral seriousness has also excited in the writer fierce tension about the very act of artistic creation.

From *Trust* to *The Messiah of Stockholm,* and throughout her critical essays, the essential divergence between the opposing forces of Hebraism and Hellenism pulses through the whole world of Cynthia Ozick's writing. In *Trust,* Ozick adduces those forces with uncommon precision and rare imaginative power. In the comparable journeys of Enoch Vand and the narrator we behold not only the initial appearance of the dialectics crucial to Ozick's fiction, but another implication of the "multifold word" that is the novel's title (309). If *Trust* is, as Ozick announced, about the failure of trust, her novel is also about the restoration of trust. At the novel's conclusion, the narrator stands on a new frontier, itself an act of trust; and Enoch Vand begins to study the Bible and the Talmud in which the term faith, the Hebrew word *emunah,* "is best rendered trust, a trust that includes accepting as God's will the inexplicable perplexities of life" (Seltzer 300). But to accept them does not entail ceasing to wrestle with them or relinquishing the "idea of becoming." It is with those perplexities and the struggle to penetrate them that the novel is concerned. More than a matrix for ideas Cynthia Ozick continues to plumb, more than a projection of a Jewish writer's involvement with Jewish history, more than a novel about a young woman in search of her identity—even more than all of that, *Trust* encompasses a journey into the interior and a voyage into the history of civilization. Various, surprising, filled with intellectual splendor, *Trust* is a contemporary masterwork.

TWO

The Insistent Sense of Recognition

Faced with divergent paths at the end of her voyage, the narrator of *Trust* follows neither of them; they remain on the same plane of her vision. But they are pursued in *The Pagan Rabbi,* Cynthia Ozick's first collection of stories. Each tale in the volume has its counterpart; each provides a different perspective, records a disparate experience. The dialectical structure of Ozick's first novel shapes not only the individual stories in *The Pagan Rabbi* but the structure of the volume itself. Informed by the storyteller's duplicate vision, the collection revives the themes present in *Trust,* often pairing them within a single tale or else matching them in two separate tales. That juxtaposition of conflicting ideas, like the narrator's reflection in the divided mirror in *Trust,* gives back a dual image of the self, the artist's sense of all identity. The controlling principle for the entire collection, Ozick's penchant for doubling had already evinced itself in the unpublished novel *Mercy, Pity, Peace, and Love* and in the evocative sketch "The Butterfly and the Traffic Light," which grew out of that novel and which was published five years before *Trust.*

History is crucial for the narrator of *Trust,* and history makes an immediate appearance in the first paragraph of "The Butterfly and the Traffic Light," in which Jerusalem serves as a contrast to the places "where time has not yet deigned to be an inhabitant" (209). A "phoenix city" with a "history of histories," a city where "no one is a stranger," Jerusalem illuminates the true meaning of the past rather than the fabricated one exemplified in the midwestern American town that is the story's setting (210). Wanting the college town to have historical allusions, the mayor named one of the town's streets after the "Bigghe diaries," a traveling salesman's forged records. And Big Road, as it came to be spelled, occasions Fishbein's lectures to Isabel. In them are elements bridging *Trust* to *The Pagan Rabbi,* adumbrations of its central thematic concerns, and two of its controlling metaphors.

One metaphor arises from the "doubleness that clung to the street," the doppelgänger every person and every object owns (213). That "insistent sense of recognition"—the dawning of the creative process, the birth of metaphor—immediately becomes attached to the Hebraism-and-Hellenism issue in Isabel and Fishbein's ensuing argument (213). For Fishbein the uniformity of lampposts in America evinces its dreary sameness, the diverse lampposts in Europe its individuality. But Isabel sees them as "some kind of religious icon" belonging to an "advanced religion," monotheism. Hers is an opinion Fishbein disputes: "The index of advancement is flexibility. Human temperaments are so variable, how could one God satisfy them all? The Greeks and Romans had a god for every personality" (214). The Jews' refusal to obey Antiochus IV's decree "to set up a statue of Zeus on the altar of the Temple of Jerusalem" caused the Maccabean War, but that "altogether unintelligible occasion," Fishbein tells Isabel, came "of missing an imagination," of not accommodating "Zeus *and* God under one roof," of forcing icons to be alike (215). To the Jews' determination to uphold monotheism in the face of severe opposition Fishbein attributes an absence of imagination: he conjures up the argument Enoch Vand and Nick Tilbeck have over personal values and abstractions.

The second metaphor emerges in one of Fishbein's lectures: "Looking at butterflies gives pleasure. Yes, it is a kind of joy . . . but full of poison. It belongs to the knowledge of rapid death. The butterfly lures us not only because he is beautiful, but because he is transitory. The caterpillar is uglier, but in him we can regard the better joy of becoming. The caterpillar's fate is bloom. The butterfly's is waste" (217). An affirmation of process, Fishbein's metaphors recall Baeck's explanation of classical religion and echo Keats's idea of beauty in the "Ode on Melancholy." There the death-moth is linked to Psyche, whose emblem Fishbein adopts. His name and his allusion to Psyche invoke Venus, the role the goddess of love played in the Cupid and Psyche story. As in *Trust*, that goddess is implicated in the creative act. And the story's epigraph—"the moth for the star"—suggests Isabel, whose name resembles that of the American moth Isabella, as the devotee of "something afar," of Shelley's muse Urania. Yoking these allusions, Ozick proclaims the process of becoming, the "work as it goes," superior to the finality of completion (A&A 54). In the confluence of her references resides the battle between Hebraism and Hellenism, the artist's dilemma and a major conflict in "The Pagan Rabbi."

In that later story Ozick explores the consequences of what Fishbein deems a "harmless affair": bringing Zeus together with God. Whereas in *Trust* and "The Butterfly and the Traffic Light" the dichotomy between Judaism and paganism is represented by two separate characters, in "The Pagan Rabbi" the conflict is an internal one—a rabbi's wrenching struggle to reconcile his attraction to two utterly disparate and discordant ways of life. Rabbi Isaac Kornfeld's predicament, like the narrator's quest in *Trust*, is broadened to include cultural and historical contentions as well. Not only does the tale provide three distinct perspectives on the same situation, not only does it afford a series of ideas and situations which are doubled and divided, it connects the turmoil suffered by the rabbi to the disquiet endured by the artist.

Like *Trust*, "The Pagan Rabbi" has an unnamed first-person narrator who seeks a solution to a mystery, the reason why Isaac Kornfeld hanged himself on a tree in a public park. But as the narrator of Ozick's first novel knows, facts are not enough; they must be judged by history. And it is to history the narrator of "The Pagan Rabbi" turns to recount the events in his life and to describe his relationship with Isaac Kornfeld. Fathers loom as large in this tale as they do in *Trust*, and their presence throughout *The Pagan Rabbi* testifies to their vital and continuing importance to Ozick's fiction. Where in *Trust* Ozick reports the narrator's quest for a father, in *The Pagan Rabbi* she emphasizes the strife between generations. That tension is manifest in "The Pagan Rabbi," in which two sons comply with their fathers' choices of careers and attend a rabbinical seminary but have reactions to their training that diverge from their fathers' expectations. Isaac's experience differed from the narrator's as well, for the seminary that recognized Isaac's "imagination was so remarkable he could concoct holiness out of the fine line of a serif," was the same seminary in which the narrator discovered he had no talent (4). Neither father regarded Greek philosophy as anything but an "abomination." Judging Socrates a "monotheist," Isaac's father nonetheless believed philosophy to be the corridor to idolatry; the narrator's father vowed philosophy brought his son to atheism and determined him to withdraw from the seminary. His subsequent marriage to a gentile was an occasion for his father to mourn his son as if dead. A lapsed Jew, the narrator furnishes one of the three perspectives on the events in the tale.

Driven to know the entire story of Isaac Kornfeld's suicide, the narrator journeys to Trilham's Inlet to see the tree on which a pious Jew saw fit to end his life. A powerful symbol of both Hebraism and Hellenism, the oak tree revives the tree in *Trust,* and the bay surrounding Trilham's Inlet is reminiscent of the filth at Duneacres: "filled with sickly clams and a bad smell," its water "covered half the city's turds" (4, 5). The cut up pieces of trees, the "deserted monuments" in the park—these recall the dilapidated garden in which the narrator of *Trust* first sees her father. In the garden and in the public park are blasted paradises—the lost idyllic Arcadia, the fallen Garden of Eden. If in *Trust* the daughter's hopes are dashed upon meeting Tilbeck, here the rabbi's crumble in the wake of deviating from a father's established beliefs. The rabbi's name embodies the conflict central to the story: Isaac refers to the trust the biblical son placed in his father and "Kornfeld" alludes to Demeter, the Greek goddess of fertility.[1] But in "The Pagan Rabbi," it is the failure of the son to trust the father's tradition and the rabbi's attraction to Hellenism that ultimately prove destructive. The conjunction of the two names, like the double implications of the oak tree, emphasize the coexistence of two desires which must forever remain embattled. Specifically associated with important biblical events and people, the oak was sacred to Zeus; and linking the tree's roots and the toes of a gryphon Ozick evokes a Greek tree of life, for gryphons function as guardians of immortality, of what is sacred, powerful, or omniscient.[2] Explicitly forbidden in Deuteronomy, however, is the worship of trees: "you shall tear down their altars, and dash in pieces their pillars, and burn their Asherim with fire; you shall hew down the graven images of their gods, and destroy their name out of that place" (Deut. 12:3). Serried with allusive and contradictory significance, the oak which the narrator describes at the beginning of the story and on which Isaac hangs himself functions as a hieroglyph of the tale just as the tree in the swamp constitutes an emblem of "Duneacres."

And as the rain, which brings revelation in *Trust,* begins to fall, the narrator of "The Pagan Rabbi" recognizes himself as "a man in a photograph standing next to a gray blur of tree," a man who "would stand through eternity beside Isaac's guilt if [he] did not run" (5). A lapsed Jew whose father died without ever speaking to his son again, the narrator identifies with Isaac's guilt: the photograph, a representation of truth, implies both men have partaken of forbidden fruit. As if to rectify that sin, the narrator runs to the woman he once loved, to the woman Isaac Kornfeld married—the woman born in a concentration camp. About to be thrown against an electrified fence, Sheindel was saved by the vanishing current, a seemingly magical intervention by God. Unlike Isaac and Sheindel's, the narrator's marriage to a gentile was childless and ended in divorce. The histories of the men, their careers as a rabbi and a bookseller, locate one man at the center of Judaism and the other at its fringes. Isaac Kornfeld, an authority on the Mishnah (the oral code of Law), was also a writer who contributed significant responsa, answers to questions on halakhic (law) topics. But his was a frenzied path to achievement, as his favorite authors, Saadia Gaon and Nietzsche, attest: one a specialist in biblical study, the other an enthusiast of the ideals of Greece, the two writers represent Isaac's antithetical passions.

The opposition between Sheindel and the narrator, however, is implied by their positions at her dining table "as large as a desert" and "divided . . . into two nations" by a lace cloth (10). As it does in *Trust,* the division into halves invokes contrary perspectives. Speaking "as if every word emitted a quick white thread of great purity," Sheindel scorns Isaac's reading "about runners with hats made of leaves," the bedtime stories that gave to animals and nature human life, the rabbi's insistence on a "little grove" for the location of their picnics (10, 13). Her derision of his darkly inventive stories—"stupid and corrupt" fairy tales "full of spirits, nymphs, gods, everything ordinary and old"—adds yet another reference to Isaac's imagination and reveals Sheindel to be, as the narrator observes, "one of those born to dread imagination." One of those born to exalt imagination, Rabbi Isaac Kornfeld writes stories like an artist inspired by a Greek muse (14, 15).

Of the notebook containing what Sheindel believes is the reason for her husband's suicide, the narrator concludes, "it was all a disappointment" (15). In fact, the notebook affords important and indispensable clues: extracts from Leviticus and Deuteronomy, a "snatch of Byron, a smudge of Keats . . . a pair of truncated lines from Tennyson," and an unidentified quatrain (17). Passages from the Bible vie with lines from English Romantic poetry and references to the classics, revealing the rabbi's unspoken desire: to reconcile a love of nature with belief in Torah. The very description of the notebook—its "wrinkled leaves," the handwriting that fills it, "oddly formed" like that of a man who is "leaning on a bit of bark"—recall Tilbeck's "wild" handwriting. To determine the tree's age, Isaac thinks of "counting the rings" just as he imagines his age "may be ascertained by counting the rings under his poor myopic eyes"

(17). The alliance between the writer of the notebook and the male muse intimates the relationship of writing and paganism. His affiliation of self and tree yokes the Mishnaic scholar to nature. That he has edited the extracts from Deuteronomy and Leviticus in transcribing them indicates a wish to alter their meaning, for they concern the renewal of the Covenant and the penalties for violating its laws. From Deuteronomy Isaac has copied, "He shall utterly destroy all the places of the gods, upon the high mountains, and upon the hills, and under every green tree." His version leaves out the injunction to burn the Asherim, to cut down graven images, to root out their name. An extract from Leviticus follows: "And the soul that turneth after familiar spirits to go a-whoring after them, I will cut him off from among his people" (16). Reminding himself of God's commandment, Isaac is then driven to record the penalty for breaking God's commandment.

Unable to penetrate Isaac's preoccupations, the narrator judges the unidentified quatrain in the notebook "cloying and mooning and ridiculous" (17). But the quatrain's last line, "The beauty of the earth is haunted still," precedes the description of the tree, a *Quercus velutina*. An Australian she-oak, it is the spirit with whom Isaac falls in love and from whose branches he hangs himself. Below the passage appears the deliberately legible announcement, "Great Pan lives" (17). Including fragments written in Greek, Hebrew, and English, the tiny notebook presents the "Pan Versus Moses" case in miniature. It begins with the consequences of transgression and ends with a firm declaration; Isaac Kornfeld implies that the Greek cult of nature and beauty should not be reviled by the Hebrew lawgiver, that Moses need not oppose Pan. That idea alludes to one in "The Last of the Valerii" and anticipates the fate of Isaac and Sheindel's marriage: in James's story the Count forsakes his wife for a statue and "communion with the great god Pan" (43). The Count's desires are echoed in Isaac's letter, which is read aloud by Sheindel when the narrator returns the notebook, secretly angry at having been cheated. Written on "large law-sized paper," the letter of self-explanation contains proofs; it resembles in form Isaac's responsa.

To choose that form to express a powerful attraction to nature is to endeavor to bring what amounts to paganism under the aegis of Judaism. And Judaism impels the rabbi to return to "human history," to his personal history: "At a very young age I understood that a foolish man would not believe in a fish had he not had one enter his experience. Innumerable forms exist and have come to our eyes . . . from this minute perception of what already is, it is easy to conclude that further forms are possible, that all forms are probable" (20).[3] His apprehension of forms precedes his pantheistic celebration of nature, the subsistence of "holy life" in "God's fecundating Creation" (21). Once the immanence of God is acknowledged, the threat of transgressing the Second Commandment vanishes. What Isaac disputes is not the injunction against idolatry but the possibility of committing idolatry: if Divinity resides in nature, worship of its beauty should yield an expanded proclamation of God's glory, not a violation of His Divine fiat. The rabbi's argument is reminiscent of the one propounded by Spinoza, to whom Ozick refers in the story. The immanence of God, that philosopher maintained, was a principle of the law: "It was Spinoza who first dared to cross these boundaries [of tradition], and by the skillful use of weapons accumulated in the arsenals of philosophy itself he succeeded in bringing both God and man under the universal rule of nature and thus establishing its unity" (Wolfson 331–32). But Spinoza's insistence upon the absolute unity of body and soul is denied by Isaac's assertion: "To see one's soul is to know all, to know all is to own the peace our philosophies futilely envisage. Earth displays two categories of soul: the free and the indwelling. We human ones are cursed with the indwelling" (21). His divergence from talmudic belief and his compulsion to unify discordant ideas is revealed in the revision Isaac attempts of the Platonic theory of Forms and Plato's concept of the soul.[4]

Interested more in humanity than in nature and believing the entire human being was active in history, talmudic Judaism declared body and soul inseparable. That monistic doctrine opposes Platonic dualism, in which the task of philosophy is to liberate the body from the soul. In the *Phaedo*, Socrates tells Simmias that "it is only those who practise philosophy in the right way . . . who always most want to free the soul; and this release and separation of the soul from the body is the preoccupation of the philosophers" (67d). But the soul, Socrates contended, belongs to an invisible realm and is imperceptible. That is the realm Isaac proclaims visible, the sight of it divine wisdom. Disputing Spinoza's conviction that Moses was ignorant of nature, Isaac concludes, "Moses never spoke to [our ancestors] of the free souls, lest the people not do God's will and go out from Egypt" (23). Since the existence of free souls was a secret kept from him, Isaac only accidentally discovered a Platonic Form, what Tilbeck called "Sacred Beauty."

It becomes incarnated in "Loveliness," to whom Isaac has addressed his letter and who is its subject. Proof of her existence is the "shape of a girl" whom he saw wading among his seven daughters in a stream and who exemplified, as Sheindel comments bitterly, the "principle" the rabbi habitually found "to cover" his proofs (25). And the memory of ample precedents for mortals "reputed to have coupled with gods," Isaac explains, emboldened his desire to "couple with one of the free souls" so as to liberate his soul from his body (28). In an erotic passage that recalls the one in *Trust*, Ozick describes the reaction Isaac has to his union with a dryad: "Meanwhile, though every tissue of my flesh was gratified in its inmost awareness, a marvelous voluptuousness did not leave my body; sensual exultations of a wholly supreme and paradisal order, unlike anything our poets have ever defined, both flared and were intensely satisfied in the same moment" (29). As in *Trust*, the sexual act occurs in a place befouled by filth and decay. But satiety brings in its wake the conviction of having been "defiled," the memory of Leviticus: "Neither shalt thou lie with any beast" (PR 29; Lev. 18:23). But a dryad is not an animal, and the dryad with whom Isaac discovers he has coupled claims she would refuse a man wishing "only to inhabit [her] out of perversity or boastfulness or to indulge a dreamed-of disgust"; to which Isaac responds, "Scripture does not forbid sodomy with plants" (32). The rabbi judges his lust for Nature with his knowledge of the Law: he attempts to bring paganism into accord with Judaism.

But the two are asymptotes and can never meet. That the rabbi's belief in *halakhah* is incompatible with the wish to abandon himself to Nature emerges in the extraordinarily imaginative interchange between Isaac and the dryad. The embodiment of paganism, the dryad Iripomoňoéià, "who shed her own light" and who plays with language, brings back the tree in the swamp at Duneacres and the narrator's dislike of words-in-themselves. As the dryad near the cottage at Brighton augured Tilbeck's disappearance, Iripomoňoéià anticipates Isaac's disappearance. The rabbi, she observes, has "spoiled" himself "with confusions"; in its separation from his soul, his body will become "crumpled and withered and ugly," the very antithesis of Sacred Beauty (33). It is the very antithesis of everything moral: " 'Where you have pain, we have ugliness. Where you profane yourselves by immorality, we are profaned by ugliness' " (33). By its very nature, the dryad explains, paganism is "all-of-a-sudden"; like Nick's name, "it goes too quick" (33). Of Isaac's soul, the soul of a Jew, Iripomoňoéià complains: "I do not like that soul of yours. It conjures against me. It denies me, it denies every spirit and all my sisters and every nereid of the harbor, it denies all our multiplicity, and all gods diversiform, it spites even Lord Pan, it is an enemy" (34).

Such a soul cannot survive among diversiform gods, nor can it worship Beauty. What the rabbi struggles to bring into consonance must perforce remain asunder, as the confrontation between Isaac Kornfeld and his soul reveals. An ugly old man wrapped in a drooping prayer shawl, his soul trudges along a road reading a tractate of the Mishnah with such absorption that the beauty of the field eludes him. Once desiring to see his own soul, Isaac now rejects it; it cares "only to be bound to the Law" (35). Divided from his body, Isaac's soul declares the dryad has "no real existence," that it was not the soul of Isaac "who clung to her" but his body (36). In angry despair, Isaac seizes his soul and shakes it, but it confronts him with the truth of his existence: "The sound of the Law . . . is more beautiful than the crickets. The smell of the Law is more radiant than the moss. The taste of the Law exceeds clear water" (36). In contradiction with himself and unable to accept his own soul, Isaac Kornfeld hangs himself with his prayer shawl on the branches of the oak whose spirit he believed would grant him immortality.

This clash between opposing aspects of the self is implicit in the story's title and in the rabbi's name. Worship of Pan cannot subsist alongside obedience to Moses: a rabbi cannot be a pagan. The idea that Form must either retreat or perish at the advance of its opposite is set forth in the *Phaedo*, which Ozick reveals is at odds with Isaac Kornfeld's desire—a reflection of talmudic monism. In her essay on James's *The Sacred Fount*, "The Jamesian Parable," published shortly after she finished *Trust* and three years before "The Pagan Rabbi," Ozick defines the meaning of self-contradiction: "He who desires to change himself, negates the integrity—the entelechy—of his personality" (69).

To be in contradiction with oneself is to be "unreal" and unreality leads to "moral self-cancellation" (70). Lured by the beauty of paganism and owning a Jewish soul, Isaac engages in an act of moral self-cancellation; and as the fragment he copied from Leviticus warns, he is "cut off from among his people."

That punishment in Leviticus is the one inflicted on Tithonus. Granted immortality when Eos asked Zeus to bestow it on him, Tithonus was doomed to eternal decrepitude because Eos forgot to ask for everlasting youth; however, he changed himself into a cicada and continued his existence apart from human life. Wanting to couple with Nature, Isaac remembered "Cadmus, Rhoecus, Tithonus, Endymion." But the rabbi forgot that radical isolation results from the negation of entelechy; he turns "after familiar spirits" and is severed from his people. That fate explains why his soul prefers the sound of the Law to that of the cricket. Both Isaac and Tithonus wither, but Tennyson's Tithonus asks:

> Why should a man desire in any way
> To vary from the kindly race of men,
> Or pass beyond the goal of ordinance
> Where all should pause, as is most meet for all. (ll. 19, 28–31)

Ravished by Nature, Isaac wanders outside the Law, and in the process, varies from the ordained source of life—the Torah, Israel's Tree of Life. The epigraph to "The Pagan Rabbi," a maxim from *Pirke Avot*, renders Isaac's story in brief: "Rabbi Jacob said: 'He who is walking along and studying, but then breaks off to remark, "How lovely is that tree" or "How beautiful is that fallow field!"—Scripture regards such a one as having hurt his own being'" (III.9). That following Pan can destroy human existence is evident in the deaths of Isaac Kornfeld and Gustave Nicholas Tilbeck, for both men perish before their lives reach natural completion.

Adherence to Mosaic law in "The Pagan Rabbi" is represented by Sheindel. Contrasting images buttress the conflict between Isaac's notion of Judaism and Sheindel's. The oak tree and the Torah as the Tree of Life, the Fence of the Law and the fence of the concentration camp epitomize the dichotomy between Hebraism and Hellenism, between life and death. And Isaac's reference to the animism that existed as a "historical illumination" within the Fence of the Law alludes to the pantheistic tendencies in the Kabbalah and other forms of Jewish mysticism that were opposed by traditional, rational Judaism—the kind of Judaism to which Sheindel adheres.[5] She has kept pure the Fence Isaac scales. His choice of Sheindel represents his Hebraism, the dryad his Hellenism—the difference between the sacred and the profane. Surrounded by the Fence of the Law, Isaac partakes of God's holy fecundity—his seven children who are reminders of God's creation.

On the other side of that Fence is the sterility of the narrator's life. Unnamed and unattached, the narrator remains as cut off as Isaac becomes from his own people. The men began their journey to that predicament in the same rabbinical seminary from which they followed two paths: one led to God's manifestation everywhere, the other to His absence altogether. Though both Isaac and the narrator loved Sheindel, neither stays with her. The attraction to Nature proves too powerful for the rabbi, and he avoids his wife to capture a dryad. The narrator, however, has divorced his wife and intends to marry Isaac's widow. But her "unforgiving" voice, her pitiless derision of her husband, the "terror of her cough, which was unmistakably laughter"—these determine the narrator not to return to Sheindel, who is as different from him as she was from Isaac (21, 37). What she deems a superfluity of imagination, a "choking vine on the Fence of the Law," the narrator regards as "possibility," "inspiration," insight (25, 23). To her claim that her husband was an "illusion," the narrator responds, " 'Only the pitiless are illusory,' " and advises her to go to the park to "consult" Isaac's soul (37). But at home he drops "three green house plants down the toilet" as she had given hers away to rid her house of "little trees" (37, 15). His gesture suggests he shares Sheindel's horror at Isaac's crossing the boundaries of Judaism into paganism even though the narrator has lived outside those boundaries. Where he will go in the future, whether he will climb over the fence to Judaism is a question Ozick characteristically leaves unanswered.

A story that dramatizes the warring drives in a human being, the simultaneous desires to follow Hebraism and Hellenism, the discord between rational mainstream Judaism and its mystical components, "The Pagan Rabbi" itself has a structure that reflects conflict: each character has an opposite, each idea an antithesis. Dividing ideas and characters, Ozick then doubles events by matching them. In her vision of the doubleness that clings to all existence is glimpsed the complexity of human life. If "The Pagan Rabbi" concerns the cleavage between Pan and Moses, the tale dramatizes the unconscious battle between father and son and the searing conflicts awakened in the Jewish artist. But those conflicts are not confined to Jewish writers. If Isaac Kornfeld "brings to mind I. B. Singer's Yasha Mazur," he also conjures up Henry James's Mark Ambient in "The Author of Beltraffio" (Knopp 29).[6] In turn, Ambient's wife Beatrice and Sheindel judge their husbands' writing products of paganism. And the description Mark Ambient offers of the rift between him and his wife pertains to Isaac and Sheindel as well:

> The difference between us is simply the opposition between two distinct ways of looking at the world, which have never succeeded in getting on together, or in making any kind of common household, since the beginning of time. They've borne all sorts of names, and my wife would tell you it's the difference between Christian and Pagan. . . . She thinks me at any rate no better than an ancient Greek. (58)

It is also the difference between Jew and Pagan. The inventiveness that produces Isaac Kornfeld's letter of self-explanation, a luminous narrative, establishes the rabbi as a writer who ushers his readers into an unknown world, one he imagines and creates. As the narrator of *Trust* observes, "whether a letter is more substantial than a chapter is moot" (378). Conjuring a realm where all of nature becomes an animated manifestation of God, Isaac Kornfeld fashions Nature into the image of God forbidden to monotheism. The Rabbi becomes the Creator's rival. In opposition with his own soul which embraces Holy Law, Isaac Kornfeld hungers after the beauty of Nature to which he attributes holiness. Two impulses contrast and collide: one impulse wants to maintain the tradition handed to the son by the father at the same time that another impulse seeks revision of that tradition. The distinction between Isaac's soul and Isaac's body—a young body inhabited by an old man, one resembling the rabbi's father—suggests the ambivalence existing between generations and reflects the dissension between the artist and tradition. Whether for a Jew or a Christian, the gulf between Hebraism and Hellenism abides, and as the narrators of Ozick's and James's stories learn, is "well-nigh bottomless" (67). The first in a collection of stories which in their deepest grain concern artists, "The Pagan Rabbi" focuses on the Jewish artist. In "The Dock-Witch" Ozick changes her lens and fixes it on a gentile.

Though she recounts his experience from a different angle, George, a lawyer and the narrator of "The Dock-Witch," shares Isaac Kornfeld's conflict; together the two stories reveal that conflict to be one common to Jew and Christian alike. As the authority on Mishnaic history cannot reconcile his love of Nature with the demands of the Law, so two impulses coexist in the lawyer. The first is rational and orderly; it has turned him into a "mad perfectionist who chewed footnotes like medicinal candy" (132). The second, a "hot liquid of imagination," impels him to transform the names of seaports into "some unbearable siren's perfume, all weedy, deep, and wild" (134). If the rabbi is fatally drawn to a dryad, the narrator of "The Dock-Witch" is devastated by a water nymph. Neither man emerges unscathed from his powerful attraction to nature, nor can either man make it congruous with the requirements of the law—holy or civil. Once a churchgoer from Ohio, George is unlike his family, a "clan of inlanders," for his love of the sea has drawn him away from the cornfields of Ohio to an apartment in New York City where he imagines the "mouth of the wide sea" and reads Conrad "far into the night" (131).

His desires opposed by his family as "ferociously as betrayal," the lawyer recalls the rabbi and the bookseller. "As a family pioneer," George finds himself seeing off relatives who are traveling abroad (131). At the dock with his uncle who is going to Greece, the narrator meets the "odd" woman who at first seems as trivial as a "crank" but who later dominates his fantasies. Her eyes "darkly ringed like a night-bird's," she chirps at him like a bird, instructs him in the "sacred rites of the pier," and urges him not to miss the "rush of milk expressed from the pith of Mother Sea" (137). When he returns to the dock with his young cousin's senior class on their way to Hamburg, she informs him: " 'You don't talk of time when you talk of Greek sailors. Greek sailors are timeless. Greek sailors are immortal' " (140). And like Isaac Kornfeld, who the narrator of "The Pagan Rabbi" thinks "was on the side of possibility," George sees himself, the "man on the dock," quivering "always at the edge of possibility," "clinging to the rim of infinity" (23, 142, 143).

As Isaac Kornfeld's apprehension of Nature's free souls precedes the rabbi's coupling with a dryad, so the impression of transcending the land's limits leads to George's merging with a water nymph. Isaac's encounter with Iripomoňoéià is "all-of-a-sudden," George's with the strange woman less sudden. He resists the "obscure" woman at the dock whose claim to clairvoyance he mocks. Nature bestows acute perception on Undine and confers immortality on Iripomoňoéià, but Nature exerts the fascination that exacts from Isaac and George their desire to participate in the world. Envisioning a pair of rats as "crouched penguins, one hurrying after the other in a swift but self-aware procession, like a couple of priests late for divine service," George boards a ferry to Staten Island and upon his return awakens to what at first appears to be a "galaxy of rats riding the top of the water" and then the sails of "galleons, schooners, Viking vessels" (147–48). Rendered feverish by the experience and "in an atavistic fit," the lawyer goes to church where, overhearing a verse read from Jonah, he retches in the vestry.

The story of a prophet who was unwilling to fulfill the divine mission of journeying to Nineveh to warn its citizens of their imminent punishment for succumbing to paganism, the Book of Jonah adumbrates George's heathen experience. For fleeing from the Lord, Jonah was punished by imprisonment in the "belly of Sheol" (the abode of the dead) for three days and three nights. A part of the prophet's thanksgiving prayer for past deliverance, the verse that causes the lawyer to throw up—"For thou hadst cast me into the deep, in the midst of the seas; and the waves passed over me"—augurs George's voyage to the underworld. In the biblical story, it is the great fish that vomits the prophet out upon dry land to salvation; in "The Dock-Witch" George's vomiting forecasts a journey further away from God's protection. Like Jonah's boarding a ship in a direction opposite from the one God commanded, George and Undine meet at the piers and turn their backs on a Jewish ship about to sail to the Holy Land. He cries, "Quick, let's hop off or we'll end up in Jerusalem"; she refuses to join the onlookers who are "dancing the ship toward the sacred soil." George and Undine symbolically sever themselves from sacred soil, from holiness.

And their ensuing union, like those in *Trust* and "The Pagan Rabbi," is pagan. Early in "The Dock-Witch" and in each encounter the narrator has with Undine, Ozick associates her with water and with trees, signals her dual identity, and links the tale to "The Pagan Rabbi." Christening herself Undine, a water nymph, the woman reveals she is also called Sylvia, a "name for a stick," a name that comes from the Latin word *silva,* a wood (149). Her laugh resembling a "flutter of leaves," Sylvia is the "starched woman" clad in a dress which "extended as crisply as the hide of a tree." Creating "dairy" metaphors for the ship's wake, Undine haunts the piers, goes "along with the tide" (140, 150). Images related to her names characterize the lovers' coupling: he is the "tide," she a "wave"; they "coruscate. Like a fish's back" (150). Later, she is "weighty as a log" and he feels as though he "had dived undersea, with all the ocean pressing on [his] arched and agonized spine" (155). This combination of tree and water recalls *Trust* and yokes it to "The Dock-Witch" and to "The Pagan Rabbi." In all three tales decay and filth identify the natural world celebrated by pantheism. What is unnatural Undine scorns: she turns off the refrigerator and the air conditioner, leaving George's apartment reeking of "decay" and "rot," the food "all gilded over with mold" (151).

"Amid the civil excrement" in Trilham's Inlet where he enjoys Iripomoñoéià, the rabbi confronts his soul. The lawyer meets his double, another man named George, after having intercourse with his wife. In both stories Ozick adopts the tradition of the doppelgänger but for disparate reasons. Dividing Isaac Kornfeld's body from Isaac Kornfeld's soul, she exhibits his opposing selves; doubling the two men in "The Dock-Witch," she reveals the narrator's secret sharer. When he first goes to the drugstore, the lawyer witnesses Undine's insensitivity toward the man, who, Undine announces, looks "just exactly like the Devil," a description she ultimately applies to her lover. About her husband, the lawyer muses: "she was perfectly correct. He was all points, like the ears of a rat—he was the driest, thinnest man I had ever seen" (153). Yet the very image he employs conjures up his vision of the "sacerdotal rats" and identifies him with the druggist. The two men share more than their thinness and their names, for Ozick implies they are both priestlike in their worship of the woman who lays claim to a dual identity. In the fate of the druggist can be glimpsed that of the lawyer. Doomed to a drugstore where "No one went in and no one came out," George consigns himself to a life cut off from others (151). That fate awaits the other George as well. In the underworld of lovemaking, he ignores newspapers for three days. He recalls Tilbeck, whose interest in fact and event is precluded by self-absorption; withdrawing from life the attorney resembles the rabbi. But George's experience partakes of the demonic. The mirror in the drugstore yields up "two straw-like creatures with pointed chins and ears and flickering eyes"—a "pair of Satans," a pair of men in thrall to a demon who renders them unable to distinguish the holy from the profane (159).

Sylvia-Undine is a Siren, a Lorelei, a witch who lures men to their own destruction. Though her singing initially propels the attorney to his office, when she sings in German, her voice "somehow blurred, like a horn heard from afar," she entices him back. Her song beckons him to the unreal world forsworn by Isaac's soul: "The dryad, who does not exist, lies. . . . Sir, all that has no real existence lies. In your grave beside you I would have sung you David's songs, I would have moaned Solomon's voice to your last grain of bone" (36). Undine's is a very different song: "My daughters shall be your lovely attendants; every night my daughters dance a round dance, they will rock you and dance you and sing you to sleep" (80–82). Those lines from Goethe's *Erlkönig* are spoken by an Erlking who lures a young child to enter a magical realm where life as mortals know it cannot be sustained, and the boy dies in his father's arms. Not only does Undine chant a deadly song, she carries a symbol of her powers, a lyre, which in *Trust* signified the realm to which that novel's narrator would plight her future. The lyre in "The Dock-Witch," however, "looked like the real thing. . . . Made out of a turtle-shell, green all over. Phosphorescent sort of. Could've been dragged up out of the bottom of the sea, from its looks" (161).

An instrument of ancient Greece, the lyre was invented by Hermes out of a tortoise shell and was an attribute of Apollo, the implement of Orpheus's music. It is the instrument Cynthia Ozick associates with the perilousness of the imagination and which she employs symbolically throughout "The Dock-Witch." At first, the lyre is connected with the lawyer, who buys a washboard on his way to the drugstore to celebrate not having been hit by a truck. "Clutching" the washboard "like a lyre," he enters the store where he mistakes Undine's tray for a real lyre; then it "turned into a thin tray fluted with golden tubes, each bloody at the tip"—an object warning against the dangers of the imagination (151). After his colleagues report the appearance at the sailing firm of a "naked" woman "covering her modesty with a lyre," he discovers she owns a real lyre, perhaps "swiped . . . from a museum" (161). Throwing the "ancient little hand-harp" through the window of his apartment when last they meet, Undine becomes the thief who robs her lover of all save her body: "I went to her docilely enough then; it was though she had broken something in me—some inner crystal, through which up to the moment of its shattering I had been able to see rationality, responsibility; light. I saw nothing now; her mouth became a wide-open window, and I hurled myself through it, whirling my tongue like a lyre" (164). Reason and determination gone, he becomes her slave destined for ruin, for she permits no release, no return from the bottomless depths of desire.

From such desire comes devastation—swift and inexorable. Undine demolishes his apartment in a fury over the phone call from his Uncle Al, an intrusion from reality, a reminder of the "noisy world almost forsworn." Heaping the fragments that remain of his apartment into mounds that rise up into "barrows . . . at her heels like the rapid wake of disappearing civilizations," she transforms his apartment into a cemetery, where, corpselike, George falls asleep. In thrall to a Siren, the lawyer has been bewitched. He ignores Circe's warning: the "Sirens by the melody of their singing enchant. . . . /They sit in their meadow, but the beach before it is piled with boneheaps of men now rotted away, and the skins shrivel upon them" (*Odyssey* 12.44–47). His final union with his Siren results in the annihilation of self that the wreckage of his apartment symbolizes. Shut of Undine, he runs to the piers where he meets her husband and where they see Undine-Sylvia metamorphosed into a figurehead on the prow of a Viking ship: "her left hand clasped a lyre, her right hand made as if to pluck it but did not, her spine was clamped high upon the nearest prow. Although her eyes were wide, they were woodenly in trance" (170). Left without a job or an apartment, the lawyer is undone. Of his double who wishes him good luck when he finds out what to do, the lawyer asks, "in the voice of a victim," "find out what?" But his double, who has "turned his side," cannot be seen and does not answer. The druggist's mirror can no longer "deliver up" the lawyer's "lost reflection" (168).

An obliteration of identity, the loss of that reflection recalls the rabbi's actual self-destruction and conjures up the divided mirror in *Trust*. In "The Pagan Rabbi" and "The Dock-Witch" Ozick links the artist's world of imagination to the worship of Pan: one story depicts the threat of idolatry confronting the Jewish artist, the other the artist's forfeiture of reality to the demonic power of art. That view of the imagination is Keatsian, and in her description of Undine-Sylvia, Ozick alludes to those poems in which Keats depicts the enthrallment to the imaginary as not only ephemeral but deadly. Her long hair, her "darkly ringed" eyes, her evil power—these suggest Undine's resemblance to Keats's nightingale, a "senseless tranced thing," to the Lady in the Meads, to "La Belle Dame sans Merci." Like the knight-at-arms, the narrator of "The Dock-Witch" is left "Alone and palely loitering"; like the poet in "Ode to a Nightingale," the lawyer must wonder at the whole experience; like Lycius, the lawyer is wasted "to a shade." The escape into the magical realm renounced by the narrator of *Trust* is explored in " The Pagan Rabbi" and "The Dock-Witch" as Ozick extends the battle between Pan and Moses into a contest between the imagination and the reason, between illusion and reality—a besetting predicament of art.

In "Envy; or, Yiddish in America" the theme that inhabits the deepest stratum of "The Pagan Rabbi," the perplexities of the Jewish artist, surfaces and becomes the chief concern. The sixty-seven-year-old Yiddish poet Hershel Edelshtein, one of Cynthia Ozick's most poignant characters, clings to his Jewish identity and, at the same time, craves recognition from a world alien to his own. He belongs neither to the generation of Jews who have grown up in the American Diaspora nor to the gentile community that surrounds him in Manhattan. Nonetheless, he fights the assaults of a generation that "courts amnesia of history," struggles against the lure, only secretly acknowledged, of a pagan culture, and lusts after immortality (74). A question posed in one of Edelshtein's poems—"*Does my way fork though I am one*"—epitomizes the poet's dilemma and that of Isaac Kornfeld, constitutes the twin paths explored by the narrator of *Trust,* and adumbrates the two routes to Joseph Brill's home in *The Cannibal Galaxy,* in which the schoolmaster attempts to reconcile the duality tht rends the rabbi and the poet (68).

Nearing the end of his life, Edelshtein is pierced by the emotion the narrator in *Trust* in her "sudden agedness" experiences at her commencement— "envy in the marrow," the "plague-fly" that "desires us against our will" (14). Alone, she envies the other graduates their bridegrooms: she hungers for the world that lies before her. A shrinking future faces Edelshtein, however. After living in America for forty years, he writes only in Yiddish and mourns its death in English. But he believes that a translator can make his Yiddish poems famous and redeem him from the anonymity of an "unmarked grave" (78). The pervasive death imagery with which Ozick describes Yiddish is consonant with Edelshtein's grief. To keep himself alive, Edelshtein lectures on the "lost,

murdered" language as if presiding "over a funeral"; those who understood
him "were specters," like his friend Baumzweig whose apartment reflects the
condition of his career (42, 43, 44). Living amid "dirty mirrors and rusting
crystal" in an "abandoned exhausted corridor," Baumzweig is also a poet as
well as he editor of *Bitterer yam* (Bitter sea), an obscure Yiddish periodical
paid for by a trust from a philanthropist who founded an organization for Yiddish letters to which notable writers once belonged. "Of the Alliance nothing
was left, only some crumbling brown snapshots of Jews in derbies"; of the periodical something is left—a few subscribers, the tiny audience for the smat-
tering of those poems by Edelshtein and Baumzweig consents to publish (46).

Shared enmity, not mutual affection, has brought the two writers together.
They hate the same person: a famous writer of stories written in Yiddish and
translated by collaborators he changes monthly. Consumed with envy, the poet
and the editor name Yankel Ostrover "Pig," "Devil," "Yankee Doodle." They
insist the storyteller is an assimilated Jew, a questionable Jew; an unkosher
Jew. The homage paid to Ostrover, his exit from the "prison of Yiddish," his
reputation as a "modern"—these are what Edelshtein covets (47). Scorning
Ostrover's subject matter—the activities of sexual freaks in Zwrdl, an imaginary village in Poland—Edelshtein imagines Ostrover owes his success to translators. In his beseeching letters to them, Ozick reveals the complex desires
Edelshtein harbors, his comical antics, his tragic failures.

From the "spinster hack," one of Ostrover's translators, Edelshtein receives
the reply: "Transformation is all he [Ostrover] cares for—and in English he's
a cripple—like, please excuse me, yourself and everyone of your generation. . . . I got caught in between, so I got squeezed. Between two organisms.
A cultural hermaphrodite, neither one nor the other. I have a forked tongue"
(55). Her metaphor recalls Edelshtein's poem. If she echoes him in her awareness that Yiddish has perished, she feels none of the Yiddish poet's grief, for to
her "whatever's in Yiddish doesn't matter" (56). But Yiddish and Ostrover
matter terribly to Edelshtein and Baumzweig, and they attend a reading given
by Ostrover at the 92nd Street Y to discover the reason for his popularity. Brilliantly witty, the scene poignantly captures the humiliation the unknown
writer suffers at the hands of the renowned one. Ozick's story-within-a-
story—Ostrover's tale about the untalented and unread poet who can only
write in the obscure language Zwrdlish and who trades his soul to Satan for
fame in any tongue—humorously encapsulates Edelshtein's situation and
looks forward to "Usurpation," in *Bloodshed*. Though the poet remains obscure, a failure at writing poems in any language, Satan consigns him to Hell
where upon completion his poems are consumed by flames. In a writer's hell,
a poet writes "only for oblivion" (60). Edelshtein flees from the lash of laughter the story elicits to a conversation with Vorovsky, another of Ostrover's
translators, a lexicographer driven half mad by compiling a German-English
mathematical dictionary. To Vorovsky Edelshtein confides his desire "To
reach," to do the very same thing the spinster hack accuses Ostrover of doing:
climbing on his translators' backs in search of fame (65). The poet's ambitions

recall Enoch Vand's goal, "to go as high as [he] can," and anticipate Joseph Brill's motto *Ad astra* (*Trust* 448; CG 55).

None of the men achieves his aims. As if aware of his fate, Edelshtein imagines another talk with Vorovsky in which the Yiddish poet shouts, "I've failed, I'm schooled in failure, I'm a master of failure!" (67). And Ozick, as she does throughout *The Pagan Rabbi*, limns the moment of recognition before a mirror. Like the glimpse George has of himself in the druggist's mirror and the horror Pincus Silver experiences, in "The Doctor's Wife," at the sight of himself in his mirror, the mirrored wall at the Y yields the painful truth. The reflection of an "old man crying, dragging a striped scarf like a prayer shawl" evokes Edelshtein's wish to have been born a Gentile, to have "God take back history," to be allowed to begin anew (67, 68). And Edelshtein's imaginary conversation with Ostrover is both a revival and a reversal of the confrontation Isaac Kornfeld has with his soul. Along with the refusal to "stop believing in Yiddish" and Jewish history is the longing Edelshtein has to divest himself of the past and acquire the accolades gentiles earn for their pagan contributions to western civilization.

And western civilization—"that pod of muck"—is Edelshtein's "sore point," the poet's "secret guilt" (41, 42, 96). The memory of a childhood experience in Kiev, where as a child he traveled with his father to tutor a "red-cheeked little boy," lingers in the poet's consciousness and emerges in Edelshtein's dreams. The poet longs to be Alexei Kirilov "whose destiny was to grow up into the world-at-large," "to slip from the ghetto," to enter the world from which Edelshtein is excluded (42, 96). Born Katz, the family Russified its name and the son was tutored not only in *Chumash* (the Pentateuch) but in Latin as well (96). Like the narrator of *Trust*, the young Edelshtein looked "through the doorway" and "crouched outside the threshold" listening to the Latin tutor chant a language, "Dirty from the lips of idolaters," "foreign," "beautiful," forbidden; alluring (81).

At the Baumzweigs', where he has taken refuge after Ostrover's reading, he has a "fine but uninnocent dream": "young, he was kissing Alexei's cheeks like ripe peaches, he drew away . . . it was not Alexei, it was a girl, Vorovsky's niece," the young woman who can read Yiddish, the translator in whom the poet has invested all his hopes (72). His unconscious confusion of the child and the lexicographer's niece, both of whom have "golden" heads and have escaped into western civilization, unmasks Edelshtein's attraction to that world (42, 94). But the dream discloses Edelshtein's fears: after the poet kissed her, Hannah "slowly tore the pages of a book until it snowed paper, black bits of alphabet, white bits of empty margin" (72). To deny the dream's revelations, Edelshtein writes a letter to Hannah in Yiddish:

whoever forgets Yiddish courts amnesia of history. Mourn—the forgetting has already happened. A thousand years of our travail forgotten. Here and there a word left for vaudeville jokes. Yiddish, I call on you to choose! Yiddish! Choose death or death. Which is to say death through forgetting or death through translation,

Who will redeem you? What act of salvation will restore you? All you can hope for, you tattered, you withered, is translation in America! (74–75)

Juxtaposing letter and dream, Ozick illuminates every crevice of the poet's mind, and Edelshtein's recognition of the motives which sparked the dream completes its analysis: "His cry was ego and more ego. . . . He wanted someone to read his poems, no one could read his poems" (75).

To find some who can, Edelshtein leaves the Baumzweigs' apartment in the middle of the night, a voyager in search of a port. The walks Ozick's characters take, from the narrator's wandering through the house at Dune-acres in *Trust* to Lars Andemening's rambling around the city's streets in *The Messiah of Stockholm*, lead to discoveries, are journeys to clarity.[7] On a "quest for consequence," the narrator and the lovers in *Trust* move from room to room; coming "to a kind of truce" with Big Road, Fishbein lectures his walking companion (*Trust* 585; PR 216). Memories and sorrows crowd Edelshtein's mind as the poet roams the snow-filled streets. A reminder of the rain in *Trust* and "The Pagan Rabbi," the snowstorm is part of the nexus of water imagery in "Envy" that is interwoven with the story's death imagery. Having symbolized both fertility and destruction in *Trust*, water in "Envy" signifies frozen aspirations, empty desolation. Baumzweig's *Bitter Sea* is almost unread. The laughter at the reading is "terrifying, a sea-wave" breaking "toward Edelshtein, meaning to lash him to bits" (61).

It is the audience's power to reduce him to anonymity that Ozick captures in that metaphor, and she exhibits its lingering resonances in the ruminations of the poet as he wanders through the snowstorm "toward Hannah's house, though he did not know where she lived" (78). A man who "had no descendants," whose "grandchildren were imaginary," Edelshtein envisions Hannah as his redeemer, a kind of descendant (78). In his remarkable imaginary letter to Hannah, Ozick not only unfolds her character's consciousness but also provides Edelshtein's immensely humorous criticism of Jewish writing in the Diaspora which broadens into a discussion of the meaning of language to tradition. Of those writers who know something about that tradition there is Ostrover—a "popularizer, vulgarian, panderer to people who have lost the memory of peoplehood" (79). Of those ignorant of Yiddish entirely, there remain the "so-called" Jewish novelists who lack any knowledge of that language save its curse words, the "ten words for, excuse me, penis, and when it comes to a word for learning they're impotent!" (79, 80). Remembering then the "beautiful foreign nasal chant of . . . Latin," he returns to Yiddish, to the impossibility of reproducing its "gait," its "prance," its "hobble" in English—to the problems of all translation. To write of the continuity, the growth, the hope, the tragedy of people living and struggling in English, Edelshtein tells Hannah, is to distort the nature of Jewish peoplehood.

Prepared at last to convince Hannah to be his translator, he dials Vorovksy but reaches Ostrover instead. His insults intensify the poet's desire to be read, and Edelshtein continues his imaginary letter to Hannah. Asserting that Yiddish divides the "Commanded from the Profane," distinguishes "between God and an artifact" and arguing for "auto-emancipation" and against mergence with the surrounding culture, Edelshtein then asserts the more fortunate situation of poets: "most are Greeks and pagans, unbelievers except in natural religion, stones, stars, body" (86). His desire to write pulls him in two directions. Only Hannah can unify them. Arriving at last under the canopy in front of her uncle's building, Edelshtein remembers his own wedding and the failed poets who held up the poles of the wedding canopy—all lovers of "America the bride, under her fancy gown nothing" (88). Edelshtein's image recalls Fishbein's opinion and reverses the meaning of America in *Trust*, making America not the country of golden opportunity, but the location for its loss. And the "piece of statuary, an urn with a stone wreath" that marks Vorovsky's building conjures up Tilbeck's amphora: in "Envy," an emblem of Edelshtein's desperate hope for immortality. But the statuary is filled with "sand, butts," emblems of waste, the waste filling Vorovksy's apartment as well. It and the urn augur the outcome of Edelshtein's quest.

Surrounded by two thousand copies of the dictionary he gave his life to compiling and which, because of a business dispute, he has to sell himself, though he does not know how, Vorovsky is fated "to swallow what he first excreted" (93). That situation mirrors Edelshtein's, and the confrontation the poet has with Hannah seals his doom. She severs herself from his and her uncle's generation; to her, "History's a waste." She denounces Edelshtein's fervent pleas: " 'It isn't a translator you're after, it's someone's soul. Too much history's drained your blood, you want someone to take you over' " (94). Worse, she compares him to Ostrover: " 'even in Yiddish Ostrover's not in the ghetto. Even in Yiddish he's not like you people' " (94). For Hannah, a writer who is "in the mainstream" is a "contemporary," one who speaks for the world-at-large, from which she excludes Edelshtein (95). Unlike the narrator of *Trust* who embraces the real and unlike Edelshtein who believes "real things" are literature's subject, Hannah admires Ostsrover for knowing a "reality beyond realism" (95). Anticipated in his dream, her condemnation of him brings Edelshtein clarity: "What he understood was this: that the ghetto was the real world, and the outside world only a ghetto" (96). At the same time, he acknowledges he is the "same as this poisonous wild girl," a man who "coveted mythologies, specters, animals, voices," a man who harbors pagan desires (96). But a crisis of insight prevails and he abandons his fantasy of being Alexei, of entering western civilization; he understands that "he was blessed" (96).

Filled with the rage of a father whose daughter has countermanded him, he slaps Hannah for renouncing history, for wanting to be rid of his generation, for denying its travail. The scene, a magnificent if lacerating enactment of the incapacity of the old and the young to imagine each other's lives, widens into one that represents the warring values—the revival of the battle between the ancients and the moderns—of contemporary culture. The impassioned altercation between Edelshtein and Hannah, however, ends the vain hopes he had of being read and culminates in Edelshtein's phone call to "Christ's Five-Day Inexpensive Elect-Plan" (87). Rapidly turning into a fervid antisemitic attack, against which Edelshtein inveighs, the comical interchange is the stuff of the Yiddish poet's ultimate tragedy. To the "eunuch's voice" that answers the phone, Edelshtein lists as those who "should drop dead" Pharaoh, Queen Isabella, Haman, King Louis, Hitler, Stalin, and Nasser (99). In response he receives a catalogue of typical antisemitic charges—"Judaic exclusivism," Jewish cowardice, abnormal eating habits, corrupt language. And Edelshtein hysterically empties into the telephone receiver his frustrated being, his lifelong fury. Shouting the names of the Jews' enemies from biblical times to the twentieth century—Amalekite, Titus, Nazi—Edelshtein cries, "The whole world is infected by you anti-Semites! On account of you I lost everything, my whole life! On account of you I have no translator!" (100). The story concludes as it began—with Edelshtein's cries unanswered.

Instructive for its account of Yiddish in America, moving because it chronicles the writer's accumulation of disappointed hopes, frustrated talents, and agonized strivings, "Envy" is richly layered. On one level the story "details the humiliating effect of America and American values on a once-fertile culture . . . . a culture that must pay constant tribute to English hegemony or lose its children and all its future" (Wisse 38–39). On another level "Envy" probes an artist's psyche, is a fiction whose provenance is biography. The interlacing of the two forms has always set Cynthia Ozick's imagination ablaze and continues to as tale after tale illuminates one form with the other, suggesting the inseparability of the writer from the work. Hershel Edelshtein becomes Cynthia Ozick's version of the poet Jacob Glatstein, a leading proponent of the group of Yiddish poets called *In Zikh* (Introspectivists).[8] Its very purpose— "to bring Yiddish poetry into the mainstream of Modern literature"—is Edelshtein's burning desire; *In Zikh*'s insistence on the "right to shake off the burden of the folk and the curse of history" the source of the Yiddish poet's ambivalence, a fact documented by Glatstein's poetry, which Ozick has translated and which reverberates in her tale.[9]

Threaded together by their emphasis on the crises arising from an uncertain identity, Glatstein's early poems link the real poet to the imagined one, to Edelshtein's concerns not to die unrecognized and to the aching awareness that only the power of the word can survive human transience.[10] If, as the young Glatstein wrote, "The wick of our generation is flickering," the sixty-seven-year-old poet laments "Yiddish, a littleness, a tiny light . . . . Sent into darkness" (42). It is a flame both poets strive to keep alight even as the desire to be a poet ignites ambivalence over the very language they celebrate. About the ghetto from which he wants to be released Edelshtein comes to understand that in it, not in the outside world, is the reality he seeks. Glatstein addresses his poet living in a ghetto: "Too bad, Yiddish poet, / you're not fated to become a fortress of quotations" (Whitman 110). And then in the last part of the poem the speaker urges the poet to "Become the watchman; guard," the preserver of the "faintest Yiddish speech" (Whitman 110–11). That conflict has forked Edelshtein's way.

Glatstein's divided desires finally left the poet no choice "but to come back, with blessing or curse, to the themes of the fathers"—the only themes, Edelshtein tells Hannah, that matter (Howe, "Journey" 76). As Edelshtein envies Ostrover's reputation, Jacob Glatstein was driven to speculate "on the curious fact that Bashevis [I. B. Singer], who was so deeply rooted in the Yiddish language, should have achieved fame through translation in a dozen languages, particularly in English, by means of which he has acquired for himself a recognized place in American literature" (17). Glatstein took I. B. Singer to task for his "tales of horror and eroticism," for his "distasteful blend of superstition and shoddy mysticism," for appealing more "to the non-Jewish than to the Jewish reader" for whom his stories "savor of a warmed-over stew of hoary old wives' tales, made alien by villainy, brutality and cynicism" (17, 18). To those complaints the poet added, "Bashevis lacks an ear for language and a sense of style" (18). In Edelshtein Ozick has revivified Glatstein; she has entered his consciousness through his poetry and she imagines his response in Edelshtein's witnessing what she observed when she reviewed *The Collected Stories of I. B. Singer*—"an accustomed celebrity who can negotiate a Question Period with a certain shameless readiness" (A&A 217). There is more. A translator of Glatstein's poetry, Ozick has translated other Yiddish poetry, and her essay on the process of translation intimates how Edelshtein came into being:

> First the translator begins, bit by bit, to discover the poet's verbal and ideational habits; then, little by little, the translator acquires the poet's obsessions. Next the translator is able to take in the ruling obsession of each single poem. Next the translator is certain he or she *inhabits* the poet, walking up and down inside the maze of the poet's convictions, conditions, tics, and itches. And then at last the translator turns into the poet. Not that the translator has 'merged' with the poet; but the one has genuinely become the other. (M&M 201)

Glatstein writes in "Genesis," a poem Ozick translated, "Why don't we start all over again / with a small people / out of the cradle and little?" (Howe, *Penguin* 458). A line in one of Edelshtein's poems asks, "Who will let me begin again" (68). The translator has acquired the poet's mind.

And the storyteller fleshes out her character's life by describing Edelshtein in images inspired by Glatstein's poetry. Standing before the mirrored wall at the Y he sees a reflection of the poetic persona that emerges in Glatstein's early poems—an aged man, a "decrepit old man" who in "On a Sunny Day" "accompanies the speaker for 'hours, days, years, centuries' " (Novershtern 132, 142). It is as if Edelshtein's mirror captures the speaker's words in Glatstein's "The Poet Lives":

> The mirror shines on your presence.
> It smooths and conceals your years. Tie the neck in flashy colors.
> Don't be afraid. The Yiddish burial-birds won't lay a hand on you.
> They will not—God forbid—salute a living poet. (Fein 163)

For Glatstein as for Edelshtein "Longing's a crooning for old men gumming sops" (Howe 464). In her translation of "Yiddishkayt," Ozick inhabits Glatstein; in creating Edelshtein she becomes Glatstein. He was appalled by Singer's making Satan the narrator of "Two Corpses Go Dancing"; and co-incidentally, it is Satan in "Envy" who invents the writer's hell (Glatstein 19).[11] Fame through translation is Edelshtein's obsession, for the Yiddish poet believes, as Glatstein wrote of Singer, that his translators gained Ostrover acclaim in America. Of Singer's translators Ozick reported: "the scandalous rumors about Singer's relation to his changing translators do not abate: how they are half-collaborators, half-serfs, how they start out sunk in homage, accept paltry fees, and end disgruntled or bemused, yet transformed, having looked on Singer plain" (A&A 223). She "wishes Singer would write their frenzied tale," she wishes "it were possible to list every translator's name" (A&A 223, 222). Writing the translator's letter in "Envy," Ozick imagined one of those frenzied tales; and she added one more translator to her list when she named Vorovsky's niece after still another of Singer's translators, Channah Kleinerman-Goldstein, who shares the first name of one of Glatstein's translators, Chana Bloch.[12]

Vorovsky's niece, however, calls Ostrover "A contemporary," while Edelshtein wonders "Who had discovered that Ostrover was a 'modern' " (95, 51). Hannah's is an opinion against which Edelshtein rails but one which has been voiced about I. B. Singer: "Yet one feels that, unlike many of the Yiddish writers who treat more familiar and up-to-date subjects, Singer commands a distinctly 'modern' sensibility" (Howe, "Singer" 107).[13] What Ozick has achieved in pitting Hershel Edelshtein against Yankel Ostrover is not only a brilliantly witty scene but a sharply delineated dramatization of an issue in postmodern criticism—whether a writer's identity matters. A subject that obsesses her second volume of tales, authentic identity is what Ozick celebrates in the poet Glatstein. As she does in "Usurpation," she recreates—she usurps—real lives for her fiction.[14] In "Envy," however, Glatstein has become Edelshtein and Ozick Glatstein. Yet this identification was misunderstood by Yiddish writers and by Glatstein himself, who died suddenly in 1971.[15] Presented with B'nai B'rith's Book Award for *The Pagan Rabbi* in 1972, Ozick delivered "a Bintel Brief for Jacob Glatstein" in which she explains that her story was intended as homage to Glatstein. Her title, a reference to the letters asking for advice from the editor of a Yiddish newspaper, "A Bintel Brief" illuminates the importance she accords biography in her fiction and affords insights into the workings of her imagination.

Echoing the precise word her character uses, she describes her feelings about the fate of Yiddish: "We did not know then that Yiddish in Europe was doomed to be murdered in the mouths of its speakers . . . that Yiddish too would become a corpse on the continent where it had flourished for a thousand years and produced at last one of the world's significant literatures" (59). Listen now to Edelshtein: "And the language was lost, murdered. The language—a museum. Of what other language can it be said that it died a sudden and definite death, in a given decade, on a given piece of soil" (42). To Hannah he writes, "Yet whoever forgets Yiddish courts amnesia of history" and at Hannah he screams, "Go get a memory operation" (74, 97). Of her own generation Ozick observes "that if we did not come to the heart and bones of the language [Yiddish] itself we would only betray it and ourselves becoming amnesiacs of history," victims of "autolobotomy" (60). Crowded with fathers, *The Pagan Rabbi* bears testimony to the meaning their lives possess for the storyteller who in her "Bintel Brief" recalls entering Yiddish as a translator: "I . . . explored my father's brains and life—and with the pursuit of each poem, I more and more recovered, and also discovered, not only what had been, but what would be, and not only the future but the present" (60). How wrenching, then, that her story was "branded" an enemy "of Yiddish and Yiddishkayt" (60). How chilling, then, that she experienced from the Yiddish audience and from Glatstein himself the force of Edelshtein's rage at Hannah: "I felt as if I had held a gift up to my mother and father, and in return they had struck me a blow on the skull" (60). Rarely have fiction and biography come together so graphically, so movingly.

Ozick explores Edelshtein's sorrows from another perspective in her essay "Toward a New Yiddish," and the interplay between the essay and the story—its painful conflicts and the essay's firm convictions—is enlightening. Commonly and mistakenly deemed an unwavering proclamation of the storyteller's artistic credo, the essay, read alongside "Envy," attests to its author's dialectical imagination, to Cynthia Ozick's capacity to entertain the irreconcilable and accept the changeable. Although the essay, which was originally delivered at a conference in Israel in 1970, grew out of the story, revives its issues, and recalls its ideas, "Toward a New Yiddish" lacks the anguished conflicts central to "Envy." In the essay Edelshtein's "secret guilt" becomes Ozick's revulsion, " a revulsion against Greek and pagan modes, whether in their Christian or post-Christian vessels, whether in their purely literary vessels, or whether in their vessels of *Kulturgeschichte*. It is a revulsion—I want to state it even more plainly—against what is called, strangely, Western Civilization" (A&A 156). Beleaguered by his failures, ridiculed by the successful story writer, and laughed at by the audience at the Y, the Yiddish poet longs to have been born a gentile, to join the surrounding culture, to be shut of what it regards as alien. In the American Diaspora, Edelshtein reflects, the "birth of a Jew increases nobody's population, the death of a Jew has no meaning. Anonymous" (77). The desire for acknowledgment from the gentile community, Ozick tells us in her essay, is a phenomenon of the American Diaspora: "Diaspora-flattery is our pustule, culture-envy our infection. Not only do we flatter Gentiles, we crave the flattery of Gentiles" (171).

Edelshtein's dilemma—the belief in Jewish history coexisting with an attraction to pagan culture—was one Ozick shared: "When at last I wrote a huge novel I meant it to be a Work of Art . . . I discovered at the end that I had cursed the world I lived in, grain by grain. And I did not know why. Furthermore, that immense and silent and obscure labor had little response—my work did not speak to the Gentiles, for whom it had been begun, nor to the Jews, for whom it had been finished. . . . Though I had yearned to be famous in the religion of Art, to become so to speak a saint of Art, I remained obscure" (157–58). But she converts Edelshtein's "chaos . . . of actuality" into an "impressionistic term, a metaphor suggesting renewal" and advocates a "new language . . . New Yiddish" (PR 96; A&A 173, 174). More than a metaphor or a cry for a "religious consciousness," New Yiddish is a clarion call for a "liturgical literature," a literature which will " 'passionately wallow in the human reality' . . . be touched by the Covenant. . . . Above all, the liturgical mode will itself induce new forms, will in fact *be* a new form; and beyond that, given the nature of liturgy, a *public* rather than a coterie form" (A&A 175). It is ultimately a universal form rather than a parochial one; it sets out to transform the "aestheticized, poeticized, and thereby paganized" novels of our time into something other than a "ceremony of language"; it aims to restore to literature a moral consciousness, a concern for human reality (A&A 164). What Ozick seeks to regenerate is what Edelshtein mourns the disappearance of—the "Jewish sense-of-things" (165).

In "Toward a New Yiddish" Ozick defines and assesses the cultural realities he faces, criticizing those like Hannah who repudiate Judaism for the narrowly parochial, the "aesthetic paganism" of Hellenism (152). Against those twentieth-century writers who claim the novel is about itself, Ozick urges Judaizing them—writing of "conduct and the consequences of conduct" (164). Against a society in which the will has ceased to matter, Ozick presses for the work of art to be "in command of the reciprocal moral imagination rather than . . . the isolated lyrical imagination" (169). Addressed to Jews in the American Diaspora, the ideas in "Toward a New Yiddish," like those in "Envy," are not limited to Jews; instead they concern contemporary culture, a culture enshrouded in the "occult darknesses of random aesthetics," an era marked by "historical amnesia" (A&A 177; Jameson 125). To use "Toward a New Yiddish" to take the measure of "Envy," discovering within the essay "clues, or cues, or concordances" to the story is to proclaim the premise of the essay the premise of the story as well (M&M x). The truth is otherwise: one probes the intricacies of a poet's desire for recognition, the other the complexities of cultural identity. In "Toward a New Yiddish" Ozick sets out to redeem our culture from its decline, to restore to Hannah's generation what it has excised.

A confrontation like the one between Hannah and Edelshtein becomes the focus of "The Suitcase," whose main character, a sixty-eight-year-old German architect, is a man of Edelshtein's generation, but Mr. Hencke has views that make him the Yiddish poet's opposite. Envisioning an encounter similar to the one in "Envy," Ozick then reverses her characters' roles. In "The Suitcase" Genevieve Lewin flirts with the world Hershel Edelshtein finds so beguiling; all the same, she attacks the retired architect not for believing in history, but for ignoring it. And Mr. Hencke, the father of her lover, harbors secret guilt not for an attraction to western civilization but for belonging to it. His is a consciousness wholly unlike Edelshtein's, but Ozick unmasks the German architect's consciousness the way she unfolds the Yiddish poet's—in dreams. A man who "no longer thought of himself as a German," Mr. Hencke, who was a pilot for the Kaiser in World War I, lives in a "yellow-brick house in Virginia" and denies any "German thoughts" save those appearing in a recurring dream. In his dream Mr. Hencke rides naked and bareback on a stallion over a meadow he remembers from his childhood, "past the millhouse, into a green endlessness hazy with buttercups" (103). Although aware of riding a stallion, the dreamer sometimes replaces the horse with his dead wife and always cries out in German, "faster, faster." The symbols in the erotic dream recall the pagan coupling in *Trust* and echo the significance Ozick accords to yellow in all four parts of that novel, but especially in part 1, where the color is specifically identified with Germany. That he unconsciously associates a pagan sexuality with his life in Germany and that he has chosen to live in a yellow-brick house in America reveal Mr. Hencke's German thoughts and suggest why, though he claims to regret it, the architect named his son after himself. Believing his life in America proof of his assimilation, Mr. Hencke has relegated to his dreams the deeper ties to his Teutonic stock.

But those unclaimed roots and the feelings consonant with them surface repeatedly during his visit to New York, where he has traveled ostensibly to see his son's art show. Arriving with his bag at "Nobody's Gallery," a name which the narrator of *Trust* would say divests its artists of real identity, Mr. Hencke is greeted by a "Somebody," the wealthy woman his son married (104). Catherine offers him the big upstairs room newly redecorated with yellow curtains. Although he disdains her for her stupidity, her invitation pulls from his "conventionally gossamer soul" the memory of the yellow buttercups, the dream-image—"one hair of the horse's mane" (105). His refusal to accept his daughter-in-law's proposal, however, elicits from his son's lover, Genevieve, the suggestion that the architect "frequented prostitutes" (108). Extremely offended, he apprehends that behind her provocation lies scorn for Germans.

The scorn escalates. Genevieve describes the crowd viewing the artist's paintings as " 'staring through the barbed wire hoping for rescue and knowing it's no use' "; the " 'terrible *precision*' " of the paintings appear to her eyes like " 'Shredded swastikas' " (108, 109). Aware "she thought him a Nazi sympathizer," Mr. Hencke judges her "full of detestable moral gestures" and eager to blame him for History, which he regards simply a "Force-in-itself, like Evolution" (109). His world-view reflects that of Schopenhauer, the philosopher toward whom Mr. Hencke "inclined" (109). Unlike Jewish historians, the nineteenth-century German philosopher considered historical events senseless and interest in them needless; any involvement in history, any stirring of social impulses were to be ignored and abandoned for fantasy, for the kind of art that most effectively transcended reality.[16] This "egoistic" and "morally cynical" philosophy is evident not only in the father of the artist, but in the artist himself, whose paintings in effect duplicate his father's labors: "everything seemed pasted down flat—strips, corners, angles, slivers" like cut-up "plans for an old office building" (White 237, 240; PR 105). In their identical names, their similar work, and their moral indifference, Mr. Hencke and his son Gott-fried are reflections of each other. The father shrugs off Genevieve's observa-tion that Jung stayed alive because he was not Jewish with the apathetic reply, "Everybody dies"; the son, supported by his wealthy wife, keeps a married Jewish mistress (108).

Mr. Hencke's subliminal hostility rises into consciousness as the architect listens to his daughter-in-law and remembers how her depressing conversation always "gave him evil sweated dreams" (110). In one of them the former pilot was in Cologne in the great cathedral where a "bomb exploded out of his own belly, and there rolled past him as on a turntable in the brutalized nave, his little niece laid out dead, covered only by her yellow hair" (110). His deepest German thoughts are sexual, warlike, and they account for his defensive-ness. To Genevieve's refusal to drop the issue of Jung, Mr. Hencke responds, " 'Gnädige Frau. . . . What do you want from me? . . . In sixty-eight years what have I done? I have harmed no one. I have built towers. . . . I have never destroyed' " (110). His return to the language he had not used since his wife's death hints at the recollections that dominate his conversation with Creighton MacDougal, whom his son has paid to talk about his paintings.

The famous critic's lecture occasions Ozick's rapier wit. The storyteller not only strips away the critic's pretensions, at the same time she humorously im-plies that the artist's work exemplifies a species of romantic religion and par-takes of the butterfly's fate—waste and death. Looking like God, according to the vacuous Catherine, the great "cultural critic" from the Partisan Review pontificates on "the art of Fulfillment," the art in which there is no "Yearn-ing," an art of "satiation," an art "for fat men" (112–13). During his inter-change with the critic, who reminds the architect of his father, Mr. Hencke talks of nothing else but Germany, of the airplanes flown in the "fierce and rigid Air Force," of its "strict teachers," the old school represented by his fa-ther (104). When the father of the artist observes his son and his mistress whis-pering to each other over a bowl of apples, the father understands an assignation is being arranged and, acting in the spirit of the old school, he un-dertakes, like God, to protect his son from sin. In fact, Mr. Hencke seeks re-venge on the Jewish woman who has released in him memories he had consigned to his dreams.

She is also linked to his son. Not only does Ozick identify the work of the artist with the architectural designs of his father, she portrays the latest effort of the son, for which he employs a metaphor recognized by his father as Genevieve's, in the precise words used to picture his mistress's coat. And in turn the coat presents a double design: "looked at one way," the coat resem-bles a "deep tubular corridor, infinitely empty, like two mirrors facing one an-other"; looked at another way, the pattern on the coat appears to Mr. Hencke as a "solid, endlessly bulging, endlessly self-creating squarish sausage" (117). Insulted by his son's mistress, the father of the artist deplores her influence, and adverts to his German memories. And when Genevieve teasingly embraces him, the pumpernickel crumb on her chin makes "some inward gate" open in Mr. Hencke and he is reminded of another field, "furry with kümmel, a hairy yellow shoulder of a field shrugging at the wind" (117). As he becomes more German, Genevieve becomes more Jewish. Her asking him if his brother-in-law made his shampoo out of "Jewish lard" in World War II, implicates the German architect in the Nazi atrocities (119). Describing herself as having a nose "like a Communion wafer," as possessing "gold inlays" that "click like castanets manufactured in Franco Spain" and breasts "like twin pomegranates. Like white doves coming down from Mount Gilead," Genevieve refers to the secret Jews, the Marranos, and to the Song of Solomon (119–20). Ozick doubles these allusions in two of Mr. Hencke's conversations: the "great lovely dove" becomes the Rumpler-Taube, an airplane in the German Air Force, and Corbusier a "secret Jew descended from Marranos" (114, 120). The architect transforms a biblical emblem of love into a weapon of war just as he converts the unfortunate and enforced secrecy of Jews into a dubious advantage.

Juxtaposing the same images in different contexts, Ozick emphasizes the hostility of the German toward the Jewish woman with whom he feels embattled. His increasing use of combat imagery hints at his final confrontation with Genevieve. The famous critic Creighton MacDougal looks "like a Junker officer," and the former pilot hears the "buzz of a biplane" spiral "out of his head" at the same time that a "saxophone opened fire" (120). As if the weapon has hit its target, Genevieve's scream rises from the bowl of apples, and Mr. Hencke "delayed and envisioned wounds." His thoughts are those of her enemy: "In his heart she bled, she bled. He stepped away. He kept back. He listened to her voice—such a coarse voice. . . . A Biblical yell, as by the waters of Babylon. Always horrible tragedy for the innocent. She was not innocent." Then he is attacked—the "saxophone machine-gunned him in the small intestine" (121). To refer to Psalm 137, to its prayer for vengeance on Israel's enemies, is to imply that Genevieve is a militant Jew seeking retribution for her people.[17]

And he identifies with his. Catherine's excitement over Genevieve's stolen pocketbook makes Mr. Hencke "nearly proud his son had chosen" Catherine as his wife and aware that like her father-in-law, she was "one whom crisis exalts" (122). Remembering the wound he received after landing an airplane with one wing half destroyed, he thinks how the experience "seemed sweeter to him than any crisis of love-making he was ever to endure" (122). Out of his meeting with Genevieve come all his hidden German thoughts, and they are those of a vigorous sexual warrior. His face mirrors his sense of himself; pock-marked, the skin on his face "was as pitted as a battlefield" (104). To Genevieve those marks look like "barbed wire" or the "ruts left by General Rommel's tanks" (120). His revenge is to turn her into the prostitute she accused him of visiting by ordering his son to give her money to replace what was stolen from her pocketbook.

Her indifference to his affront prompts him to confess he has not come to New York only to see his son's show but also to board a ship bound for

Sweden. But she accuses him of covering a journey to Germany with a lie about Sweden. Behaving as if she had charged him with stealing her pocketbook, he throws open his suitcase, a bag parallel to hers, and rummages "through the depth of his new undershorts" to prove his innocence. It is for his dreams and his German thoughts that he feels guilty.[18] Over them Genevieve is victorious and she returns to her husband, leaving the father of the artist to burn "in the foam" of the memories that remain in his "tenuously barbule soul, for which he had ancestral certitude" (127). At the end of "The Suitcase," however, it is Genevieve's ancestral certitude that prevails, and Ozick matches the Jewish woman's victory with the Yiddish poet's failure.

The generations are at war in the paired tales; doubling and dividing in each of them and between both of them, the storyteller, as she does in "The Pagan Rabbi" and "The Dock-Witch," provides conflicting perspectives, competing voices. If the two Gottfrieds disapprove of each other, they fundamentally resemble one another: artists whose first names suggest lives free of God, their last name brings to mind the German word for hangman. The relationship between father and son a presence in all four stories, "The Suitcase" is the only one to center on a father's consciousness. When he tells his son the Jews are a "superior race," the father of the artist excludes them, as Hannah does in "Envy," from the mainstream and revives the issue of racism in the later nineteenth century. In his reawakened German thoughts, the architect echoes the nineteenth-century antisemitic writers who extolled the "virtues of ancient German paganism and military vigor" as characteristics of the "Aryan mentality" (Seltzer 633). Indifferent to history, the aging German architect is more closely allied to the young Jewish translator; but the translator's fierce rejection of the Yiddish poet parallels Genevieve Lewin's behavior with the older Gottfried Hencke. His world, in turn, is the one Genevieve Lewin conquers and the one which Hershel Edelshtein feels has conquered him. Like the Yiddish poet, Genevieve precipitates an exchange which rapidly pits Jew against Gentile. But her namesake is the patron saint of Paris who defended the country against the Huns and the Franks; and Ozick intimates the Jewish woman ultimately triumphs over the German, a kind of Hun from World War I.

To the opposing perspectives on history she provides in "Envy" and "The Suitcase," Ozick adds the personal histories of Dr. Pincus Silver and Elia Gatoff, the main characters of "The Doctor's Wife" and "Virility." Neither man succeeds at making a real history or in constructing a viable future, but for varying reasons. Diverse in tone and execution, the two tales are yoked by similar concerns that accord to the themes present throughout *The Pagan Rabbi* a further dimension and augur the storyteller's future preoccupations. Into "The Doctor's Wife," a deeply moving and starkly realistic tale, Ozick interweaves thematic allusions to stories by Chekhov and James and her own apprehension of the philosophic and psychological implications of the Second Commandment. The tale, though its characters are Jews, illuminates not the sense of Jewish identity but the dynamics of an obsession. Dr. Pincus Silver, nicknamed Pug by his family, nurtures an illusion of his own conscious creation, devotes himself to it exclusively, and ends mired in the isolation that a compulsion exacts, his opportunities for future happiness destroyed. That powerful and chilling theme commands Cynthia Ozick's attention. Exploring the "most metaphoric depths of Commandment," the storyteller transcends the issue of Hebraism-and-Hellenism and arrives at the psychological mainspring of an *idée fixe* (A&A 123).

"The Doctor's Wife" involves two days, as decisive as those the narrator spends at Duneacres, in the life of a man about to turn fifty. Dr. Pincus Silver regards women's bodies as "their life's blueprints" and scorns his sisters for submitting to predetermined existences, for their ordinary marriages to men he cannot keep apart (177). Surrounded by the "pitiful ignorance" of his family, the incessant fury of his father, and the "Bedlam, waste, misery" in his waiting room, the doctor treats his patients, advises family members, manages to distance himself from the "old recurrent groan of life," and remains single (180, 181). Like John Marcher in James's "The Beast in the Jungle," Pincus Silver is convinced "that his most intense capacities, his deepest consummations, lay ahead" (183). As he rides through the streets with one of his brothers-in-law the night before his momentous birthday, the doctor is reassured by the "childlike fragrance" of lilacs which fills the air and which promises future fulfillment. But Ozick's allusion to Chekhov's "Doctor Startsev" augurs the obverse. During the spring, the "scent of lilac wafting from outside," Dimtry Startsev is introduced to Catherine Turkin, who seems to him the "very breath of springtime" and who so greatly attracts him that he takes seriously her joke that they meet in a cemetery (Chekhov 228). Longing for love "at whatever cost," Startsev proposes to Catherine but is rejected (234). More troubled by his hurt pride than by her refusal, the doctor assesses his feelings the way Pincus Silver does: "Nor could he [Startsev] believe that his dreams, his yearnings, his hopes had led to so foolish a conclusion, like something in a little play acted by amateurs" (236). His irritation with the provincials matches Pug's attitude toward his family; as Pincus Silver remains aloof from humanity even though he attempts to unify others, so Dimtry Startsev "met many people, but was intimate with none" (237). Years later, stripped of the illusions that caused her to turn him away, Catherine evinces genuine gratitude for his love and urgently seeks his understanding. Rather than seize that response as a fresh opportunity, a means to change an otherwise empty life, the doctor chooses never to see her again: he acts in the Turkins' garden the way Pug behaves at his birthday party.

Pincus Silver's fate, Ozick suggests, replicates that of Dimtry Startsev: "He lives alone. It is a dreary life, he has no interests" (242). Time inflates Doctor Startsev's egotism into grandiosity, as the narrator of Chekhov's story reveals when he describes Startsev driving his troika: "It is an impressive scene, suggesting that the passenger is not a man, but a pagan god" (241). The allusions to stories by James and Chekhov, both of whom provide related perspectives on the unlived life, become in Ozick's revisionistic reading elements of an arresting obsession, the storyteller's version of idolatry. The emotions that create it emerge in Pug's thoughts later that night when the doctor has an autumnal vision of his life. Unpermeated by the scent of lilacs, the air seems more "like the breathing of a vindictive judge" as Pincus Silver mourns his lost youth and recounts his losses (187). Lying on his back facing the ceiling, the visible symbol of an inner barrier, he reviews two decades of his life—twenty years of wasted talent, of emotional passivity, of awaiting some miraculous event. At twenty he felt "singled out for aspiration, for beauty, for awe, for some particularity not yet disclosed"; at thirty he judged this notion a youthful contrivance, a boyish imagining (188). Nonetheless, he envisaged himself "an open plaza . . . waiting to be overcome by a conquest," an event like the one James's Marcher anticipates. The necessity of deed, the evolution of individual personality—these vital developments the middle-aged doctor has replaced with mere yearning.[19] For that reason, he entered the fourth decade of his life "still without a history" and fell in love with a woman whose photograph he had seen in a biography of Chekhov. Entitled "Unknown Friend," the photograph extracts from Pincus Silver his complete adoration, which results in his failure ever to find a palpable and identifiable woman (188).

In this worship of a woman in a photograph around which he constructs a consuming fantasy that resists the intrusion of real possibilities, Pincus Silver recalls Marmaduke, the hero of James's "Maud-Evelyn." Drawn into the parents' grief over the child who died at fourteen and whom he has never met, Marmaduke spends his life imagining a relationship with the girl in the parents' photograph; believing he had married Maud-Evelyn, he stays faithful to her memory. Ozick alludes to "The Beast in the Jungle" and "Maud-Evelyn" not to usurp their themes but rather to interpret and thereby revise them. If James was haunted by the plight of the living dead, Ozick is drawn to the aetiology of that predicament. Emotional impoverishment, she repeatedly shows, is inevitably the consequence of a ruling illusion. Surrendering to the power of an image, like Marmaduke, the doctor arrests his life. But his identification with Chekhov, who was also a doctor, establishes Pincus Silver as one of Ozick's artists. A "bachelor up to the last minute," Chekhov married when he was fifty. Included in Ernest J. Simmons's biography of Chekhov, the biography in which the photograph of Unknown Friend appears, is a famous letter in which Chekhov describes his painful struggle to overcome his youthful slave-like mentality. His affecting account of how he had to press the "slave out of [himself] drop by drop" until he could wake up one morning and feel "real human blood," not the blood of a slave, coursing in his veins testifies to an internal tyrant's terrible power (Simmons 175). Chekhov's example notwithstanding, Pug never liberated himself from his mind-forged manacles. Instead, he awaits the miracle promised by romantic religion. His infatuation with the photograph of a woman anonymous even to Chekhov's biographer is charged with significance.

That Pincus Silver falls in love with an unnamed woman exposes his illusion; for as Enoch Vand observes, "there is no proof of being, outside of one's own mind . . . except for the solidly indisputable fact that one's friends call one by name" (*Trust* 178). Because of "her tormenting anonymity," because she is "sitting nameless" in a photograph, because "if she spoke he would not understand," Pincus Silver can sever Unknown Friend from his sisters, whom he regards as "no more than ovum-bearing animals" (188, 189). Like a writer he invents a personality for the woman and contrives a life for her; the doctor imagines the woman he desires and then worships his own creation. The recognition that it has enslaved him, has darkened his future, brings determination: "the doctor resolved to throw away the biography with its deeply perilous photograph. . . . what he meant by this was that he must throw illusion away. All the photographs of the mind—out! All the photographs of hope and self-deception—out! Everything imprinted, laminated, sealed, without fruit, without progress or process—out! Immobility, error, regret, grief—out!" (189).

Even as he resolves to change, he relieves himself of the responsibility for changing and like one of Baeck's completed men, resigns himself to an unalterable fate, to the idea that he "was sterile by default," to the knowledge that "his life was a bone" (189). His chilling discovery becomes a license for stasis (190). On the morning of his birthday, he meets his sister Frieda at the supermarket and learns she has invited an available woman to his party. At that news the "indoor garden" grows "corrupt and vicious," and he spends the rest of the day prior to the birthday party "dutifully" gluing the "daring chin of Unknown Friend" to the "unimaginable face of the guidance counselor" (194, 197). His pleasure at the blue handle of his shopping cart, the color which to the narrator of *Trust* seems "the bare color of impatience, the color of the thing deferred" and his fixation on the mind's photographs decide the outcome of his momentous fiftieth birthday. Despite his desire for separation, he attempts "unions" at his office. But the glimpse he catches of himself in a mirror, a vision not unlike Edelshtein's, delays his arrival at the party where Pug feels choked with Gerda Steinweh and forced to hide "his coldness" (198). While his sister introduces Gerda to him, he laments inwardly, "Life, life, where are you, where did you go, why didn't you wait for me? Let me live!" (202). His cry reverberates the truth of Strether's declaration in Gloriani's garden in the fifth book of *The Ambassadors*—"It doesn't so much matter what you do in particular, as long as you have your life." Her sense of contrast—the growth of Strether's awareness as opposed to the collapse of Pincus Silver's—determines Cynthia Ozick to transform James's "story of conversion" into a study of arrested desire (Wegelin 96).

Unwilling at fifty to liberate himself as Strether does at age fifty-five, Pug becomes a conscious dissembler when he uses the features of Unknown Friend against Gerda to contrive the image of a marriage he has developed in the darkroom of his mind. A recrudescence of illusion now externalized and made more unshakable in its purposeful falsity, his lie drives him away from the very life he had pleaded for earlier. His portrayal of an imaginary wife, "An emigré. A fugitive," differs from his perception of real women, whom Pug disdains because they "have no categories," and provides an exact if unwitting portrait of himself (205). "One of those 'interior' refugees," like Enoch Vand, "who seem always to be fleeing . . . the persecutions of ordinary life" and who practice the "cult of a single idea," the doctor rejects Gerda, severing himself from "human deed and human history-making" and sacrificing his future (*Trust* 69; A&A 191). That it is irredeemable is achingly apparent in the last sentence of the story, for Pincus Silver, whose last name links him to photography, is "captured" by the deluded photographer and forced to listen to another of his impossible schemes as the doctor's fateful day, the first of the new decade during the season of renewal, ends blighted by his panting after a chimera.

It is the tyranny of illusion, the sacrifices it demands, and the failures it promotes that Ozick penetrates in "The Doctor's Wife." In "Virility" she satirizes the brilliant, though ephemeral, success of an illusion. The perils of paganism link "The Pagan Rabbi" to "The Dock-Witch," the conflict between generations "Envy" to "The Suitcase." In "The Doctor's Wife" and "Virility" a lie determines the futures of the main characters. Matching thematic similarities in the two tales, Ozick sunders them in tone and balances the grimness of one with the playfulness of the other. "Absorbed in the notion of waiting," Elia Gatoff reaps its benefits, but postponement ambushes Pincus Silver. For disparate reasons, neither man succeeds in constructing a future; if one has excised his history, the other never made one.

The future, however, frames "Virility," which is told by a "centagenerian" who relates a tale from his very distant past (221). It was a time "when a poet—a plain . . . and rather ignorant man—was noticed, and noticed abundantly, and noticed magnificently and even stupendously" (222). Of the present the one-hundred-six-year-old narrator observes, "Now it is the stars which dictate fame, but with us it was *we* who made fame, and we who dictated our stars" (222). Envisioning a future bereft even of the memory of Byron and Keats and preoccupied with "moon pilots, and mohole fishermen, and algae cookies, and anti-etymological reformed spelling," Ozick satirizes not only the idea of fame but the destiny of high art and the present fashionable indifference to history (221). Her aged narrator begins his tale just as the narrator of "The Pagan Rabbi" does, in the present. Visiting Edmund Gate's grave the way Isaac Kornfeld's friend travels to Trilham's Inlet to see the tree on whose branches the rabbi hanged himself, the narrator of "Virility" is then driven to return to history to recount the reasons Edmund Gate "jumped off a bridge" at twenty-six (269). He was born Elia Gatoff and began life less auspiciously than Isaac Kornfeld. A boy during "Czarist times," Elia was sent to live with an old aunt in Liverpool on a forged passport until his family could be reunited there (223). But a pogrom murdered the entire family and it fell to Tante Rivka, an "intellectual spinster," to care for and teach her great-nephew. To support him she worked in a millinery shop "sewing on veils"—an occupation that becomes metaphoric in "The Sewing Harems"—and taught the young boy English. He rewarded her toil with abandonment and journeyed to America unaffected either by the fate of his family or the future of his aunt.

Ambitious to be a poet, Elia arrived in America wanting "contact with written material" and came to the office of the narrator's newspaper for a job, which he was given despite his lack of preparation and in spite of his indifference to his past (225, 224). Rapidly divesting himself of it by taking the narrator's name, Edmund Gate, Elia Gatoff becomes an impostor and Cynthia Ozick posits a theme with which the first novella in her second collection is concerned and which continues to appear throughout her fiction—the issue of impersonation. His adopted name, a "name suitable for the language" in which he is eager to write, severs him from Edelshtein, who celebrates Yiddish even as he covets fame. The self-named poet more closely resembles—he anticipates—the orphan Lars Andemening, who chooses his name from a dictionary. Dictionaries, though, play a strikingly different role in "Virility," for the margins of their pages initially serve as the paper on which Elia composes his poems. Asked about that practice, the fledgling poet responds," 'I like words. . . . I wouldn't get that just from a blank sheet. If I see a good word in the vicinity I put it right in' " (229). It is the "ceremony of language" taken to its most ludicrous extreme. And it goes along with the poet's separation "from the moral life" as is evident in the lack of concern Elia has for his aunt's poverty or for her unanswered letters (A&A 245). This witty and disdainful portrait of a would-be poet recalls Euphoria Karp and the other word-manipulators in *Trust* who, indifferent to the meaning of words and untouched by the "consequences of conduct," are drawn to words merely for their own sake (A&A 164). In Gatoff's clumsy conglomerations of words culled heedlessly from the dictionary Cynthia Ozick ridicules what elsewhere she argues against—the pure form of classical aesthetics.

That is the form the poet embodies: "he held his torso like a bit of classical rubble" (237). Propelled by unfailing self-esteem, undaunted by the uniform rejection greeting him everywhere, Elia is sustained by an "odious resiliency" and obsessed with an *idée fixe* as purposeful as Pug's is purposeless (235). The doctor's nickname, however, more closely approximates the poet's pugnacious spirit and large body. They elicit from a woman the regard and succor Edelshtein cannot wrest from Hannah, who dashes his hopes for fame through translation as resolutely as Margaret supports the confidence Elia has in his future recognition. With a "miraculous change in his history"—the change Pincus Silver awaits—comes the preeminence that shocks the narrator upon his return from the war and causes his sister Margaret to credit Elia's "genuine manliness" for bringing success. Ozick wryly suggests that masculinity, not talent, promotes a writing career: "The element in him that partook of the heathen colossus had swelled to drive out everything callow—with his blunt and balding skull he looked . . . like a giant lingam: one of those curious phallic monuments one may suddenly encounter, wreathed with bright chains of leaves, on a dusty wayside in India" (244). After the publication of his first volume of poetry, titled *Virility* by Margaret, *Virility II* and *Virility III* follow rapidly, along with an infant whom Margaret names Edmund. Increasing masculinity is wed to growing fame. And Margaret cultivates it; dressing Elia like a prize fighter, she arranges a lecture circuit "to Paris, to Lisbon, to Stockholm, to Moscow" (254). Hotly pursued, wildly praised, the poet is more photographed than read since only the title of his books has been translated. Having depicted the sorrows of the untranslated in "Envy," Ozick then illustrates their irrelevance in "Virility." Acknowledgment, she indicates ironically, follows not understanding or accessibility or even merit; fame is solely a product of virility. That accounts for the critical opinion that praises Edmund's poetry for being " 'Seminal and hard. Robust, lusty, male. Erotic' "; that explains why the poet is thought to be " 'The Masculine Principle personified, verified, and illuminated' " (254).

To his virility Ozick joins his literary fertility, for the birth of his children accompanies the publication of his poetry. In turn, it is judged by his masculinity: "The poet and the poems were indistinguishable" (257). In an ironic twist, the storyteller separates them and renders Elia as "sterile" as Pug claims he is "by default"; she links the two men in their common act of impersonation. A confrontation between the narrator of "Virility" and the poet exposes Elia's lie just as a lie devolves from the meeting between Dr. Silver and the guidance counselor. The widely acclaimed poet is an impostor: writing under a name stolen from Edmund Gate, Elia Gatoff had published poems usurped from letters written by Tante Rivka. Elia's confession, however, is induced not by a "fit of conscience" or grief over her death but by her "last bunch of letters," the end of his poems and his career. Credited with amazing literary productivity, Elia Gatoff has in fact only turned out two babies, Edmund and Gate, who do not even bear their father's real names. They belong to the narrator, and he becomes an avenger, forcing Gatoff to make a public confession and to publish the rest of Tante Rivka's poems under the right name. *Flowers from Liverpool* appears with a picture of the poet on the cover of the volume. The narrator judges Tante Rivka's poems "sublime," the "crest of the poet's vitality," thinks them "as clear and hard as all the others, but somehow rougher and thicker, perhaps more intellectual" (264). But the sex of the poet determines the critics' response. Extravagantly praised when they were believed written by a man, the poems are now regarded "Thin feminine art," "Choked with female inwardness," the poet, the owner of a "spinster's one-dimensional vision," an instance of "Distaff talent, secondary by nature" (266).

In "Previsions of the Demise of the Dancing Dog," an essay she published during the same year as "Virility," Ozick argues in behalf of Tante Rivka and against the "idea of literature-as-physiology" (A&A 267). What the reviewers of her poetry are guilty of is attributing to a body that which is body-less. They are "adherents of the Ovarian Theory of Literature, or, rather, its complement, the Testicular Theory" (A&A 266). Of her personal experience with those theories the essayist remembers:

> I came to the university in search of the world. . . . I wanted Experience, I wanted to sleep under bridges—but finding that all the bridges had thickly trafficked cloverleaves under them, I came instead to the university. I came innocently. I had

believed, through all those dark and hope-sickened years of writing, that it was myself ("myself"—whatever that means for each of us) who was doing the writing. In the university, among my colleagues, I discovered two essential points: (1) that is was a "woman" who had done the writing—not a mind—and that I was a "woman writer"; and (2) that I was now not a teacher, but a "woman teacher." (A&A 265–66)

About Tante Rivka's collection the reviewer writes: "There is something in the feminine mind which resists largeness and depth. Perhaps it is that a woman does not get the chance to sleep under bridges. Even if she got the chance, she would start polishing the piles. Experience is the stuff of art, but experience is not something God made woman for" (267).

God, the reviewers imply, made woman for childbearing, a process frequently compared to the genesis of a poem. To that notion of creativity Ozick replies in her essay: "It is insulting to a poet to compare his titanic and agonized strivings with the so-called 'creativity' of childbearing, where—consciously—nothing happens" (A&A 270). In "Virility" she yokes the publication of poetry and the birth of children, equating for the purposes of satire the conscious "labor of art" with an "involuntary" process of nature (A&A 271, 270). Essay and tale interact, reverberate each other's ideas, or as in "Envy" and "Toward a New Yiddish," balance one idea against another. The essayist concludes "Previsions of the Demise of a Dancing Dog" with a glimpse into the future when laughter might be our response to the "quaint folly of obsolete custom" (283). And it is to the future she turns at the end of "Virility," to the "curious incident" at Edmund Gate's grave. There what appeared to be a woman was disclosed to be a man dressed in women's clothes who declared himself to be Edmund Gate—a testimony to the quaint folly, now obsolete, of adhering to stereotypes and judging by physiology.

That is a judgment both Elia Gatoff and Pincus Silver make. His lie exposed, Gatoff is shorn of the accolades that affirmed his masculinity; without them he stands "in the middle of a floor without a carpet, puzzled, drunk, a newspaper in one hand and the other tenderly reaching through the slot in his shorts to enclose his testicles" (223). Neither the doctor nor the fraudulent poet can distinguish body from intellect, although that is, Ozick maintains, a distinction essential to a "humanist society" (283). Such a society turns out "human beings" instead of "role-playing stereotypes," such a society rejects "false barriers and boundaries . . . segregationist fictions and restraints"; such a society repudiates a "politics of sex" (A&A 283, 288). Ozick's is a "classical feminism—i.e., feminism at its origin, when it saw itself as justice and aspiration made universal, as mankind widened to humankind—rejected anatomy not only as destiny, but as any sort of governing force" (A&A 288).[20] What the storyteller champions is not "the new" feminism but traditional feminism, and it is to the traditional, not to the experimental, she turns for the source of innovation in art.[21]

At their nub, all the stories in *The Pagan Rabbi* are concerned with art and tradition. Knowledge of her tradition is what the narrator of *Trust* gains when she meets her father; in *The Pagan Rabbi* the father is omnipresent and he incarnates the idea of tradition against which the artist struggles. Isaac Kornfeld's father considers the philosophy his son studies an "abomination"; Edelshtein's father regards Latin, the language that charms his son, evidence of an "apostate family" (3, 81). Mr. Hencke disdains his son's idleness, and Pincus Silver's father, whose "fury rose with him in the morning and went to bed with him at night," stays awake to yell at his son (186). Alive, Edmund Gate's father "had disliked" his son "completely," but the absence of Elia Gatoff's father results in his son becoming an impersonator (239). A complicated human and artistic predicament, that clash between the generations inevitably becomes part of any writer's quest for self-definition. More and more such confrontations as those in *The Pagan Rabbi* become the focus of the storyteller's attention as she continues to urge tradition upon the individual talent and, at the same time, to engage in an enduring dialectic with the patriarchs of that tradition. That she has adduced the conflict between religious belief and the religion of art, lamented the disparagement of history, and reinvigorated the idea of tradition has occasioned the observation: "Cynthia Ozick, a writer not infrequently compared with Flannery O'Connor, may be judged by posterity our T. S. Eliot. . . . Ozick . . . is a writer who surveys waste, idolatry, compromise and the meretricious; and, with Eliot, she is a writer who proposes a sterner, and an older, way" (New 288). Seeking like Eliot to restore to literature its nourishing ties to the past, she evinces, along with her belief in the treasures of the past, an "anxiety of influence." Her first volume of tales embodies that anxiety in the tension between the generations, in Isaac Kornfeld's and Hershel Edelshtein's competing desires, in Pincus Silver's ruling illusion. The very structure of *The Pagan Rabbi*—its juxtaposition of tales with antithetical ideas—attests to the endeavor to examine the tradition from which her tales evolve. Ending *The Pagan Rabbi* with "Virility," a tale whose subject is impersonation and whose satirical elements summarize the vital concerns of the entire volume, Ozick anticipates the first tale in *Bloodshed*, in which she continues to explore the meaning of tradition and the barriers to authenticity.

THREE

The Dread of Moloch

In Cynthia Ozick's first volume of stories Pan battles Moses for the souls of a rabbi, a Yiddish poet, and an attorney; or else a doctor and a would-be poet yield to dissemblance and imposture. From *The Pagan Rabbi* emerge competing ideas, the tension excited by dual perspectives and the strife over an inherited tradition. In *Bloodshed* the storyteller is preoccupied with the betrayal of that tradition. The characters in her second volume of stories have either shorn themselves of the Judaic heritage or they exist only on the margins of Judaism. Depicting the obverse of cultural rootedness, Ozick explores the implications of cultural rootlessness, its divestiture of "historical freight," its spuriousness as a source of liberation, its guarantee of "outsideness" (A&A 155, 162). In "Toward a New Yiddish" she states unequivocally that the "annihilation of idiosyncrasy assures the annihilation of culture" (A&A 168). Dante, Shakespeare, Tolstoy, and Yeats, she maintains, "did not intend to address the principle of Mankind; each was, if you will allow the infamous word, tribal. Literature does not spring from the urge to Esperanto but from the Tribe" (A&A 168). *Bloodshed* reflects that conviction: meditations on tradition, the four novellas are "tribal." If Jews are the concern of these tales, their betrayals of the Mosaic idea exemplify the effects brought about by the loss of cultural integrity and the negation of the self: the weakening of tradition. To that principle—that innovation *is* traditional—Ozick hews in *Bloodshed*. It is the principle she adduces in "Innovation and Redemption" and one which has transformed not only the potentialities of American Jewish writing but has established her as a leading contemporary innovator. "Toward a New Yiddish" urges the revival of traditional values; *Bloodshed* depicts the consequences of repudiating them. Like the stories in *The Pagan Rabbi,* the novellas in *Bloodshed* are paired. They afford contrasting views, they impart disparate perspectives; they illumine the ambivalence coextensive with truth.

I

To introduce Stanislav Lushinski as a "Pole and a diplomat" is to suggest his ambivalent identity, to conjure up Isaac Kornfeld, a pagan and a rabbi (15). In "A Mercenary," historical event has determined Lushinski to welcome the paganism of the tiny African country he represents. Its "thick night-blossoms excited him," for in Poland he lived in a "flag-stoned Warsaw garden." Unaware of the names of flowers, he "was hardly conscious that these heaps of petals, meat-white, a red as dark and boiling as an animal's maw . . . the lobe-leafed mallows, all hanging downward like dyed hairy hanged heads from tall bushes at dusk, were less than animal" (15–16). The lush blossoms, the dense foliage, the exotic perfumes of the land he perceives as mammalian—these divide it from the "roil of Europe" from which he has fled. From the "girls he pressed down under the trees" he learned the language of the small African country; from the African rendering of the Bible, "curiously like a moralizing hunting manual," the young Lushinski learned syntax. The book in the Bible that stresses God's mercy and forgiveness, Jonah "seemed simple-minded in that rich deep tongue," more like a detailed description of a fish than an example of God's mercy (17). But Lushinski's escape to Africa recalls Jonah's flight from God's presence to Tarshish, a land which "connotes luxury, desire, delight. . . . 'a distant paradise' " where God is unknown (Ackerman 235).

A native of the land Lushinski has adopted, Lushinski's assistant compares his boyhood to the diplomat's and in the parallel events of their lives, Ozick establishes them as secret sharers and ultimately unmasks the mystery—the man the diplomat claims to have killed—at the core of Lushinski's existence. If Stanislav Lushinski has traveled to Africa and learned its argot, Morris Ngambe holds an Oxford degree in political science and talks to the diplomat in his office—"this atmosphere almost of equals" (18). But his assistant's "ecstatic boyhood" was filled with games, boys hanging upside down from tree-branches, with indulgent aunties (23). The ritual cannibalism of Morris's mother, a worshiper of "plural gods" and a believer in animism, transformed her into the goddess Tanake-Tuka, a goddess who "could perform miracles" (18, 20). Having partaken of the "principal sacrament, the nose," Morris prays "to his mother's picture"—to an image Sinai forbids (19, 23). What has drawn Lushinski to Africa emerges in a television interview. As if recounting a legend and not the real history of his boyhood, Lushinski begins, "Once upon a time, long ago in a snowy region of the world called Poland, there lived a man and his wife in the city of Warsaw" (25). Alluding to the evil Slavic witch Baba Yaga from whom, in one tale, two lost children fled through a wilderness, the diplomat hints at what is to follow—the all too real terror of his escape from the Nazis through the forests of Poland when he was six years old. The horror-filled Polish forest resembles the forest encompassing Morris's village, a forest "with all its sucking, whistling, croaking, gnawing, perilously breathing beasts and their fearful eyes luminous with moonlight" (23).

And the peasants' attempt to give Lushinski to the Germans is parallel to the attack on Morris in New York by a rust-colored chow. The young Lushinski gouged out the eye of the ferocious bulldog Andor, who "had chewed-up genitals and vomit on his lower jaw," and then threw him against his master whom the dog killed (28). Designed as mockery and parody, Lushinski's story elicits laughter and disbelief not only from the television audience but from Morris Ngambe. Only Louisa, the diplomat's German mistress, does not doubt her lover's veracity, for she has often shaken Lushinski out of nightmares and comforted him with the reminder that he was now a "figure the world took notice of" (29). In this role Louisa resembles Morris's motherly aunts who gave Morris the confidence that he "would one day weigh in the world" (24). His relationships with his mistress and his assistant imply the diplomat's wishes to have been born someone else. On the telephone, Lushinski addresses Louisa first as Tanake-Tuka then Lulu; she "mothered him and made him eat" (21). She resembles Morris's transformed mother. Lushinski's mother considered German "the language of the barbarian invaders, enemies of all good Polish people," but Lushinski has a German mistress. Her "large fine nose" recalls the powers Morris attributes to his mother's nose; a "German countess," Lulu has less strength than the goddess and submits to every wish of her lover, though she knows how the word Jew "restored him to fear" (41). Like Genevieve Lewin in "The Suitcase," Lushinski is attracted to a pagan world; like Genevieve he insists on the importance of history, but unlike her he does not return to a Jewish world.

What the parallel hangings from Lushinski and Morris's boyhoods—one a brutal torture inflicted by the peasants who strung Lushinski from a rafter by his wrists, the other an exercise devised by the village men to stretch the muscles of a boy's neck—establish is the reason Lushinski has fled that world. What the two incidents juxtapose is the received idea of civilization in Europe against the conventional notion of the untamed life in Africa. Acutely sensitive to the inexorable facts of history, Ozick has woven into the fabric of her story allusions to those texts that reflect the aftermath of historical event and that disclose the outcome of personal decision. The tale of Lushinski's escape through the forests of Poland is an obvious reference to, even a recreation of, Jerzy Kosinski's *The Painted Bird*.[1] On one level, "A Mercenary" provides commentary on the failure of Kosinski's narrator to become morally involved in the events of his life. The dark-skinned and dark-eyed narrator of Kosinski's novel looks like a gypsy the way Lushinski did, and both lads had fair-skinned and blond parents who were forced to leave their children with peasants. Afraid of the Germans, the peasants put the six-year-old boy out and he entered the forest to escape his pursuers. *The Painted Bird* charts the experiences of the boy as he wanders alone from one Slav village to another in flight from the Holocaust. Never identifying his narrator as a Jew, Kosinski simply reports that others consider the "olive-skinned" boy a "Gypsy or Jewish stray" (2). Though she alters their form for her own purposes, Ozick includes several episodes from *The Painted Bird* in "A Mercenary." Lushinski's revenge on the bulldog Andor, for example, conflates three separate events from *The Painted Bird*, a castration and the blinding of a plowboy. Hung from a ceiling in a farmer's house and left to dangle over the vicious dog Judas, Kosinski's narrator denies being Jewish and, for a time, begins to believe in the power of Christian prayer. Then he is hurled into a manure pit and loses his ability to speak. His dreams of himself as a German officer, his learning to take revenge, his transformation into a Stalinist and an atheist, his refusal to acknowledge his parents upon their return—these betray his conscious attempt to become someone else. Kosinski concludes his novel ambiguously, leaving the boy's future uncertain. Suffused with nightmarish brutality and violence, *The Painted Bird* celebrates the triumph of individual will, not the survival of a people.

Where Kosinski's tale ends, "A Mercenary" begins. In chronicling the diplomat's life after the young Lushinski escaped to Russia, Ozick concentrates on the "consequences of conduct," what for her is the true concern of fiction (A&A 164). That she has combined two of the episodes in Kosinski's novel with an allusion to the blinding of the monstrous Cyclops in the *Odyssey* as well as an allusion to the killing of a dog in the Jacob and Esau narrative revises the significance Kosinski accords to the events in *The Painted Bird*. He names his dog Judas and suggests his narrator is like Christ. Ozick strips the allusion of its Christian associations and replaces them with classical and Judaic overtones. Instead of becoming Christlike in overcoming a lawless monster, Lushinski resembles the hunter Esau whose descendants were cut off from the world.[2] Adverting to Kosinski's narrator, Ozick portrays the outcome of the process by which a different life is appropriated to one's own.

Morris Ngambe's mental annexation of another continent, brought about by a departure from Africa and an education at Oxford, is a reflection of Lushinski's history, the assistant's experiences in New York an emblem of the exiled. Despite his firsthand knowledge of Africa, Morris Ngambe is judged ineffectual and obtuse by the Secretary of State, to whom the diplomat's assistant says, "there is no contradiction between the tribal and the universal" (33). That statement conjures up the distinction Ozick makes in "Toward a New Yiddish." To declare the tribal and universal fundamentally the same, Ozick avers, is to annihilate culture (A&A 168). To aspire to the apotheosis of a private moment is to act on a pagan impulse; it is to follow the "religion of Art" (A&A 165). Morris's impression of the Secretary of State is illustrative: "The ugliness, the defectiveness, of some human beings! God must have had a plan for them if He created them, but since one did not understand the plan, one could not withhold one's loathing. It was not a moral loathing, it was only aesthetic" (33). Uninterested in biography—"he did not care about the consequences of any life"—Morris turns whatever he studies into poetry (42). It, Ozick argues in "Toward a New Yiddish," "shuns judgment and memory and seizes the moment"; it allows the diplomat's assistant to regard Hitler as a mad genius who "saw how to make a whole people search for ecstasy," to imagine the German Final Solution "an aesthetic solution" (A&A 169; *Bloodshed* 42; A&A 165). Morris Ngambe is an incarnation of paganism and the embodiment of Stanislav Lushinski's deepest desires, all that Sinai assails.

The Sinaitic commandments yoke the Jew to deed, involve him in history. To a historical catastrophe Lushinski attributes his freedom: "Every survivor is free. Everything that can happen to a human being has already happened inside the survivor. The future can invent nothing worse. What he owns now is recklessness without fear" (37). But Lushinski is frightened by the words "peasant" and "Jew" and insists on one topic of conversation with Lulu— death and the record of it. Like Enoch Vand, Lushinski favors the "Accretion of data." If Enoch reminds the narrator of *Trust* that "history is a judgment on what has happened," Lushinski tells Lulu that "something liturgical" is *"what really happened"* (38). And what is liturgical, Ozick explains in "Toward a New Yiddish," is "in command of the reciprocal moral imagination" (A&A 169). Lushinski, however, believes "there are no holy men of stories . . . only holy men of data." They write books like Raul Hilberg's *The Destruction of the Jews* and Elie Wiesel's *Night,* the sources and documents the diplomat reads (38). To Lulu's inability to separate stories and sources he counters, in Enoch's fashion, " 'Imagination is romance. Romance blurs. Instead count the numbers of freight trains' " (38).[3] But the title of Hilberg's book irritates Lulu, and she protests, " 'It isn't as if the whole *world* was wiped out. . . . It wasn't *mankind,* after all, it was only one population' " (38–39). Hers is an opinion Ozick discusses in her essay, "Cultural Impersonation," wherein she interprets Matthew Arnold's desire to be civilized as the wish to belong "to the locally prevailing mythos—to the West as Christendom," to the mainstream of civilization from which Arnold and Lulu exclude Jews (A&A 134).

And she excludes herself from their passion for history, which she hates as much as she knows the diplomat hates "being part of the Jews" (40). The very mention of the word Jew drives him to bathe, and his ritual suggests baptism, allies him to Disraeli, a baptized Jew who represented another race, and recalls Enoch Vand, whom Allegra calls Disraeli (*Trust* 69). If he shares some of Enoch's convictions, Lushinski resembles his assistant. The ritual to mark Morris's coming-of-age, the occasion on which a garland of mallows was wreathed around the tribe-god's member, "its lulu," and when the fourteen-year-old boy was led into the forest for a sexual initiation, is matched by Lushinski's excitement over the mallows, European perennials, and his choice of a German mistress whom he calls Lulu. Juxtaposing the experiences of the two men, Ozick unmasks Lushinski's wish to have become a man in the forest of the African village rather than in the woods of Europe. She establishes the means by which an identity is fabricated. That Ozick was especially preoccupied during the 1970s with the subject of impersonation is evident in the many references she makes to the Jacob and Esau story in her essays. In "Toward a New Yiddish" she describes Norman Mailer's flight from a Brooklyn *shtetl* as his transformation into Esau; in "Cultural Impersonation" she yokes Mark Harris's *The Goy* to John Updike's *Bech,* proclaims the two books examples of cultural impersonation and even titles her review "Esau as Jacob" (A&A 130–137). Itself a history, the biblical tale concerns deceit and immorality and traces the destinies of two personalities, the origins of two peoples.

Those nations are, in "A Mercenary," the continents of Europe and Africa. Allusions to *Robinson Crusoe* and Conrad's "Heart of Darkness" and *A Personal Record* appear early in Ozick's novella. That Crusoe leaves his father's house without parental approval, receives a warning from a comrade's father, who uses Jonah as an example of why Crusoe should not go to sea; that at nineteen he journeys to Africa and ends up a slave are auguries of Lushinski's fate. They are buttressed by and combined with Ozick's allusions to Conrad.

He recorded his determination to travel to Africa in his autobiography and included in "Heart of Darkness" the human heads which at first seem to be posts with round carved balls, like the hairy hanged heads of the lobe-leafed mallows in "A Mercenary." Interweaving imagery from "Heart of Darkness," to which Europe and Africa are central, and elements from the Jacob and Esau story, Ozick adds a further dimension to Lushinski's history. Neither the diplomat nor his assistant shrink from disparaging Europe. Lushinski declares himself an African and tells Lulu, " 'I don't want Europe' " (41). And Morris, whose last name is reminiscent of Niambe, the African god of the sky, calls New York a "wilderness, a jungle" and Europe the "Dark Continent," a "hellish and horrible" place from which "you fled . . . you ran like prey into shadows" (41, 42). In "A Mercenary" Ozick locates the heart of darkness in Europe and makes its counterpart the unrestrained paganism of Africa, reversing the thesis of *Through the Dark Continent*. Henry Stanley contrasts Africa, a continent on which pagans devoted to idolatry lived, with the "boundless treasures" of European life; Ozick exposes the derivation of those "treasures" and presents postwar Europe and its unfathomable savagery as the extreme form of paganism (81). If Enoch Vand's life in Europe constitutes a period in the wilderness, then Lushinski's fascination with Africa is a sojourn in Edom.

The color red along with the imagery of roundness, knives, and halves identify the African village with Edom, a word meaning "red." Condemned by the prophets for wickedness and corruption, Edom became a synonym for Rome in later rabbinical literature. The color of the round mallows, the horrible chow, and the jackals running in Morris's forest, red is used by Ozick to describe her characters as well. Lulu is a "great rosy woman"; the young Italian man with whom Lushinski is rumored to live in Geneva has red hair, and the Secretary of State is envisioned by Morris as an "old, carmine-colored, creased and ugly man" (17, 33). Imagining Africa, Lulu pictures a "red stalk of bird-leg in an unmoving pool" (41). In "Heart of Darkness" the sun, "dull red without rays and without heat," is adjoined to death; and Marlow designates as "red-eyed devils" violence, greed, and desire (17). Conrad's imagery limns the erotic and untamed country to which Lushinski has attached himself: a pagan land, red like Edom, inhabited by Esaus who are impure, a land where the Covenant is unknown and where Morris's mother was cooked in her own milk.[4] From the Jacob and Esau narrative comes the meaning of the round objects, the "dense sweetnesses of so many roundnesses" that Lushinski feels "native" to and that Morris's "perfectly rounded" forehead reflects (16, 18). Born holding on to the heel of his twin, Jacob was thought to have formed the "ancient circle motif" with Esau, a circle like the one made by Eve and the snake.[5] And the lentils for which Esau sold his birthright are round because "mourning rolls from one person to another" (Plaut 177). The biblical images embody loss—the Fall, death, mourning—and they are deployed by Ozick, along with her reference to the knobs in "Heart of Darkness," to mark Lushinski's adopted African country as Edom, a hell appropriate for someone who has sold his birthright for a heap of lobe-leafed mallows.

Reminders of the life Esau led, knives appear throughout "A Mercenary,"
and Ozick joins to their ability to kill their capacity to divide, introducing into
her novella the imagery of halves that in her novel *Trust* symbolizes the
Hebraism-and-Hellenism controversy. A knife was the instrument used to
murder Morris's mother; Lushinski's nose "could have sliced anything"; and
the diplomat thinks his assistant uses knives "for buttering scones," an adumbration of Ozick's *Puttermesser*, a name meaning "butter knife" (22, 51). But
the letter Morris sends Lushinski is a "blade between them," a "severing" (51).
The letter divides the diplomat from his assistant and reinforces the novella's
imagery of halves. "Exactly half Lushinski's age," Morris possesses a language
that "was an observant, measuring, meticulous language." Lushinski's left eye
recalls the language: "This pupil measured and divided, the lid was as cold
and precise as the blade of a knife" (18, 17, 22). His eye is an emblem of the
diplomat's life. Pronouncing the word "starve" like a "half-pun," Lushinski
travels in America for a "half-year" (36, 44). Contrary to the halforisms that
indicate how Enoch Vand lived the first half of his life, which culminates in a
Return, the halves in "A Mercenary" emphasize how Lushinski spends the second half of his life—divided from the Covenant.[6]

Having run from his tormentors through the dark and perilous forests of
Poland, Lushinski dreads what he is, what he was hated for. His terror impels
him to flee like Jonah from God's presence and to regard Europe as the
twentieth-century's heart of darkness. To escape it Lushinski becomes "a der-
vish of travel" and fills his suitcase with " 'Several complete sets of false papers . . . passports for various identities . . . and a number of diplomas in
different languages' " (36). Lushinski's suitcase conjures up Mr. Hencke's. An
image from the preface to *Bloodshed* suggests the significance of both suitcases: "Stories cannot carry suitcases stuffed with elucidation" (9). Mr.
Hencke's and Lushinski's suitcases are their own elucidations. Crammed with
various identities and diplomas, only two of which are not forged, Lushinski's
suitcase establishes the diplomat as a man in flight, as an impersonator who
belongs nowhere. To hang toy ribbons and medals on his fake officer's uniform and to ring a scarlet cord around the bill of his cap is to repeat the "ma-
neuvers he invented for his toy soldiers" as a boy. Dressed in such a costume,
Lushinski journeys to Rhineland where he is welcomed (25). Like the narrator's dream of becoming a German soldier in *The Painted Bird,* Lushinski's
uniform manifests the desire for acceptance at any cost and in any place.

In New York Morris Ngambe "brooded about impersonation," remembers Tarzan "investing himself with a chatter not his own," and knows himself
to be "self-duped, an impersonator" (46). When he questions Lushinski about
sincerity, Lushinski tailors his response to fit Morris's expectations: " 'Sincerity is only a maneuver, like any other. A quantity of lies is a much more sensible
method—it gives the effect of greater choice. Sincerity offers only one course.
But if you select among a great variety of insincerities, you're bound to strike
a better course' " (47). Designed to accommodate what his assistant wants to
hear, Lushinski's answer betrays the willingness to " 'jump into someone else's

skin' " and make it fit, to become a Tarzan (47). What Lushinski knows himself to have become is represented in his self-portrait, the "head of a cormorant," which he draws while the representative from Uganda reports the diplomat's fabrication of "dangerous adventures for make-believe pirates who exist only in his fantasies" (49). A bird that seizes its prey under water, the cormorant is designated unclean in Leviticus and Deuteronomy (Lev. 11:17; Deut. 14:17). Other impure birds are referred to in "A Mercenary": on the airplane leaving Africa after the war he has invented, Lushinski pictures the "tarred roofs of the guerilla camps" as the "dark nests of vultures," and Lulu imagines herons inhabit Africa (35, 41). Those birds recall Kosinski's painted bird, which "circled from one end of the flock to the other, vainly trying to convince its kin that it was one of them. . . . The painted bird would be forced farther and farther away as it zealously tried to enter the ranks of the flock. We saw soon afterwards how one bird after another would peel off in a fierce attack. . . . When we finally found the painted bird it was usually dead" (50). At the end of Kosinski's novel "some inner force" restrains the narrator from leaving his parents; he becomes the painted bird, "which some unknown force" pulled "toward his kind" (241). Ozick reverses the significance of the painted bird; for unlike the bird, drawn to its kin and driven to remain with them, the cormorant, the vulture, and the heron are birds destined to dwell in God's wilderness—away from all kin.

Those are the birds Isaiah claims will appear in Edom on the day of God's vengeance and those are the birds Ozick lodges in the African country. They are related to the painted gourds belonging to Morris's father. Together the birds and the gourds reveal the outcome of the decisive flight Lushinski makes from his Jewish self. The godlike painted gourds are pagan versions of the gourd God prepared "to deliver" Jonah "from his grief." When the fish disgorged him, the prophet was rescued, but the diplomat identifies with a bird that habitually swallows fish and destroys them. The protective shade of Jonah's gourd has become the painted and hollowed-out gourd housing the murderer's knife in Morris's village, and Lushinski understands he is unacceptable to God, undeserving of His protection, and destined to endure His vengeance in desolation and devastation.

Morris's realization in New York, a "city of Jews," is parallel. Knowing that he is "Mdulgo-kt'dulgo in exile," an imposter "made not new but neuter, fabricated," he writes to Lushinski in Africa (50). About a Japanese who murdered twenty-nine people at the Tel Aviv airport and then partially circumcised himself in a Jerusalem prison, Morris speculates:

> Here is a man who wishes to annihilate a society and its culture, but he is captivated by its cult. For its cult he will bleed himself.
> Captivity leading to captivation: an interesting notion.
> It may be that every man needs to impersonate what he first must kill. (51).

Her character answers a question the storyteller poses in the preface to *Bloodshed*: "Why do we become what we most desire to contend with?" (12). Both

Cynthia Ozick and Morris Ngambe echo William Blake, who in *Milton* and *The Four Zoas* limns the labors of the poet Los against Urizen, Blake's avenging lawmaker. Of Los shrinking from his task of setting limits to the ruin of Urizen Blake writes:

> Pale terror seized the Eyes of Los as he beat round
> The hurtling Demon, terrifid at the shapes
> Enslavd humanity put on he became what he beheld
> He became what he was doing he was himself transformd. (Erdman 331)

To become an impersonator is to identify with the oppressor.

In Africa aware that "Morris saw him as an impersonator," that his assistant had "uncovered him," "had called him Jew," the "Prime Minister's gaudy pet" sits "on a blue sofa before an open window" and is cast back into the past: "under the shadow of the bluish snow, under the blue-black pillars of the Polish woods, under the breath of Andor, under the merciless palms of peasants and fists of peasants, under the rafters, under the stone-white hanging stars of Poland—Lushinski. Against the stones and under the snow" (51, 52). The passage alludes to Wiesel's memoir, a "source" in which Lushinski discovers truth. In *Night* Wiesel recounts the harrowing time he spent in concentration camps, the death of his God, the loss of his desire to live, the destruction of his soul. Two of his experiences are alluded to in "A Mercenary"—the death of a child by hanging and the abandonment of corpses by the S.S. "Then," Wiesel writes, "the train resumed its journey, leaving behind it a few hundred naked dead, deprived of burial, in the deep snow of a field in Poland" (94). If Wiesel's soul was murdered in the death camps, Lushinski murdered his soul in Poland: "Against the stones" of his "flag-stoned Warsaw garden" and "under the snow" that deprived the dead in *Night* of burial lies the real Lushinski.[7]

Captivated by Africa, the Lushinski at the end of "A Mercenary" knows himself to reside in the land of burning pitch described by Isaiah, the land on which the "line of confusion" and the "stones of emptiness" are stretched, the desolate land inhabited by the impure cormorant (Isa. 34). That land Ozick depicts mainly in red and blue, the dominant colors of the large map of Africa that Marlow peers at in "Heart of Darkness." The colors of the countries Kurtz's parents come from, the red and blue map supports Marlow's contention that "all Europe contributed to the making of Kurtz."[8] Marlow's judgment of Kurtz is Ozick's of Lushinski. Exchanging the savagery of Poland for the paganism of Africa, Lushinski becomes a mercenary, the Prime Minister's gaudy pet—a well-paid slave kept for pleasure.

In "A Mercenary" Ozick explores with uncommon acuity the reasons for impersonation and its consequences. That she specifically mentions Chekhov in the preface to *Bloodshed* recalls the famous letter he wrote in 1889, to which she refers in "The Doctor's Wife," a story which ends in a deliberate act of dissemblance—a theme central to the Russian writer's work.[9] Attributing to the need to falsify a sense of one's own worthlessness and fear, Chekhov shows, in his later stories, how one lie heads inescapably to the next lie, how lying requires the sacrifice of freedom.[10] Feelings of inadequacy and childhood experiences with an abusive adult had two seemingly paradoxical consequences for Chekhov, the assumption of a false personality and the condition of moral slavery.[11] Pursued by cruel adults as a child, Lushinski ends by identifying with them. Africa becomes an adult version of Poland, only with a crucial difference: Lushinski transforms himself from the person who was terrified into the person who terrifies. He makes a war ostensibly to raise prices: he victimizes as he was once victimized. History, the memory of the past, and Lushinski are, as he tells Lulu, " 'One and the same' " (38). As if to signal where "false gods . . . may lead their victims," Ozick has attached to "A Mercenary" an epigraph from Joseph Goebbels: "Today we are all expressionists—men who want to make the world outside themselves take the form of their life within themselves" (Rosenfeld 79). The first of the stories in *Bloodshed* concerned with the problem of Jewish identity after the Holocaust, "A Mercenary" makes plain that a fabricated identity neither liberates nor ennobles: "cultural accommodation" succeeds only in victimizing (Rosenfeld 78).

Published in 1970, four years before "A Mercenary," the second and title story of *Bloodshed* is wed to the volume's first novella.[12] Not an impersonator, Bleilip calls himself a "secularist": "The secular Jew is a figment; when a Jew becomes a secular person he is no longer a Jew" (A&A 169). But Bleilip feels himself to be "part of society-at-large," a situation Ozick describes in "Toward a New Yiddish" as tantamount to vanishing: "If he [the Jew] does not judge what he finds, if he joins it instead, he disappears" (*Bloodshed* 59, 58; A&A 166). Though related to "A Mercenary" thematically, "Bloodshed" begins, as "The Pagan Rabbi" begins—with a journey "out of New York." Of significance in "A Mercenary," the halves in "Bloodshed" are crucial. They determine the story's structure, they signal the story's fundamental conflict.[13] In fact, "Bloodshed" is divided in half; in turn, each half contains matching episodes and repeating images which ultimately expose the central character's intentions, the reason for the unaccountably heavy pockets of his coat. And the halves connect Bleilip to Lushinski, another man with a secret. Both men resemble Enoch Vand, whose absorption in counting the dead after the Holocaust approximates the attraction Bleilip has to the survivors, whom he regards as comprising a "town of dead men" (60). Wanting to penetrate the mystery of the town's inhabitants, Bleilip conjures up the narrator of *Trust*, who must travel to Duneacres to uncover the truth of her existence.[14] Unlike the ruins that fill Huntingdon's grounds, however, "everything in [the hasidic town] was new or promised" (55).

Bleilip's sojourn to his cousin's "half-built house" in a community where "everything was unfinished," where even the frozen puddles are "fresh-smelling, mossy," takes on all the contours of a symbolic journey from the very beginning. That he considers the "town of the hasidim" alien is evident in his first glimpse of his cousin Toby, who Bleilip thinks is a "convert," an ordinary girl who has been transformed into something "freakish" (55). To his questions about whether she likes her life, one he, a lawyer and a professional fund-raiser, thinks insular and primitive, she responds " 'Why do you keep asking? Don't you like your own life?' " (56, 58). Including himself in "society-at-large," away from her *shtetl*, he thinks he enjoys his life "excessively," but as Yussel observes, Bleilip is " 'looking for something. He wants to find' " (58). He and the hasidim exemplify the difference between the "Jewish idea and the world-at-large," between cultural rootedness and cultural marginality (161). That Yussel has survived the death camps arouses special expectations in Bleilip. From a survivor, Bleilip, "wanted some kind of haze, a nostalgia for suffering perhaps"; he presumed survivors had a "certain knowledge the un-scathed could not guess at" (58, 59). But his attitude toward the hasidim is sharply divided. Believing Toby "crazy to follow deviants, not in the main-stream even of their own tradition," Bleilip is nonetheless "lured" by the very group of Jews he thinks "actually christologized" Judaism by forcing every-thing "to go through a mediator" (59). A "rationalist, a *mitnagid . . .* purist, skeptic, enemy of fresh revelation, enemy of the hasidim," Bleilip flushes with excitement when he learns the town has a rebbe (59). One half of the attorney professes to be a rationalist, the other half is drawn to the miraculous. In "an atavistic fit," the lawyer in "The Dock-Witch" goes to church just as Bleilip travels to the hasidim.

Their new town betokens renewal, but Bleilip imagines himself surrounded by a "crowd of ghosts coming down" (60). His sentiments are explained by his assumptions. As he and Yussel turn toward the schoolhouse to attend *mincha*, the evening prayers, Bleilip is startled by the sight of Toby entering the dark-ened door of her house with her "two pairs of boys with golden earlocks," for it is "as if a beam of divinity had fixed on her head, her house" (61). Scorning the hasidim for their mediators, he envisions his cousin the owner of a divinely protected and blessed existence, a gift from the Messiah. Bleilip, Ozick sug-gests, has come to the hasidim to discover the effects of belief, to understand why the survivors continue living; to look for a savior. That he ascribes unique knowledge to the hasidim proves he has mistaken the "hasidic part [of Juda-ism] for the historic whole" (A&A 162). A movement that transformed and dominated Jewish religious life throughout the nineteenth century, hasidism proclaimed devotion to the *zaddik* (righteous person, or the hasidic rebbe) and his teachings as the corridor to inner redemption.[15] The rebbe brings to his reading of the Torah passages from the Talmud and other sources, and the tra-ditional texts receive the fresh interpretations that induce a religious act of in-tense personal devotion—spiritual elevation. It is that experience that Bleilip means to observe as he fits "his haunches into a boy's chair" and tries to catch a glimpse of the rebbe, whose face, Bleilip imagines, is a "patriarch's face—the father of a large family" (61, 62).

Bleilip's analogy of rebbe and father is telling, and it constitutes another instance of Ozick's preoccupation with the father and child relationship. The key to self-knowledge in *Trust*, the father in "Bloodshed" signifies God, the Patriarch—the essence of Judaism. After they finish *mincha*, Bleilip and the other men move to a long table to read Torah; as if to separate himself, Bleilip sits in a folding chair "away from the men" (62). Initially regarding them as apparitions, Bleilip is "stunned" that the men "were not old." His awareness of their piety and the strangeness of their language diminish him: "a month short of forty-two . . . he felt like a boy; even his shoulder-blades weakened and thinned" (62).

A mixture of Hebrew and Yiddish, the men's language conjures up in Bleilip the memory of his grandfather, whom the fundraiser imagines hanging "from the ceiling on a rope . . . mischief-maker, eager aged imp. The imp came to life and swung over Bleilip's black corner" (62). If his grandfather is an imp, the "hasidim (refugees, dead men)" are "ghosts" sitting "as if already in the World-to-Come, explicating Scripture (63, 62, 63). Elevating the hasidim to the security of salvation, to the Messianic Era when, the rabbis believed, men would lead a pristine spiritual existence, Bleilip reduces himself to an ignorant child and construes the survivors' suffering as the price paid for admission into a new world permeated by a superior joy and governed by divine justice.[16] Their text is Leviticus 16, the chapter of the Torah devoted to the Day of Atonement. Of singular importance, that day commemorates the receiving of the Tablets of the Law and is the climax of the religious year when those who have successfully atoned for their sins experience *t'shuva*. A book referred to in Hebrew by its first word, *Vayikra* (And He called), Leviticus is the first text studied in *cheder* (elementary religious school). That Bleilip feels like a child in a yeshiva listening to a reading from Leviticus 16 suggests his situation in the story: the boy who has just begun to learn Torah differs from the sanctified men who know its teachings.

Bleilip hears them read *Yoma* (the Day, the fifth tractate of the order *Mo'ed* in the *Mishnah*) "through the web of a language gone stale in his marrow" and Ozick renders the text as he interprets it. Although Yom Kippur imparts a message of harmony with God and among human beings, Leviticus 16 and *Yoma* are concerned with legislation for the Day of Atonement, with the rituals surrounding the scapegoat. On the Day of Atonement the *kohen gadol* (High Priest) performs an intricate sacrificial service on behalf of the community. Picking a disk from an urn, the high priest determines, from what is inscribed on the disk, which of two goats will serve as the scapegoat, the goat to be sent to Azazel, and which one will function as a sin offering for the Lord. Ozick compresses that procedure, infusing it with dramatic intensity. First the High Priest "changes his vestments" and immerses his body in the ritual bath, and then the blood of the priest's bullock and that of the slaughtered goat is sprinkled on the altar eight times. At last, the goat for Azazel is touched by the High Priest, who "confesses the sins of the whole house of Israel, and utters the name of God, and pronounces the people cleansed of sin" (63). The fate of the goats scrapes Bleilip "to the edge of pity and belief, he pitied the hapless goats, the unlucky bullock" (63).

His pity expands to include the "God of Israel" whom he identifies with his grandfather: he reinvokes the imagery he had employed to piece together his dead grandfather's face and replaces his grandfather with the God of Israel, "whom he saw as an imp with a pitted nose dangling on a cord from the high beams of the Temple in Jerusalem" (63). The imp and the God of Israel conjure up Lushinski suspended from the rafters of a shed, and all three recall Isaac Kornfeld hanging from the branches of a tree and the hanged child in *Night*. In "Bloodshed" the suspended imp marks Bleilip's loss of faith: "What God could take the Temple rites seriously? What use does the King of the Universe have for goats? What, leaning on their dirty tablecloth—no vestments, altars, sacrifices—what do these survivors, exemptions, expect of God now?" (64). Bleilip's vacillating attitude toward the survivors is matched by a fluctuating response to the reading. Mishearing that a piece of red wool will be tied on the goat designated for the Lord, he reveals his ambivalence. In *Yoma* the red wool marks the goat designated for Azazel; when the goat reaches the cliff, half of the yarn is tied to the goat's horns, the other half to the rock. The purpose of the scapegoat and the symbolism of the yarn emerge in *Yoma* (6): "When the he-goat reached the wilderness, the crimson turned white; as it is said 'Though your sins be as scarlet, they shall be white as snow.' " A redemptive act in *Yoma*, the idea of the scapegoat is interpreted by Bleilip, who initially responds to the text with pity and belief, as an act of useless bloodshed. Moved to the edge of faith, Bleilip retreats to the center of doubt and despair, whereupon he identifies the rebbe. Noting his posture and his "funny flat nose," Bleilip concludes that the rebbe is a "self-stabber," the opposite of Morris Ngambe who "stabbed" (64). But the rebbe's nose connects the rebbe to Bleilip's grandfather, to the God of Israel. The shared images—the nose and the yarn—in "Bloodshed" and "A Mercenary" connect the two tales. As she does in *The Pagan Rabbi*, Ozick pairs stories and juxtaposes ideas. To the problem of post-Holocaust Jewish identity she renders three responses—Lushinski's, Bleilip's, and the rebbe's.

Unlike Lushinski, the rebbe does not dissemble; but Bleilip distorts. His perception of the relationship between the rebbe and the men is illustrative: "Bleilip . . . saw that the rebbe was their child, they gazed at him with the possessiveness of faces seized by a crib, and he too spoke in that mode, as if he were addressing parents, old fathers, deferential, awed, guilty. And still he was their child, and still he owed them his guilt" (64). Though he believes the hasidim christologize, Bleilip is the one who christologizes. It is Bleilip who imagines the nativity scene and attributes to the men's respect for the rebbe the adoration of those who have come to worship the infant Christ. And it is Bleilip who misconstrues the goat on which the red yarn belongs. In his discourse the rebbe conflates the prayer of the High Priest for the people of Sharon in the Talmud with the scapegoat's fate as it is reported in *Yoma*. The rebbe's version of the people's prayer, which alludes to the Eulogy of the High Priest in the apocryphal Wisdom of Ben Sira, stresses the peacefulness once brought by atonement. Then a community's guilt was transferred to the scapegoat and thereby removed. Now, the rebbe reflects, "For animals we in our day substitute men" (65). Summarizing the various ideas of Azazel—"wilderness . . . hell itself," a place for "demons"—the rebbe interprets the word as "instead of."[17] The pity aroused in Bleilip for the slaughtered goat is the rebbe's: "Who did not think: *how like that goat I am! The goat goes, I stay, the goat instead of me.* Who did not see in the goat led to Azazel his own destiny?" (66).

Applying his explanation of Azazel to the darkness of the present, the rebbe registers his response to the Nazi abattoir: "instead of freedom we have the red cord around our throats, we were in villages, they drove us into camps, we were in trains, they drove us into showers of poison, in the absence of Messiah the secular ones made a nation, enemies bite at it. . . . all our prayers are bleats and neighs on the way to a forsaken altar, a teeming Azazel. Little fathers! How is it possible to live" (66, 67). That despairing thought has propelled Bleilip to the town of the survivors and Lushinski away from Covenant. But the rebbe's inquiry alludes to Ezekiel's—"how then can we live?" (33:10)—and it intimates that the prophet's consoling vision is the rebbe's: life breathed into dead bones, the renewal of the covenant.[18] A counterpart to the one Bleilip has with Yussel, Bleilip's confrontation with the rebbe contains a "rigid truth" which illuminates the fundraiser's "darkly hidden" intentions and the rebbe's fundamental convictions.

Addressing him as "visitor," the rebbe demands Bleilip identify himself. Like a "schoolboy in a schoolroom," the former lawyer speaks "his own name" and admits to himself that he is "only a visitor" who wants "only what he needed, a certain piece of truth, not too big to swallow. He was afraid of choking on more" (67). Out of that desire he had come to the town where Yussel seems like a "guide," a "tourist office" (58, 57). In the rebbe's name for Bleilip, which recalls the one Tilbeck gives to his daughter, and in Bleilip's sense of Yussel, Ozick echoes the distinction she makes in "Toward a New Yiddish": "A visitor passes through a place; the place passes through the pilgrim. A visitor comes either to teach or to learn, or perhaps simply and neutrally to observe; but a pilgrim comes on purpose to be taught renewal" (A&A 154). The town's ancient traditions and newness establish the town as the location for the fresh beginning promised by *t'shuva*, but coming because of his interest in an "unfamiliar" community, Bleilip has not come as a pilgrim. He has come, the rebbe understands, out of a "certain idea" of the hasidim (68). That idea, gleaned from his narrow reading, includes legends of miraculous deeds, the notion that "some Rabbis achieved levitation, hung in the air without end," the way Bleilip imagines his grandfather and the God of Israel in the schoolhouse (68). His attraction to the magical instances the lawyer's ambivalence; declaring himself a rationalist and deemed an atheist by the rebbe, Bleilip evinces his belief in magic (67). But the magical does not engage the rebbe, who sets no store by it and who attributes to " 'influences. . . . Turnings,' " the profoundest import, the possibility " 'That a man can be turned from folly, error, wrong choices. From misery, evil, private rage. From a mistaken life' " (69). These convictions constitute for Rabbi Leo Baeck the "distinctiveness of Judaism," a "religion of ethical optimism" which Baeck deems unique because "despite the prevalence of wickedness in this world, it [Judaism] does not succumb to mere indifference to, or resignation in, this world"

(*Essence* 84, 85). The rebbe articulates Baeck's idea of *t'shuva* using the same word Ozick employs in "Toward a New Yiddish": " 'Happen' implies history, 'become' implies idea; both imply *teshuvah*, a turning" (A&A 164–165). In the rebbe's optimism, in Bleilip's despair, and in Lushinski's retreat into paganism, Ozick renders contrary psychological reactions and antithetical theological responses to the human condition after the Holocaust.[19]

As if to recoil from the rebbe's phrase, "a mistaken life," Bleilip reverts to the "language of a kind of rhetoricized sociology," and characterizes the rebbe and his community as a "human relationship," a social response to a "root" situation—which is to say, a "superficial" one (*Bloodshed* 69; A&A 156). The fundraiser calls himself a "secularist," denies that his life is mistaken, that he is "in despair"; in his reply is all of the defensiveness he displayed to Toby in the first half of the story. That conversation and the one Bleilip has with Yussel match the lawyer's encounter with the rebbe in the second half of the story. From those meetings come the unwelcome insight consonant with that quickened in Lushinski by Morris Ngambe's letter. Adopting the psychological power of the doppelgänger, Ozick brackets together "A Mercenary" and "Bloodshed" and invokes two disparate sets of figures through a convention she repeatedly draws upon. In the tale of the diplomat and his assistant, the doubles are mirror images and their final confrontation unmasks Lushinski; in the clash between the man who no longer practices law and the one who upholds Torah, religious law, the opposing self, at first unrecognized by Bleilip, lays bare in him masked elements of despair and destructiveness. The ultimate source of the doubles in "A Mercenary" and "Bloodshed" is the Jacob and Esau story, which proves to be the key to the two fictions and which is deployed to incarnate their converging themes, the preponderant concern in the collection—the powerful tendency in Diaspora Jewry to subvert its own identity.

The plastic gun, whose glint recalls the "glinting hooves" of the sacrificial animals in the Temple and which Bleilip has hidden in his pocket, provokes the rebbe's outcry, " 'Esau! Beast! Lion' " (70). To the rebbe Bleilip is a "devourer" who "would eat" them "up," a lawless cannibal, an Esau involved in bloodshed (67, 68). And Esau occupies a central place in the rebbe's sermon: "Which of us would slaughter an animal, not for sustenance, but for an idea? Which of us would dash an animal to its death? Which of us would not feel himself to be a sinner in doing so? Or feel the shame of Esau?" (65).[20] That reference to Esau, a man who lived by the sword—a hunter and a murderer— suggests that Bleilip, like Lushinski, has relinquished his birthright. If the visitor reminds the rebbe of Esau, Bleilip's pockets bring back a memory of a "certain rebbe" who "believed every man should carry two slips of paper in his pockets": "In one pocket should be written: 'I am but dust and ashes.' In the other: 'For my sake was the world created' " (69–70). The opposite messages reinforce the structure of halves in the story, echo the purpose of the two goats—one for Azazel, the other for the Lord—and recall the two-work-permit custom of the Nazis. Demonically contrived to divide those Jews who were to be murdered immediately from those the Nazis secretly planned to murder later, the horrendous custom fostered, at the very least, false hopes; but on those occasions when Jewish men were issued these permits to use at their own discretion, to decide the fate of their family members, the custom implicated the men in murder.[21] Separating those who were allowed to live temporarily from those doomed to die immediately, the work-permit system approximates the rebbe's interpretation of the world devoid of Messiah: "we are assigned our lot, we are designated for the altar or for Azazel, in either case we are meant to be cut down" (66).

Humiliated like a child caught with a "forbidden toy," Bleilip is amazed by the rebbe's clairvoyance; the "seer" orders Bleilip to "disgorge," to empty his own pocket of the real gun—"An actuality, a thing for use." Unexpectedly, the rebbe declares the toy the thing "we have to fear: the incapable" (70, 71). Of the toy gun Ozick writes in the "Preface": "Like the rebbe in 'Bloodshed,' I am more afraid of a gun that is 'merely' a symbol than I am of one that can really go off. . . . Auschwitz was so devised that, thanks to Zyklon B, not a drop of blood was made to flow; Auschwitz, with its toy showerheads, out of which no drop fell. (' "It is a toy we have to fear," ' says the rebbe.)" (7). That which is incapable in itself of killing is the most lethal instrument, for its ability to deceive removes fear and replaces it with vulnerability.

Alone with the rebbe in the schoolhouse, Bleilip thinks, "how dim the bulbs, dangling on cords" (71). He visualizes the bulbs the way he envisioned his grandfather and the God of Israel. They had coalesced with the rebbe in Bleilip's mind when Bleilip envisioned his grandfather's nose attached to the God of Israel and then suddenly knew which was the rebbe—the "man in the work-cap, with a funny flat nose" (64). It is after the rebbe penetrates his secret that Bleilip perceives the bulbs not as images of magical levitation but as the source of light which has afforded him a brief view of the rebbe's power. The imagery of hanging objects establishes an affinity between "Bloodshed" and "A Mercenary" and affirms their disparate relationship to *Night,* in which the snow and the hanging child signify the death of God and Wiesel's soul. Running through the snow of Poland to the sun in Africa, Lushinski forsakes his God and renounces his identity; but the survivor in "Bloodshed," a man whose hands—"two fingers missing, the nails on the others absent"— were deformed at Buchenwald when the Nazis immersed his arms in ice up to the elbows, has reaffirmed the Covenant despite his ghastly experience (64). Lushinski, the rebbe, and Yussel, whose name and that of his wife recall Tibi and Yossi, the two boys in *Night* who want to keep together for strength, represent two views of life after the Holocaust, two answers to the question the rebbe poses in his sermon, "how is it possible to live?" (*Night* 68). At the heart of contemporary Jewish theology, that issue encompasses not only post-Holocaust problems but all contemporary problems with faith and doubt.

Bleilip's journey does not result in renewed faith; but Bleilip's hope had been "only for a glimpse of the effect of the rebbe. Of influences. With these he was satisfied" (72). Repeatedly and insistently denying his life is mistaken, the fundraiser betrays his despair. The scarred trigger and the smelly barrel of the real and recently fired gun implicate him in bloodshed, for he has killed a pigeon, one of the two birds in Leviticus designated fit for a burnt offering (1:14). To be content with an awareness of "influences" is to express, at the very least, a longing for an acquaintance with another way of life. A visitor, a tourist from society-at-large, Bleilip has declared himself "marginal man, wanderer and guest," an "ideological outsider," a rootless person with the "hopeless destiny of obscurity" (A&A 155, 154, 158). That he is lured by the hasidim discloses Bleilip's desire to witness the lives of those whose beliefs have brightened the darkness of futility with the incandescence of hope. Throughout "Bloodshed," Ozick associates Bleilip with darkness, the hasidim with light: his purposes are "darkly hidden," theirs brightly illumined since Sinai (58). During his sermon, the rebbe tells the men that their visitor "fills the studyhouse with a black light" (68). His toy gun, the gun the rebbe fears, is described as a "black plastic thing," the real gun "Dark, no gleam" (69, 71). The capable gun, a monstrous and heavy thing, lacks the "gleaming" presence of Toby's new refrigerator; the halos of light formed by the "golden earlocks" of his cousin's sons and the "beam of divinity" on his cousin's house are wholly unlike the "black corner" of the schoolhouse Bleilip occupies (56, 61, 62). Residents of a new town redolent with freshness, the hasidim shun the despair the rebbe descries in Bleilip. That despair has driven him to purchase the guns, to toy with the idea of suicide, to journey to the town of the hasidim in quest of possibility which, the dim light bulbs and the end of the story imply, remains only a possibility.

The opportunity for renewal is informed by the optimism that animates Judaism, to which the principle of life is critically important: bloodshed constitutes a cardinal sin against God and forfeits a place in the world-to-come.[22] A predominant color in "A Mercenary," red in "Bloodshed" signals the presence of life and the destruction of it. Toby's "large red face" most plainly bears, in Bleilip's mind, the stamp of the hasidim, and Yussel's mention of the town's rebbe enlivens Bleilip: "instantly a wash of blood filled his head" (57, 58). The story's avatar of affirmation, the "red-bearded" rebbe articulates in his sermon the momentousness Judaism imputes to the life-force:

> Was there no one present in the Temple who, seeing the animals in all their majesty of health, shining hair, glinting hooves, timid nostrils, muscled like ourselves, gifted with tender eyes no different from our own, the whole fine creature trembling—was there no one there when the knife slit the fur and skin and the blood fled upward who did not feel the splendor of the living beast? Who was not in awe of the miracle of life turned to carcass? (66)

But the act which brings that miracle to an end occasions the deep red fluid of bloodshed, the sin committed by Esau.

Of decisive significance to "A Mercenary" and "Bloodshed," Esau and the imagery coexistent with his history appear again and again in the two tales,

establishing a congruence between them and intimating the fates of their protagonists—to reside not in "Jacob's tent" but in Esau's wilderness (70). Both
fictions dramatize "what it is to think as a Jew"; however, Ozick avoids depicting that idea from a fixed standpoint. Her mind is nothing if not dialectical; she never permits the values she assigns to principles to remain constant
and immutable. It is for those reasons that she situates the rebbe in the center
of Judaism and Lushinski and Bleilip at its edges. From their positions she discloses two defining components of the Jewish Idea—the elevation of the life-
principle and the implication of humanity in history. That themes and images
are common to the narratives commend them as a pair, a hallmark of Ozick's
fiction and one evident in "An Education" and "Usurpation," in which the
most essential element in the Mosaic vision comes to the fore.

II

The third fiction in *Bloodshed* marks a turning point in the collection. Bearing
important thematic resemblances to "A Mercenary" and "Bloodshed," "An
Education" is specifically yoked to "Usurpation (Other People's Stories)," for
the other title of "An Education" might very well be "Other People's Parents"
or "Other People's Religions"—different kinds of usurpations. "An Education" was written, Ozick tells us, "immediately" after *Trust* and published
nine years before "Usurpation" and eight before "A Mercenary" (*Bloodshed*
4). That the storyteller placed "An Education" in the middle of her second
group of stories suggests she avoided ordering *Bloodshed* chronologically for
a deliberate reason—to have the tales lead progressively to a "point," to tender
"usurpation" as the very "incarnation" of the collection's "*idea*" (8). A main
concern of "An Education" and "Usurpation" is the injunction against idolatry. To the Second Commandment the rabbis imputed the profoundest import, declaring the prohibition of idolatry " 'equal in weight to all the other
commandments of the Torah,' " identifying a Jew as anyone who " 'repudiates
idolatry,' " and determining that even under the threat of death a Jew must not
worship idols (A. Cohen 5, 6). The Second Commandment is one to which
Ozick repeatedly returns. Her "dread of Moloch" leads her not simply to de-
nounce idolatry but to imagine its attractions and its perils; to investigate all
its facets, psychological and intellectual; and, ultimately, to reinterpret the
commandment crucial to Jewish identity (12). Of the ways to repudiate it the
first half of the volume illuminates two. From the last half of the volume comes
a double view of a more serious transgression—the invention and veneration
of idols. Brilliantly witty, "An Education" and "Usurpation" brighten the
somber tones of "A Mercenary" and "Bloodshed" and conclude *Bloodshed*
with the defining characteristic of the Mosaic idea.

    At the end of *Trust* that is one of two paths open to the narrator. Eighteen,
her brain "deliciously loaded with Horace . . . and even more deliciously with
Catullus," Una Meyer enters her college Latin class; by twenty-four she has

acquired a "master's degree in Classics and most of a Ph.D." (76). Two years older than the narrator of Ozick's first novel, Una has decided which path to pursue. "An Education" begins where *Trust* ends. Calling the protagonist of her novella Una, Ozick incorporates into the name a prevision of her character's history. An allusion to *The Faerie Queene,* the name Una recalls at least two characters in Frank O'Connor's stories, which Ozick read after she finished *Trust.*[23] "So pure an innocent," the Una in Spenser's poem signifies Truth awaiting liberation from Falsehood, Deceit, and Hypocrisy and union with Holiness. Like Spenser's Una, Una Meyer is pure and innocent: her face full of "innocence and ordinariness," she "has kissed no one but her parents" (75). As naive emotionally as she is sophisticated intellectually, she, too, must be rescued by a knight. Ozick's allusions to Spenser's maiden are witty and ironic, the references to O'Connor's protagonists exact and proleptic. The triangle in which Una Meyer involves herself conjures up the one in "The Frying Pan" where Una, her husband, and Father Fogarty destine themselves to "die as they had lived, their desires unsatisfied" (157). A distaste for marriage and her confidence that "there was nothing left for her to learn" lead Una MacDermott in "The Sorcerer's Apprentice" to have an affair with a married man which culminates in the loss of a lover and in Una's wondering "what lesson . . . she had failed to learn" (355). Not only does Una Meyer share Una MacDermott's distaste for marriage but she is also convinced that "there were no new revelations to be had" (80).

Of the old ones there are the "very obscure" Latin verbs that take the genitive, the case expressing an unchanging and exclusive relationship, the kind unfamiliar to Una but which she scorns because unlike the narrator of *Trust,* "nothing bored her more than married couples" (76, 79). To "contemplate" one's mind as "tenderly" as Una does is to invite the fate of O'Connor's heroines; not to have "improved" at twenty-four is to welcome the stasis Ozick accords to Hellenism (76). Calling herself a "Platonist" who believes "in the perfectibility of man," Una argues against the idea of "cultural relativity" (78). When her friend Rosalie introduces Una to Clement and Mary Chimes and tells her about their card catalogue, Una thinks she has discovered perfection. What Una fails to understand about Clement is that in changing his name from Chaims, the word meaning life in Hebrew, to Chimes, "like what a bell does," he signals his cultural relativity (80). Clement's new name alludes to the bells in Wiesel's *Night:* "Everything [At Buna] was regulated by the bell. . . . Whenever I dreamed of a better world, I could only imagine a universe with no bells" (69–70). In effect, Clement has transformed his name from one meaning life to one promising death.

For him the word "Holocaust" means nothing more than an opportunity to pun: of "Heidegger and the Holocaust" he makes the joke, Heidegger and "the Holy Ghost" (80). That Ozick refers to Heidegger in this context adds another dimension to the title of her story. A member of the Nazi party for a year, Heidegger cultivated "educational reform" in the classroom as the "model for society," a concept of education valued by the Nazis who invoked "Greek paideia to justify . . . their racial-elitist notions of Kultur" (Eiland 280). The philosopher's fascination with language, Heidegger's attempt to discover a new language for philosophy and to place Man over against God—these approximate Clement's interests.[24] Unconcerned about the meanings of words, an "emancipated" Jew to whom Rosalie is bringing a "four-pound ham" and who has enrolled in the Union Theological Seminary, Clement Chimes is "egalitarian with kings and serfs" and "on the Israeli situation . . . pro-Arab" (80, 81).

His enrollment in the seminary, his wife's name Mary, their decision to call their child Christina "after the heroine of James's *The Princess Casamassima*"—these suggest an attraction to Christianity (92). But Clement proudly declares himself an "anarchist," though he possesses neither the ardent convictions of the anarchists in *The Princess Casamassima* nor their capacity for deed. Like Gustave Nicholas Tilbeck, Clement believes in "Nonaction" and "Stasis," what for Leo Baeck characterizes the Greek world view.[25] Although Clement is "working on the sources of Paul Tillich's thought," he complains that the theologian's book, *The Courage to Be*, is "evasive" and "ambiguous" (86, 92). In that book Tillich addresses what Clement calls the "problem *of* the Self," and he might have discovered in *The Courage to Be*, had he not evaded it, an unambiguous definition of courage. To affirm "one's essential nature," Tillich avers, is "always" to have "the courage to be as a part and the courage to be as oneself in interdependence" (*Bloodshed* 92, 88; Tillich 4, 89–90). According to the theologian's terms, Clement has neither the courage to affirm his true being nor the courage to participate in the world, which is why he advocates "*in*action" (88). Although Clement identifies with the excommunicated Jewish philosopher Spinoza, Tillich discovered in the philosopher's work ideas alien to the young man—the central element in the "doctrine of self-affirmation," a decisive "striving toward something" (212).

The man who lacks the courage to be himself is the man who changes his name and who disavows his heritage. Clement Chaims has not sold his birthright; he has disclaimed it. Ozick records his pursuits sardonically and Lushinski's tragically, for the diplomat's fate evokes sympathy, the theology student's merits scorn. In opposition to the importance Lushinski attaches to history is the Chimeses' desire "to learn to dispense with the past," to regard it as an "old skin" to be "shed . . . now and then" (97, 96). Rootless culturally, Clement is blighted creatively; unable to complete his work at the seminary, Clement cannot progress past the title page of his book, *Social Cancer: A Diagnosis in Verse and Anger*.[26] Sundering themselves from a heritage with a "precept of loving the stranger" enables the Chimeses to think nothing of keeping slaves (M&M 279). To their self-proclaimed slave, they are exemplars of perfection—her idols. The daughter's search for a father in *Trust* is in "An Education" given a new twist when Una in effect re-fathers herself. Crucial to *The Pagan Rabbi*, the relationship between fathers and children is signaled in the second and third sections of "An Education" when Ozick refers to *King*

Lear and *The Princess Casamassima*. In both Shakespeare's tragedy and James's novel, the family occupies center stage.

That Una identifies her first meeting with the Chimeses as the "one that came just when [she] had decided there were no new revelations to be had" conjures up Bleilip, the "enemy of fresh revelation." That the Chimeses, Rosalie, and Una read *King Lear* aloud on the beach augurs the role she plays with them, though Ozick ironically reverses it when Una plays Regan, Lear's selfish and ungrateful daughter. A Christian play in a pagan world, *King Lear* unfolds the aftermath of Lear's self-made destiny, focuses on the parent-child relationship, the marriage involved in it, and dramatizes the necessity of endurance.[27] The moral seriousness of Shakespeare's play points up the emptiness of the Chimeses' world and the callowness of Ozick's protagonist. Lear's momentous question "Who is it can tell me who I am?" is followed by his discoveries, his increasing "recognition of what he has done, and beyond that, of who he is" (Blissett 105). His is an education that rewards and redeems. For Una it is otherwise: her endurance brings not increased awareness but further bondage (90).

The forces that move Una to reject her essential freedom are her belief in the perfectibility of man, her "rapture without a fault," her "sense of illimitable possibility"—all of which she attributes to the Chimeses (81, 82). A Platonist, Una "has just swallowed Beauty" and, like the Allegra Vand of *Brighton*, the graduate student worships Sacred Beauty. Tilbeck is revived in Clement Chimes, a pale and reduced version of the lover who extracts from Allegra a portion of her wealth. If Tilbeck is the initiator in *Trust*, Clement is the self-appointed tutor in "An Education." His course in the Problem of the Self promotes "*in*action. Nonaction. Stasis" (88). To fulfill Clement's requirements, Una ceases working on her dissertation. An opponent of marriage, she no longer gives a "damn" about the "Etruscan Aphrodite," a reminder of the goddess who haunts the pages of *Trust*. Instead, Una stops "looking at the world in terms of [her] own self-gratification": she follows Clement's advice and gratifies the Chimeses' desires (88). The reason for Ozick's ironic allusion to *The Beggar's Opera*, which Clement has promised they will do on their next excursion to the beach, is evident when Mary opens act one of the Chimeses' opera with a song about an empty larder and the family's dearth of funds. Because he seems "very stern, almost like a father," Una behaves like Clement's dutiful daughter and bicycles to the market and buys the food. When the Chimeses' real daughter is born, Una regards the infant as a "combination of two perfections," "some sacred object" to whom she owes devotion (92).

That the Chimeses name their daughter Christina after the heroine of James's *Princess Casamassima* alludes to the family theme in Ozick's novella and heightens the meaning of Una's education. Revising elements from that novel the way in *Trust* she reverses the significance of events from *The Portrait of a Lady*, Ozick engages with Jamesian sources as if involved in a dialogue with the Master. He, too, was preoccupied with the education of his protagonist who, like Una Meyer, falls "in love with the beauty of the world" (62,

72, 44). A man for whom the "prospect of new experience—a sensation for which he was always ready to exchange any present boon," Hyacinth Robinson is enveloped in the Princess's aura the way Una is in the Chimeses'. At Medley Hall, however, "there was a world to be revealed to him," an opportunity to fulfill what he craves most of all—"to be initiated" (182, 299, 164). An ironic allusion to the Chimeses' exploitation of Una, the "beggars' opera scene" in *The Princess Casamassima* constitutes part of its world—"London's grimy, sooty, gin-soaked, under-privileged life" (Edel 118). Where Ozick humorously depicts the willing surrender to imagined power, the Master characterizes with "complete accuracy" the "dynamics of power, the relationship between idealism and the manipulation of people" (Edel, *Middle Years* 123). Both writers fill their tales with fantasized parents, and their demands on Hyacinth and Una are decisive. If Hyacinth is adopted by the Princess, he is committed to obey the resolute anarchist Diedrich Hoffendahl, the father figure who exacts the youth's sworn oath to murder a Duke.[28] Of even more relevance for Ozick's purposes is the mythic pattern Lionel Trilling detects in *The Princess Casamassima*—the common childhood fantasy of imagining parents different from one's own.[29] Ultimately the stuff of tragedy for James's hero, that fantasy is invoked by Ozick for disparate reasons. When compared to the irresolute and inactive Clement, the ardent revolutionist Hoffendahl, to whom Hyacinth pledges his life, illuminates the motivations of Ozick's irony; for if Una relinquishes a portion of her life to her adopted father, the reasons have nothing to do with honor. She has grown up with the advantages of education; Hyacinth is a bookbinder from the slums, the illegitimate son of an English peer and a French seamstress. But he is a "youth on whom nothing is lost," and she one on whom almost everything is lost. Nearly complete, her formal education contributes very little to Una's judgment of the Chimeses' machinations. If Hyacinth spends a week at Medley Hall and discovers the "wine of novelty, of civilisation," Una arrives at the Chimeses full of that wine and then tastes its lees (325).

Enthralled to her adopted parents, she forgoes her Fulbright, takes over Mary's responsibilities for Christina, writes Clement's letters, works at Woolworth's so he can write, pays a "good chunk of the rent," prepares breakfast, and sometimes feels "that maybe she wasn't an imposition on the Chimeses after all" (93). Hers is an education in enslavement. That Una professes repugnance for marriage remains ironic: she performs all the chores of a married person. Then she meets the equivalent of her namesake's knight, the student in her college Latin class who was ignorant of the genitive case. Once a "failure at conjugation," Boris Organski has become a medical student, a profession well-suited to his name, and his accidental meeting with Una is converted into a witty allusion to book 1 of *The Faerie Queene*, in which a distressed maiden awaits rescue by a knight. Una Meyer's knight instructs the Latin expert in the genitive case. To his invitation that she become his mistress Una "giggles. It sounded just like Mary's giggle" (105). It recalls Tilbeck's laugh and anticipates Sylvia-Undine's "tumble of laughter" (PR 141). A characteristic of Pan, the laugh identifies Una with her pagan gods and implies she thinks life with them is tantamount to enjoying the delights of Arcady.

But as Enoch Vand observes and as Boris Organski points out, "every Eden has its coil of treachery." Unlike Una he thinks the Chimeses "worse than perfect." He tells them their child is "malnourished"; he protests their maltreatment of Una (105). In turn her "perfect" parents complain about her obsequiousness, her cooking, her stupidity about the Fulbright; and when she returns from seeing Boris, they "speak to her very sternly" like the parents of a daughter who has an objectionable boyfriend (107). To this situation Boris, an inept classicist, has but a single response: "Abandon fantasy." The medical student diagnoses Una's obsession and prescribes a dose of reality (113). That divides him from Una and suggests why the storyteller includes in her novella the halves that pervade her first novel and that appear throughout *Bloodshed.* Clear signs of the "Pan Versus Moses" brief, the halves in "An Education" are associated with the Chimeses and Una from the beginning of their relationship "at half-past four in the afternoon" in the "very core of August" (80). Having agreed to come "in halfies" with the Chimeses, Una does "practically half [Clement's] work" because, as Boris observes, her eyes are "half shut" and she believes the Chimeses to be "right in the middle of being alive" (198, 94, 113, 86). If she giggles the way Mary does, Una has "mastered [Clement's] intonation to the life" (113). Any time spent away from the Chimeses, Boris retorts, makes her an "Ungrateful girl" (114). Ozick's ironic allusion to *King Lear* calls attention to the storyteller's reversal of its theme in "An Education." Blind to the Chimeses' ingratitude the way at first Lear is to Cordelia's loyalty, Una is attracted to Boris's "long attractive nose" and the "long, stiff nostrils that stared downward like an extra pair of eyes" (115). An emblem of his clear-sightedness, Boris's nose adumbrates the rebbe's and suggests Boris's attachment to the Ideal rather than the Idyll to which Una is drawn.

But as any student of the classics should know, even in Arcady there is death. A portent of that eventuality occurs when Christina is hospitalized and Una witnesses the "terrible sight" of Clement and Mary "at war" (116). Pages are ripped from *The Princess Casamassima,* a hassock bursts in the fight, discharging "cloud-bits . . . like little roaming mice" (119). Emblems of time's voraciousness and signs of the Death-in-Arcady theme, the micelike bits rising from the Chimeses' hassock and the shredded pages of *The Princess Casamassima* augur Christina Chime's death. A champion of the Real, the medical student's evaluation of the scene is unerring and complete: " 'An attack, yes. An attack of guilt' " (117). But Una accepts responsibility for Christina's illness and dutifully clears away the plunder the next day (120). Under a heap of newspapers she discovers Clement's manuscript—a title-page with the author's name. Unlike Boris's, Clement's "Diagnosis" is incomplete. Although she has worked at Woolworths so Clement could write, Una denies even this glaring evidence of her exploitation. Despite the sight of Christina's coffin descending into a small cut in the earth, Una thinks "of a dog burying a bone," of the young dog playing in the sand on the shore of the state of Connecticut the day her relationship with the Chimeses began. Una's recollections are commensurate, and they bring in their train not thoughts about the end of her association with the couple but remembrances of its inception.

It spite of Boris's admonitions, Una cannot forget the Chimeses. She continues to expect the two of them "to jump out at her from a newspaper," perhaps "repaired and reconverted by fresh educations," as the presence of a rabbi at Christina's funeral might indicate. Neither repaired nor reconverted by her education, Una refuses to marry Boris because " 'there's no education in it' " and decides to complete her Ph.D. at a midwestern university because she can write her dissertation on "The Influence of the Greek Middle Voice on Latin Prosody"—a topic that requires "no travel, foreign or internal" (124, 125). A winner of a Fulbright to study "certain Etruscan findings in southern Turkey," Una Meyer ends up on the "faculty of a small college in Turkey, New York" surrounded by colleagues who are "invincibly domesticated." At one of their parties, Una is reunited with Rosalie Orenstein, a teacher at the high school bordering the campus of Una's college. In the histories of the two teachers—one a widow, the other single—Ozick wittily contrasts the results of the Chimeses' "instruction in life-values." For the teachers of those values Rosalie has contempt. " 'Anybody,' " she tells Una, " 'could see right through them' " (126). But that is the reason Una continues to admire the Chimeses: "They were like a bubble that never broke, you could look right through and they kept on shining no matter what. They're the only persons I've known who stayed the same from start to finish" (126). She echoes the opinion the narrator of *Trust* expresses about Gustave Nicholas Tilbeck, but Una ends not on a threshold but where she began.

Her knowledge of the genitive case flawless, she arranges a marriage between Boris and Rosalie. A decade later, middle-aged, still unmarried, and troubled by her gums, Una visits the Organskis and observes their "house held no glory and no wars" (127). To her request for news about the Chimeses the Organskis' daughter answers, " 'Ding dong' "; and alluding comically to *The Tempest* and Ariel's song for Ferdinand's drowned father, Ozick links the endings of "An Education" and *Trust* (27). A guest at weddings, the narrator of *Trust* evinces her interest in marriage on the last pages of the novel; but the forty-two-year-old Una, who visits her married friends, lacks the "passion for ordinary human entanglement" (A&A 292). The contrary marriages of the Organskis and the Chimeses—emblems of Hebraism and Hellenism and the alternatives lying before the narrator of *Trust*—most closely approximate for Una the attributes of imperfection and perfection.

The desire for perfection hinders the "process of becoming" (Baeck, J&C 218).[30] Elements in a theme whose permutations and modulations Ozick continues to explore, the central importance of cultural rootedness and the dangers of idolatry are in "An Education" enforced with wit and vigor. The issue of Jewish identity bridges "An Education" to "A Mercenary" and "Bloodshed." The implied warning against idolatry joins the third fiction in *Bloodshed* to the last, a "story written against story-writing; against the Muse-goddesses; against Apollo. . . . against magic and mystification, against sham and 'miracle,' and, going deeper into the dark, against idolatry" (10, 11).

The idea that story writing can be a corridor to idolatry, that the very act of writing is perilous, derives from a long tradition in Judaism that stretches back to biblical literature, a large part of which is given over to the injunction against idolatry: "The Bible conceives of idolatry as the belief that divine and magical powers inhere in certain natural or man-made objects and that man can activate these powers through fixed rituals. . . . Idolatry is nothing more than the worship of 'the work of hands' " (Kaufmann, *Religion* 14–15). Denouncing Israel's idolatry, the prophet Hosea identifies the objects man creates with his pursuit of Canaanite gods. That the propensity for idolatry was connate with man's mind was a conviction held by the rabbis, who believed that the Evil Inclination, the *yetzer ha-ra*, coexisted in the imagination alongside the inclination for good and was responsible for idol worship. Although the sages thought the Torah an "antidote" to the evil *yetzer* and the "principal safeguard" against idolatry, they "did not think that the Torah was able, so long as it was in the possession of man, to uproot the Evil Inclination completely" (A. Cohen 92, 382; Urbach 472–73). The properties of idols, idolatrous images, objects of veneration—these are set forth in *Avodah Zarah*, the tractate in the Talmud devoted to idolatry. Because the human imagination was thought capable of producing those images, the primacy of human reason was affirmed and the imagination mistrusted.[31]

That imaginative writing can be a corridor to idolatry is implied in the Book of Enoch and in Moses Mendelssohn's *Jerusalem*. The misdeed of Penemue, the fourth angel in Enoch, was to demonstrate writing:

> he caused the people to penetrate (the secret of) writing and (the use of) ink and paper; on account of this matter, there are many who have erred from eternity to eternity, until this very day. For human beings are not created for such purposes to take up their beliefs with pen and ink. For indeed human beings were not created but to be like angels, permanently to maintain pure and righteous lives. Death, which destroys everything would have not touched them, had it not been through their knowledge by which they shall perish. (69:10)

Unnatural activities, writing and written communication are regarded as acts against God. The ceremonial law of Judaism, not writing or visual presentation, Mendelssohn argues, provides guidelines for behavior and ensures memory of truth and history: "images and hieroglyphics lead to superstition and idolatry. . . . there is nothing lasting, nothing enduring about them [man's actions] that, like hieroglyphic script, could lead to idolatry through abuse or misunderstanding" (118–19). To value the human intellect over deeds is to be an idolator: "The war upon paganism was at the same time a war upon the idolatrous deification of reason, the faith that rational knowledge could save man. Moral goodness shall redeem, not the power of the intellect!" (Kaufmann, "Biblical Age" 92). What that power enables the storyteller to do is invent her own world and in the process emulate the Creator; usurping His place, she replaces it with the work of her hands and falls prey to idolatry.

The injunction against idolatry is the afflatus of "Usurpation." Indeed, in the preface to *Bloodshed,* Ozick worries "whether Jews ought to be story-tellers," wonders whether the "Commandment against idols" warns "even ink," and concludes of her tale: "I had written 'Usurpation' in the language of a civilization that cannot imagine its thesis" (10). Against her apprehension—that the writing of stories is an offense against the Second Commandment—is her "lust after stories more and more and more" (12). But such a conflict, though Ozick claims it for Jews, "is at least as much Christian as it is Jewish," and the "phenomenon Ozick addresses with great vigor and freshness is a very old phenomenon, as old as Hellenistic Alexandria, home of the first of the many recurrent literary 'modernisms' " (Bloom, CO 3). It is a phenomenon lying behind "Envy" as well as "Usurpation," which begins with a scene reminiscent of one in "Envy." Like Hershel Edelshtein, the narrator of "Usurpation" listens to a renowned writer read a story she wishes were her own.[32] "Drawn not to the symbol, but to the absolute magical act . . . to what is forbidden," the narrator of "Usurpation" recalls the Yiddish poet and his secret desire for western civilization (134). But in "Usurpation" Ozick is concerned with the "relation between the usurper and the idolator" (8). What obsesses her tale is the writer's clash with tradition; what signals that conflict is the presence of the father. Even the "prey" of "Usurpation," Bernard Malamud's "The Silver Crown," concerns a father whose son, a teacher, seeks a cure for his dying father from a miracle-working rabbi (7). Promising a magical, healing silver crown, the rabbi extracts the teacher's money and the father dies, but the rabbi exposes the lifelong hatred the teacher has harbored against his father. Riveted by the "magical parts" of the famous writer's tale, the narrator contemplates the ways she would have construed the account in the newspaper: "Perhaps the sick father would have recovered. Perhaps the teacher would not have confessed to hating his father" (134). The narrator suggests the underlying theme of Ozick's story, the storyteller's concern for the father as transmitter of tradition and preserver of continuity, values Ozick adduces in her essay "Innovation and Redemption."

However, the narrator of "Usurpation" longs to give up the God of the Jews, "who cannot be imagined in any form," for a "magic God" who will permit her to "make a little god, a silver godlet, in the shape of a crown, which will stop death, resurrect fathers and uncles" (135). The unholy desire for "everything anti-Moses" lures her; the ability to usurp the role of Creator captivates her (135). She considers the possibility of burning the famous writer's manuscript, "freeing the crown out of the finished tale" for her own use; but she fears producing a "conflagration of souls out of lust for a story!" (135). At the same time, she thinks "A typewriter is a volcano. Who can stop print?" (135). Associated with divinity in both the Hebrew Bible and in Greek mythology, fire signaled the presence of God and His indignation: Yahweh manifests Himself in fire and is the "devouring fire" that will consume the idolators (Deut. 6:24). Small wonder, then, that the rabbis used the metaphor of fire for the *yetzer ha-ra*.[33] Prometheus, whom Ozick calls the ultimate usurper, became the Creator by stealing fire and giving it to humankind; and her allusion to Vulcan severs the act of writing from Hebraism and joins to the imagination the Roman god of volcanic fire and metalworking and the furnace god, Moloch. That is why the narrator knows that even her fantasy of lighting a match to wrest away the crown "is too powerful a magic" (135). As the famous writer reads the last word of his story, she is accosted by another writer with the "face of a goat"; mistaking her for an official, he foists his manuscript on her, tells her to have it read by the known author, and then vanishes (135).

In the guise of critic and "unfamiliar with the laws governing plagiarism," the narrator robs the goat of his story just as he complained the famous writer had (139). Ozick wittily links her narrator and the writer who approaches her to Pan, the Greek god who had goat's horns and legs, and both writers to the renowned writer, who stole his tale from a newspaper. To employ legal language to describe imaginative writing is to emphasize the conflict between writing and the law; it is to establish the idea that the storyteller usurps God's role and becomes an idolator—a person who breaks the ultimate law. Or, as the narrator humorously puts it, "here I am, brazenly giving away stories that are not rightly mine. . . . What if, by the time *this* story is published, at this very moment while you are reading it, I am on my back in some filthy municipal dungeon?" (139). Her story, ostensibly a retelling of the goat's, is in fact based on elements gleaned from Malamud's "The Silver Crown" and David Stern's "Agnon: A Story," and her vision of those tales constitutes the story-within-the story, the moral point of "Usurpation." Filled with "masks and tricks of metaphor and fable," the goat's manuscript, "A Story of Youth and Homage," is intended to be "interpreted on several 'levels' " (139, 138). All of them are scorned by the narrator: even as she pretends to summarize the manuscript, she begins to revise it. Transforming three of Malamud's characters—the rabbi, the teacher, and the father—into three writers, Ozick turns the silver crown into a symbol of her narrative's central conflict.

In the goat's story, an American student has come to Jerusalem professing to study Torah at a yeshiva. Arrogant, young, and unpublished, the yeshiva student really wishes to become like the old and famous writer whom Ozick, in her preface, identifies as S. Y. Agnon. Not having "read a word the Nobel Prize winner has written," the unacknowledged writer seeks to "usurp" the old writer's "place" (140). For that, the famous writer counsels, the student must become a "true *ba'al ga'avah*. . . . The self-righteous self-idolator. . . . the man whose arrogance is godlike, whose pride is like a tower" and who is "so audacious and yet so ingenious that [he] will fool God and will live" (141). To his advice the old writer admonishes, " 'All that is not Torah is levity' " (141, 142). But the student "wishes to usurp the place and power of another writer" and obediently places on his head the crown of a "predecessor," the Hebrew poet Tchernikhovsky. Immediately, stories crowd the student's brain, "His own; yet not his own" (149). Mistaken for the famous writer, the student is blessed by the *Rosh Yeshiva*, the head of the yeshiva; but the student fears having to produce a story and runs to a deserted alley. There he encounters the ghost of Tchernikhovsky, who reminds the wearer of the crown that he is not its rightful owner. He struggles to remove the crown, but dies of a heart attack, ending the narrator's version of his story with the final word the famous writer uttered at his reading, "expired." In the humorous tale of the student and the two writers in Jerusalem lies the serious point of "Usurpation."

The world is perceived differently by the poet Tchernikhovsky and the old writer of Jerusalem, and in his explanation of how he came to possess the crown reside the two conflicting world views at the heart of Ozick's novella. An "admirer," especially of the old writer's tale "about why the Messiah will not come," the poet's ghost came to bring a crown, to have the old writer assume a dead poet's "eminence" (145). But the tale admired by the ghost, Agnon's "Fable of the Goat," sharply diverges from "Before the Statue of Apollo," which Agnon was reading when the ghost appeared. Revising it in "Usurpation," she makes the fable into a lament over the "tarrying of the Messiah"; but in the original story, the sick old man has a goat slaughtered and destroys with it his chance for salvation. Ozick humorously reverses Agnon's intentions and has a young man die in "Usurpation," and she transforms Agnon's goat, an agent of redemption, into a follower of Pan. Judging the fable the Nobel Prize winner's best, the ghost of Tchernikhovsky at the same time misconstrues the point of the tale and is satisfied "that the Messiah is prevented from coming" (145). And the Hebrew poet's poem suggests why, for it celebrates not the appearance of the Messiah but that of the Greek god Apollo. The two writers' divided interests are in Ozick's tale part of the Hebraism-and-Hellenism controversy.

It is present as well in the old writer's description of the ghost: "He was a completely traditional ghost, you could see right through him to the wall behind. . . . The wall behind . . . held a bookcase, so where his nose appeared to be I could read only the title of a tractate of the Mishnah" (143). Usurped from the story "Agnon," Ozick's account of the ghost differs from Stern's. Where Stern's student first sees Agnon learning *Avodah Zarah*, Ozick's old writer reads Tchernikhovsky's most pagan poem; instead of the ghost, he sees the title of an unnamed tractate. Replacing the ghost's nose—a pagan emblem in "A Mercenary"—with the writer's vision of the tractate, Ozick forges a link between the old man and Torah. In "Before the Statue of Apollo," Tchernikhovsky recounts the chasm dividing the Torah of the speaker's father from the "cult" of Apollo. The "first among those who return" to worship the Greek god, the "god of life's joy, its riches and splendour," the poet names Apollo God of Israel, claims His followers transformed him into a harsh lawgiver and bound Him "with the straps of their phylacteries" (Silberschlag 98). Tchernikhovsky's is a poem that pays pagan homage to a Greek god. Of the poem's inventor the old writer observes, "All that pantheism and earth-worship! That pursuit of the old gods of Canaan! . . . All pantheists are fools. . . . How can a piece of creation be its own Creator?" (144). Not only does he repudiate Tchernikhovsky's Hellenism, he refuses the poet's crown, offering it instead to the student who has come in quest of fame.

Out of Tchernikhovsky's biography Ozick creates a keenly humorous and immensely ingenious character who embodies her point about idolatrous writers. From his birth in 1875 until his death in 1942, the Hebrew poet "wrestled with the problem of Hellenism" and was "overwhelmed" by "that ever-present dichotomy"—the one between "Jew and Greek" (Silberschlag 46–47). That the poet could not in fact have met the old man's "yeshiva standards" is evident in the way the young Tchernikhovsky learned Torah—without knowing Leviticus, the book with which the Jewish children traditionally and symbolically begin. As a youth Tchernikhovsky judged the Pentateuch and the *Odyssey* similar; his later preoccupation with translating the classics into Hebrew and his affair with a Greek girl concretized his attraction to Hellenism. Not "of the soul," the poet's Zionism was, according to Eisig Silberschlag, a "matter of self-identification," a reaction to a brief but harrowing imprisonment by the Czarist police and a grateful gesture to the rabbi who secured Tchernikhovsky's release (*Bloodshed* 146; Silberschlag 13, 20). Imagining the student dead from angina pectoris, the disease which ultimately killed the Hebrew poet, Ozick yokes the two.

The trajectory of S. Y. Agnon's life diverged sharply from that of Tchernikhovsky. If the poet was beset by divided loyalties, the storyteller "wanted to write within the tradition and not in conflict with it" (Miron 23). Born in Buczacz in eastern Galicia on the Ninth of Av—the day in the Hebrew calendar when the First and Second Temples were destroyed and when, according to Jewish tradition, the Messiah will be born—Agnon began life in an orthodox Jewish family and was educated accordingly.[34] In 1924, he settled in Jerusalem, the "city of his heart. . . . [his] adopted city," a "new birthplace" (Band 25). His was not the Zionism of a Tchernikhovsky. Nor did the "poet of revolt" share the storyteller's convictions: "For Agnon tradition and literature were identified with Torah and the way of life prescribed by it" (Miron 23). Agnon incarnates the Mosaic idea, Tchernikhovsky, the pagan pursuit of Canaanite idols.

To that dichotomy the various significances of the silver crown and the pattern of hot and cold imagery are profoundly relevant. Listening to the old writer explain the idea of the *ba'al ga'avah*, the student grows "as cold now as a frozen path, all his veins are paths of ice"; wearing the crown, a "coldness . . . stabs into his brain" and he hears plots, titles, characters "inside his steaming skull" which is "boiling" and "teeming" with usurped tales (142, 149). That imagery characterizes the ghost as well: his strength "is equal to a snowflake" and he prescribes a vial of nitroglycerin to relieve "burning in the chest" (153, 151). The will to write, an act of usurpation and an impulse governed by the inclination toward idolatry, resembles the metaphor the rabbis attached to the evil *yetzer*. But they also compared the Torah to fire, a recollection of the fire at Sinai, and likened man's relationship to the Torah in imagery of fire and ice: "The words of the Torah are compared to fire, for both were given from heaven, both are eternal. If a man draws near the fire, he is burned [or derives benefit]; if he keeps afar, he is frozen."[35] That one is "frozen" when divided from Torah explains the narrator's fear of magic: "Forbidden. The terrible Hebrew word for it freezes the tongue—*asur;* Jewish magic" (134). Unprotected by the Torah's warmth, Tchernikhovsky and the student inhabit the icy realm of idolatry. To reign there is to wear the crown of Apollo, the "Lord of the Silver Bow," whose wreaths of laurel leaves honored victors. That is the crown Tchernikhovsky chose; that crown feels to the student like a "cargo of helium" and supplies him "with a ready-made bibliography" (148, 149). His sensation recalls the narrator's: "I rose like a heated gas, feeling insubstantial, and went to press my head against the cold side wall along the aisle. My brain was all gas, it shuddered with envy" (136).

Repeated references to crowns are made in The Ethics of the Fathers, a tractate which possesses special importance in the Talmud and which illuminates the significance of the father in "Usurpation." The sages assert man's chief interest in life should be study of Torah. In chapter 1:13 of The Ethics Hillel warns, "And he that puts the Crown of the Torah to his own use shall perish."[36] In declining Tchernikhovsky's crown for the crown of the Law, the old writer escapes the fate of the *ba'al ga'avah* "whose pride is like a tower." Ozick's allusion to the tower of Babel is apposite and recurrent; for the legend of the tower penetrates to the heart of the affinity the storyteller envisions between writing and idolatry. "Man's boundless arrogance" is instanced in the legend of the tower because it displays the human desire "to storm heaven," to be godlike, "to rule the world" (Kaufmann, *Religion* 294). If the pious writer in Jerusalem rejects the crown Tchernikhovsky received "from Ibn Gabirol. Via ouija board," the old writer unreservedly admires the eleventh-century poet and philosopher: " 'Ibn Gabirol! Sublime poet, envied beyond envy, sublimeness without heir, who would not covet the crown of Ibn Gabirol?' " (154–55). Ibn Gabirol's poem "The Royal Crown" and Tchernikhovsky's "Three Crowns" reveal the difference between the two poets. Included in the Sephardic prayerbook for the Day of Atonement, "The Royal Crown" proclaims the greatness and splendor of God and stresses the insignificance and vanity of man.[37] God reigns supreme in Ibn Gabirol's poem, but the crown of Beauty exceeds the crown of the Torah in Tchernikhovsky's poem, which makes the poet a "crowned individual" (Silberschlag 6). To replace the crown of the Torah with the crown of the poet is to have chosen Apollo over God, which is why the crown Tchernikhovsky receives resembles a fish forbidden to Jews—a "fish without scales" (155).

That Ozick portrays the Hebrew poet as a ghost and that he alludes to *Hamlet* when he explains why the old writer naps—" 'To sleep, perchance to dream' "—signal the thematic concerns of "Usurpation." What seems like a witty and ironic aside from the ghost of Tchernikhovsky is in fact another instance of usurpation in the story, for he refers to the soliloquy in which Hamlet ruminates on life and death: "Man in his aspect of bafflement, moving in darkness on a rampart between two worlds, unable to reject, or quite accept" (Mack 241). Hamlet's situation defines Tchernikhovsky's, the poet's abiding attraction to the irreconcilable worlds of Hebraism and Hellenism, neither of which the poet could totally embrace or entirely forsake. And the ghost of Tchernikhovsky also conjures up the ghost of Hamlet's father, the bond between father and son secured from the very beginning of Shakespeare's play. Both ghosts are preoccupied with a crown, and in each case, the crown is an emblem of ambition. Because of that Claudius killed the king: "I am still possess'd / Of those effects for which I did the murder— / My crown, mine own ambition, and my queen" (III.3.53–55). The ghost of Hamlet's father appears in order to lay the charge of revenge, but the ghost of Tchernikhovsky visits the famous writer in Jerusalem to confer upon him the ambition of a *ba'al ga'-avah*. Ingeniously revising the purpose of the ghost in Shakespeare's play, the storyteller transforms in her tale the dramatist's play-within-the-play.

If that is symbolic of the problem pervading *Hamlet*, the story-within-the-story in "Usurpation" holds the moral truths of the novella. But Hamlet's early eulogy of man—"What piece of work is a man, how noble in reason, how infinite in faculties . . . in apprehension how like a god"—is from Ozick's point of view that of a *ba'al ga'avah*. Accepting the limitations to which human beings are subject and recognizing "that a divinity shapes our ends," Hamlet provides commentary on the student's death in "Usurpation," for like those who schemed " 'to circumvent God' " in Shakespeare's play, the student aspired to heights beyond the boundaries set by God (Mack 256). That is the reason the narrator of "Usurpation" gives for his death: "I killed off the student to punish him for arrogance. . . . The goat was a *ba'al ga'avah!*. . . . only a *ba'al ga'avah* would dare to write about 'religion.' So I punished him for it. How? By transmuting piety into magic" (157–58). She deems religion a subject only the self-idolator would venture to write about; but having decisively separated magic from Judaism earlier in the story and having confessed her lust for the "absolute magical act," she questions the difference between religion and magic and concludes, "Whoever intends to separate them ends in proving them to be the same" (134, 158).

And with that statement Ozick returns to the tale with which she began "Usurpation," and doubling events from the story-within-the-story, she resolves her narrator's conflict.[38] "As if by magic," the narrator finds the goat's address on the next-to-last page of the manuscript. Though she mocks the name of his street, "18 Herzl Street, Brooklyn, N.Y. A street fashioned—so to speak—after the Messiah," the narrator admonishes the reader to ignore any significance attached to Herzl, affirming her "hatred of metaphysical speculation" and her "contempt for significant allusions, nuances, buried effects" (159). Her warning of course only calls attention to every implication buried in the goat's address. Deriving Herzl Street from the name of the "battered synagogue . . . Congregation Theodor Herzl" in "The Silver Crown," Ozick adds to Malamud's name for the synagogue the number eighteen, the numerical equivalent of the Hebrew word *chai* or life (Malamud 5). Her use of gematria (the numerical value of letters and words) is what the narrator calls Jewish magic: "And yet with what prowess we [Jews] have crept down the centuries after amulets, and hidden countings of letters" (134).[39]

To dismiss the significance of the goat's address is to emphasize a "concern" for "practical action," but in describing the street of the Messiah the narrator belies her own protestations:

> It was a place where there had been conflagrations. . . . The sidewalk underfoot stirred with crumbs, as of sugar grinding: mortar reduced to sand. A desert flushed over tumbled yards. Lintels and doors burned out, foundations squared like pebbles on a beach: in this spot once there had been cellars, stoops, houses. The smell of burned wood wandered. A civilization of mounds—who had lived here? Jews. There were no buildings left. A rectangular stucco fragment—of what? synagogue maybe—squatted in a space. There was no Number 18—only bad air, light flying in the gape and gash where the fires had driven down brick, mortar, wood, mothers, fathers, children pressing library cards inside their pockets—gone, finished. (159).

In the midst of the ruin, the goat appears the way his address had—"as if by magic" (160). Greeting the goat precisely as the old writer had hailed Tchernikhovsky's ghost "in the story that never was," the narrator identifies with the old writer, signals her disapproval of the goat, and once again smashes together pilfered elements. Living in a synagogue bereft of its scrolls and abandoned by Jews, the goat inhabits a place fit for a pagan writer. In the narrator's brief journey to 18 Herzl Street, Ozick transforms elements from *Trust* into ones appropriate to the theme of "Usurpation." Where Tilbeck, the "one who needed wine," dwells in a "ruined abbey" located in a crumbling Arcady, the goat, an imbiber of "Schapiro's kosher wine," has settled in the charred remains of a synagogue (*Trust* 512; *Bloodshed* 161). And Tilbeck knows his daughter "has come for a taste" of him exactly the way the goat divines the narrator's interest in him—" 'because of the crown' " (161). That the fire has reduced a synagogue to rubble, eradicated the numerical equivalent of life, left only a desert with the "clear sacrificial smell of things that have been burned" identify the goat's habitation (160). It stands as a humorous counterpart to the desolation in "A Mercenary."

A symbol of Pan, the goat conjures up the Hebraic sacrificial goat Azazel in *Bloodshed* and the wilderness to which it was consigned. The goat in "Usurpation" resides in the biblical locale for punishment where fire appeared to signal the presence of the Lord, to manifest His wrath, and to destroy idols. But the goat cares only for his story, about which the narrator comments: "It's all fake. . . . What I mean by fake is raw. When no one's ever used it before, it's something new under the sun, a whole new combination, that's bad. A real story is whatever you can predict, it has to be familiar . . . no exotic new material, no unexpected flights. . . . The only good part in the whole thing was explaining about the *ba'al ga'avah*. People hate to read foreign words, but at least it's ancient wisdom. Old, old stuff" (163). The narrator's distinction is one Ozick makes in "Innovation and Redemption": "Innovation in art is not rupture. Innovation in art is not the consequence of the implantation of 'wholly different' expectations. Innovation in art means the continuity of expectations" (A&A 243). However, the narrator of "Usurpation" is attracted to magic, and it induces her to discover the source of the famous writer's story. Identifying with the old writer in Jerusalem, all of whose unpublished manuscripts were burned in a tragic fire in 1924, the goat throws his manuscript into the stove.[40] The juxtaposition of the two events evinces Ozick's irony, and the storyteller names the rabbi jailed for selling fraudulent crowns "Saul" and depicts him as "like Tchernikhovsky" in a photograph, making them doubles. Their twin fates suggest Cynthia Ozick's view of the Hebrew poet's involvement with the magic of Hellenism and revises Malamud's tale of the faith healer Rabbi Lifschitz who escaped punishment. The predominant imagery of crime and punishment in "Usurpation" buttresses the conviction that magic is against the Law.

That the storyteller risks transgressing those laws and that miracles do not belong to Judaism are the lessons of the last and unstolen tale in "Usurpation." It was written by the rabbi who ended up in jail for the invention of a magic crown, the source of the famous writer's story. A fake rabbi, Saul is an unpublished writer, the author of only one story, which concerns God's refusal to perform miracles even during the Holocaust. Ironically reversing the narrator's transformation of him into a *ba'al ga'avah*, the goat imitates the old writer's gesture in the story-within-the-story and places the false rabbi's crown on his visitor's head, implying that the narrator has become the *ba'al ga'avah*. Brilliantly rendered in "immigrant English," Saul's narrative of a father's attempt to save his son from being gassed by the Germans in a death camp not only overturns the son's dilemma in "The Silver Crown" and demonstrates the lack of miracles in Judaism, but also raises the inescapable issues of what the Covenant means after the Holocaust and what warrant there is for writing about it.[41]

To rescue his son from being gassed by the Germans in the death camp, a father considers putting another boy in his son's place, but hesitating about the law governing such a situation, the father asks the old rabbi in the camp. Of the father's decision the rabbi says, " 'Instead of Isaac, Abraham put a ram. And that was for G-d. You put another child, and for what? To feed Moloch. . . . The law is, Don't kill' " (170). The father changes his mind, but his faith, which "Ha-shem" regards as "a very great miracle," brings not the divine intervention that rescued Isaac but God's decision to make "an end with miracles," and "after this the destruction continues, no interruptions. . . . until millions of bones . . . goes up in smoke" (170, 169, 170–71). The logical conclusion to that parable is "For the sake of one life, the whole world is lost." But Saul's story conflicts with what the sages have written—"If you save one life only, it's like the whole world is saved"—and proves "that if you talk miracle, that's when everything becomes false. . . . No stories from miracles! No stories and no belief" (170, 171). But magic determines the rest of Ozick's tale, for levitation takes over, releasing the "false rabbi Tchernikhovsky" from the "tin prison of his frame" and propelling him "to the ceiling as if gassed." From his elevated position, he directs the narrator to choose between "The Creator or the creature. God or god. The Name of Names" or "Apollo" (176). Like the real Tchernikhovsky, she picks Apollo, and wearing the crown of the *ba'al ga'-avah*, she doubles the student's experience—usurped stories gush from her. They knock off the goat's crown, but her crown, struck by the strips of leather which the false rabbi's beard has turned into, falls off and slices her forehead. The leather thongs of the phylacteries with which Tchernikhovsky saw fit to bind God in the last line of "Before the Statue of Apollo" become in "Usurpation" the instrument for punishing an idolator. The narrator joins the goat Alex, the "name of a conqueror, Aristotle's pupil, the arrogant god-man" (177).

Appending to her tale the observation that after death when paradise is entered, story writers will be in a "cage" where they will be taught "All that is not Law is levity," Cynthia Ozick echoes the old writer in Jerusalem who proclaimed that statement the "truth to be found at the end of every incident" (177). Ozick confirms in the final image of the story the fundamental conflict between story-writers and Torah. In the imagined scene of Tchernikhovsky and the old writer in paradise, the storyteller depicts the fate of the writer who denies his Jewish identity. The pious writer murmurs psalms and "snacks on leviathan," an allusion to the day of judgment when the power of good will defeat evil.[42] But Tchernikhovsky "avoids the congregation of the faithful" and "eats nude at the table of the nude gods . . . his sex splendidly erect." Betrayed by the mark of the covenant, he cannot gainsay his identity and the "Canaanite idols call him, in the language of the spheres, kike" (178). His companions antisemitic Canaanite idols, Tchernikhovsky repeats in paradise the choice he made "in life . . . the god of poetry, Apollo" (11).[43] The final prison image in "Usurpation" embodies the concerns of the entire volume—the assaults against Judaic law.

And the apprehension that story-making can lead to the worship of idols prompts the argument Ozick advances in "Literature as Idol: Harold Bloom," which was published in 1979. The narrator of "Usurpation," like Tcherni-khovsky, chooses Apollo, but in her essay Ozick argues fiercely against that choice when she takes the critic Harold Bloom to task for being a "system-maker," even an "idol-maker." Unambiguous and unequivocal, Ozick's remonstrance against Bloom's theories when seen in light of the narrator's conflict in "Usurpation" illuminates the storyteller's practice of expressing ambivalence in fiction and decisiveness in essays. Often the essays' themes are irreconcilable with the storyteller's tales. The idea that Cynthia Ozick worries over in "Usurpation"—that literature itself "is an idol"—constitutes the thesis of her essay, "Literature as Idol" (A&A 196). What the goat in her tale desires is what Harold Bloom has devised: " 'revisionism' is a breaking off with the precursor; a violation of what has been transmitted; a deliberate offense against the given, against the hallowed; an unhallowing of the old great gods; the usurpation of an inheritance by the inheritor himself; displacement. Above all, the theft of power" (185). Like the narrator of "Usurpation" who values "ancient wisdom," Ozick proclaims "modernism and belatedness" enemies of Judaism, for they "look to break the bond with the old and make over" (*Bloodshed* 163; A&A 195). It is Bloom's idea of "misprision," the symbolic killing of precursors, that for Ozick is the opposite of the "Jewish view," which holds that "it is only through such recapture and emulation of the precursor's stance, unrevised, that life can be nourished, that the gift of the Creator can be received, praised, and fulfilled" (A&A 195).

Breaking the chain of tradition, the linkage of the old and new, competing with God—these acts belong not to the Jewish Idea but to Bloom's invention of "magic." But magic is precisely what the narrator of "Usurpation" lusts after, and the fire imagery that is present in "Usurpation" is the imagery with which Ozick describes Bloom's lexicon: "Listed nakedly, the Bloomian glossary has the ring of engineers' shoptalk. But this is to miss—because of the smoke it gives out—a chance of sighting the burning bush. The glossary is the girandole—the scaffolding out of which the Bloomian fireworks erupt. And what the fiery wheel writes on the sky is, after all, a single idea: discontinuity" (A&A 185). The critic's theories offend the Second Commandment: emphasizing the "hubris of the poet," to whom Bloom vouchsafes the "temerity to usurp the Throne of Heaven," Bloom himself has the audacity to become a *ba'al ga'avah* (A&A 197). Ozick's fundamental rejection of Bloom's theories, then, has to do with the conclusion the narrator in "Usurpation" reaches, that the supreme Father cannot be slain, even symbolically, that aestheticism can never replace ethics. The narrator's choice of Apollo over the Name of Names in "Usurpation" is in "Literature as Idol" overthrown when Ozick denounces the very thing her narrator embraces. Onto Harold Bloom Cynthia Ozick affixes one half of her own conflict: he embodies an unacceptable desire lodged in herself.

Though she seeks "to reproduce a purely transmitted inheritance, free of substitution or incarnation," though she strives not "to compete with the Creator" and to maintain an unbroken "chain of tradition" descending from God's revelation at Sinai, the storyteller risks violating those values when she creates her own world and rebels against her predecessors (A&A 195).[44] The many references and allusions to fathers in "Usurpation"—the idea the narrator has of having the sick father in "The Silver Crown" recover in her own story, the allusion to *Hamlet*, the false rabbi's story—suggest simultaneously the desire to emulate the patriarch's stance and the wish to displace it. A metaphor for inheritance, continuity, law—all that the artist can subvert—the father in "Usurpation" symbolizes an ineluctable conflict. Such strife inhabits the deepest layer of the novella, as its other title and the reference to *Hamlet* imply. In an interview in 1985 Ozick movingly suggested a possible reason for her novella's other title, "Other People's Stories": "But the most hurtful moment of my life was when my father said to me once, 'Other people's books and other people's children,' at a certain point when I was writing and writing away on *Trust* and not publishing anything and having all my eggs in that basket and having no other eggs that were operative" (Interview with Kauvar 386). Her remarks shed light on the theme that originates in her first novel, pulses through her fiction, and culminates in *The Messiah of Stockholm*. The ending of "Usurpation" is conditioned not only by her dread of idolatry and her desire to adhere to the teachings of the patriarchs but by her enduring "lust after stories." "Usurpation" unfolds the last and most serious betrayal of Judaism and then upholds obedience to its decisive commandment. In that confirmation resides Ozick's conviction in a more strenuous moral experience and a meditation on the loss of values and beliefs threatening contemporary life. Concerned as they are with rootlessness, disbelief, and idolatry, the fictions in *Bloodshed* pertain directly to our times. In her second collection of stories Cynthia Ozick invites us to examine the basis of our attraction to discontinuity, our rupture with tradition, our eschewal of the moral life. In short, she urges us to relinquish our idols.

FOUR

The Uses of Fantasy

From the resolution in "Usurpation" spring the conflicts animating *Levitation: Five Fictions*.[1] In them Ozick considers the resolution she reached in *Bloodshed*, explores the shifting implications of that resolution, establishes its multiple perspectives, and ends by attenuating its finality. She resembles the narrator of "Usurpation" who declares her conclusions "less logically decisive" than those of other writers. Their boundary is Ozick's frontier. The laws that govern the complexities of her fiction resist codification, for every story offers alternative positions and none of them is ever completely overwhelmed. If the narrator of "Usurpation" is drawn to the magical and the fanciful—to what is forbidden—the "five fictions" in *Levitation* conjoin the inventive to the moral. Not only does Ozick balance two meanings contingent upon each other, but she contrives her metaphors so that they are double-natured. Such metaphors pervade *Levitation,* in which the fantastic proves especially useful in unmasking motivation and in revealing moral truth. In *Bloodshed* the emphasis is on the tribal; in *Levitation* the stress shifts to the nature of the artistic imagination. Indeed, the five fictions in *Levitation* are like five paintings hung in an imaginary gallery, portraits of artists in the act of imaginative creation.

I

Ozick begins her study of artists' lives in the title story, a tale about two married novelists. The Feingolds joke about being "secondary-level people," but their tenderness toward the victimized and their attraction "to bitter lives" allow them not to face the reasons for their own obscurity (7). Lucy believes she and Feingold have "the same premises," but from the very beginning of "Levitation," Ozick clearly differentiates Lucy's premises from Feingold's. Always aware "he did not want a Jewish wife," Feingold married a "minister's daughter" who "became an Ancient Hebrew" the way Allegra Vand became an Ancient Greek. His marriage conjures up Edelshtein's "culture-envy" and is itself a cultural statement, not unlike Clement Chimes's new name.[2] In "An Education" and "Levitation," Ozick makes plain that the failure to succeed is tied to the denial of a heritage. Unknown and excluded from the ranks of famous writers in New York, the Feingolds delight in their productivity. On one principle they concur: the "importance of never writing about writers" (4). Their interests, however, betray a more fundamental disagreement. Inclined "to speculate and ruminate" and "tempted to write solipsistically, narcissistically, tediously, and without common appeal," Lucy has written a novel "about domestic life" and reads only Jane Austen's *Emma* (5, 4). She recalls Lulu in "A Mercenary," but the novelist's sense of herself as a "stylist" is reminiscent of the word manipulators in *Trust*. Professing to be an Ancient Hebrew, Lucy is as indifferent to history as an Ancient Greek.

But Feingold is drawn to history and "event," owns volumes and volumes of Jewish history, and writes "about Jews" (4). His attraction to the Middle Ages—one of the darkest eras of Christian Europe when Jews were persecuted, humiliated, and massacred—is significant on many levels of the story.[3] He has chosen as the subject for his novel Menachem ben Zerach, a survivor of a fourteenth-century massacre in Spain: "From morning to midnight he hid under a pile of corpses, until a 'compassionate knight' (this was the language of the history Feingold relied on) plucked him out and took him home to tend his wounds. . . . Six thousand Jews died in a single day in March. . . . It was nevertheless a triumphant story: at the end Menachem ben Zerach becomes a renowned scholar" (4–5). That Heinrich Graetz's *History of the Jews* is the history on which Feingold depends illuminates his personality and clarifies issues crucial to the story.[4] For the nineteenth-century historian, the Middle Ages were exemplary: "Enslaved a thousand times, this people [the Jewish people] still knew how to preserve its intellectual freedom: humiliated and degraded, it still did not become a horde of gypsies nor lose its sense for the lofty and holy; expelled and homeless, it built for itself a spiritual fatherland. . . . post-talmudic Jewish history . . . knows no Middle Ages, in the pejorative sense of the word, which is afflicted with the symptoms of intellectual stupor, brutishness, and religious madness" (Graetz, *Structure* 136–37). The massacre to which Feingold refers began on the Sabbath with mobs of people demanding either the death of Jews or their conversion to Christianity. Of importance to the historian is the twenty-two-year-old Menachem ben Zerach who was rescued by a "compassionate knight" but lost his entire family in the massacre. Vowing, when he recovered, to devote himself to talmudic studies, Menachem ben Zerach wrote a compendium of theoretic and practical Judaism, but "did not rise above the mediocrity of his times" (Graetz 144–45). Captivated by the massacre, Feingold is drawn mainly to the compassionate knight for whom the novelist plans to write a journal, thereby converting the knight into a writer who, as Lucy observes, is really Feingold himself.

That he has unearthed the source for his novel from Graetz's version of Jewish history is ironic, for the nineteenth-century historian was nothing like the novelist. The novelist identifies with a Christian knight and is married to a gentile woman whose apathy toward history contravenes Graetz's idea of Judaism. It was important to the historian not only because he believed it "negates paganism" but because it proved "the utter insignificance of paganism as far as truth is concerned as well as its damaging effect on society" (*Structure* 66).[5] Inveighing against Greek morality and Hellenized Jews, Graetz proclaimed Christianity the "arch-foe" of Judaism and deemed the Jews' suffering responsible for their deep involvement with their religion, their blood a sanctification of Judaism. His impassioned opinions, his focus on biography rather than on neutral historical forces, his talent as a writer—these imbue Graetz's account with power and vitality. They are precisely what Feingold and Lucy lack: "Anonymous mediocrities. They could not call themselves forgotten because they had never been noticed" (8). Attracted to the powerful Christian knight, Feingold reveals his fascination with power; engrossed in the events of the Middle Ages—its "blood libels," host desecration myths, the Fourth Lateran Council, the Crusades—he links himself to martyrdom and impotence. Trusting Graetz's history of the Jews, Feingold rejects the historian's beliefs.

His interest in the Middle Ages notwithstanding, Feingold married a minister's daughter whose attitude toward tradition significantly resembles his own; but her alienation from her father's faith makes Lucy's a more decisive denial of tradition. Feingold's wife has refused her father's gift of transmission. In fact the minister's reading of a psalm determined Lucy to convert to Judaism, yet to her "Jews and women . . . were both beside the point." Nonetheless, she married a Jew, took his faith as her own, and "supposed the inner life of a housebound woman—she cited *Emma*—to contain as much comedy as the cosmos" (9, 8). She perceives that cosmos with "huge, intent, sliding eyes, disconcertingly luminous" (4). Her eyes and her resemblance to a "tall copper statue" look forward to her realizations at the end of the story (7). But in her description of Lucy, Ozick alludes ironically to Saint Lucy, the virgin martyr of Syracuse who was killed when her betrothed denounced her to the authorities as a Christian. The legends accruing to her and the beauty of her eyes, which Saint Lucy is thought to have torn from her head as protection for her suitor, account for the meaning of her name and the significance of her emblems. They are eyes and a lamp, symbols of divine light and wisdom, reflections of her name ("light"). Naming her character after such a saint, Ozick implies that Lucy has martyred herself not out of religious faith but for an allegiance to a man whose religion she finds irrelevant. Lucy Feingold possesses none of her namesake's attributes.

She more closely resembles Jane Austen's protagonist at the beginning of *Emma,* the only book Lucy reads. Jane Austen records the growth of her heroine's morals, the progress of Emma Woodhouse's perceptions, the young woman's burgeoning comprehension of the world and the human beings who inhabit it.[6] Her novel focuses on marriage, is unconcerned with religious issues, and provides sharp commentary on Lucy Feingold and her world.[7] Like Lucy's, Emma's world is narrow; both women judge people by their power, which in *Emma* is manifested by class and property. If Ozick calls attention to Lucy's eyes, Austen dramatizes Emma's misperceptions, which diminish with moral progress. Lucy, however, makes less and less moral progress as Ozick's story proceeds, and the marriage that ends *Emma* happily and represents the fulfillment of its protagonist's maturity is in "Levitation" exposed as a relationship based on conflicting premises. Unable to leave her father even to marry Mr. Knightley, Emma is as attached to her father as Lucy is detached from hers. If the adoration Emma lavishes on her father is, as Mark Schorer believes, an "emotional insufficiency," the breach between Lucy and her father is a cultural deficiency (106). In short, Emma's Knightley enlightens, but Lucy's "compassionate knight" does not. The novelist who judges *Emma* exemplary stops short of finding in it a paradigm by which her own moral life is put to test. Juxtaposing Lucy Feingold and Emma Woodhouse, Cynthia Ozick engages in a dialogue with Jane Austen and revises the outcome of her novel.

Although the Feingolds believe themselves devoted to the imagination and fancy themselves "children with a puppet theater," they are in fact "addicted to . . . counterfeit pity" because it is another manifestation of power. Unnoticed in New York and separated from their parents who rarely venture a visit to the perilous city, the novelists arouse no curiosity in anyone: "no one said their names . . . no one ever asked if they were working on anything new" (7, 8). Lucy explains their predicament as the fate of those "sunk in a ghetto"; but Ozick suggests that their detachment from their families and their traditions have rendered the Feingolds powerless to make themselves known (8). "To study power," they invite a number of luminaries to a party; none of them attend, but the Feingolds unexpectedly learn about power from the refugee a friend brings to the gathering. Divided into three party-rooms which shine "like a triptych," the Feingolds' apartment emphasizes the tripartite structure of "Levitation" and befits the story's concern with artists (9). The guests in the dining room, their costumes and conversation, strike Feingold as "a falsehood, even a figment"; choking with disappointment, he tells the "blank-eyed" Lucy, " 'My God . . . do you realize *no one came*,' " by which he means none of the powerful. In despair he joins the guests in the living room, and Lucy "crossed no-man's-land to the dining room" (11). Then someone asks Feingold to light his fireplace and the flame illuminates the face of Feingold's friend from the seminary. Instantly, Feingold wants "to talk about God. Or, if not God, then certain historical atrocities" (11). That the fire kindles such desires recalls "Usurpation" in which fire is associated with God's presence. Their unused fireplace and unburned Sabbath candles indicate God has been snuffed out of the Feingolds' lives. Suffused with the bright light from the fire, the living room "seemed" to Feingold "dense with family," but Lucy "saw that everyone in the living room was a Jew" and felt "uneasy," the way she had when Feingold's friend from the seminary conducted her conversion. Ozick divides Lucy from the guests in the living room and allies her with the ones congregated in the dining room. It is filled mostly with gentiles and "unruffled, devil-may-care kind" of Jews, those who attend "studio showings of *Screw on Screen* on the eve of the Day of Atonement" (12).

Of those Jews—"normal . . . with sense"—Lucy approves. To Feingold's tales of historical atrocities she imputes a spasm "of fanaticism" which she tries to silence (12). But "Feingold was waiting for a voice," and it comes from the refugee. Lucy does not listen to him; she scrutinizes him, and that allows her to identify him as a refugee. His eyes hidden "in their tunnels," his "nose like a saint's. The face of Jesus," the refugee reminds her of her father (13). At first luminous, then blank, Lucy's eyes wheel around the room taking in all the Jews and coming to rest on the man with the hidden eyes. They seem blind, Lucy's all-seeing. His voice conjures in her a vision of the scene in Genesis where the "voice of the Lord God" walks in the Garden and calls to Adam (14). She identifies the refugee with her father: reflections of God, the Supreme Father after the Fall, they foreshadow her alienation from the Jews in the living room. But the voice of the refugee commands attention "to modern times," to the time when "the eyes of God were shut," the time which Feingold has ignored and about which Lucy can feel nothing.

Dividing herself from the Jews, she questions their perpetual intensity, wonders whether it comes from their chosenness, and concludes they are immured in self-pity. The refugee's horrifying memories evoke nothing but a "mind-picture" in Lucy: for her the Holocaust is "only a movie," a "hillside with multitudes of crosses, and bodies dropping down from big bloody nails"—multiple crucifixions (14). She dismisses the Holocaust and the Crucifixion as examples of martyrdom and judges the refugee to be a preacher like her father. Listening to her father read a psalm, she fancied herself an Ancient Hebrew and converted to Judaism. Now she Christianizes the refugee, renders him indistinguishable from her father, merges Judaism and Christianity, and sunders herself from both. Indifferent to the brutal reality of the survivor's memories, Lucy likens his voice describing the victims to an artist carving "stone . . . like sculptures." She transforms his harrowing story into an aesthetic experience.[8]

Her name, the implication of the refugee's words, the repetition of the stone imagery to describe the Jews before being murdered by the Germans— these allude to Spenser's *Faerie Queene,* a work to which Ozick refers in "An Education" and "Puttermesser: Her Work History, Her Ancestry, and Her Afterlife." The name of the Virgin martyr of Syracuse, Lucy is the name of the dowerless maid abandoned by Amidas and married by Bracidas in book 5 of *The Faerie Queene* (5.4). That book, which explores "justice as it can be perceived, understood, and exercised in the difficult human scene which the Proem describes," diverges from the refugee's perception of the present and the past (Williams 159). Through an analogy of the altered heavens, Spenser compares the life of this world to golden antiquity: "And all this world with them amisse doe moue, / And all his creatures from their course astray, / Till they arrive at their last ruinous decay" (Proem, 6). Just as the Golden Age has "become a stonie one," men who were at first created on earth are now converted into stone (Proem, 2). They live in a transformed world, a world without justice—the attribute Spenser believes most resembles God. Evoking Spenser's imagery, Ozick ingeniously converts its meaning in Lucy's version of the refugee's story.

Unlike Spenser, the refugee condemns the past: " 'Yesterday . . . the eyes of God were shut . . . shut . . . like iron doors' " (13). Spenser's golden age is

Ozick's iron one, a time when neither justice nor piety prevailed. What Lucy envisages are victims as lifeless statues. What Ozick alludes to is the thirdsection of Spenser's proem, which implies that God's closed eyes—His injustice—permitted death in a region that was originally a birthplace: "And men themselves, the which at first were framed / Of earthly mould, and form'd of fleshly bone, / Are now transformed into hardest stone" (Proem 2). The central symbol of justice in book 5 of *The Faerie Queene* is the temple of Isis, a goddess who is united with Diana and Venus as well as with all the great goddesses. To Isis Spenser attributes a predominant role in establishing justice because she was able to temper cruelty with love.[9] But in Lucy's ensuing illumination, Ozick severs the goddess from justice and attaches her instead to the erotic sensuality of paganism. Usurping from Spenser, Ozick refashions his materials so that they serve her contrapuntally.

The stone imagery recalls the end of "A Mercenary," where stones mark the burial place of Lushinski's soul. But Lucy imagines the Jews before they are slaughtered "as if they were already stone" until all at once the room of Jews floats upwards, leaving Lucy "alone at the bottom . . . while the room floated upwards, carrying Jews" (15). At the beginning of the story, the "party washed and turned like a sluggish tub; it lapped at all the walls of all the rooms"; all of the guests seemed "afloat in a tub" (9, 10). Toward the end of the story, the living room "ascended. It rose like an ark on waters" (15). Lucy's "mind-picture" invokes the flood in Genesis when the "ark . . . rose above the earth," saving only Noah and those who accompanied him. Ozick transforms the biblical event into a levitation to separate Lucy from the Jews, to imply that they and the refugee, like Noah and the people in the ark, have recovered Covenant and will be renewed. The image discloses Lucy's dawning realization: the convert belongs neither to Judaism nor to Christianity. To that tradition Noah and his generation prefigure the end of time when only those who take refuge in faith will escape God's judgment.

The levitation estranges Lucy from the Jews, excludes her from the "glory of their martyrdom," and that produces her second "illumination," the memory of being in a city park "early in May" where she witnessed Messinian and Calabrian peasants sing and dance (16). Their "suggestive" dances, their "erotic" songs, sung "in a dialect of archaic Greek," their exaltation of the "Madonna of Love," their pipes and bicycle bells—these suggest a pagan May Day celebration, which was "famous for its orgiastic revels."[10] Including in the scene in the park a reference to the "bells the priests used to beat in the temple of Minerva"—the temple of the ancient Italian goddess and patroness of the arts was especially popular with artists and poets—Ozick connects paganism to art and establishes Lucy's second illumination as emanating from the "religion of Art" (A&A 163). Beholding that religion, Lucy "is glorified . . . is exalted," for as a pair of dancers intertwine and extol the Madonna, "giver of fertility and fecundity," Lucy comprehends that "Astarte will always be reinvented," that she is "eternal" (*Levitation* 18; A&A 197). From her second illumination Lucy learns she has relinquished the pulse of nature, the garden of Aphrodite, the miracle of everything: "true religion"—all for the "God of the Jews" (18).

At first obliquely and then more directly, Ozick associates Lucy with Aphrodite, weaving the imagery connected with the goddess of love into the texture of Lucy's thoughts. The triptych formed by the three party rooms, the guests standing "in the niches of a cathedral," the conversation flowing like a river with "new eddyings" swallowing it and "swirl devouring swirl," Lucy silent like a copper statue, her sense that the levitating Jews have left her "below the floorboards"—these precede her second illumination (9, 10, 15). Aphrodite's connection with the garden and with the sea are well known; but the remarkable breadth of Ozick's knowledge of mythology becomes apparent in the variety of her allusions to the rituals and iconography belonging to the worship of the goddess who haunts the pages of the storyteller's books. It is to the tripartite temple facade in the Aphrodite temple at Paphos that the Feingolds' three party-rooms advert; and it is the small bronze statue of the goddess atop a copper bar in a sanctuary on Cyprus that Lucy's appearance recalls.[11] In the *Iliad* Aphrodite's flashing eyes, strikingly similar to the novelist's luminous eyes, make Helen recognize the goddess. An early hymn likens the goddess to the Mother of the Mountain to whom the goat belongs and who appears in Lucy's recollection. Even Aphrodite's vivid attire is revived in the long "violet-colored" skirt Lucy wears to the party. Picturing herself in the earth below the floorboards, Lucy enters nature, the domain of the gods. In her final illumination she attains a glorification—a pagan deification of nature which she embraces as eternal truth.

That anchors her in the earth and severs her from the Jews, whose eternal truth resides upward in a place so high as to be unvisualizable and, for Lucy, almost inaudible. Emerging from beneath her illumination, she strains after the faint voices of the Jews in the living room; but she knows they mainly speak of the Holocaust. In unabashed boredom she recoils from the atrocities of the Holocaust, considers Feingold diminished, and joins to the repetitive horrors of the death camps her father's iterated hymns, dismissing them all as "tiresome" (19). From the room in which she has been "abandoned" like Spenser's Lucy, the novelist turns in "relief" to the dining room where the "humanists"—all of them "compassionate knights"—congregate and discuss "The Impact of Romantic Individualism," but the real impact has been made in the living room where "All the Jews are in the air" (19, 20).[12] The levitation that ends the story echoes Bleilip's beliefs about the hasidim, is part of the story's complex pattern of flight imagery, and parallels the ascension of the Jews in "Usurpation," in which the fate of the Jew who chooses Apollo over the Name of Names is made plain. In "Levitation" Lucy exchanges the God of the Jews for the gods of the pagans and remains on earth while the Jews soar overhead. The opposing movements of rising and falling correspond to the distinction between hearing and seeing. At each critical juncture of the story, mind-pictures or sensory memories are what enable Lucy to decode an event or to decipher her feelings about it, and imagery of light always accompanies those moments. She scrutinizes her surroundings, she derives pleasure from looking; she relies on her eyes to confirm her religion. In "The Structure of JewishHistory," Graetz sets forth the fundamental divergence between the pagan and the Judaic conception of the divine: "To the pagan, the divine appears within nature as something observable to the eye. He becomes conscious of it as something seen. In contrast, to the Jew ... God reveals Himself through a demonstration of His will, through the medium of the ear. . . . Paganism sees its god, Judaism hears Him; that is, it hears the commandments of His will" (68). A vivid illustration of Graetz's cognition, Lucy resembles the Homeric Greeks, who did not distinguish between the word "see" and "know" etymologically, thus merging the two mental faculties (Onians 18). Ultimately, Lucy's great, luminous eyes finally cannot follow the ascending living room as it sails upward, carrying the Jews to the air where they escape her sight altogether.

What propels them there is the power of words endemic to Judaism. Possessing a God who can neither be visualized nor "confined in any temple" and about whom "it is not permitted to make an image or a work of art, or even to have an idea," Judaism, Ozick implies, rejects the fixity and finality characteristic of Hellenism, which, in her metaphor, remains bound to the earth (Baeck, "Two World Views Compared," *Pharisees* 138). Their experiences at the party mark the distinctions not only between their religions but between Lucy's and Feingold's writing, which is inextricable from the novelists' respective attitudes toward tradition. Anchoring Lucy to the earth, Ozick indicates the limitations to her imagination as well. Urged forward by the refugee's voice, Feingold is impelled upwards beyond the boundaries of what he can visualize into a realm where he must imagine the unimaginable. Lucy's fantasy of the levitation along with the allusion to Genesis revives Ozick's description of the couple early in the story: "They wrote not without puzzlements and travail; nevertheless as naturally as birds" (4). That Feingold is later imagined by Lucy aboard the ark with the Jews suggests Ozick's simile refers to Noah's two birds in Genesis (8:7)—the white dove and the black raven—one a messenger bearing glad tidings of Jerusalem's survival, the other a devourer feeding on carrion.[13] To journey upward is to ascend to freedom and redemption; to remain on the earth is to be a fallen bird deprived of flight. In Ozick's metaphors of flight are resonances of withdrawal, of ambition, of redemption.

Their common images and themes commend the last tale in *Bloodshed* and the first in *Levitation* as a pair. In "Usurpation" and in "Levitation" Ozick unfolds from two separate consciousnesses the perplexities confronting the writer. If "Usurpation" affirms the preponderance of the Name of Names, "Levitation" depicts the magnetism of Aphrodite and the old gods. One tale depicts the writer's tie to tradition, the other the writer's separateness from tradition. The contradictory forces of a dialectic, the fictions coalesce in their informing ideas: they uphold the absolute necessity of the father's transmission, the link in the chain of tradition. Art that denies it and yields only beautiful forms is "aesthetic paganism," the art emanating from Hellenism. Redemptive art possesses an inherent moral value: "Implicit in redemption is everything against the fated or the static: everything that hates death and harm and elevates the life-giving" (A&A 246). Related to the flight imagery in "Levitation," the verb "elevates" underscores the direction from which Ozick's imagination draws sustenance. Bridging *Bloodshed* and *Levitation*, "Levitation" heralds the themes reverberating throughout the third volume of Ozick's stories and constitutes the first artist's portrait, one strikingly different from those in "Shots" and "From a Refugee's Notebook."

Lucy's notion that history is harmful to Feingold and has reduced him is reversed in "Shots," in which the attachment the narrator has to photography reflects her commitment to history and her capacity to restore memory. The largeness of import Ozick accords to the father throughout her work reveals the primacy of the legacy he hands down, a conviction in total consonance with the Hebraic tradition. Like the fundamental irony involved in the title of her first novel, the title of her story plays on two meanings of the word "shot." By producing a photographic record of what is seen, the photographer's shot preserves life; by killing his prey, a marksman's shot shatters life. The competing senses of the word appear repeatedly throughout the story; they are deployed to incarnate the story's essential conflict, and they are illustrated precisely by two photographs. The unnamed narrator, who is a photographer, carries an old photograph she calls the Brown Girl in the "pocket of her blouse" and "in a pocket of her mind": "I *could* keep her *even though* she was dead . . . I could keep her, just as she used to be, because someone had once looked through the bunghole of a box and clicked off a lever" (42). However, at a public symposium she attends, her camera captures the very moment the simultaneous translator is killed; and her photograph, preserver of time, registers "death the changer, the collapser, the witherer" (41).

Both pictures mark a photographer's intimate involvement with time. The narrator's accidental discovery at age eleven of an old and browning photograph suddenly brings awareness of time's existence and recalls the passage at the beginning of *Trust* where, after her commencement exercises, the graduate inadvertently learns how time is revealed and recognizes the moment as the beginning of knowledge. At first, Brown Girl evokes the young narrator's wish to defy time: "if only she had been halted, arrested, stayed in her ripeness and savor!" Older, the photographer realizes that what she had seen in the photograph "was time as stasis, time at the standstill, time at the fix; the time . . . of Keats's Grecian urn" (40, 41). Linking the fixed time of Keats's urn to the arrested time in a photograph, Ozick establishes a congruence between art and photography and intimates the dilemma of both: like the figures on the urn who are immobile, imperishable, and unfulfilled, the photograph rescues a moment from the ravages of time, but consigns it to unchangingness, the "curse of perpetuity" (CG 76). Stasis is what the narrator of *Trust* equates with monomania and magic. Stasis and magic are what Ozick ascribes to aesthetic paganism. Art and photography possess the ability to preserve life by representing it; yet their magical powers are potentially perilous, for they can become idolatrous. Having linked art and photography, Ozick renders their apt connection into her central metaphor.

Her metaphor is transformed into a parable about art when she recounts the relationship the photographer has with Sam, a married, tenured professor of South American history.[14] Their story demonstrates the deep affinity existing between art and history and examines the fate of the artist. The narrator meets Sam when she is assigned to follow him through some public symposia he is chairing. Although at first she "didn't care about one thing in Sam's mind," she becomes infatuated with him, attends to everything he says, and finds herself wanting more. Ozick relates the narrator's infatuation with Sam to the photographer's discovery of photography: "I came to photography as I came to infatuation—with no special talent for it, and with no point of view" (39). After meeting Sam's wife, the narrator reflects that infatuation comes on like a "bullet in the neck" (51). A bullet in the neck is how the simultaneous translator, whose picture she took, was murdered, and she thinks telling Sam how "between the exposure and the solution, history comes into being" would make her "bleed, like a bullet in the neck" (52). The appearance of that phrase within the contexts of infatuation, photography, and history raises vexing questions.

And the ambiguity implicit in the story's title persists. Immediately after Sam tells her that his wife Verity is so remarkable that he will never have a mistress, the narrator, though "silent about the orphaned moment" they are living, asks to take his picture "under a dripping linden tree" so that she "can keep him forever," the way she has kept Brown Girl, the way Pincus Silver has kept Unknown Friend (53, 54). Although the narrator has mused that history comes into being during the process of photography, her picture now seems "finished on the spot" (54). The photographer's infatuation with history does not generate history; the photographer stops time but she "shoots" history. Her photograph of Sam, who "now resembles a Greek runner resting," recalls her reference to the time of Keats's urn (54). Both the urn and the camera possess fixative powers: they stop time's erosion but suppress the very movement in life that leads to fulfillment and decay. And the picture of Sam under the wet linden tree symbolizes the meaning of history, for the linden, whose heart-shaped leaves account for its traditional erotic overtones, was respected as a guardian of pregnant women and regarded as a life-index. Mostly present when Sam and the narrator walk, rain, as it does in Trust, signals moments of revelation.[15]

In addition to the rain, Sam's "big blue umbrella, with a wooden horse's head for a handle" recalls imagery from Trust, to which the horse is important and in which blue and yellow are predominant colors. The narrator of "Shots" first mentions Sam's blue umbrella after she introduces her relationship with Sam in the context of the Brown Girl: "Knowing this—that now will become then, that huge will turn little—doesn't cure" (42). Struck by her "strange" preoccupation with an umbrella Sam "hasn't owned for a whole year," she remembers the umbrella as part of the time when she did not "care about one thing in Sam's mind," but the umbrella hints that "now will become then" (43). Their "faces . . . rivers," Sam and the narrator walk in the rain "without an umbrella" before she takes his picture beneath the linden tree and sees his and Verity's apartment. Like the narrator of *Trust,* the unnamed photographer-narrator learns about history from a couple; and as in Ozick's first novel, it is photography that brings recognition. In *Trust* Ozick compares the discovery of the girl's history to the unreeling of a "slow-motion camera"; in "Shots" the narrator, older than the girl, takes the picture that will enable her to restore the important moment (*Trust* 581). The photographer not only witnesses history, she preserves it. The pursuit of the elusive bluebird of happiness and the untamed sexuality engaged in by Tilbeck in *Trust* are, in "Shots," relinquished for art. In the novel and in the fable, a tree affords realization.

By associating Sam—an allusion to the last biblical judge—with the dripping linden tree, Ozick suggests that history clarifies the past, vitalizes the present, and presides over the future; by having Sam invite the photographer to observe his life with Verity, Ozick reveals that history's truth is enacted in the palpable reality of time, not in the factitious rendering of time. After the narrator sees Sam and Verity's apartment, watches Verity sewing, and sees what her "polishing and perfecting" fingers have achieved, she concludes, "Verity resurrects." Indeed, Verity resurrects a dead nun's brown clothes, dresses the photographer in them, and converts her into a living "period-piece": the work of truth differs from the effort of representation. Her image reflected in the mirror attached to a bedroom door, the narrator sees herself "all in brown, as brown as leaves" and identifies with the Brown Girl: "I'm the Brown Girl in the pocket of my blouse. I reek of history. If, this minute, I could glide into a chemical solution, as if in a gondola, splashed all over and streaming with wet silver, would the mirror seize and fix me, like a photographic plate?" (56–57). Her gaining awareness before a mirror recalls George's experience in "The Dock-Witch"; and using the same words to describe herself and Brown Girl, the photographer yokes her fate to the girl's in the photograph and suggests she and Brown Girl are doubles.

Eleven years old when she discovered the Brown Girl, the photographer suddenly saw her age into a "melancholy" spinster, not because of the "distinct little parallelogram" between her nose and mouth but because the "face faded out" and the "woman turned to ghost." The picture revealed the photographer's intention "to obliterate her," but the narrator understood she had seen "death . . . coming" in the faded out face (41). Twenty-five years later, staring into a mirror, the thirty-six-year-old photographer sees the same aging spinster's face and thinks about growing old, about dying. "Lovesick" and "dreamsick" the way Brown Girl must have been and tripping "over . . . [her] nun's hem," the photographer seizes her camera—an "ambassador of desire," a "secret house with its single shutter," a "chaste aperture," a "dead infant," the "husband of" her "bosom"—catches the reflection of Sam's and Verity's heads, "negatives of each other . . . in their daughter's mirror," and shoots into them, exposing them, making them "stick forever" (56–57).[16]

If verity and history are negatives of each other, married to each other's reflections, they can experience the better joy of becoming the print that defies time's dominion, and the photographer who has reproduced their image has contributed to history. However, the photographer's "intimate involvement with the subject matter necessitates detachment" from it, and her photograph freezes the "spontaneity of life without leaving traces of his presence" (Arnheim 150–51). Though affecting the way we view ourselves, though expanding our knowledge, though recovering our experiences, the inevitable isolation of the artist engenders her remoteness from the events of ordinary human life and alienates her from the essential judgments of history. The photographer-narrator of "Shots" has chosen Art over Life; in her infatuation with history she fails to make history in the most ordinary, quotidian way—by living out her humanity.

In 1975, two years before "Shots" was published, Ozick described the photographer's dilemma in an essay, "The Riddle of the Ordinary," when she explicated Yeats's "The Choice." The choice, she said then, "is the choice between pursuing the life of Deed, where acts have consequences, where the fruit of experience is more gratifying than the experience itself, and pursuing the life of Art, which signifies the celebration of shape and mood . . . and finishes out a life in empty remorse" (A&A, 204). Noting the "multitudinous" ironies of Yeats's position, Ozick intimates those at the end of "Shots." "Ravished by the last century's faces" and drawn to photography because it is "*literal* . . . [and] gets what's *there*," the photographer-artist becomes infatuated with history. But infatuation, unlike the "love that sticks," the "wedding-glue" that holds history and truth together forever, is "unilateral" and places the photographer under a "special spell . . . in thrall to [a] cult," excluding her from the course of history's events (*Levitation* 40, 52; A&A 26; *Trust* 419; and *Levitation* 53). Wedded to truth, history begets continuity and ensures the future; photography fixes the images of history and truth into the "very photographs that fickled into period-pieces," but without these period-pieces, history and truth cannot "stick forever" (*Trust* 109). The competing ideas at the end of "Shots" reflect the problematic nature of art, and the story continues to shimmer in ambiguity.

The relationship of photography and history and the necessity for continuity persist in the two fragments that constitute "From a Refugee's Notebook." Published in 1973, "Freud's Room," the first fragment, bears as important an affinity to "Usurpation," which was published the same year, as to "Levitation" and "Shots." Spanning a six-year period, the fictions record Ozick's evolving ideas about art. The "Redactor's Comment" that precedes "Freud's Room" and "The Sewing Harems" discloses the source of the fragments and their title. Found "behind a mirror" in a "vacant room-for-rent" on the west side of New York City, the notebook containing the fragments recalls the kind a student from "an earlier generation" and "another country" used, though the "author, of European, or perhaps South American origin, remains unidentified." That the fragments have been written by a refugee suggests they will contain truths as powerful as those uttered by the refugees in "Bloodshed," "Usurpation," and "Levitation."

"Freud's Room" introduces the unidentified narrator: a person who has never visited Vienna because of an antipathy "to any land which once suckled the Nazi boot," but who has nonetheless "dreamed over photographs of those small rooms where Sigmund Freud wrote his treatises . . . met with his patients . . . and kept . . . his collection of ancient stone animals and carved figurines" (59). The "literal-minded" refugee describes two photographs of Freud's room. One is of Freud sitting at his desk surrounded by books and "hundreds of those strange little gods." Though at first glance the second photograph seems to be filled with "Victorian clutter," upon a closer look, the picture reveals that everything in the room is necessary—"Especially the gods. The gods, the gods!" Divided in two by a lamp pole, the photograph produces a "curious juxtaposition" of the stone gods Freud collected and the couch where he analyzed his patients. Seeing through the photograph, the narrator apprehends that the stone gods "represent the deep primitive grain of the mind Freud sought," that the patient "on the couch was an archaeological enterprise," that Freud lusted "to become a god absolute as stone" (59, 61, 60, 60, 61). For the narrator, the "camera completes the half-language of appearances and articulates an unmistakable meaning" (Berger 129). Gazing at a photograph, the refugee-narrator reaches her conclusion the same way a historian who has seen the actual room recognizes that Freud's "partiality for the prehistoric," fondness for archaeological metaphors, and passion for collecting antiquated objects "testify, reluctantly and eloquently, like a dream, to the mind of their owner" (Gay, FJOG 39).

And that mind, Ozick wrote in "The Hole/Birth Catalogue," an essay she published one year before "Freud's Room," "had it backward," for it "limited humanity to the grossest designs of the flesh" and "came finally to 'discover' what [Freud] called the 'death instinct.' . . . And in choosing the centrality of death, he reinvented as instinct what the priests of the Pharaohs took to be ontology. . . . he put death before life" (A&A 256). What she divines in Freud's theories emerges in a later essay, "The Biological Premises of Our Sad Earth-Speck" (1978), in which Ozick, using images similar to those in "Freud's room," joins "Spirit—or Imagination, which means Image-making, which is to say Idolatry" to stones, tyrants, and kings (A&A 234). The men in history whom the refugee lists as sharing Freud's wish to become a god—the Pharaohs, Napoleon, Hannibal—are idolators; that Freud is among them reveals another facet of Ozick's remonstrance against the Viennese psychoanalyst. In fact, throughout his life Freud identified with Hannibal and longed to surpass him.[17] Envisioning him as another man who lusted after godhead,

Ozick's refugee once again relies on history to illuminate the nature of Freud's mind and implies that Freud became one with "Spirit" and contravened nature: "then up rears monstrousness" (A&A 234).

The monsters he unearthed—"everything barbarous and dreadful and veiled and terror-bearing: the very tooth and claw"—he claimed for the Unconscious, which he "peopled . . . with the devils of Id and Ego and Superego . . . who cavort unrecorded in our anatomies while we pretend they are not there" (63). Ozick's refugee rejects Freud's perception of a magical grotesque realm, for she prizes "verisimilitudes: the lifelike, the anti-magical" (62). Her disavowal of idolatry, her aversion to "make-believe," and her attention to the moral dimension of history identify the refugee-author of the fragments as one of Ozick's innovative artists. Writing in 1987 about the source of fiction in "The Young Self and the Old Writer," Ozick reveals her lingering quarrel with Freud: "The Unconscious is what Freud made up. No one can prove or disprove it. The Freudians claim that the dream-life is its proof; but to pin the name Unconscious on the dream-life is a tautology, not a proof" (166).

Clearly in accordance with nature, not rising out of some dark hellish realm, the source of fiction goes with "the diurnal rhythm of things"—all that Freud, unlike Moses, sought to stop (63). In that attempt, Freud chose "revenge against Judaism's declared life principle," against the Mosaic Idea itself (A&A 256). Art that defies that idea descends into idolatry, confounding not only redemption but sanity itself, as the refugee's speculation on the "draw of the irrational" makes clear: "Freud was lured by what was clearly not 'sane.' . . . Is the scientist, the intelligent physician, the skeptical philosopher who is attracted to the irrational, himself a rational being?" The difference between Freud, the archaeologist of the unconscious, and Gershom Scholem, the historian of Jewish mysticism, Ozick concludes, is that Scholem composed his historical volumes "with bookish distance and objectivity" and Freud's "historical laboratory" was really the demesne of a physician whose bent toward the prehistoric led to his desire for absolute godhood (*Levitation* 63; Gay, FJOG 39).

The photograph of Freud's room becomes the transparent picture through which the narrator glimpses Freud's imperceptible motivations: it is as if Ozick had used the camera and the photographs it takes to pan the landscape of the entire Freudian enterprise. And the value of Scholem's historical investigations, which refashioned the way an entire people looks at itself, over Freud's archaeological endeavors emerges unmistakably in "The Fourth Sparrow: The Magisterial Reach of Gershom Scholem," in which Ozick again invokes the language of photography: "Freud is a peephole into a dark chamber—a camera obscura; but Scholem is a radiotelescope monitoring the universe, with its myriads of dark chambers. . . . Scholem, whose medium was history, touched on the very ground of human imagination. . . . Where Freud thought fit to end, Scholem begins" (A&A 139). Where Freud sought fit to end was in the identification of the beasts that inhabit the unconscious and in the recovery of an individual's prehistory from the detritus of the unconscious; but as Enoch Vand in *Trust* explains, "We call the things we don't remember [man] making, prehistory . . . before history there was no man, there were only beasts" (397–98). With "Freud's Room," Ozick adds another portrait to the gallery of artists in *Levitation*, determines art to be inextricable from history, and raises once more the disquieting issue of idolatry.

The refugee's concern for maintaining the ordinary rhythms of life, the refugee's scorn of Freud for disrupting them as well as for reinventing the principle of death are in "The Sewing Harems" embodied in the very metaphors the refugee claims to "despise." To declare oneself, as the refugee does, literal-minded, impatient "with figures of speech," ignorant of art, and unable to appreciate music is to gainsay possession of an imagination and to proclaim fact the agent of one's pen. All that the refugee disclaims "The Sewing Harems" continually displays; its first sentence immediately establishes the fragment as a parable, "drenched in metaphor": "It was for a time the fashion on the planet Acirema for the more sophisticated females to form themselves into Sewing Harems."[18] The refugee's pen unleashes a Swiftian reflection on the self-indulgence of so-called enlightened women in Acirema, America spelled backwards, and on that country's choice of artifice over naturalness. Just as Swift's depictions of Lilliput and Brobdingnag have lessons for Gulliver, the refugee's description of the planet Acirema possesses moral truths for its readers; just as Swift's savage tone in "A Modest Proposal" demonstrates his deep moral concern for humanity, Ozick's satirical tone in "The Sewing Harems" marks a profound regard for continuity.

Because they consider children the "most regressive forces on the planet," unwelcome interrupters of personal development, interferers with the "most profound ideals," hindrances to "ecological reform," promoters of "pollution," and frustrators of "rational population reduction," the females of Acirema have organized Sewing Harems in order to prevent conception without relinquishing sexual delight: "What the Sewing Harems sewed was obvious. Do not visualize quilting bees, samplers, national flags." The "last ice age" has availed the Acireman women "of imperva molecules" so that they can sew their own bodies painlessly and soon after, rent themselves out to men for whatever pleasures they can devise save cutting the stitches for "bodily entry" (69, 65, 66). The virtuosity and reliability of the stitches notwithstanding, a considerable number of pregnancies occur; and according to contractual agreement, the children became the common property of "equal mothers" (67). Hired by all the cities on the planet, the Sewing Harems fared poorly in "the underdeveloped countries," where they were rarely found and where less innovative practices prevailed. Nonetheless, the influence of the faddish Sewing Harems was felt everywhere, and natural motherhood became an infrequent practice, enabling "self-respecting individuals . . . to add to their goodness via self-improvement and self-development." Since "they were taught that they were at the root of the planet's woes" and deemed "pariahs," the children of the Sewing Harems turned themselves into "irrational demons," "idolized motherhood," married only one another, developed a "notorious talent for obscene stonecutting," and transformed the Madonna of Love in "Levitation" into a "Superior Goddess" called "Mom." To her was attributed a single role—nurturing the "urge to spawn." From their worship of her came the birth of more savage pariahs. Idolators, the offsprings of the Sewing Harems not only murdered sewn women, they erected "religious statuary" in the "shapes of huge vulvae" to honor their goddess. Life on the planet continued in this way until technology improved the thread for sewing, making it virtually unsnippable, ensuring the permanence of the stitches until death. Owing to the scientific advances, the outcasts became the "only source of mothers" and "bred like monkeys . . . until the great stone vulvae covered the planet from end to end" (70, 71, 72, 74).

The inhabitants of the planet Acirema have contravened nature; they have transformed the ordinary into the extraordinary and have made experience of the self the center of life, an end in itself. In the daily lives of the Aciremans, continuity, the root and ground of any society, has ceased to matter. Ozick's parable not only traces the implications of the Freudian attitude toward women but addresses those radical feminists whose zeal for egalitarianism eventuated in the very segregation they sought to dispel. And going deeper, "The Sewing Harems," like "Levitation," "Shots," and "Freud's Room," concerns art. With consummate wit, the parable clarifies and dissolves the commonly held view that childbearing is tantamount to the artist's toil.

If Ozick satirizes the avoidance of "*the* event of the race" in "The Sewing Harems," in "The Hole/Birth Catalogue" she argues that "To make of the giving-birth a lifelong progression of consequences is to make a shrine of the act" (257). Demonstrating that Freud's famous declaration, "Anatomy is destiny," leads inescapably to the conclusion "The destiny of anatomy is death," Ozick considers the lives of women born into a culture that enjoins them to think of themselves "as a hole; the *Ur*-hole, so to speak," and imposes on them duties that have nothing to do with their brief participation in the events of childbirth (260, 251). To be a creature who expels "an infant out of her hole," is to wear a "cloth tube cut off at the knees instead of two cloth tubes cut off at the ankles" (251). Such a creature can often be found "sewing another cloth tube" and living the life the "hole in her body dictates," a life that reduces her to a hole and thrusts her "into a nullity" (A&A 251, 252). Although "The Sewing Harems" contains no mention of Freud, the planet Acirema is clearly a place where females have defied the destiny Freud envisioned for them; they have sewn their own vulvae rather than make clothes for children.

The second fragment from the refugee's notebook answers the mad letter writer whom Ozick quotes in her essay. He accuses women of "overpopulating the earth and ruining our ecology," he warns them of the "animosity toward . . . over-whelming womb-output! Toward . . . selfish spawning," and he predicts the reverse of what the pariahs enact—the derision and murder of pregnant women. To his railings, Ozick responds, "The death instinct, having given up on the primal father, is ganging up on pregnant women." Because he limited women to the role of childbearers, Freud made them into "disgorgers of corpses" and "nullified [them] into an absence" (A&A 258, 259, 255, 257). Stripping from women all importance save for what emerges from their vaginas makes them destroyers; removing from women the desire to procreate guarantees the annihilation of humanity. Taken to either extreme, the issue of childbirth becomes a "species of idolatry." In Ozick's sewing metaphor reside conflicting moral truths. If in "The Hole/Birth Catalogue" sewing signifies the constricted lives led by women, in "The Sewing Harems," the activity mirrors their self-indulgence, the opposite of what Verity achieves: her sewing resurrects the past and ensures continuity. Imbuing the same metaphor with differing significations, the storyteller advances one idea and then ventures a contrary one. Such incongruities are glossed over by other writers; in Ozick they are heightened. Tributaries from Ozick's river of ideas, "Levitation," "Shots," and "From a Refugee's Notebook" swell into divided currents which meet again and form a confluence in "Puttermesser: Her Work History, Her Ancestry, Her Afterlife" and "Puttermesser and Xanthippe," the chronicle with which *Levitation* ends.

II

When her biographer begins to recount her "work history," "ancestry," and "afterlife," Ruth Puttermesser is thirty-four, a lawyer, "something of a feminist," though not a "crazy" one. Two years younger than the narrator of "Shots," the attorney lives the way the photographer does, alone "among other people's decaying old parents," enraptured with "last century's faces" (21, 40). She shares the photographer's desire to preserve history. In "slippers left over from high school," Puttermesser roams the "same endlessly mazy apartment she had grown up in" and keeps "weeks' worth of Sunday *Times* crossword puzzles" to work on "indiscriminately." Her desire to remain in her parents' apartment, her absorption in facts, her fascination with puzzles, her drive to study—these, her biographer tells us, do not describe an "egomaniac out for aggrandizement"; they reveal that Puttermesser "was looking to solve something, she did not know what" (21–22). Like the "mazily interconnected" upper rooms at Duneacres in *Trust*, which promise to unlock the mystery of the narrator's origins, the apartment Puttermesser inhabits, her crossword puzzles, and her relationship with her father augur a quest similar to the one undertaken by the narrator of *Trust*. And the antithesis between law and art, a prevailing one in Cynthia Ozick's fiction, continues to inform the Puttermesser tales.

Puttermesser's "personal history" testifies to a clash between the law and the imagination. Hired by a "blueblood Wall Street firm," Puttermesser, who "had a Jewish face" and spoke without any trace of "regionalism," believes herself "indistinguishable from the others" and detects "little discrimination" in the firm, though "three Jews a year" are disqualified for promotion (37, 23, 26, 25). At such moments Puttermesser's thoughts about Dreyfus are significant, for his obliviousness to the upsurge in antisemitism was connected to his assimilation into a society to which he was loyal and in which he felt secure. A warning to assimilationists who sought to become undifferentiated people in the modern world, the Dreyfus case prompted many Jews to return to Judaism and rekindled the Zionist idea.[19] From Dreyfus's fate comes a historical lesson like the one Tchernikhovsky learned in paradise. Although Puttermesser never denies her Jewishness, she remains in the "back office," hunting up "all-fours cases for the men up front," noting the exclusion of Jewish men from athletic clubs, observing the men's growing anxiety at not being moved into the front offices, and witnessing the men's departures from the firm she is convinced discriminates neither against Jews nor women. At her farewell meal with the firm's partners at a club barring women, she becomes aware of their antifeminism; their "anthropological" interest in the "rites of her tribe" confronts her with their antisemitism. In her next job with New York City in the Department of Receipts and Disbursements, she discovers civil bureaucracy, patronage lists, and witnesses the transience of power. Consigned to the ignominy of the Municipal Building, the brainy Ruth Puttermesser works for a commissioner who cultivates "bluebloods," pursues boating, and understands nothing. Of Puttermesser's situation, her biographer writes: "Now if this were an optimistic portrait, exactly here is where Puttermesser's emotional life would begin to grind itself into evidence. . . . Puttermesser would end her work history abruptly and move on to a bower in a fine suburb. This is not to be" (25, 27, 31).

Away from the Municipal Building, the lawyer studies Hebrew grammar in bed. The "permutations of the triple-lettered root" elate her. The capacity of the Hebrew verb's three letters to "command all possibility simply by a change in their pronunciation, or the addition of a wing-letter fore and aft" impresses her "as a code for the world's design." That three-lettered verb suggests the reason for the story's tripartite title and the significance of the number three to her work history (23). If the triple-lettered root promises to reveal to Puttermesser the world's plan, "indissoluble, predetermined, translucent," she envisions the "idea of the grammar of Hebrew" as a "trinity" which, her biographer observes, transforms her "brain into a palace, a sort of Vatican" filled with "resplendent" triptychs (24). An apt analogy for Puttermesser's brain, the Vatican Palace houses such collections as the Greek and Roman sculpture museums, the Museo Pio-Clementino, the Sistine Chapel, and the Gregorian Museum of Pagan Antiquities. That Puttermesser's brain resembles a treasure-house of art implies her allegiance to it; that statues from the Hall of Muses, Greek vases from the Etruscan Museum, and frescoes of Michelangelo crowd her mind intimate that pagan art is among the riches lodged in her intellect. A visual equivalent of it are the Hebrew prophets and pagan sibyls occupying the ceiling in the Sistine Chapel; representing her divided mind, they indicate the direction from which, in "Puttermesser and Xanthippe," the lawyer will fall.

"Rooted bleakly" in her "gray" cell inside the Municipal Building, the city attorney's imagination rises beyond it, and the clash between the law and her fancy brings forth a "luxuriant dream, a dream of *gan eydn*"—a "reconstituted Garden of Eden, which is to say in the World to Come" (28, 31). That paradise for the righteous was for the rabbis a place distinct from the terrestrial Garden. The Tree of Life stationed in the center and filled with a myriad of trees, *gan eydn* was thought to consist of seven divisions corresponding to the seven classes of the righteous who in turn were ranked by degrees, "one higher than the other," and allotted an appropriate dwelling in paradise. To its third division belong the great scholars whose devotion to the study of Torah provided them in paradise with the "solution of the intellectual difficulties which had beset them on earth."[20] Whatever division they occupy in *gan eydn,* the righteous will be served the flesh of Leviathan at a feast.

In "Bloodshed" Ozick alludes to the survivors studying Scripture in paradise; in "Usurpation" to the paradisal banquet. In "Puttermesser" she incorporates into the lawyer's dream of *gan eydn* the reward accorded to the third class of the righteous and changes the principal course of the banquet, transforming the traditional vision of paradise into a mirror of her character's psyche. Instead of snacking on Leviathan and studying Scripture in the World to Come, Puttermesser imagines herself sitting under a tree in Eden in "an uninterrupted forever," indulging in an endless supply of fudge and reading library books "sans librarians and fines." Just as the pious scholars in paradise will solve the intellectual problems that perplexed them on earth, so if Puttermesser "still does not know what it is she wants to solve, she has only to read on." Fancying herself among the third class of seven in *gan eydn,* she reinvokes the number three to which she attributes a key to the world's plan and which signals her intellectual explorations in paradise (32).

There she will read such trilogies as Sigrid Undset's *Kristin Lavransdatter* and Dmitri Merezhkovski's *Christ and Anti-Christ,* books related to the problems besetting Puttermesser on earth: Undset's heroine and Ozick's rise against their fathers' wishes and in the last volume of his trilogy *Peter and Alexis,* Merezhkovski attempts a synthesis of pagan and Christian beliefs. "Insatiable Puttermesser," comfortable in Eden and unafflicted by eye fatigue, will study, along with Roman law, "religions of ancient civilizations," the histories of China, Russia, and Iceland. She will peruse three biographies: one of Beatrix Potter, an independent woman like herself, another of Lytton Strachey, a biographer who revolutionized the art of writing biography, and one of Walter Scott, a lawyer who turned his efforts toward literature the way Puttermesser does in her dream of the World to Come.

"To Postulate an afterlife" is to play "a game in the head" and enter the realm of fantasy, where the reality of facts ceases to matter. Attorneys, Puttermesser and George in "The Dock-Witch" find themselves caught between the law and their imaginations. The governing force of George's reveries is paganism, that of Puttermesser's the Jew's need to "own a past." Discovering herself "in the world without a past" with a mother "born into the din of Madison Street" and a father "nearly a Yankee," Puttermesser not only presupposes an afterlife, she "dares to posit her ancestry." Her biographer records a conversation between Puttermesser and her Uncle Zindel, from whom she is learning

Hebrew, assures us the lawyer has "not much imagination" and "is literal with what she has," and then reveals Zindel died before Puttermesser was born. Called into being out of her need to "claim an ancestor," Zindel is her fancied surrogate father who, unlike Puttermesser's father, possesses a tradition to transmit. Ruth Puttermesser and Una Meyer adopt other fathers but for different reasons. To see hers, a former *shammes* (a synagogue sexton), the lawyer travels to the outer fringes of New York the way the girl journeys to Duneacres (32, 36, 38, 35–36).

Before she can learn about the triple-lettered root, Puttermesser must climb "three flights of steps" and wait for Zindel to boil the "single egg" he brings up from a Cuban grocery each evening. At first Zindel tells Puttermesser her name "Butterknife" is a "joke"; then he contrasts the one name—*messer*—Jews have for a knife with the plethora of names others have: "By them they got sword, they got lance, they got halberd. . . . cutlass, pike, rapier, foil, ten dozen more." Finally, he fastens to Puttermesser "Judaism's declared life principle": "A *messer! Puttermesser*, you slice off a piece butter, you cut to live, not to kill. A name of honor, you follow" (*Levitation* 33, 35; A&A 256; *Levitation* 34–35). In Zindel's explanation is a law crucial to Judaism. And the storyteller connects to the "wings" of Zindel's eyes the flight imagery that prevails in *Levitation:* the *shammes* envisions Puttermesser airborne, like the Jews in "Levitation," "voyaging" to Israel over the "Tomb of the Patriarchs." To the image of flight and the number three Ozick links the egg; they coalesce into a metaphor for Covenant, the code for the world's design. Reminiscent of the cosmic egg in *Trust*, Zindel's hard-boiled egg adds to the associations in Ozick's first novel the egg's significance in the Jewish tradition. Placed on the Seder plate at Passover—the festival commemorating the exodus of the Israelites from Egypt and celebrating their emergence from bondage and idolatry—the egg is a reminder of the original festival offering, a symbol of spring.[21] And the bulk of an egg is the most common of all measures in the *halakhah*.

Because her father refuses to obey *halakhah*, Puttermesser thinks he is an "anti-Semite." But she fancies the legendary Zindel a repository of the "holy letters"—the three letters to which are anchored a "whole language, hence a whole literature, a civilization even." He is the provenance of her legacy, he "is all her ancestry." Of the world that is, there is only the "blank" of America, the void around which her assimilated parents weave their lives. Inside the Municipal Building, its windows filled with the view of lower Manhattan, Puttermesser sits in her cell while dusk darkens the Brooklyn Bridge: "The bridge is not the harp Hart Crane said it was in his poem. Its staves are prison bars" (36, 37, 38). Born into the America Crane envisioned as the New Jerusalem, the lawyer "strains beyond the parents," beyond the "blank" of a New World to the "teeming" of an ancestry, a tradition, a sure identity. To know herself, to learn her name, the narrator of *Trust* must uncover her past and discover her father; to own a past, to learn the meaning of her name, the lawyer has to invent an ancestor and secure a link in the chain of tradition. The product of her fancy, Zindel epitomizes the freedom of the imagination, its power to redeem the past and so ensure a future. Declaring Puttermesser an "essence," not an "artifact," her biographer detaches herself from the lawyer's life, announces the lawyer "is henceforth to be presented as a given," and concludes this chapter of Puttermesser's life. But the last line of the story—"Hey! Puttermesser's biographer! What will you do with her now?"—promises another chapter of Puttermesser's biography (36–37, 38).

What Puttermesser's biographer does next is the subject of "Puttermesser and Xanthippe," a novella in twelve parts. Echoing the tripartite division of "Puttermesser," part 1 of the novella, "Puttermesser's Brief Love Life, Her Troubles, Her Titles," reveals that her biographer has predicted the lawyer's future accurately: "Puttermesser will always be an employee in the Municipal Building. She will always behold Brooklyn Bridge through its windows; also sunsets of high glory, bringing her religious pangs. She will not marry. . . . The difficulty with Puttermesser is that she is loyal to certain environments." In fact, the forty-six-year-old civil servant's situation remains unchanged: still avowedly single and fervently intellectual, Puttermesser feels "attacked on all sides." Her married lover Morris Rappoport has left her; she has developed periodontal trouble. Worse: "Her office life was not peaceable. . . . She had fallen." Once daring to posit an afterlife and claim an ancestor, Puttermesser now "dreamed an ideal Civil Service" (31, 77, 81, 85).

Rappoport abandoned her after she read aloud to him in bed from Plato's *Theaetetus* instead of making love. Indeed her choice of Plato over Rappoport humorously illustrates his observation that "she had the habit of flushing with ideas as if they were passions." In the first chapter of her biography, Puttermesser is described as studying Hebrew in bed and finding in its triple-root a "code for the word's design"; in "Puttermesser and Xanthippe" the lawyer adopts Plato's dialogue on knowledge as a model for the intellectual's life. The passage Puttermesser reads from the *Theaetetus,* itself part of a trilogy, glimpses her fate; for the philosopher Thales, who fell into a well while looking up to study the stars, exemplifies the distinction Socrates makes between a life devoted to philosophy and life as it is commonly lived, especially in courts of law.[22] Puttermesser identifies with the philosopher's situation, but fails to understand its irony—the radical difference between philosophy and law. Surveying "the landscape of the bureaucracy," the lawyer falls into its wells of succession because she is unaware of what is taking place before her own feet: the Idea, not the quotidian, captures her (99).

The idea of the *Theaetetus* seizes Ozick as well, but if Ruth Puttermesser misses its irony, her creator misses none of it; and Ozick's brilliantly imaginative use of Plato's dialogue illuminates the deepest recesses of "Puttermesser and Xanthippe." What is knowledge is the question around which the dialogue is constructed; but Socrates shows the three answers given to the question are wrong and indicates that the theme of the dialogue *"is not knowledge but the possibility of error, which is grounded in the 'similarity' of the 'Same' and the 'Other' insofar as they are ruling beginnings. This similarity has its mimetic counterpart in the similarity of Socrates and Theaetetus, who are playfully made to represent the 'Same' and the 'Other'* " (Klein 145). One of the novella's themes is the fall into error, and in the tale of Puttermesser and her counterpart the golem, who is named after Socrates' shrewish wife, Ozick roots error in the failure to recognize the fundamental alikeness of the Same and the Other. She employs Plato's dialogue contrapuntally throughout her novella, and it is for this reason that the *Theaetetus* is referred to at the very beginning of "Puttermesser and Xanthippe"—to herald the presence of the Hebraism-and-Hellenism controversy that in the novella is a battle between the Ideal pursued by the philosopher and the Real which should govern the lawyer.

A passion for philosophy is congruent with Puttermesser's love of the law, even though Socrates sharply differentiates the two ways of life, celebrating the freedom of philosophers and lamenting the slavery in courts of law. Of the philosopher he observes, "his mind . . . is borne in all directions, as Pindar says, 'both below the earth,' and measuring the surface of the earth, and 'above the sky,' studying the stars . . . never lowering itself to anything close at hand" (121). Of the necessity for men to live a righteous life, Socrates explains, "we ought to try to escape from earth to the dwelling of the gods as quickly as we can; and to escape is to become like God, so far as this is possible; and to become like God is to become righteous and holy and wise" (173e). Rising and falling are central to "Puttermesser and Xanthippe," and in part 1, Ozick uses the two movements to describe Puttermesser's office life— the "fact of the Ladder itself." At first the lawyer deems it appropriate "that the Top Rung of law school should earn you the Bottom of the Ladder," but Puttermesser has "fallen" between the "heights of direct mayoral appointment" and the less lofty "rungs of the Civil Service." A "fathomer" familiar with the "tunnels" the City's "money . . . rolled through," the Puttermesser of part 1 has "traveled upward" and migrated downward. Nonetheless, she "loved the law and its language. She caressed its meticulousness. She thought of law as Apollo's chariot" (25, 83, 84).

Her descent in the Municipal Building is parallel to her moving downtown from the capacious dwelling in the Bronx to a cramped apartment on East Seventy-First Street after arsonists ravaged her home on the Grand Concourse and burned away her childhood. Of her "early mental growth" there remain her youthful compositions which her mother has preserved in Florida, reaffirming her daughter's need to own a past. And the narrator's pithy phrases, "Loss of bone, loss of Rappoport, loss of home," yoke her troubles—the destruction of her childhood, the departure of her lover, the disease of her gums. Called "uncontrollable pockets" by the dentist and "the dread underworld . . . [where] a volcano lay, watching for its moment of release" by the narrator, Puttermesser's gum disaster suggests the unruly passions that lurk behind the attorney's love for the law's orderliness. Puttermesser's "voice was like Cordelia's"; like Lear's daughter, Puttermesser "disdained assertiveness" and "was not aggressive." "Diffident" and "polite," she shuns the aggrandizement of force; yet in her apartment, where she discovered the "power to stimulate green bursts," she dreams of Cordelia's obstinacy in the face of tyranny, of the authority to construct an ideal Civil Service. Instead of the imprisoning staves of the Brooklyn Bridge, Puttermesser now envisions the "long patchwork-colored line of joggers, breathing hard above the homeland-hugging green waters." Instead of remaining "under a middle-sized tree" in the World to Come and passively taking in fudge and books, Puttermesser now imagines herself atop the highest rung of a utopian Civil Service, commanding its polity and securing its patriotism (80, 79, 84, 83, 85, 32).

But a harbinger from the Civil Service that *is* brings the lawyer news of her fall, her "ignoble" dismissal from the Department of Receipts and Disbursements. "Deprived of light, isolated, stripped, forgotten. An outcast," Puttermesser protests the injustice in a letter to the mayor, Malachy Mavett, Ozick's pun "for *Moloch ha Moves*, the Angel of Death" (Sarah Blacher Cohen 108). No reply comes and Commissioner Turtleman evicts her from her office, shoves her into an office where she can no longer see the Brooklyn Bridge, and directs her to take up her post in "the lowliest ranks of Taxation." In a humorous and telling allusion to the *Theaetetus*, the narrator comments on Puttermesser's new position, "It was an unlikely [one] for a mind superfetate with Idea" (87, 90). The connection between ideas and children is made by Socrates when he describes ideas as the "offsprings born" of one's "own soul" and himself as the midwife; he likens the knowledge of a midwife to the "tending and harvesting" of plants and his art to discerning the difference between a "mere image, an imposture, or a real and genuine offspring," between a "wind-egg" and truth (150d, 149e, 151e). Ozick's allusions prove proleptic; for "determined . . . to be responsible for life," Puttermesser has crowded her new apartment with plants and dragged in "great clay urns." Simulating the activity ascribed to midwives by Socrates, Puttermesser then acts as the midwife to the offsprings of her own soul—a golem and an ideal Civil Service. Whether they are "wind-eggs," as Socrates designates the falsehoods which in their fruitlessness are like unfertilized eggs, emerges in the remainder of the novella, but in adverting to that passage in the *Theaetetus*, Ozick implies the risk inherent in Puttermesser's activities. If Puttermesser's golem is fertile in the Platonic sense, then the golem is prohibited by Judaic law, for the dietary code forbids Jews from eating a fertilized egg, even one "tainted with the minutest jot of fetal blood" (80, 100).

Knowledge of the various ideas about the golem, a being who was thought to be magically created and whose conception developed from the exegesis of the kabbalistic work, *Sefer Yetsirah* or *Book of Creation*, enables full understanding of this richly traditional and strikingly imaginative figure in "Puttermesser and Xanthippe." The sparks of "metaphoric vitality" in the Kabbalah ignite the furnaces of Ozick's imagination, and its shaping power reconceives a unique figure created from many historical legends. Though the lore about the golem changed with time, certain fundamental convictions about it and the meaning of its making persisted. The idea of the golem in Judaism,

Gershom Scholem explains, is joined to "the ideas of the creative power of speech and of the letters" (K 351). In fashioning a golem, the adept was believed to have attained mastery over the secret knowledge of God's creation and to have participated in the ritual of initiation, to which was attached the symbolism of rebirth, owing to the idea that a golem was buried in the earth from which it also rose.

Early versions of the legend conceived of no practical purpose for a golem, whose invention was alleged to be a product of thought and a measurement of the adept's achievement. Later legends about the golem's corporeality engendered a practical and redemptive figure who served a master. Producing a golem not only confirmed man in his likeness to God but also rivaled God's creation of Adam and admonished the adept against idolatry with the letters written on the golem's forehead, for erasure of the letter *alef* from *emeth* (truth) left the word *met* (dead), which demolished the golem in an act symbolic of its creator's limitations. Other legends posited a dangerous golem of "prodigious strength" and growth "beyond measure," and they warned that "unless this tellurian force is held in check by the divine name, it rises up in blind and destructive fury" (Scholem, K&S 202). The rich matrix of beliefs from which this legendary kabbalistic figure springs makes its appeal to an imagination as protean as Ozick's unsurprising; but the golem Cynthia Ozick has imagined, a figure who implicitly represents the triumph of fantasy over reason and who is shaped from various elements of tradition and cloaked in contemporary garb, is astonishing psychologically and artistically.[23]

Witness the way she introduces the golem into the story and depicts Puttermesser's response to the unformed figure who has been fashioned. The naked girl slips into the paragraph following Puttermesser's brooding over Rappoport and imagining a daughter "memorizing Goethe's *Erlkönig*." In "The Dock-Witch" the sirenlike Sylvia sings the fourth stanza of *Erlkönig*—the lines about the Erlking's daughters—to the lawyer. Puttermesser recalls not the fourth stanza of the poem but the last stanza, in which after reporting his vision of the Erlking's daughters, the boy dies in his father's arms. The dead child transfixes Puttermesser, who "was not yet reconciled to childlessness"; a firm believer "in the uses of fantasy," she imagines daughters. Nonetheless, her memory of the dead boy in *Erlkönig* intimates her subliminal awareness of the fancy's peril, against which Ozick juxtaposes the facts in Rappoport's *Times,* now "as heavy as . . . a dead child" (92). Facts in newspapers only intensify Puttermesser's awareness of the corruption filling the city. She is unlike the narrator of *Trust,* who constantly reads newspapers and renounces magic; in imagining a magical being to effect her utopian dream, Puttermesser is akin to the narrator of "Usurpation."

With wit and perspicacity, Ozick unfolds in the paragraph following the one in which Puttermesser ponders the injustice and violence reported in the *Times* her discovery of a dead girl in her bed. Lacking an explanatory transition, the paired paragraphs, which obfuscate the boundary between reality and fantasy, replicate the free-associative process of thinking and exhibit the dynamics of the imagination. Puttermesser's struggle to prevent the ascendancy of fantasy over reality is depicted in the refusal to acknowledge the girl's resemblance to the imaginary daughters "who were Puttermesser as a child." The avowed rationalist summons reason to account for the girl's body, even as the lawyer continues to "move around and around the bed," engaging in the ritual for golem-making, and even though she recognizes the "body had a look of perpetuity about it, as if it had always been reclining there, in Puttermesser's own bed" (92–93). That look of perpetuity suggests the child's body as an external simulacrum of Puttermesser's interior sorrow over her lost childhood. Her movements mimic those in the traditional instructions for creating a golem and recall the practices Socrates prescribes to test an argument's validity, specifically whether man is the measure of all things and whether knowledge is sensing. Relying on the analogy of midwifery and the birth of ideas, Socrates subjects the argument to the traditional custom which took place after the birth of a child to determine whether it should be brought up: "and now that it is born, we must in very truth perform the rite of running around with it in a circle—the circle of our argument—and see whether it may not turn out to be after all not worth rearing, but only a wind-egg, an imposture" (169a). The procedure Socrates requires serves as commentary on the one Puttermesser adopts. Ozick invokes two rituals to reflect the tension between the Judaic conception of a golem and the Platonic apprehension of an idea to imply that the creation of a golem, which makes man godlike, is the creation of the image Socrates distinguishes from a real child and, therefore, partakes of idol-making.

That she brackets together the golem-maker and the artist as rivals of the Creator is evident in the storyteller's description of Puttermesser intent upon finishing "the thing" while wishing herself to be an "artist or sculptor"; for in reaching "out a correcting hand" and "forming and re-forming the savage upper lip," Puttermesser has completed, with her "own handiwork," a kind of Baal, a figure not unlike the idolatrous molten calf. Puttermesser names her creation Leah, which in Hebrew means "wild cow" and which intimates the conjunction of golem and idol, implicating the lawyer in idolatry. Not until the thing is completed and writes, "I am made of earth, but also I am made out of your mind" is it apparent that Puttermesser has fashioned a golem (94, 93, 94, 95, 98).

The golem's words reflect the early belief that golems were products of the psyche; but Puttermesser, who has virtually memorized Gershom Scholem's essay, "The Idea of the Golem," ignores what she has read when she creates a golem by herself. Included in Scholem's essay is a medieval commentary on the *Sefer Yetsirah* which repeats the talmudic injunction that a "sword is upon the scholars who sit singly, each by himself, and concern themselves with the Torah" and which explains why golem-making required two or three adepts (K&S 176). That Puttermesser departs from this rule affirms her isolation, suggests her hubris, and augurs peril. Her decision to name the golem Leah because "she had always imagined a daughter named Leah," the golem's desire to be called Xanthippe, the name of Socrates' shrewish wife, and the golem's claim, "I know everything you know . . . I am made out of your mind," imply that Puttermesser, like Socrates, has delivered the offspring born of her own soul—an opposing self (96–97).

Like the narrators of "Usurpation" and "Shots" and the author of the two fragments in the notebook, the lawyer purports to have "pruned out allegory, metaphor," to have shunned all manner of mysticism, to have sustained a "clean" and rational intellect—"immensely sober, pragmatic, unfanciful" (99–100). Having breathed life into a tellurian creature, Puttermesser is ambivalent about keeping it even though she knows that in the past golem-makers were "reasonable" men "of biting understanding," scholars, leaders (100). She identifies with the Great Rabbi Judah Loew of Prague, "a learned quasi-mayor," who created a golem to redeem the Jews of Prague. Unlike the literal-minded refugee who remembered that the Rabbi of Prague was "devoured by his own creation" and who speculated "that the quarry is all the time in the pursuer," the lawyer designates the golem's creators "scientific realists, serious scholars, and intellectuals" and repeatedly denies that golem-making is irrational. She is entranced by the rational basis of this activity; it is in accord with her passion for law—both Judaic and civil. That a golem "cleansed Prague of evil and infamy, of degeneracy and murder, of vice and perfidy" increases her wonder. Judah Loew's golem in particular fascinates her, for she has read how the famous rabbi "climbed a ladder"—the very metaphor she employs for the Civil Service—to reach the golem's forehead in order to erase the *aleph* and render the golem lifeless (101, 100).

The history of golems crowds her brain, and she uses each historical occurrence of golem-making to conclude that it arose not from "untrammeled figments or romances," but from the most rigorously analytical and logical thinking. Justifying the rational and pragmatic basis of golems, and at the same time assuring herself there was nothing irrational or fanciful in it, Puttermesser releases herself from any shame at what she has concocted and allows the golem to stay. Nowhere in her fiction does Ozick present the conflict between the law and the imagination so humorously, and her dazzling wit deepens the reader's insight into Puttermesser. Because the lawyer denies fantasy and feeling, she cannot recall fabricating a golem. During her "introspective stride"—a repeating motif in Ozick's fiction—up Lexington Avenue, Puttermesser weighs the golem's future. Despite her crooked tooth (another element of resemblance between the two), the golem promises to "ameliorate" her maker's "woe." Indeed, woe fills Puttermesser's life as the attorney continues her flight downward at her office. If her enemies Marmel, Turtleman, and the mayor are joined by their identical rings and by their "politics and loyal cunning," Puttermesser and Xanthippe are yoked by their resemblance to each other and by their comical struggle against the prevailing "Spoils Quota." Puttermesser's mode of estrangement finds its counterpart in Xanthippe, "a kind of foreigner herself," and the golem's style begins to infect the lawyer's (107, 111, 117).

Busy at the typewriter, the golem induces Puttermesser's wonderment: "Was Xanthippe writing a novel? a memoir?" Ozick suggests that the golem, like her maker, is a writer. The letters Puttermesser composes protesting her dismissals from Receipts and Disbursements and from Taxation embody a writer's vision of injustice and the craving to excise it. In her imaginary letter to Mayor Mavett, Puttermesser unconsciously produces a draft of the "*PLAN* for the Resuscitation, Reformation, Reinvigoration & Redemption of the City of New York*" (123). To call Marmel "the hollow accuser" is to make him Satan and to label him a dunce, the "God of this World" to whom Blake's epilogue for *The Gates of Paradise* is addressed. And Puttermesser includes in her letter lines from Whitman's "Mannahatta," which ask "for something specific and perfect for [his] city" and describe its "million people—manners free and superb—open voices—hospitality" (Murphy 485–86). It is in poetry that she discovers answers to the city's problems. Puttermesser the lawyer becomes Puttermesser the writer, and the growing unfairness in her world and her increasing reliance on the golem induce the lawyer to imagine writing the letter in which she achieves a "clarification . . . no: a clarity. She was shut of a mystery. She understood; she saw" (119).

Puttermesser understands and sees she has created a golem for the same reasons Rabbi Loew had—as an agent of redemption to preside over civil reforms. The Great Rabbi's accomplishments inspire her: "Old delicate Prague, swept and swept of sin, giving birth to the purified daylight, the lucent genius, of New York!" (120). Like Feingold she ponders past atrocities—the blood libels of Prague—but the lawyer dreams of the power to reform and restore the present. And the blueprint for that, Puttermesser discovers, has been drawn up by the golem in two days: "It was as if she had encountered this *PLAN* before—its very language." What she cannot recollect is the actual creation of the golem; but the reality of the *PLAN* forces her to acknowledge that it could not have been produced by a "mere forward apparition" and to remember the feverish speed with which she performed the rites for making a golem: "she had whirled from window sill to window sill, cracking open clay plant pots as though they were eggs, and scooping up the germinative yolks of spilling earth" (121, 122). The beginning of Puttermesser's knowledge, limned by Ozick in egg and clay imagery, echoes the beginning of the *Theaetetus,* when Socrates invites the young man, whom he closely resembles, to tell what knowledge seems to be. To clarify his objection to Theaetetus's first answer, Socrates chooses clay as an example. It would be "ridiculous" to assume, he explains, "that the questioner can understand from our answer what clay is, when we say 'clay,' no matter whether we add 'the image-makers' or any other craftsmen's" (147a). Soon after that statement, the philosopher resorts to an analogy between midwifery and harvesting, between a wind-egg and something fruitful. It is to that egg and to the egg Zindel tapped when he began to teach Puttermesser Hebrew that the lawyer's endeavors allude.

Ruth Puttermesser has become like the scholars Scholem describes, those who studied together for three years in order to understand how to create the world (K&S 175–78). To the traditional clay from which golems were said to rise Ozick attaches the egg to which accrue cosmic associations. The invention of a golem and the four parts of the PLAN conjure up the first four *Sefirot,* the images of God in His mode of creation, as set forth in the Kabbalah.[24] Its teachings hold that the world emanated from God and that the golem was sometimes understood to be a "creation of thought" (Scholem, K&S 188). In her wish to follow Socrates, the lawyer turns herself into the image-maker he describes, a midwife to a wind-egg. The philosopher's attempt to discover the meaning of knowledge in the *Theaetetus* is in "Puttermesser and Xanthippe" the route to idolatry. Identifying the attorney with the Greek philosopher, Ozick implies that Puttermesser is an exponent of Hellenism who proceeds according to the dictates of Hebraism. The harvest of that guiding principle, Xanthippe declares herself Puttermesser's "amanuensis" and announces that "Creator and created merge." Having always insinuated they are doubles, the narrator now establishes Puttermesser and Xanthippe as different aspects of the same self and their likeness divulges the significance of the golem's two names. Because "only Xanthippe could gainsay Socrates," because Leah means "wild cow" in Hebrew, and because the Rite of Leah in the Kabbalah promises redemption and "the regeneration of the light after its total disappearance," the golem is the representative of Puttermesser's unacknowledged self and the illuminator of her inner cosmos (Scholem, K&S 152).[25] The repeated references to Xanthippe as the offspring and the servant of Puttermesser's brain indicate that the golem's vaunted visionary restoration of city includes citizen as well.

A persistent form in Ozick's fiction, the doppelgänger takes on added complexity in "Puttermesser and Xanthippe" when Ozick transfers to her idea of the double her version of the Platonic conception of "being" and "becoming." Socrates reveals to Theaetetus that "nothing exists as invariably one, itself by itself," that "everything is always becoming in relation to something," that the word " 'being' should be altogether abolished," that things do not stand still, and that change arrives in the form of twins—" 'being made' " and " 'being destroyed' " (157b). It is this twoness of being, the "eidetic Two," that accounts for the Platonic idea of the "Same " and the "Other," the notion Ozick adopts to depict the relationship between Puttermesser and Xanthippe. In the *Theaetetus* (and in the *Sophist*) it becomes apparent that something is other only in relation to something else: *"Nothing could be what it is if it were not the* same; *and, on the other hand, there could not be any multiplicity of beings without 'the Other.' The 'Same' and the 'Other' are* both *indispensable for the understanding of what is"* (Klein 63). Hence the similarity of Socrates and Theaetetus, who represent the "Same" and the "Other." Hence the necessity of Xanthippe, who reveals that which *is* to Puttermesser: "Two urges seeded you," the golem tells her maker, "I am one, this is the other. A thought must claim an instrument. When you conceived your urge, simultaneously you conceived me" (124).

But Puttermesser is "afraid of the last page" of the plan, of "falling into the mouth of the Destroyer." The slyness powering Xanthippe's eyes as the golem proclaims the coalescence of herself and her creator augur Puttermesser's "blatant destiny," which the narrator reveals at the beginning of part 6, "Mayor Puttermesser" (123, 124, 126). That destiny is predetermined by Xanthippe's steady growth and by the golem's role as campaign manager of Puttermesser's mayoral candidacy, for the increasing size of a golem and its potential for becoming a kind of sorcerer's apprentice contain the seeds of its master's destruction, which Ozick foreshadows in Puttermesser's worsening periodontal troubles. They do not afflict the golem, and she names Puttermesser's party ISPI, "Independents for Socratic and Prophetic Idealism." An artist is hired to design a poster: "It shows an apple tree with a serpent in it. The 'S' in ISPI is the serpent. Puttermesser has promised to transform the City of New York into Paradise. She has promised to cast out the serpent" (128). But the name of the party and the poster portend an outcome unforeseen by Puttermesser. The party's identification with Socrates locates its ideals in Hellenism, but the presence of a serpent augurs the downfall of Puttermesser's Utopia. If Mavett, the Angel of Death, "is routed" on election day, his flight downward, along with the presence of the serpent in the apple tree, is an omen for the triumphant new mayor whose paradise is seeded with the germs of its own disintegration.

At first, however, her success allows the mayor to exercise her new found power and to take revenge on her accusers Turtleman and Marmel by firing them precisely the way they dismissed her. Her ideology now begins to "succeed for her in aggrandizing force" (84). Her voice is no longer like Cordelia's. The realization of her dream notwithstanding, Puttermesser is disconcerted by the move uptown to Gracie Mansion, for her new home reminds her of her lost apartment in the Bronx, of the destruction of her past. And the "antique dresser with gryphon feet" in the bedroom Xanthippe chooses presages another loss. Reminiscent of the gryphonlike roots on the tree from which Isaac Kornfeld hanged himself, the dresser's gryphon feet recall those "gryphons or monsters guarding all the roads to salvation, mounting guard over the Tree of Life" (Eliade, *Patterns* 291). Ozick intimates that Puttermesser, like Hercules in the garden of the Hesperides or Jason in Colchis, will have to kill the monster barring the road to salvation. In her frenzy to appoint commissioners and executives, Puttermesser ignores a warning about the potential monster she has created—the golem's "sprightliness." Instead, the mayor is intent on recruiting "noble psyches and visionary hearts": she yearns to make poets and novelists, not lawyers, the legislators of mankind and envisions writers in charge of paradise. Tempted to staff the "highest echelons of City management" with "multiple members of the genus golem," Puttermesser fancies herself their creator.

If her hubris leads her to imagine she is godlike, her ideal civil service ennobles her; for the redeemed city, like its author's mind, "upholds the values of

the conventional, the orderly, the traditional." Suffused with the light of reason, the city "has shut the portals of night." But the incessant growth of her
golem and the reflection the mayor has that "she is the golem's golem" foreshadow the dawning recognition of another and less rational self and portend
the opening portals of night in paradise. A signpost along that path is the persistence of Puttermesser's periodontal problems: "she who had abolished
crime in the subways was unable to stem gum disease in the hollow of her own
jaw." Called a volcano waiting for release earlier in the story, the deteriorating
gums are premonitory of the explosion that begins when Rappoport comes to
Gracie Mansion to congratulate Puttermesser, to convince her they should try
again. Noticing the absence of his avocado tree, whose earth Puttermesser
took to make the golem, in her new quarters, he understands the tree's fate
indicates her desire to dispose of him entirely. Nonetheless, he congratulates
her on her "Utopia. Garden of Eden." That the avocado tree, which is valued
as an aphrodisiac, is missing from the mayor's Eden ultimately proves ironic,
for Rappoport's discovery of Xanthippe comically results in Rappoport's
becoming her first lover, an event that hastens the mayor's expulsion from
paradise. His "teeth," his "reddish mustache," his "wide welcoming nostrils,"
his "briefcase bulging with worldly troubles"—these, the narrator suggests,
elicit the golem's responsiveness, the desire for an ordinary Jewish man rather
than the Greek philosopher the golem's double prefers. When Puttermesser
returns from a meeting, she finds her former lover in bed with her golem,
and the narrator ironically comments, "Eros had entered Gracie Mansion"
(135, 136, 138).

Ozick weaves into her tale mythological allusions to the birth of Eros from
the world-egg, his companionship with Aphrodite, his youth, and the peril he
brings.[26] The golem's birthplace in an apartment where "little blue fish-tiles
swam around the walls," where the "toilet seat cover had a large blue mermaid painted on it," and where even the "toilet's flush handle [is] made of
light blue plastic" suggest the presence of Aphrodite, to whom the color blue
was sacred and whose connection with the sea is well known (80).[27] When
Xanthippe buys Puttermesser a blue bedspread, Ozick suggests blue as their
emblem. Later in the tale, the mayor's allegiance to Aphrodite is hinted at
when the mayor pays tribute, in the "Blue Room" of Gracie Mansion, to an
astronaut for looking "into the bosom of Venus" (142). Ruth Puttermesser has
fashioned a golem from traditional Jewish texts, but like Aphrodite, the lawyer
has brought forth a wild god of love and procreation whose "uncontrolled
sexual passion could be disturbing to ordered society" (Graves, GM 1, 58). In
"Levitation" the Madonna of Love induces Lucy to sever herself from the
Jews; in "Puttermesser and Xanthippe" Aphrodite causes Puttermesser to fall
from the Eden she aspired to replicate.

And Eros inflames Xanthippe's ardor, the subject of part 8, aptly titled
"Xanthippe Lovesick." As the golem's fervor intensifies, so does the perception of Ruth Puttermesser's less solitary self. The narrator's opening question—"What happens to an intensely private mind when great celebrity

unexpectedly invades it?"—invites a comparison of Puttermesser and Xanthippe. Though Puttermesser has "only desires as strong and as strange as powers," though she "finds virtue to be intelligible," though "her desires are pristine," though "she has cast a divinely clarifying light," the virtue the golem possesses is doubtful, her desires less than pristine, her dark gloom palpable. One creature is cerebral and disciplined, the other passionate and unruly. If perfection generates the fame that gratifies Puttermesser, they also bring in their train a sense of the imperiled, the expectation of some resolution. And the finale Puttermesser awaits inheres in the golem's erotic languor, a connection that is indicated by Ozick's deft juxtaposition of the two sentences, "it is as if she [Puttermesser] is waiting for something else: for some conclusion, or resolution, or unfolding" and "The golem is lovesick" (139).

The narrator suggests unbridled eroticism has its roots in childhood, for Xanthippe is "two years old and insatiable." Into the traditional belief in a golem who runs amok Ozick interweaves her psychological insight: writing that she lusts after the "higher world. Office and rank. Illustrious men," the golem expresses the mayor's unarticulated desires and recalls the frenzied golem Rabbi Loew had to destroy. Xanthippe's hot blood cannot be cooled; once the golem thirsts, "she ravages and ravages." Throwing her pen into the East River, she rebels against her creator and presages the dissolution of Puttermesser's dream, an end to the Garden of Eden, which Ozick foreshadows in the freshly shattered Attic urns and the burgeoning "jungle of graffiti"—emblems of the city's ebbing halcyon days (143).

The presence of the golem's irrepressible sexual desires, a counterpart of Puttermesser's "uncontrollable pockets," is a significant departure from the kabbalistic doctrine that proclaimed the absence of such drives. A footnote in the Scholem essay Puttermesser has nearly memorized contains an explanation, ascribed to Rabbi Loew, for the lack of sexual desire in the golem: "The golem had to be made without generative power or sexual urge. For if he had this urge, even after the manner of animals in which it is far weaker than in man, we would have had a great deal of trouble with him, because no woman would have been able to defend herself against him" (K&S 194, n2). Ozick, however, has imagined a golem endowed with sexual impulses, and Puttermesser's detailed knowledge of the potentially calamitous nature of such a golem and the mayor's awareness that the "City is diseased with the golem's urge" make the delay in returning Xanthippe to the elements of her formation especially meaningful. Xanthippe's desires propel the golem to the heights— "high politics! Lofty officials! Elevated bureaucrats"—which in turn accelerate the mayor's fall. Regardless of the golem's utter destructiveness, irrespective of her cognizance that "The turning against the creator is an 'attribute' of a golem, comparable to its speechlessness, its incapacity for procreation, its soullessness," Puttermesser is ready to gainsay a golem has no soul, no procreative powers. She counters what she has read with the conviction that "having laid hold of life against all logic and natural expectation," the golem must inevitably "dream itself a double." But the simile Puttermesser fashions, the "panting furnace that cries out for more and more fuel, that spews its own firebrands to ignite a successor-fire," conjures up Moloch, the furnace-god (144, 145).

Yearning herself for a daughter "that can never be," Puttermesser cannot fault Xanthippe: "Shall the one be condemned by the other, who is no different?" The "Same," Socrates tells Theaetetus, exists only in relation to the other. But Puttermesser weeps because she knows the golem's tellurian element must be contained, because the golem runs over the city, because stories about "a madwoman on the loose, venomous against authority" are rife, and most of all, because she knows she must dismantle her creation. She is dilatory, she excuses the golem's rampages; she resists the undoing (145). It is Puttermesser's realization of a kinship with Xanthippe that manifests Ozick's insight into the warring forces of the human heart: its pagan erotic desires coexist alongside the Judaic call to conscience. The furious intensity of Xanthippe's unleashed passions attests to the fate of Puttermesser's suppressed desires. Now understood and accepted by her double, Xanthippe's eruptions are nonetheless a product of a primitive and violent will that Puttermesser sorrowfully grants must be stemmed, and so she writes Rappoport for help. In her offer to appoint him Commissioner of Receipts and Disbursements, she replicates one of the political deals that engendered her dream of an ideal civil service. But she must secure his assistance in luring the wanton Xanthippe back to Gracie Mansion.

Waiting for her to return to the bed where Rappoport lies ready to enact the first step of the golem's undoing, the downcast mayor stands alone behind Gracie Mansion imagining "she can almost descry Orion's belt buckle" and counting one rising plane after another, "each with its sharp beams like rays scattered from the brow of Moses, arching upward into the fathomless universe" (149). Garnering allusions to Hebraism and Hellenism, Ozick illuminates the interconnecting passageways of her character's psyche and the forces that agitate it. A pursuer of the Pleiades, the gigantic hunter Orion and the constellation of stars named after him reflect the fate of the mayor and her enormous golem, for like the hunter, Puttermesser aspired to the stars and fell from their heights. The shape of the constellation, a quadrangle containing seven stars with three stars running in a straight line in the center—Orion's belt—presents the two numbers crucial to the mayor's history. Puttermesser had circled the golem seven times and breathed life into it; uttering the three letters of the Name of Names; and imprinting on the golem's forehead the three letters meaning truth in Hebrew, she rivaled the Creator. Three is the predominant number in both Puttermesser tales. The three stars in Orion's belt compel the lawyer to remember the Covenant; the Greek stellar triad images her betrayal of that Covenant. Yet the stars belong to both dispensations. In both, the rising of Orion in the east signifies the onset of autumn; the setting of Orion's quarry, the Pleiades, closed "the essential activities of the year" (Austin 241). Puttermesser's mayorship is ending. And as the Mosaic triad, Orion's belt recalls God's question to Job—"Can you bind the chains of the

Pleiades, or loose the cords of Orion?"—and marks the beginning of the mayor's return to the Mosaic Idea, Puttermesser's dawning realization that the universe God created is as fathomless as He is. Recognizing she has yearned for His power and succumbed to idolatry, Puttermesser awaits Xanthippe's arrival so that she can dismantle her golem and once again yoke herself to Covenant.

The undoing of the golem is preceded by a description of its graveyard "fenced off by black iron staves" in a small park with an "upward-flying fountain" in the "shadow of City Hall." Marked by "vivid rectangles of red geraniums" that are evident to the civil servants as "the crimson slash that with wild brilliance cuts across the concrete bitterness below," the burial site symbolizes the fate of the mayor's untamed self. The red geraniums, "those great Stonehenge slabs of the Twin Towers" and the "standing Zither that is Brooklyn Bridge" rise behind the flower bed: they illuminate the meaning of Puttermesser's relationship to Xanthippe (151). Because they grow wild, geraniums symbolize earthiness, but Xanthippe's blood-colored blossoms also suggest those Greek mythological flowers thought to be stained by their god's blood. And the Stonehenge slabs, whose meaning the younger Puttermesser fantasized she would discover in Eden, befit Xanthippe, who "breathed outside history" and whose "barrow" captures the prehistoric overtones of Stonehenge: a sanctuary built to secure relations with ancestors who, projected into stones, became "masters of fertility and prosperity" (Eliade, *History* 1, 118). At the end of "Puttermesser," the narrator likens the "staves" of the Brooklyn Bridge to "prison bars"; near the conclusion to "Puttermesser and Xanthippe," the bridge—Hart Crane's "Terrific threshold of the prophet's pledge"—is seen as "the standing zither," the instrument played in the Psalms to praise God as the Creator and Lord of history (*Levitation* 150; Crane 4).

With the vision of Xanthippe's gravesite indelibly in mind, the reader follows the meditative Puttermesser and the talkative Rappoport in their ritual undoing of the golem until the last scenes of revelation are attained. The reversal of the golem penetrates to the core of "Puttermesser and Xanthippe," for the ritual simultaneously conjoins psychic truths to the meaning of Judaism. Unaware of her secret dictates, possessed by the craving to abolish injustice, and outcast by all, Puttermesser fashions a golem singlehandedly: she ignores the warnings against creating such a creature alone and the explanations Scholem provides of the "tension which the creative process arouses in the creator himself"—the danger of the creator's hubris turning against God (Scholem, K&S 191). Now Puttermesser must consciously follow the instructions for returning a golem to its element, and she includes Rappoport in the act. They walk counterclockwise around Xanthippe just as Rabbi Loew had walked counterclockwise with his disciples when the golem of Prague had to be undone; but Puttermesser "weaved round Xanthippe on the floor, as if circling her own shadow" and "could not help glancing down into the golem's face" (154, 155). Even in her white velvet shroud, Xanthippe still resembles a child, and though formerly speechless, she protests her destruction in a "child's voice, pitched like the pure cry of a bird" (155).

In creating a silent golem who at first only writes and later speaks, Ozick conflates two kabbalistic conceptions for her own symbolic purposes. According to Scholem, muteness in golems was not always the rule: golems endowed with speech proclaim the sinlessness of their creators, and golems deprived of speech indicate that "the souls of the righteous are no longer pure" (Scholem, K&S 192–93). Some Kabbalists regarded speech as the highest human faculty, "the mother of reason and revelation." Others dissociated it from reason to mark the separation of man from image. Ben Sira's golem, who was very similar to Adam, spoke to warn his makers against succumbing to idolatry (Scholem, K&S 192, 178–79). Empowered with speech just as she is about to be returned to the earth, Xanthippe cries, "it was you who created me, it is you who will destroy me" (156). To Xanthippe's fervent plea—"Life! Life! More!"—Puttermesser responds bitterly, "Too much Paradise is Greed," and she proceeds unflaggingly with the ritual undoing. Although at first Puttermesser cannot recollect her "fabrication" of the golem, although she was convinced she had "helplessly, without volition come upon" it in her bed, and although she considered it "some transient mirage, an aggressive imagining" or an "apparition," she now beholds her golem before her feet "like [her] own shadow," the bleating of Xanthippe's "little bird's cry" still resonant (121, 122, 156).

The reverberations of bird imagery are everywhere in the novella, but they reach a crescendo in this scene as Ozick augments the contradictory forces she has incorporated in her golem. When Socrates teaches Theaetetus the difference between "having" knowledge and "possessing" knowledge, the philosopher evokes the image of captured birds in an aviary for "the varieties of knowledge" (197b, 197e). In hunting for knowledge, a mistake can be made: a wild pigeon can be seized instead of a tame one.[28] A kind of wild bird, Xanthippe protests plaintively when she is about to be undone and is reminiscent of the bird sacred to Aphrodite. Athough its connection to Aphrodite betokens life, the bird's association with sirens promises death. Alluding to Greek ideas of birds, Ozick adds to them the significance accorded to birds in the Hebrew Bible: their creation is a high point in Genesis, and their ability to fly registers their freedom, their roles as messengers between Heaven and Earth, the potential for redemptive journeys. A harbinger of redemption, Xanthippe is also an omen of danger.

In undoing her golem, Puttermesser understands that she is forfeiting a part of herself, and this realization makes the reversal difficult. When she substitutes "returned" for Rappoport's "Dead" after he has erased the magical letters from Xanthippe's forehead, it is evident that Puttermesser has completed the ritual of initiation and has attained the adept's cognizance—that the golem's return to earth symbolizes rebirth. But the initiation is fraught with danger and Xanthippe's revelation is complicated, as the golem's other name, Leah, and the narrator's description of her indicate: "Huge, sly Xanthippe, gargantuan wily Xanthippe, grown up out of the little seed of a dream of Leah!" (156). In the Zohar, the Rite of Leah constitutes an expression of messianic hope, and the little seed of Leah alludes to the law of the organism, "to the image of the seed that bursts and dies in order to become wheat" (Scholem, K&S 113).[29] As Xanthippe, who "alone could gainsay Socrates," the golem unearths Puttermesser's buried self, and as Leah, the golem promises salvation.

Xanthippe's white velvet shroud conjures up the garment of light in Genesis, for the creation of a golem was thought to imitate the creation of Adam. That Rappoport covers her after she has spent her ardor, that he becomes her first lover after commending Puttermesser on her "Garden of Eden" are reminders of the fall. Originally protected by the garment of heavenly light, Adam was forced to hide his nakedness with leaves from the Tree of Knowledge after he lost his innocence and God replaced his garment of light with the garment of skin. Magic makes an appearance in the kabbalistic rendering of this event "as a knowledge serving to veil Adam's nakedness," and it is "a demonized magic, which came into being with the earthly corporeity resulting from the Fall and is bound up with the existence of the body" (Scholem, K&S 175). The conception of a dangerous golem arises from Adam's forfeiture of a spiritual garment for a material garment which, according to the Kabbalists, magically binds Adam to the earth and necessitates two garments for the Torah as well. Leah's white velvet shroud, suggestive of the garment covering the Torah or *Shekhinah* (Divine Presence), symbolizes its mystery as well as its spirituality, and suggests Puttermesser's initiation into the conundrum of creation augurs a fall from God's grace.

It is, therefore, not fortuitous that the sprightly Xanthippe resembles a child even to the end. Her longings, primitive and passionate, are desires lodged in Puttermesser. Haunted by her lost childhood and the daughters never to be, Puttermesser invents a golem who enables her to reclaim her childhood and "own a past." The seed of Leah bursts for the golem-maker's harvest, releasing a hidden self, but Puttermesser must tame its turbulence and reshape her future. Inflamed by insatiable desires, the golem is possessed by an ardor so "terrible" that she is called a succubus—a female demon whose generative powers, according to the *Zohar,* were "misused." Those powers are related to the warning against idolatry inhering in a golem, which accounts for Puttermesser's muted fears about the last page of the PLAN. Full consciousness comes when the golem runs amok in the Utopian city and, true to form, destroys her creator. In the ideal are the means to its destruction: "Eden disintegrates from too much Eden. Eden sinks from a surfeit of itself" (156). Aware that the plan has become an idol and herself its worshiper, Puttermesser, whose first name means faithful in Hebrew, relinquishes her Platonism and returns to monotheism. Unlike Una Meyer, a Platonist and a perfectionist troubled by her gums, Ruth Puttermesser confronts the meaning of her education and the implications of her illusions. If she has achieved knowledge contrary to the conclusion Socrates and Theaetetus reach—that the soul and its experiences do not afford the truth of all things—she also dismantles an essentially noble and humanitarian idea. The inventor of a visionary city and an imaginary being, Ruth Puttermesser, like all of the central characters in

Levitation, is an artist beset by the conflicts her creator ascribes to the enterprise of art. None of its perplexities is resolved in "Puttermesser and Xanthippe." If the PLAN simultaneously creates a perfect city and turns the mayor into an idolator, in the absence of the PLAN the city lapses into its former corrupt and ungovernable state.

Mayor Puttermesser undergoes periodontal surgery; its aftermath reflects her honed consciousness, for when the surgery is over, "the roots of her teeth are exposed. Inside the secret hollow of her head, just below the eye sockets, on the lingual side, she is unendingly conscious of her own skeleton" (158). Present all along and called volcanic, Puttermesser's periodontal problems represent buried desires; like the irrepressible Xanthippe and the roiling city, Puttermesser's gums are "uncontrollable." In her extraordinary devotion to the intellect, Puttermesser has denied herself ordinary and vital emotions. A life that evades personal passion, Ozick suggests, ignores the tutelage of nature and humanity's inescapable contingency on it, and the growing inwardness of such a life can foster the drive for perfection that turns into a surrogate for God. But lacking that drive and the imaginative forces to propel it, humanity unleashes its fury and its depravity. It is for these reasons that the ordinary blood-colored geraniums, reminiscent of Puttermesser's bleeding gums, breed disease of one kind or another in whomever touches them; it is for these reasons that the novella concludes with Puttermesser, like Marius in the ruins of Carthage, calling plaintively, "O lost New York! . . . O lost Xanthippe."

A tale about the conquest of self, the redemption of the past, the values of tradition, and the struggles against veneration, "Puttermesser and Xanthippe" is a biography of an artist. Recounting the events in Puttermesser's life, Cynthia Ozick explores the nature of creativity, the contours of the imagination, the paradoxes of art; she harnesses in her last novella the prevailing themes of *Levitation.* Its five fictions in one form or another all concern artists whose portraits disclose convictions essential to the storyteller's art. Of history's importance to Ozick there can be no doubt. About the value of tradition to the artist she is unwavering. To the artist's imagination, however, she attributes disquieting desires—the Faustian aspirations that betoken a Fall. But descent is preceded by flight, an organizing metaphor of *Levitation.* The predominance of rising and falling in Ozick's third collection of stories is heralded by its first and title story. In "Levitation" the power to ascend "to the sublime" belongs to Hebraism, to Hellenism the dark slide into the earth, the wild and voluptuous realm of Pan (M&M 212). Ending with the Jews' redemptive levitation and Lucy's earthbound paganism, the first tale in *Levitation* prefigures the last, in which a Jew's skybound aspirations collapse into idolatry—art's besetting danger.

Against the fluid and the life-giving, idolatry stops the current of continuity and leaves in its stead stagnant and shrinking waters, the stasis Baeck imputes to romantic religion. Throughout *Levitation* Ozick upholds the necessity for maintaining a reservoir of tradition and designates the father its agent of transmission. He or his equivalent appears in each of the fictions and embodies the relationship Ozick forges between art and tradition. The break with her father's faith augurs Lucy's eventual disavowal of an adopted tradition as well, but the photographer's allegiance to a professor of history who is himself a father strengthens the bond between the artist and tradition. Scrutinizing Freud's room, the refugee declares its inhabitant a man "who wished to be a god"; but the discoverer of psychoanalysis credited to the "opposition be-tween successive generations" the "whole progress of society" and judged the degree of separation from parental authority the measure of an individual's maturity ("Family Romances" 41). The father from whom Sigmund Freud thought independence necessary is the parent on whom Cynthia Ozick de-pends for a cultural patrimony. For that reason, no fathers appear amidst the sewing harems, whose resistance to children reflects indifference to continuity. The presence or absence of a father, the attachment to him, or the abandon-ment of him—these signal conflicting attitudes toward the idea of tradition and its value to the artist. Beginning with a tale in which the transmission of-fered by a father is refused, *Levitation* ends with a chronicle in which that transmission becomes the means to rival God, the father. Incarnated in the di-vergent meanings of the stone imagery in Ozick's third volume of fiction is the antithesis between two traditions, the dichotomy between Hebraism and Hellenism.

From Lucy's vision of the stony Holocaust victims to the photographer's image of Sam as a statue, to the stone gods in Freud's room and the great stone vulvae covering the planet Acirema, to Zindel's "flat stone roof," and finally to the Stonehenge slabs behind the flower beds marking Xanthippe's barrow, stones sometimes represent the power of ancestry, sometimes the forbidden and reverent devotion such objects command. Inhering in Freud's stone statues and the statuary on the planet Acirema is the magic of idolatry, but stone burial monuments provide evidence of ancestors, of the "dead being 'fastened' to the stone so as to be used as an instrument for protecting and enriching life" (Eliade, *Patterns* 220). Like the pillow of stone, the one which revealed to Jacob the ladder to heaven and the God of his ancestors, the stone covering Zindel in "Puttermesser" and the allusion to Stonehenge in "Puttermesser and Xanthippe" are reminders of God and the Tablets of Law and "bear the mark of some spiritual force" (Eliade, *Patterns* 220). They implicate the artist in history and tradition. And history and tradition are the stony truths of *Levitation*.

FIVE

The High Muse of Fusion

The first fiction in *Levitation* ends with a flight to redemption, the last with a descent into truth—the recognition the downhearted Puttermesser has that in venerating perfection she has aspired to forbidden heights. *The Cannibal Galaxy* begins with the meditations of a melancholic former astronomer, Joseph Brill, on the enduring situation of his life, "consorting with the Middle" (6). Movement upward and downward bulks large in Ozick's fiction. Always exercising its fascination upon her imagination, the imagery of rising and falling became the controlling metaphor of *Levitation* and *The Cannibal Galaxy,* the signal of their shared and underlying conflicts. And those were born in *Trust.* The strife between Pan and Moses persists in Ozick's second novel, which the storyteller wrote more than twenty years after her first one and in which she struggles to resolve at last the dispute between Hebraism and Hellenism. Endeavoring to merge the contributions of western culture with the legacy of Judaism, she seeks peace between the embattled kingdoms of artistic imagination and moral responsibility. To the portraits of artists in *Levitation* Ozick adds the biography of Joseph Brill, the principal of a school he has named and whose curriculum he has designed.

Echoing the speaker's situation in Yehuda Amichai's poem "Half the People in the World," one of the novel's epigraphs, Joseph Brill, a fifty-eight-year-old bachelor and schoolmaster, "has set forth on the roads made only for returning" and is caught "between the kid and the angel of death," between "halves that are so well matched" (Carmi 570–71). Amichai's metaphor not only characterizes the divided Brill but glimpses the prevailing pattern of the novel's imagery of halves, which in *Trust* points to the contest between Pan and Moses. The halves are hieroglyphs of the duality of Brill's life. Born "in the very middle of the Rue Rosiers" and "launched into the Middle of his time in every sense," Brill, in his "late middle age," remains in the Middle as the principal of a school located "in the middle of ashen America" and divided into two sides (6, 5). His belief "in the prevalence of ash," his image of himself as a "lost shell," his equating "the-things-that-are" with "the-things-that-might-be"—these bear the stamp of a "melancholic, a counter of losses" (5, 3). And his private name for the school's lake—Edmond Phlegethon—exemplifies the doubleness predominant in the novel, its contrapuntal Hebraic and Hellenic imagery. Phlegethon alludes to the biblical River of Fire present in Daniel's vision of the four beasts (7:10), to the Book of Enoch in which men are burned at the River of Fire (18, 19), and to the Greek "Fire-flaming" river of Hades described by Circe in book 10 of the *Odyssey*. A biblical emblem of divine judgment and punishment, the river flowing out of the Styx recalls the reason Odysseus journeys to Hades—to question the prophet Teiresias. Occurring at the beginning of *The Cannibal Galaxy,* the allusion to the Phlegethon anticipates the future of the main character and constitutes a metaphor for his belief in divine punishment, a reflection of the principal's own ashen history.

The casting of Joseph Brill's life began in a flat in Paris not far from the fish store his father owned to which there were two routes from home: the most direct way through the Jewish quarter and the "roundabout way," a tantalizing excursion leading past the Musée Carnavalet (8).[1] Emblems of two separate worlds, the two ways to the *poissonnerie* vivify the binary allegiances Brill has from the very beginning of his life. Pleased by the Vieille du Temple, a "street called after the overrun and rubbled lost Temple of Jerusalem," the young Joseph is allured by the Musée Carnavalet, its courtyard enfolded in "stone wings," its gateways decorated with "stone masks," its interior housing "mysterious stone ladies" (7, 8). One of those stone statues captivates him the first time he enters the museum and mistakes the stone figure of the Jewess Rachel, the nineteenth-century French actress, for "Rachel the mother of Israel" (9). His error testifies to a private wish for a unified sensibility, for the peaceful coexistence of art and Judaism. But his mother knows a "pagan hall had enticed him, an image had ensnared him" (9). The second time he steps into the Musée Carnavalet he discovers paintings of Madame de Sévigné and her daughter the Comtesse de Grignan. Not until he is older, however, does he learn that the mother's passion for her daughter had turned Madame de Sévigné's "prose into high culture and historic treasure"(11).

The path he followed as a youth, the roundabout way is an analogue to an event recounted by Henry James in *A Small Boy and Others,* and the parallel episodes advert to the buried theme in *The Cannibal Galaxy*—the evolution of the artist. What James remembers of his youth are two ways of getting home, one of which provided a "sphere of a different order of fascination . . . with more vivid aspects, greater curiosities and wonderments" (*Auto.* 16). What Ozick does with James's excursion is convert it into Brill's roundabout way. If James presents "his early life . . . in a dual light," Ozick depicts the twin forces governing the life of young Brill: "inserted wedge-like" into their "young allegiance," Europe "was to split the tender organ into such unequal halves" (xiii, 22). But Brill and James do not share the same divided loyalties. James celebrated "the thrill of an aesthetic adventure," his "instinct to grope for" the "earliest aesthetic seeds" of his life (95). Of those the portrait of Madame Vigée-Lebrun and her little girl, like the paintings of Madame de Sévigné and the Comtesse, contributed to the "beginning of so much that was to be." The "Parisian adventure," the "aesthetic evolution," the "general sense of glory"— these are the memorable events of James's youth. The Master's mother never called her son's aesthetic discoveries idolatrous. Indeed James, not Brill, was "permitted independent visits" to the museum "during which the house of life and the palace of art became so mixed and interchangeable—the Louvre being . . . the most hushed of all temples" (198–99). James's hushed temple is Brill's pagan hall.

At the Sorbonne as well as at the Musée de Carnavalet, Brill is "maddened . . . with idolatrous joy." It increases when he meets Claude, the "aesthete" whom Joseph admires for "his worship of beautiful things and beautiful words" (12, 14). The exponent of Hellenism, Claude gives Joseph a copy of Pierre Louÿs's *Aphrodite* and urges him to relinquish his "stupid Israelite squeamishness," which Louÿs claims characterized the tradition that attached to love the "ideas of lewdness and immodesty" (CG 13; Louÿs ix). In his novel the sculptor Demetrios worships the beauty of his own statue Aphrodite so exclusively that he desires nothing else; he separates spirit from sensuality, becomes responsible for the death of Chrysis, who he thinks is a Jewess, and uses her corpse as the model for his statue, "Life Immortal." Though Louÿs argues that the value the Greeks placed on love—the "most virtuous of all sentiments and the one most prolific in greatness"—affirmed their superiority, Demetrios renounces the love of a woman for the beauty of art (xv). He worships an idol of his own making. *Aphrodite* is an emblem of Claude's identification with the Greek world, and Brill's friendship with Claude recalls the relationship between James and his brother as it is recorded in James's *Autobiography*. Alluding to that bond, Ozick implies that Claude fosters Joseph's Hellenism. The aesthete takes the young Joseph to London to hear a "certain old writer" read from a book not to be published in his lifetime; and Brill hears his future predicted as he squirms in a room filled with men holding hands. In *The Middle Years* James describes a parallel incident, the "banquet of initiation," at which he reveled in the joys of his developing artist's mind. Ozick replaces James's delight with Brill's fear.

That she conceived of the old writer as pagan emerges in "The Laughter of Akiva," Ozick's novella on which *The Cannibal Galaxy* is based and which preceded it by three years.[2] In "The Laughter of Akiva" the old writer is E. M. Forster, the book he reads from *Maurice*. Although Ozick does not call the writer by name in *The Cannibal Galaxy*, she indicates who he is, and her choice is telling. In the passage read by the old writer is "the casting of Joseph's own life"; in her essay on Forster's *Maurice* in *Art & Ardor* Ozick intimates why (15). What Forster "fell in love with" at school was "Hellenism," what he believed in was the "holiness of the goddess of fertility," and what his heroes, "genuinely won to the Greek ideal of the body," were betrayed by was a "capricious and false Hellenism" (A&A 65, 73, 67). Forster's immersion in it strips his novels of religious truth, makes "his notion of Religion, which is pagan in the sense of fearfulness, imbued with the uncanniness of *lacrimae rerum*, un-human, without relation to the world of men" (A&A 77). Venerating that Elysian Field " 'where even the immoral are admitted,' " Forster placed his temple there, not upon Mount Moriah, and so ended with the "isolated lyrical imagination" belonging to a pagan (A&A 76). It is that imagination the old writer in London possesses.

But his speculation—that Joseph will become a teacher—is vexing, and on the boat-train returning home, he protests to Claude, but his special kiss frightens Joseph, invoking Leviticus, and Joseph rejects his friend. In mockery, Claude names Joseph "Dreyfus" and deepens Brill's isolation. Outsideness and antisemitism—these, Joseph's teacher Rabbi Pult claims, are the "legacy" of the Enlightenment. Drawn to Hebraism and Hellenism, Brill becomes an out-sider, an Other.[3] By developing the feeling of otherness into creative vision, James liberated himself from the sense of estrangement: "so *other*—that was what I felt: and to *be* other, other almost anyhow, seemed as good as the prob-able taste of the bright compound wistfully watched in the confectioner's window; unattainable, impossible, of course, but as to which just this impos-sibility and just that privation kept those active proceedings in which jealousy seeks relief quite out of the question" (*Auto.* 101). For Brill it is otherwise. Claude's betrayal taints the "side of the mind" lured by the illuminations of literature and history, and drives Joseph to forsake the "human adventure" for "the cold, cold skies" (16).

Astronomy is not so distant from Claude's gift or from the *poissonnerie* as Brill supposes; for Aphrodite transformed herself into a fish, a symbol of the sea's fertility, and was the muse of astronomy, Urania. An image of the Greek goddess of love, fish is to Judaism sacramental food. In *The Cannibal Galaxy* Aphrodite is an emblem of Claude's and Joseph's friendship, itself a reference to the relationship between the two artists Claude Lorrain and Paul Brill. Con-joining an artist and a biblical figure in her character's name, Ozick augurs Joseph Brill's hope to link Scripture to art in a Dual Curriculum. Both the bib-lical Joseph and the painter Brill left their homelands to achieve success in an-other country. The artist, a predecessor of Claude Lorrain, who at first rejected the naturalistic approach to landscape for the elevated and classical style and finally reconciled the ideal mode with the naturalistic, was best known for his accomplishments in painting distance and panorama in landscape.[4] But the young astronomer realizes neither the gains of the biblical Joseph nor the harmony of the northern painter: Joseph Brill cannot accom-modate the distances of astronomy to the earthly landscape of the quotidian. His vocation is an apt metaphor of the heights associated with both his name-sakes, and it recalls Enoch Vand's ambitions "to go high." A scientist, an as-tronomer whose name harnesses allusions to Scripture and art, the architect of the Dual Curriculum has a history that mirrors the tension his name suggests.

Joseph Brill followed a bifurcated path, part of which led him, like Edelshtein, to the "allure of Gentile culture," part of which yoked him to the spirit of Judaic law. In the "middle of the war" when his family and Rabbi Pult were captured during the roundup of the Parisian Jews, Brill was miraculously rescued from the Holocaust by nuns who concealed him in a convent's sub-cellar, where he was surrounded by a priest's library. Among its volumes Brill finds Edmond Fleg's *Pourquois je suis Juif,* the chronicle in which Fleg recounts his abandonment of Judaism and his journey back to it.[5] Of Fleg the priest had written, "The Israelitish divinely unifying impulse and the Israelitish ethical inspiration are the foundations of our French genius. Edmond Fleg brings together all his visions and sacrifices none. He harmonizes the rosette of the Légion d'Honneur in his lapel with the frontlets of the Covenant on his brow" (22). In fact when he was twenty, Fleg, like Brill, became part of a circle of aesthetes at the Sorbonne and Jews "ceased to exist" for him (Fleg 25). It was the Dreyfus Affair that determined Fleg's decisive return to Judaism and occasioned the recognition of a twofold identity—"absolutely Jewish and absolutely French." Of his ambivalence Fleg concluded: "This is the Jewish enigma of to-day; I shall not be able to solve it until a later time" (59). And so Brill comes to understand that in possessing two minds, he is "like Edmond Fleg": Fleg's dilemma, the tug between two loyalties, is Brill's. In the depths of the subcellar, the astronomer ascertains the means to unifying his two minds: a "school run according to the principle of twin nobilities, twin antiquities. The fusion of scholarly Europe and burnished Jerusalem" (27).

Out of his "majestic dream of peace" comes a vision of the "civilization that invented the telescope side by side with the civilization that invented conscience," a paradisal scene inspired by Isaiah, a scheme akin to Puttermesser's PLAN (27). The solution to the artist's predicament glimmers in such reflections, as Brill's observation of the matching dark green leather-bound volumes of Corneille and the talmudic tractate *Ta'anit* (Fast) affirms. Juxtaposing a passage from Proust's *Sodome et Gomorrhe* against one from the *Ta'anit,* Brill concludes that "two such separate tonalities . . . could between them describe the true map of life" (28). He adds to Puttermesser's a second key to the world's design. But a glimpse of the map of Brill's life is provided when a fifteen-year-old girl detects Brill in the convent's cellar and inadvertently ambushes him just the way another child will after the war. His forced emergence from the depths of the cellar to the heights of a hayloft, which he inhabits for the rest of the war, ends his intellectual aspirations and turns him "into a beast of the field." Living among cows, he "snuggled close to their swelled udders, between twin flanks," and the cows "seemed to him more intelligent than the man and woman who were preserving his life." He revels in the seasons, bathes "in a metal barrel that gathered rainwater" in the spring, and delights in the "icy and pure" water, the "velvet clots of emerald algae" (33). Like the pagan wedding party in part 2 of *Trust,* Joseph Brill celebrates nature and surrenders to it his will to engage his intellect as well as his desire to pursue the stars.

To imagine him one of the "bestial forms" he associated with the legacy of the Enlightenment is to intimate that Brill is both a child of the Enlightenment and its victim. Repeating the word "beast" to describe the period of Brill's life in the "wilderness of meadows," Ozick alludes to the Joseph narrative in the Bible and to that unforgettable tale, James's "The Beast in the Jungle," to which she turns in her essay "The Lesson of the Master." The essay, which was published a year before *The Cannibal Galaxy*, chronicles her fateful identification with Henry James, whose essential note, Ozick reveals, she misheard entirely and "irrevocably" because she expected the "great shining Beast of Sacred and Sublime Literature" to spring (A&A 295). Instead "all the beasts of ordinary life . . . the beasts that are chained to human experience" pounced. A warning against homage to genius, "The Lesson of the Master" inextricably binds, through the repetition of the word "beast," art to life. More largely, the essay uncovers the conflict between art and moral responsibility that is the underlying theme of her second novel and suggests that during the period she was writing *The Cannibal Galaxy*, she was in search of a way to cut the Gordian knot. Her allusions to the biblical Joseph, who learns that his fate is said to have been that he was torn by a beast (Gen. 44:23), and to the beast John Marcher awaits foreshadow Brill's future. When the war ends, the astronomer returns to the observatory where he judges himself, though still a young man, incapable of discovery, unfit for the heights of astronomy, "middling" (34). His inner conviction governs his outer perceptions. Finding everything "middling"—"his sisters, his degree, the observatory"—he becomes middling on another continent. In the "middle of America," housed once again in a hayloft, and the principal of a school he deems mediocre, Brill ignores the beasts of ordinary life and waits for the beast of genius to spring.

The Jamesian echoes in this section of *The Cannibal Galaxy* are telling: they imply Ozick's overarching concern with locating the moral sense in the House of Art, and they juxtapose Hebraism against Hellenism. When she was writing *The Cannibal Galaxy*, Ozick was preoccupied not only with two cultures but with James's later work. To France, the setting of Brill's youth, she attributes a significance other than the one the country had for James. Of Strether in Paris James writes: "It has been as yet for the most part but a land of fancy for him—the background of fiction, the medium of art, the nursery of letters; practically as distant as Greece, but practically also well-nigh as consecrated" (*Ambassadors* 301). It is to the relationship between John Marcher and Strether that Ozick turns in her thesis on parable in the late Henry James and in "The Lesson of the Master"; she embodies in Joseph Brill the traits with which James endowed Marcher and Strether. Like Strether, Brill thinks how the "Mediterranean, Europe's old puddle. . . . lapped at the isles of Greece" (17). But her youthful description of Strether and Marcher, the one Ozick set forth in her master's thesis, suggests how Brill evolved: "Strether is Marcher's fulfillment, is what Marcher *could* have been. Realization, when it at last overwhelms Marcher comes too late. . . . Man . . . must act—neither speculate upon his fate, nor conjecture grim ontologies, nor anything else." Yoking the three men, Ozick intimates the clashing forces in *The Cannibal Galaxy*.

Brill attempts to unify them by instituting his Dual Curriculum at The Edmond Fleg Primary School.[6] His decision to journey to another continent where he plans to make his dream a reality recalls the experience of his namesake. Descent and ascent—the prevailing movements in *Levitation*— pervade the biblical narrative and *The Cannibal Galaxy*. Thrown into an empty grain pit by his brothers and imprisoned in a dungeon in Egypt, the biblical Joseph—often thought of as the first Hebrew in Diaspora—gained freedom and attained success because of his skill at interpreting dreams. But Brill's pattern of descent and ascent reverses the biblical Joseph's. In his *nox perpetua* Brill dreams of the "waters of Shiloh springing from the head of Europe," a "Sorbonne grown out of an exiled Eden"; in his ascent from darkness that dream dissipates (36). "Shifting rays of lampless television," the cadenced enumeration of his losses—these supersede his illuminations (41).

And they increase his addiction to melancholy catalogues. Every spring during the season of rebirth he writes the refrain from Villon's poem, "The Ballade of Dead Ladies" on the blackboard—"Mais où sont les neiges d'antan?" (40). Rather than remember his past, the way James does in *A Small Boy and Others,* as the "boundless fruitage of that more bucolic age" and regret "in particular . . . the peaches *d'antan* . . . the sticky sweetness of which . . . childhood seems to have been steeped," Brill worships at the altar of loss (42). In "The Laughter of Akiva" the schoolmaster Reuben Karpov scrawls "Invictus" on the board. Karpov's triumphs are Brill's losses. Submitting to the fate he envisages for himself, the fate Brill ascribes to being "born into the Middle, the sea of monsters that was—*coup de hasard*—his own time," he conquers his own soul (41).

The location of The Edmond Fleg School—the "green slope" on one side of it rising "to meet the beach and the almost empty lake," the other side "deserted fields" overgrown with uncut grass, wild flowers, and weeds—reflects the halves predominant in its principal's life (43, 4). A numberer himself, Brill's "best teacher" is Ephraim Gorchak, a man who likes lists best, "especially of place names and journeys" like those in Numbers which recount the sojourns of the children of Israel and record the forty years of wandering (41, 43). Including Numbers 33:10 in her text, Ozick not only exemplifies Gorchak's mechanical method of teaching, she imparts to her novel's metaphors of lists and halves a special significance, one it shares with *Trust*. As they do in her first novel, the lists and halves in *The Cannibal Galaxy* conjure up the period of wandering in the desert, the place of transgression and chastisement, a trial of faith. Stationed amidst the " 'drift' or 'wilderness,' " The Edmond Fleg School, like the biblical desert, becomes the "locale of a period of purification and preparation for the achievement of a new goal," but not the goal itself (Talmon 51, 63).

And Joseph Brill knows how distant he is from the "galaxies; the other life, the Unknown, he might have endured" had he not been content to remain in the Middle (41). As if to retain the vestiges of his dream, he adopts *Ad astra* as his motto and fancies himself the "god" of his students' mothers, whom he sees as "nature's creatures . . . vehicles instinct with secretion," "suppliants" at whom he wields his scepter (40). The principal's vision of himself—Ozick's brilliantly ironic allusion to the biblical Joseph's dream of the sun, the moon, and eleven stars bowing down to him (Gen. 37:9)—as "of the elect" is epitomized in Brill's motto, *Ad astra*. Failing to reach the stars himself and sub-sisting on the stale learning in his memory, Joseph Brill means to attract luminaries, to snare genius. Then a philosopher, Hester Lilt, the brilliant "im-agistic linguistic logician," registers her daughter in Brill's school and reawak-ens in the principal the wish "for the return of beauty and burnished hope" (47, 53). Startled by her resemblance to Madame de Sévigné, Brill searches for the duplication of the mother's genius in the daughter. At first Beulah appears to be the child of genius Brill has longed for, but her weakness on the scriptural side of his curriculum confounds his expectations. Though the mother "dealt in scrutiny and commentary," the child is undistinguished. Though the mother writes that "language without consequence, i.e., the 'purity' of babble, is in-conceivable in the vale of interpretation," the child is mute and impassive. Her hair "divided into two round bronze curls," an ironic counterpart to her school's curriculum, Beulah is regarded by Brill as a hopeless failure, a futility; by Hester an example of the latency of genius, the basis for her theory of ed-ucation (54, 48, 72).

At Hester's symposium, "An Interpretation of Pedagogy," she attacks the "mechanistic" predictions of psychologists, their judgments "from early per-formance," their denial of the "essential 'unsurprise of surprise,'" which suf-ficed not only for art, but even more for the human configuration" (66). In her description of Hester Lilt's paper in which "analogies, allusions, hypotheses," are "heaped up," in which "strange links . . . between vivid hard circumstance and things that were only imagined" are woven, in which her "fables" are like "paintings," Ozick implies that Hester Lilt is another of the artists in *The Cannibal Galaxy* (67).[7] She embodies a version of the artistic imagination that is distinctly Hebraic, that transcends the apprehension of the imagination Ozick has reached elsewhere, and that anticipates the conclusions she reaches in "Metaphor and Memory," an essay which extends the fundamental thesis of Hester Lilt's *Metaphor as Exegesis*. Brill, however, believes Hester Lilt is "con-nected" to him by the "true and horrific Middle" and is a "looking-glass," but it soon yields back a mysterious reflection (49). He labors to understand the meaning of her name: "*Leyl*, night. Lutes of the night; night-music. Or that succubus to small boys in the ghetto, Lilith the night-demon" (51). In "The Laughter of Akiva" the philosopher is named Marla Salem, and Ozick's dou-ble allusion to Hawthorne's *Scarlet Letter* directs attention not only to Haw-thorne's Hester but to "The Custom-House," the "psychological autobiography" Hawthorne attached to his novel (Baym 266). Hawthorne's and James's autobiographies—expressions of formative experiences in the two writers' lives—are distinctly relevant to Ozick's novel and afford keen insight into the imaginative processes at work in *The Cannibal Galaxy*. Early in "The Custom-House" Hawthorne tells of "the divided segment of the writer's own nature," which he declares is completed into a "circle of existence" through writing—a mode of self-discovery, of "bringing [the writer] into communion" with himself (4–5). The Dual Curriculum is Brill's means to a unified nature, but it fails. The turbulent lakeside of the school and the unyielding authority the principal imposes on it are like two streams which cannot flow into a confluence and are fated never to be fashioned into a "continuous circle."

Artists must inevitably contend with authority, with patriarchs, those "stern and black-browed Puritans," whose attitude toward the imagination is epitomized in the words of "one gray shadow" of Hawthorne's "forefathers": " 'A writer of story-books! What kind of a business in life,—what mode of glorifying God, or being serviceable to mankind in his day and generation,— may that be?' " (10). Though they are scornful, forefathers exert their influence; as Hawthorne remarks of himself, "strong traits of their nature have intertwined themselves with mine" (9–10). The voices of these forefathers continue to reverberate. They are the authorities whose attributes neither Hawthorne nor Ozick can entirely elude, and they are the forces against which the two writers struggle. In the custom-house and in the Dual Curriculum they labor to reconcile themselves to the past, to achieve a consonance of moral responsibility and artistic endeavor, to accommodate to their longing for private fulfillment their moral imperatives.

Their shared views of art, the nineteenth-century novelist's conjectures about "meaning in general," his creation of Hester Prynne who possesses in common with Hester Lilt a "freedom of speculation" in eschewing "the world's law" as "no law" for her mind—these must have been what Ozick found so compelling in The Scarlet Letter (Feidelson 10; SL 141). In part The Cannibal Galaxy reflects her reading of Hawthorne's novel; in turn it illuminates hers, establishing a dialogical relationship between the two novelists and their texts. That significance is the presiding concern of "The Custom-House" is evident in the scene in which "Hawthorne himself contemplated the letter, so that the entire 'romance' becomes a kind of exposition of the nature of symbolic perception" (Feidelson 10). The discovery of the letter by the surveyor and his efforts to decode it exemplify the epistemological emphasis of "The Custom-House": gazing at the letter the surveyor thinks, "Certainly, there was some deep meaning in it, most worthy of interpretation, and which, as it were, streamed forth from the mystic symbol" (25). Like the surveyor, Hester Lilt deciphers the world through metaphor. The opposition to metaphors and symbols in the custom-house produces an environment "little adapted . . . to the delicate harvest of fancy and sensibility" and fixes the malleability of the writer's imagination (27).[8]

It is the conflict between his aspirations and the constraints imposed by his patriarchs that prompted Hawthorne to write in his preface to Mosses from an Old Manse of his resolve "at least to achieve a novel that should evolve some deep lesson." An impulse not unlike Hawthorne's stirs Ozick's sensibilities. Hawthorne ultimately escapes his "doom" to the Salem Custom-House and its stern, disapproving ancestors to become "a citizen of somewhere else" where he can devote himself to the imagination away from moral censure (34). The Cannibal Galaxy is on one level Ozick's response to Hawthorne's escape. What Hawthorne judged alterable, Brill accepts as final. Had he not forsaken the universe "because others were better at it," had he not, as Hester Lilt accuses him, "stopped too soon," the Middle might have ceased "to be a reality of his life." He could have ripened the "best harvest of his mind"; he could have been a "citizen of somewhere else," a denizen of the heights (SL 34).

Where Brill is all entelechy, Hester is all expectancy. Seizing on the midrash of the Destruction of the Temple and the laughter of Akiva, the talmudic scholar who began his studies at age forty and who celebrated the unpredictable, the philosopher exposes the "hoax of pedagogy." To judge "from early performance," she explains, is to weep as Rabbi Akiva's three colleagues did when they saw the fox running on the barren Temple Mount and accepted the desolation of Uriah's prophecy as final. Akiva realized the fulfillment of Uriah's prophecy secured the redemption of Zechariah's (66). What Akiva welcomed is what the pedagogue should welcome; "exactly that which appears most unpredictable . . . the surprise which, when it comes, turns out to be not a surprise after all, but a natural path"(68). The pedagogue who predicts "from the first text," not from the second; from the "earliest evidence," not "from the latest"—that pedagogue mires himself in immobility (68).

The idea of a fixed destiny is the Greek idea of fate, the opposite of redemptiveness, the *t'shuva* promised by Torah, or the distinction Leo Baeck makes between romantic and classical religions. Assaulted by the philosopher, the "mythos of cause-and-effect . . . the reality-as-given" represents her commentary on the hypothesis of psychological determination which she finds as reductive and erroneous for art as for life. (Hers is another voice Ozick raises against Freud.) To claim the philosopher's speculations belong only to the realm of Jewish education is to dismiss their urgency for the dilemma besetting contemporary culture, to sever them from their muse of fusion. Hester Lilt is among the kinds of artists Ozick juxtaposes in the novel; indeed, she echoes Hester Lilt's convictions when she redefines innovative art: "a redemptive literature [is] a literature that interprets and decodes the world" (A&A 247). And so Ozick confronts that old perplexity—the choice between life and art—to avert the need for raging in the dark. The girl who at the end of *Trust* stood on the threshold of her future before Enoch Vand and Gustave Nicholas Tilbeck, the two heralds beckoning her in opposite directions, has become in *The Cannibal Galaxy* the harbinger of their union.

Vand and Tilbeck represent separate poles of attraction, the Jew proclaiming his belief in history as judgment, the gentile declaring his credo Sacred Beauty. In *The Cannibal Galaxy* the age-old dichotomy between Hebraism and Hellenism is made to apply to more than the split between the Jewish and Gentile civilizations; the battle has become a metaphor for art itself. In the differences between Hester Lilt and Joseph Brill lies a distinction among the kinds of imaginations Ozick explores in the novel. Hester speaks of "stopping too soon," Brill of the Middle. Hester appeals to the second text, Brill to the first. Hester invokes latency, Brill allows only for genius. What Hester reviles as hoax, Brill caresses as truth. He exemplifies the "philosophy of finality" disdained by Rabbi Leo Baeck. And Baeck's description of the synthesis achieved by Greek antiquity adds to the nuances of the Middle: "Its logic . . .

is the logic of the middle term; the results are known in advance and are presented as the given point of departure. . . . always in the middle. . . . And here, too, in conjunction with this, we have the artist, the skeptic, and the sophist, the busy sophist who finds his realm in the doctrine of the dual truth and dual morality" (*Pharisees* 134). Stirred by Baeck's perception of the middle term, Ozick nonetheless struggles against the rabbi's notion of the artist's realm.

Whereas she once regarded the imagination as the "enemy of the moral life and of moral seriousness," as threatening idolatry, her creation of Hester Lilt, whom Ozick quoted in an interview, demonstrates her fresh cognition:

> in Judaism you have the greatest demand made on the imagination, to imagine essence without attribute, without portrait—"I am that I am," so that to state a contradiction, a conflict, between imagination and Judaism is really erroneous. Where the contradiction comes in is when you—I'm quoting Hester Lilt—stop too soon, when you speak of the imagination that creates things in competition with God, a thinginess imagination, an art imagination, a systems imagination, a mammalian imagination. The mammalian imagination results in idol-making. The higher imagination, the imagination that can imagine the unimaginable, the imagination that invented monotheism—this posits God. (Interview with Kauvar 395)

In the several portraits of artists in *The Cannibal Galaxy,* the storyteller paints the various imaginations she delineated in her interview. The Dual Curriculum does not exemplify the dual truths and dual moralities Baeck associates with the artist; instead, Brill's idea is the fruit of Ozick's revised conclusions about the imagination. The principal's idolatry resides not in the heights to which the principal aspires, nor in his Dual Curriculum, but in his stopping too soon.

Which is to say, his obsession with the middle has become an idol. In "exile from the word" himself, he misinterprets Beulah Lilt's silence as that belonging to a "deaf-mute" (52, 56). But in *L'Exil de la Parole,* the book to which Hester calls the principal's attention, André Neher adduces the ontology of silence, its essential ambivalence in the Bible, the absolute silence of Auschwitz, the challenge of silence, its relation to the "key word" in Jewish thought (237). "Perhaps" signals "optimism" and "potentiality"; in the risk of silence, Neher concludes, lies its power and its hope—the "uncompleted" (237). Overlooking the potentiality latent in Beulah's silence, Brill ignores the "Jewish option of hope" in Fleg's "vertically oriented dream," and so the principal of The Edmond Fleg School removes from his lexicon the key word in Judaism (Neher 144). His exile from that word places an embargo on his future; his exile from *parole* returns him to an "aural culture . . . the most significant loss of all" (M&M 167).[9] The inventor of a dual curriculum is wed to neither of its ideals. He dreams of being swung by the telescope at Mount Palomar up toward the "vast mirror . . . that sucked in the reflections of the stars" where he affirms what he already knows and what the "calm flat image of Hester Lilt's smile" reflects: the philosopher does not recognize him, does not include him among the stars (55). At first a looking-glass he felt himself "capable of staring straight into," Hester Lilt appears in his dream as part of the "terrible cold-ness" of the cosmos, a "long finger tapping" (49, 71).

Her disapproval coalesces with Claude's: "It was as if someone had set on him, for the second time (Claude was the first), a sacred stain" (75). The prin-cipal thinks of her as "A Brahmin among untouchables, red-stained in her brow's precise center"; her apartness ignites the "scarlet flare of his own bright dream: serenity, absorption, civilization, intellect, imagination" (75). Ozick aligns her Hester to Hawthorne's and adds to the multiple meanings of the scarlet letter—"art as inspiration, art as transcendental symbol, and art as verbal construct or form"—art as interpretation (Baym 269–70). Brill's mem-ory of the passage from Louÿs's *Aphrodite*, which Claude once made his friend memorize, stirs the principal's "Orphic melancholy" (75). In *The Cannibal Galaxy* Brill copies a "fragment of the fable from *Aphrodite*—"The Tale of the Enchanted Lyre"—on the blackboard and in "The Laughter of Akiva" Karpov writes the first three lines from Tennyson's "Come Down, O Maid" on the board—both image the conflict between art and life which Ozick re-veals herself to have experienced in "The Lesson of the Master" (1982). Dis-tant from life's ordinary and quotidian events and from both kinds of art—Hester's Hebraism and Claude's Hellenism—which he had once longed to combine, Brill "felt the thoroughness, the repletion, of the curse of perpetuity. Hydra-headed replenishment. Keats's urn, but overflowing" (76).

Symbol of unchangingness and lifelessness, Keats's urn haunts the story-teller's imagination; Ozick refers to the urn overtly and implicitly throughout her work.[10] In *The Cannibal Galaxy* the stilled time on Keats's urn mirrors Brill's plight; like the lovers on the urn, he remains frozen in sameness, "for ever panting," forever unfulfilled. However, Ozick's allusions to Keats, like those to James and Hawthorne, mark not only an engagement with the poet, but variance from him. If Keats corrected Shelley's "little circumscribe[d] straightened notion" of the world as a "vale of tears" and characterized it the "common cognomen of this world among the misguided and superstitious," Ozick proclaims Keats's *"sense of Identity,"* which the poet considers "the purpose of forming the *Soul* or *Intelligence,"* insufficient and so emends his cognomen—"The Vale of Soul-Making"—to "The Vale of Interpretation."[11] If Keats calls the *"world* a School instituted for the purpose of teaching little children to read," designates the *"human heart. . . .* the teat from which the Mind or intelligence sucks its identity," and names the "System of Soul-Making" the "Parent of all the more palpable and personal Schemes of Re-demption," the Soul, man's "altered nature," Ozick envisions a School instituted for the purpose of teaching little children to combine the "provings and alterations and perfectionings" that form human "Identity" with the stan-dards that enable humanity "to make ultimate distinctions" and will itself to "right conduct" (M&M 27).

In such a school, redemption inheres in the unexpected, the capacity for change. To "look for the unexpected in everything" is, for Brill, to "negate"; for Hester Lilt, it is to "negate nothing" (82). The principal shares the pagan rabbi's dilemma, though Brill believes it is the philosopher who has given birth to a contradiction of herself. Determined to detect the "amazing mother" lurking in the daughter, Brill summons Beulah to his office. Under the "portraits of the three sages"—his photographs of Freud, Spinoza, and Einstein—he attempts to penetrate her impregnable silence. But her "absence of language" confounds him, her "stony eyes" provoke him (84). Linking the unfurled future of a young child to the shrinking one of a man in late middle age, the principal proclaims the child as well as himself void of genius. Quoting Hester Lilt, he cites the trio of venerable men as examples of genius, of men "who were never in contradiction with themselves," men who "never stopped too soon" (84, 85).

And so he writes off the philosopher's daughter. His curiosity halts, he abandons his dream of genius; he lapses into "his schoolmaster's grief." On the sand near the Phlegethon, he fathoms Tithonus's hell and shudders at the prospect of dwelling forever among immortal youth, of "dying of lack of death" (86). Sunk into the sand, the empty shells—lifeless reminders of Aphrodite—prompt Brill's determination not to "vary from the kindly race of men," but to join it by marrying. The scene of the principal's decision is also the scene of Brill's defeat. Once in pursuit of Aphrodite Urania, Joseph Brill aligns himself with Aphrodite Pandemos. Once in quest of the stars, he plummets to the sand. The vessel of Venus's birth place is in the *Zohar* and in Jewish mysticism the *kellipot*. "Husks" of evil, the source of dross, the shells represent the "dark forces" of the *sitra achra*—"the other side" (Scholem, K 125, 138).[12] Though they eventually were thought to be the life-force, the nurturers of lights in the Lurianic Kabbalah, it is clear that "those primeval shells" in *The Cannibal Galaxy*, the "life in them cleaned out, scooped, eaten, decomposed," are emblems not of life, but of the "last links of the chain of emanation where all turns to darkness" (CG 86; Scholem, K 125).[13] The glimmering dawn on the beach of the Phlegethon brings not the illumination Hester Lilt can provide in the "blindness" of their telephone conversations but a dark realization. Feeling "himself both hidden and exposed" during his talks with Hester, Brill remains as impregnable as her daughter proved to be (88). The mother, however, questions the consequences of his anecdotes and instructs him in the interpretation of narrative and the language that inhabits it. She teaches, in other words, the literature of redemption. But he never penetrates the secrets of her life, its "simplest datum" (88). Even the identity of Beulah's father is never made plain to him. A visit to the philosopher's home, where he witnesses an ordinary birthday party, strips away the last shred of his urgent interest in Beulah: he dismisses the "orphan of the future" as the "mystical salvation" of the philosopher (92).

In his office, the orphan of the past feels the "severe stare of genius" from "his three hanged men" whom he had yoked "on the wall behind him. . . . like suns, to warm his back. Freud, Spinoza, Einstein. The mind, the universe, the abyss between" (94–95). The trio of hanged men conjure up the hanged gods described by Frazer. But the mention Ozick makes of the three men in "Toward a New Yiddish" and her allusion to the scene in *The Scarlet Letter* where Hester Prynne and Pearl visit Governor Bellingham's mansion reveal the significance of the photographs. Here, then, is the description of the portraits adorning the hall extending through the mansion: "On the wall hung a row of portraits, representing the forefathers of the Bellingham lineage. . . . All were characterized by the sternness and severity which old portraits invariably put on; as if they were the ghosts, rather than the pictures, of departed worthies, and were gazing with harsh and intolerant criticism at the pursuits and enjoyments of living men" (72–73). That Brill clearly feels the harsh criticism of his departed worthies, his modern forefathers, is evident; what they represent is anticipated in "Toward a New Yiddish."

In that essay Ozick discusses the careers of Freud, Spinoza, and Einstein in the context of exile as "cultural opportunity" (155). She disputes George Steiner's claim that "outsideness" is "most within the 'genius of Judaism' "; she disclaims his portrait of the Jew "enabled by otherness" (155, 156). But Steiner's observation that the "tenor of modernity" owes substantially to Einstein and Freud survives, though Ozick has revised Steiner's conclusions considerably, in the trio of sages to whom Brill attributes genius (146). Unable to attain genius himself or to accept its latency in a child, Brill concludes, "He was nothing beside these sages. . . . he lived in the abyss," the abyss Einstein represents (95). To connect himself to Einstein is to inhabit a universe where truth is relative, where the speed of light is the only absolute. But Freud's determinism and Spinoza's emancipation are as relevant to the nature of that abyss as Einstein's theory. The tenor of the post-Enlightenment accounts for outsideness: it fosters Joseph Brill's contradictions and Joseph Brill's failures.

Inured to the Middle, Brill seeks escape from otherness and entry into ordinariness. Tall—he was always attracted to the heights—and many years his junior, Iris Garson, the new clerk-receptionist, captivates him because of her normalness. Like the photographer in "Shots," Brill is prey to infatuation and lured by "insubstantial mismatchings"—the chimerical longings he imputes to his divided soul (57, 61). His attitude toward women betrays scorn and fear; he regards females the way Pincus Silver does, and concludes they are unreliable, "chaotic, disorderly" (40).[14] As for the women to whom he is drawn, they are never "appropriate": he "recoiled" from such women (57). To fabricate tales, which "all had the gauzy sliding wink of Claude," of an unforgettable, lost sweetheart is to evade suitable women, to awake one day to see "he was older than he had ever been before," to face what Hershel Edelshtein and Pincus Silver behold in their mirrors (58, 59).

Brill's lies, however, recall Lushinki's. Escaping from the "roil of Europe" to another continent, Lushinski pursued "little round brown mounds of . . . girls" whom he "pressed . . . down under the trees" (*Bloodshed* 16). Leaving his "middling" life in Paris for the middle of another continent, Brill longs to follow the Nigerian dancer Dyduma Mbora "to Africa, to fold himself into knife blades of equator-heat for the sake of her wood-brown cheeks and berry-dark lips and polished mahogany thighs!" (61). The principal's resemblance to the diplomat is suggestive, the fictions' interconnecting metaphors revealing. In "The Laughter of Akiva" Ozick calls the Nigerian dancer Dyadya Ngambe and intimates the significance she attaches to the relationship between Lushinski and Brill. The image of the hanging boy, which in "A Mercenary" links the childhoods of Morris Ngambe and Stanislav Lushinski, is the "trick" in *The Cannibal Galaxy* that elicits only a "diffident near-smile," from Beulah Lilt. Marking her separation from the laughing children, her smile mystifies the principal, but that episode and his infatuation with the Nigerian dancer incarnate the ecstasy of paganism (72).

Brill withdraws from the restraint and responsibility of Judaism when he marries Iris Garson and only dangles "on the rim of infatuation" with Hester Lilt (77). He chooses a pagan goddess instead of a Jewish heroine. The fleet-footed and winged messenger of the gods and goddess of the rainbow that touches both sky and earth, Iris bears a resemblance to the Harpies and the birdlike sirens.[15] The heroine Esther, the biblical name for Hester, delivered her people from destruction; in Jewish legends, she is named after Venus, the morning star whose light outlasts that of other stars. Brill refuses the light of deliverance, and Ozick's description of Iris implies to what Brill is allured. Named after the goddess who was known to do others' bidding, Iris Garson recalls Xanthippe, the sirenlike golem. The link between Iris and Xanthippe is forged in Ozick's depiction of Iris: "Her teeth were bright but crooked, and this crookedness struck his still-foreign vigilance as a curiosity. . . . The ceiling light over his desk tapped this stuck-out front tooth and gave him back indecipherable impish semaphores" (103). Those are the impish signs he follows like a sailor in the trail of a siren's song.

That Brill is drawn to a young woman whose name alludes to a Greek goddess and who conjures up sirens recalls the delegation of mothers who come to his office: "Sirens moaning afar, perilous" (95). The enchantresses' songs belong to the forces of nature and are conjoined to the songs of the birds with which sirens are traditionally linked. That tradition animates the principal's thoughts, for the mothers are not only sirens, they are "egrets twittering over their nestlings," "motherhood red in tooth and claw" (40). Laced together in the novel's tapestry are various images of flight and ascent to which bird imagery is related. Infusing the novel's themes with doubleness, Ozick imparts to each image a double meaning. If birds signal the power and beauty of nature, the bird is also an image of peril. Brill hears Hester Lilt's voice as the "dark bird's caw of dark Europe"; he sees Iris Garson surrounded by the students' mothers "as if she was some curious little bird from a far continent" (108, 121). Reflections of nature's robustness, the children are "like a yardful of geese," Aphrodite's emblem, or else "like colorful starlings" emitting "high birdcries" (40, 71).

The embodiment of freedom, the bird is an emblem of the "poetry side" of Brill's life, the side Ozick links to literature and to storytelling in "Innovation and Redemption," the side Ephraim Gorchak scornfully connects to "dreamers. . . . mooning out of windows" (A&A 246; CG 43). "Worthless" because they ignore his lists and stare out windows, the dreamers are apt to see the bird whose "tail brushed the windowpane like an upside-down broom": dreamers succumb to the power of the imagination (43). Theirs are the souls in the vale of interpretation who recall Psyche, whom the Greeks often associated with a bird, which in *The Cannibal Galaxy* is yoked to art and to Claude. Speaking with a "certain birdlike emphasis," Claude once awakened Brill to the aesthetic treasures in the Louvre where, when he returns many years later, he is lured on by the "perfumed cave under Claude's wing" (146, 131). But Hester Lilt's birds assault him. At the end of the novel when Brill finally reads Hester's manuscript *Structure in Silence*, he discovers that its last section, "Schoolmistresses," is "about the pelican and the stork," about birds and their young. As if to mark a final distinction between the philosopher and the principal, Ozick turns his mockery of motherhood into the philosopher's accusations. Usurping "one of Brill's own tellings," Hester claims the pelican is an "Ideal parent," the stork a "conscientious parent." To them, not to the principal's "cockatoo teachers," the philosopher contends, belongs the title "Schoolmistresses," the nurturing of "distinction" in little ones (158, 113, 158).

The pervasive bird imagery in the novel, which is associated with sirens as well as with children and their mothers, helps explain why Brill remains a bachelor almost all his life, why he pursues only inappropriate women. When at last he meets a truly appropriate woman, her last name conjures in him thoughts of the succubus Lilith. Flourishing in the wilderness, Lilith was ultimately banished to the sea where she became a water nymph. That female demon, it was believed, seduced men into sin, threatened lives, as well as destroyed children by drinking their blood and sucking the marrow from their bones.[16] Joseph Brill's imagining women as sirens or else as the night-demon, who is akin to them, embodies not only Brill's fears but Brill's desires. In this he resembles the narrator of "The Dock-Witch." A reflection of the negative attitude of the rabbis' divided feelings about women, the positive represented by Eve, the night-demon and the siren instance the doubleness of Ozick's motifs and exemplify Brill's polarized self.[17]

One part of it is drawn to the woman who deals in scrutiny and exegesis, and it is to her that Brill announces his plan to marry Iris Garson, his decision "to become ordinary" (110). But Hester Lilt pierces the illusion that he was ever extraordinary: " 'You don't proceed. You're glued in place. You're a man who stops too soon. You deduce the future from the present. All despots do. You're stuck' " (110). And she penetrates his motivation for marrying: " 'It's not a wife you want. It's not a child you want. It's yourself. . . . Yourself continued. Yourself redeemed. . . . You want to know how to manage fate' "(112). Her interpretation of his "May and December" marriage unleashes the fury of his self-defense, and he reduces her ideas to an act of Lilith—to cannibalism of her own child (110). A hung-up telephone is the philosopher's irrefutable response, but Hester Lilt's acceptance of a post in Paris yields one more loss around which Brill weaves his plans for a descent into normality. He discovers it high in an attic where Iris Garson lives above a "large noisy Greek family" (106).

The fish dinner she prepares for him, the rainbow which is her namesake's emblem and that of the Covenant, her role as messenger in Greek mythology—these cast him back into his past when in his father's *poissonnerie*, the young Joseph "had sometimes heard his father remark on the iridescence of the scales of the ordinary *morue,* how a fish could become a mosaic of rainbows" (12). Then Brill took the observation his father made to be mean sympathy for the "poetry side" of his son's life. Now the fish signifies normal fertility, and the mosaic of rainbows has become the constraint which, Neher maintains, enclosed humanity and the earth in "limits which sent them back upon themselves," rendering the earth a "closed universe" (102). That Iris represents more than contact with ordinariness is suggested by the "indecipherable impish semaphores" produced by Brill's ceiling light as it strikes her crooked front tooth. They recall Thoreau Purse's eyeglasses "twinkling light like semaphores," and the affinity between Iris Garson and the girl's Charon in *Trust* implies that in *The Cannibal Galaxy* Iris is the "ferryman who is part of every story" (*Trust* 448, 550).[18] Indeed the "black and red" Phlegethon and the "radiance, which [Iris] shook out like wings opening," suggest that the end of the principal's thirty-fourth commencement ceremony is the beginning of Brill's voyage to Hades (118, 121). His dwelling on the realm of the dead, his counting his losses—these constitute a version of Baeck's idea of romanticism in which the dead events of mere experience render the past unsurpassable, devoid of history, "finished": the cleaned out shell of an unlived life.

To recover history, Brill journeys to Paris with his new family; but the ABCs, the three sisters who escaped a catastrophe of history, "resisted memory" and are as "far from history" as Iris is (133, 128). Because "memory burned in his kidney," he makes his way to the convent, but the "dark life of the subcellar" is closed to him, its paradise lost, the nuns "themselves by now far from history; silent; dead" (128, 129). Transfixed before the convent gates, Brill concludes, "France was Egypt: the principle of Principal Brill's eclipse from the stars" (129). He returns to the Musée Carnavalet, but he can no longer find the statue of Rachel and so he counts another loss. Perceiving nothing save a glimmer of Madame de Sévigné's likeness to Hester Lilt, he determines not to "fish her up out of the belly of Paris" or to recoup Claude, the distinguished "critic of painting, drawing, sculpture" (129). If France is Joseph Brill's Egypt, Paris is his underworld. Of the Musée Carnavalet he concludes, it "had nothing for him" (130). Headed down the Rue des Rosier, he turns away from the window when the bus reaches the "street of his father's life" (130). The effort to regild the dream his life scraped away has failed.

But the "spoor of Claude" lures him to the Louvre even as the "familiar anxiety over being late" for Rabbi Pult tugs his consciousness in a contrary direction (131, 130). Reaching the galleries of the Louvre, he remounts the stream of time, which thickens the sense of loss he suffered in the Musée Carnavalet. In the majestic museum, Brill climbs upward to the top of a huge stairway where the Winged Victory is "mounted on a height of rubble" (131). "Headless, armless, an invisible sea-wind tossing her dress," the marble statue is the Nike of Samothrace. The goddess Ozick has chosen as the first to greet Brill's eyes is the one who was the symbol of decisive victory for the gods, the statue "erected to celebrate a victory won at sea" (CG 131; Burkert 284). In *The Cannibal Galaxy,* however, the Winged Victory is an ironic reminder of Iris Garson. Linked to the Styx, Brill's Winged Victory promises not the conquest of death but the assurance of it, celebrates not accomplishment but bodes failure. Two other statues—a "glowing torso of Apollo" and the Venus de Milo—revive events from the aesthetic side of the principal's life (131). When he comes to the Winged Victory, Brill is all atremble, before an "azure Isis on a throne of gold," all affright: "He had a terror of these images and idols" (131). That Ozick envisages Isis as the goddess arousing Brill's intense fears is not fortuitous. A nature goddess, Isis was eventually worshiped as a powerful and inclusive goddess to whom the functions of all goddesses were attributed so that she became the exemplar of them all. The universal mother and mistress of all magic in Egyptian mythology, Isis was known to the Greeks as Demeter, the goddess to whom Ozick alludes in her first and second novels.

The collation of pagan spectacles Brill beholds in the Louvre makes keen the indistinct fear he felt in the Musée Carnavalet: in the great rooms of the Louvre "It was as if there had never been a Hebrew people, no Abraham or Joseph or Moses. Not a trace of holy Israel" (131). Those halls offered "so many things at once" to James; walking in them he discovered "not only beauty and art and supreme design, but history and fame and power, the world in fine raised to the richest and noblest expression" (*Auto.* 196). And it was in one of the Louvre's galleries that he had his "immense hallucination," the "dream-adventure" in which Henry triumphantly routed a "dimly-descried figure." The figure Brill imagines in the "incandescent twilight," which suffuses the room with "beauty and light," is Beulah Lilt; but when he calls to her, she "took him in as if he had a flaw" (131–32). Brill's experience in the Louvre proves as "immense" as James's in the Galerie d'Apollon and as "appalling." But James's "final recognition" resulted in "life-saving energy," the feeling of power the Master felt in Europe and the "sense of glory" he derived from art. Brill's "dream-adventure" leaves Brill not animated by personal power but depleted by personal loss.

Yet the Ozick who weaves Jamesian strands into the warp of her fabric is the Ozick who intertwines diverse ones in the woof. That she alludes to Stransom, Marcher, and Strether in her story about a man who like them is preoccupied with loss and fate indicates her congruence with James. That she transforms what links the men into what ultimately divides them divulges her variance from James. In the preface to "The Altar of the Dead" James reveals his intention was to explore the effect of loss on individual sensibility and to "mate" with George Stransom John Marcher, who is "condemned to keep counting with the unreasoned prevision of some extraordinary fate" (*Art* 246). Of Marcher, James explains: "I seemed to see him start in life—under the so mixed star of the extreme of apprehension and the extreme of confidence . . . his having to wait and wait for the right recognition; none of the mere usual and normal human adventures . . . appearing to conform to the great type of his fortune" (246). Where Marcher's career "resolves itself into a great negative adventure," Strether's impels him "to press the spring of a terrible question. *Would* there yet perhaps be time for reparation. . . . The answer to which is that he now at all events *sees*." *The Ambassadors* is James's "demonstration of this process of vision" (1–2).

Ozick alters significantly the events in James's stories and the implication of those events, revising their conclusions, revealing her reading of James's texts while at the same time converting them in a "newer and richer saturation." If James provides George Stransom with his roll-call of the dead, Ozick gives to Brill the *Ta'anit*—the talmudic treatise that lists the fast days commemorating misfortune. If the date of Mary Antrim's death keeps Stransom from doing little save mourning, the lie about a dead sweetheart prevents Brill, for a good part of his life, from marrying. If Stransom's candles, the emblem of his worship of the dead, are called, when a different candle appears, a "new star," the symbol of Brill's veneration of the heights *is* the star (*Eight Tales* 114). But Stransom's roll-call is just that, a list of names; Brill's enjoins its readers, with the legends it includes concerning the redemption of Jerusalem, not to despair. James designates Stransom and his companion in grief a "pair of pagans of old alluding decently to the domesticated gods." Ozick provides her counter of losses with an opponent who challenges his gods. One storyteller ruminates over the dynamics of loss, the other over the ways to surmount it.

What Brill shares with Marcher is the insurmountable, the horror of it being too late. Neither attends to the admonishments against their inaction; one awaits the sudden surprise, the other condemns it. And so their beasts differ: the principal has been forced to live like one, but the man "to whom nothing whatever was to happen" has evaded the urge to live. Strether, whom Ozick envisioned early in her career as Marcher's fulfillment, is a "man of imagination" and in *The Ambassadors* James traces the progressive growth of his character's awareness (3). Strether's "moral scheme of the most approved pattern which was yet framed to break down on any approach to vivid facts" does indeed break down in Paris, and affords the experience of conversion, the "drama of discrimination" (7). In the European scene itself, Strether sees the reverse of Marcher's unlived life, life lived to the fullest. In Paris, then, Strether and Brill have contrary realizations because James and Ozick learned the lesson of Europe differently, and that because of the war. Joseph Brill's moral scheme solidifies because of the images and idols that surround Brill in the Louvre; he fancies Paris as the belly of Jonah's whale, a dark underworld, not a "bright Babylon." And he returns to America lacking what Strether has gained.

In conflating traits from the three characters—Stransom, Marcher, and Strether—and reconceiving them, Ozick depicts in Joseph Brill a sensibility belonging to a failed artist. Despite the fact that Brill survived the European devastation, he attends not to the promise of redemption in Rabbi Pult's *Ta'anit* but to its commemoration of despair. His obsession with genius is his idol, more resolute and more perilous than the statues he fears in the Louvre. Capable of the higher imagination, the one that invents the Dual Curriculum, the principal's rage for order transforms Joseph Brill's dream into a system. Brill's becomes the "systems imagination" that competes with the Creator. And Ozick, plucking from James the elements of an unlived life, offers him in return a portrait of an artist resigned to his doom. She shares with James full consciousness, "blest imagination"—that drew her to him, that excites her divergence from him.

It is with considerably less than full awareness, however, that Brill imagines what he might have said to Beulah had she "stopped for him" in the Louvre (134). Insight ends where projection begins: "Beulah . . . what a grief you are in the world, to have fallen short of the heights! . . . to be what you are, dry and plain, without a will, without a fire, flat, flat, flat, what good is it, defeat after defeat, nothing behind, nothing ahead, never to accomplish, never to distinguish yourself, to be the ordinary article while your mother's brain burns and burns!" (134–35). A passage from "The Lesson of the Master" in which Ozick confesses her, and echoes Brill's, mistaken apprehension of the Jamesian dictum adjoins to the schoolmaster's erroneous notions of genius that of the writer's: "Now the truth is it [the early achievement of mastery] could not have been done, even by a writer of genius; and what a pitiful flicker of the flame of high ambition for a writer who is no more than the ordinary article! . . . no writer, whether robustly gifted, or only little and pale, should hope for this implausible fate" (A&A 296). These misapprehensions are instructively similar, and they coincide with the misjudgments of Brill, the father.

Ravished by genius, the principal attends to his son's first text. "Bright-eyed . . . ambitious beyond anything," designed "to go high," Naphtali and his "ingenious" lists . . . categories, divisions, classifications, types" portend a second, and less auspicious text—one more like his father's (139, 148). Where Brill habitually counts the losses he incurred during the war, Naphtali compiles a "Biographical Scrapbook" containing the "life-story, from birth to death, of every person who ever had anything to do with the American Revolution" (140). Where the young Joseph dreamt of founding a school, the young Naphtali dreams of becoming a teacher. The father disdains the chaotic, the disorderly; the son "loved orderliness" (148). But the son's "protean" nature renders the pedagogue's "judgment from early performance" a nullity. Naphtali decides not to teach but to major in business administration, not to study at the Sorbonne but to enroll in Miami University.

Ultimately, Naphtali journeys, as his father once did, to another place where instead of founding a school to "bring together all his visions," he "thought he would found companies, induce them to accrete, and then forcibly amalgamate them." His is not the high dream of fusion; it is a scheme for launching "empires." The father has, like Puttermesser, brought to life a creature who devises a plan, one for transportation on the ground: "He would resuscitate cross-country land mobility, commanding untried alliances among

buses and trains; he would air out the crackling grease of the bus-stop cafe-
terias that lay across the breast of the nation; he would wash the windows of
the dozing trains; in the cities he would plant twin silver tracks in black urban
asphalt, and bring streetcars to life again" (159). That is not the higher imagination; it is the imagination of a "system-maker" (A&A 187). "Nature's
prank of duplication" has proven "to be true without exception" (73, 72).

If Naphtali confirms his father's belief in nature's doubleness, Beulah Lilt
annihilates the schoolmaster's conviction of nature's predictability. Having
once imagined confronting the philosopher's daughter with her defeat, the
principal, when he is nearly seventy-six, is confronted instead with her brilliant
success. His grief over the irretrievable remains a constancy, his "first losses"
accustomed burdens. Then he is weighed down by fresh loss when he sees the
screen of his television aglow with the "stupendously lit" eyes of Beulah Lilt.
Not only has she been widely acclaimed as a leader of a new school of painting
in Paris, not only have her stony eyes become "polished . . . green stones," but
she tells her interviewer she has no memory whatsoever of her schooling in
America. Unlike the schoolmaster who professed his curriculum had a "base in
theory," the artist, her hair "held by two butterfly pins," claims only to have
"called a series of her own paintings Caryatids" (145). Stunned by her inability to recall the Dual Curriculum, Brill is startled that the art critic who discusses her work is his boyhood friend. Claude declares the artist's success
owed to the " 'latency . . . of Idea,' " to her " 'indisputable subject' " (146).
Taking Naphtali as a "witness," Brill travels to the Guggenheim to see an exhibition of Beulah's paintings (147).

In the halls of the Louvre Brill brooded over Beulah's failures; in the
Guggenheim he stands before her accomplishments. The successful artist, he
concludes, "had no 'indisputable' subject," but in his hotel room, he apprehends an unquestionable truth. Despite his youthful desire to set Jonah and
Koheleth beside Corneille and Racine, he ignored the words of Koheleth. Not
knowing "which one shall prosper, whether this seed or that or whether they
both *shall be* alike good" (Eccles. 11:6), the principal assumed he could foresee
a child's future. His is the guilt arising from the "sin of withholding his hand"
(149). It was Pult who recounted that at forty Akiva, when he *still did not
know anything*," had asked, "*And who polished this stone?*" It is Brill who at
seventy-six asks, "Who had polished those green stones?" Akiva was provided
with an answer from Job: "*The waters wear away the stones*" (149). Brill
shares with Job "his flesh's pain" but not his ignorance of sin (Job 14:19). The
two motifs—that of the hand and that of the stones—thread their way
through *The Cannibal Galaxy* and culminate in the apprehension that seizes
Brill in his hotel room, just as his experience in the Louvre brought in its train
an aching realization. But consciousness of loss has been overtaken by consciousness of sin. In reviving Brill's memory of Pult and Akiva, Ozick yokes a
central fact of Akiva's life to a prevailing theme in the Joseph narrative—the
achievements of the unpromising—and severs Joseph Brill from both.

A motif in the biblical Joseph's life to which positive and negative associations accrue, the hand in *The Cannibal Galaxy* is emblematic; standing in the

principal's office in The Edmond Fleg Primary School is a Bristol chair with "only one arm, which ended almost shockingly in the replica of a wooden hand." Made variously to grip a "runner's torch," or to hold a "wooden bowl of artificial fruit, including a glass apple turned golden by the insertion of an electric bulb," the Bristol chair behind the principal's desk is the kind which has a wooden hand supplied with a "painted glass globe of the world" but without its customary cross (18). Adorned by the wooden hand, the chair was elevated "into a sort of sculpture," and it is as a piece of statuary that the chair holds significance in the novel (18). The globe of the world, the runner's torch, the golden apple—these symbolize the triumph of power and authority. Alluded to in *Trust* and in "The Pagan Rabbi," the Greek runners are signs not of triumph but of strife. That the upturned hand of the Bristol chair in Brill's office seems "appalling, a deranged artisan's mad thought" when Beulah's silence conquers the principal foreshadows his ultimate defeat at the end of the novel (84). Once a throne on which he felt himself to be the mothers' "ruler . . . their god . . . their gleaming seated Buddha," the Bristol chair becomes, near the end of the principal's life, the bench of his desolation: "curled in the Bristol chair, his hand on the hand that held the globe," he knows "he had been ambushed by Hester Lilt" (40, 161, 162).

That recognition clashes with the significance the hand has in the Joseph saga, where it indicates power and prosperity (Gen. 39:3, 9). A manifestation in the Bible of God's participation in human life, His power, and His protection, the hand also heralds His punishment. In *The Cannibal Galaxy* Ozick integrates into her powerful symbol the biblical senses of the hand as they appear in Job and in Koheleth: the man who has withheld his hand is at the end of his life the man from whom God has withdrawn His hand. Brill's awareness is Puttermesser's: the principal and the golem-maker have endeavored to know the unknowable and have rivaled Him "who does great things beyond understanding" (Job 9:10). Had he read Hester Lilt's manuscript, *On Structure in Silence,* "fifteen years ago" when it was delivered to him "BY HAND" to his office, he might have understood what he has beheld in Beulah's paintings: "the colors, the glow, the defined darkness, above all the forms of things—all these were thought to be a kind of language" (157, 156). Had he read André Neher's book when Hester urged him to, Brill would have recognized that silence ushers in the "culminating moments of human creativity," that silence is the "tangible sign of potentiality stored up in the reserves of the human being," the "tension . . . which precedes the splendor" of the artist's act (Neher 39, 40, 39). The Beulah Lilt who becomes "THE PAINTER OF THE YEAR," whose "face seemed . . . more like a heavy statue than a photograph," whose "eyes were green stones splendidly polished"—that Beulah evolved from the "poetry side" of the principal's life, sprang from the school's "green and watery and airy landscape" (151, 118, 59). The painter exemplifies the third sort of imagination Ozick limns in the novel—the "art imagination." As Beulah's career makes plain, the art imagination brings fulfillment, but requires a retreat from Hebraism, and so among the images that celebrate the painter's achievement are ones that discountenance it. The name of the married land in Isaiah (62:4), no longer "Forsaken" nor "Desolate," the painter's name signals success but does not wed Beulah to Brill's dream of fusion. Rather the derivation of the name constitutes another allusion to *The Scarlet Letter*, for both Hester Lilt and Hester Prynne have daughters whose names originate in Scripture but who are caught in the pagan elements of nature.[19]

Nature's lush greenness incarnates those elements in *The Scarlet Letter* and in *The Cannibal Galaxy*. At first the color of both Rabbi Pult's leather-bound *Ta'anit* and the "old priest's volume of Corneille," green comes more and more to instance the forces of nature in Brill's life and in Beulah's. The color links the principal's past to the present. In the paradise of the subcellar the color symbolized for Joseph Brill his dream of combining the binary traits of his intellect; in the middle of another continent, the principal lives near an "empty side field," a "tumbledown meadow, weed-frilled green" that is "hairy with unmown grass" (4). Reminded of his past idealism, he is struck by the "after-school muteness and greenness," the "density of greenness" of his "boyhood mind" that exploded in the courtyard of the Musée Carnavalet (79, 129). The green world of Brill's boyhood and Beulah's childhood is akin to the "green natural world" of Hester Prynne's daughter (Hoffman 345). To mimic her mother, Pearl takes "some eel-grass" and imitates, "as best she could, on her own bosom . . . the letter A,—but freshly green, instead of scarlet" (121). As Beulah's stony green eyes are the artist's emblem, so the green letter becomes Pearl's: "the mother-forest, and these wild things which it nourished, all recognized a kindred wildness in the human child" (139). Greenness reflects the vitality of the natural world, which in *The Scarlet Letter* and *The Cannibal Galaxy* is a world where the "morally undirected energies of life" are tied to the "power of fecundity, and its derivative power, that of the imagination" (Hoffman 345). Not "subjugated by human law, nor illumined by a higher truth," nature is "wild, heathen": until Pearl receives "human patrimony," she "must remain a Nature-spirit," a pagan (SL 131; Hoffman 348). Without an identifiable patrimony, Beulah produces a series of paintings, "Caryatids"—a bridge to the pagan gods of nature.

That Ozick attaches special significance to the female statues used as columns of the temple built for Artemis is evident in her referring to the statues in her first novel and in her writing the poem "Caryatid," which she published the year she finished *Trust*. The poem's concluding lines are strikingly relevant to Beulah:

> She that raised Diana's hall
> cannot comprehend its fall:
> rebel
> holding up a pebble.

Though she denies her leadership of a revolutionary art movement, the sucessful painter rebels from her past when she disregards the Dual Curriculum. Beulah Lilt shatters Joseph Brill's dream just the way Barby McCormick, the daughter in Ozick's early story "Stone," shatters her father's idols. But the identity of Beulah's father remains as enigmatic as the background of the painter's mother. Hester Lilt "was all future," Joseph Brill all past (92). That is why he correctly judges the philosopher: "she cut the thread of genesis. . . . In the end she would have no use for his Dual Curriculum, his two civilizations, his radiant antiquity." To be removed "from any remnant of history" is to be shorn of its judgments. If Hawthorne regards patrimony as Pearl's salvation from paganism, Ozick attributes to the mysteriousness of Beulah's patrimony the failure to receive the father's gift of transmission, a "linking meant to be carried forward into the horizons of the farthest future" (22). And so the "orphan of the future" repudiates the "Jewish cultural side of her education," which she forgets, severs herself from a "sense of a moral civilization," and upholds in its stead the Temple of Diana (CG 92; Interview with Kauvar 381).

At The Edmond Fleg Primary School, Beulah trailed behind Corinna Luchs, the "leader of the pack," whose first name alludes to the Greek poetess who wrote narrative lyrical poems for a circle of women, foretelling in one poem the high success of women married to gods. These allusions to Hellenism—the caryatids, the Greek poetess—account for Beulah's resplendent green stones. They wed her to the aesthetic side of Brill's past, to the "courtyard emblazoned with statuary," to the "stone beauty," to the "stone steps" of the convent, to a "certain deep stone-littered dell" not far from the simmering Phlegethon (8, 9, 57, 118). They link her to the Greek urns in the Louvre, where Brill imagined seeing her, and to the aestheticism of his boyhood friend Claude. That explains why Ozick chose to make Beulah Lilt a painter; *that* is responsible for the overarching importance of the "forms of things" Brill beholds in her paintings.

Though Hester Lilt avows the "purity of babble is inconceivable in the vale of interpretation," though her daughter's "transmogrification of forms: strange violent quick tongues" are thought "to be a kind of language," the shapes in Beulah's paintings, "sometimes like gyres," allude to Yeats's gyres, those symbols of dissolution, and to the Tower of Babel, the supreme example of idolatry (148, 156). To the world of Babel Neher assigns the "suffocation of the word," the "conversion of nature into artifice," and the "establishment of the concentrational society" whose characteristics are reminiscent of an idol, as Ozick defines it. Of the concentrational society Neher writes: "the power of invention springs not from the human spirit but from the thing itself, which generates its own system, determines its own laws, prescribes its own language to which the whole world must submit and which has nothing in common with the languages of the world outside" (104, 105). The human inventiveness that raised the Tower of Babel is what sundered humanity from the Divine and what provoked Him to confound human speech. Beulah's luminous forms, evidence of her accomplishments as an artist, are the achievements of someone in exile from the word.

In connecting Beulah to Claude, who worships at the altar of Sacred Beauty, in endowing her paintings with the splendor of pure form, in electing to make Beulah a painter instead of a writer, and in attaching to her hair emblems of Psyche, Ozick divorces Beulah from Hebraism and allies her with Hellenism. Symbol of the imagination, the butterfly is Ozick's image of completion: the imagination generates the wonder of art, but its fulfillment "belongs to the knowledge of rapid death" (PR 217). *The Cannibal Galaxy* is Cynthia Ozick's meditation on the life of the imagination, a theme that obsessed the poet to whom the storyteller repeatedly refers. She alludes to Keats's "Ode to Psyche" when she describes Beulah's paintings as "phantasmagorical windows," when she depicts Brill's diminished imagination as he dozes "before the glimmering casement" of his television, and when she charts her departure from the poet's realm of the visionary imagination which, his early ode reveals, he trusted and revered (156). The "worshipper of Psyche" vows to shield his imaginary vision from reality, to build a temple to the Greek goddess of the soul in "some untrodden region" of his "mind" (Perkins 226).[20] The exponent of monotheism can exalt only the Supreme Being. The "vale of soul-making" is suggestive, it is even inspiring, but it is insufficient. And so is the "vale of interpretation": "She [Beulah Lilt] had forgotten her childhood in the Curriculum that was his [Brill's] treasure and his name. . . . She labored without brooding in calculated and enameled forms out of which a flaming nimbus sometimes spread" (162).

That is not the "nimbus of *meaning*" Ozick accords to redemptive art; it is the nimbus of glory surrounding the head of a pagan god (A&A 246). Like the surveyor of the custom-house, the painter escapes her "doom" to her "forefathers," retaining not even a "haze of memory," and becomes a "citizen of somewhere else." "Amongst other faces" and in an atmosphere exempt from moral obligation, she ripens the "best harvest" of her imagination and becomes an aesthete (SL 34). Proof against doom, Beulah's course is not proof against dissension. If the absence of her father seems to signal the artist's essential freedom, it is rather the sign of moral deprivation. If the painter labors "without brooding," she replaces interpretation with "calculated and enameled forms." If hers is not a "systems imagination," it is an "art imagination." Neither posits the higher imagination; both result in idol-making. However triumphant Beulah Lilt's second text is, it cannot be said to represent the victory of Hebraism over Hellenism, nor indeed their convergence. Endeavoring to combine the treasures of the two civilizations, Ozick rekindles the dispute that inflamed their separation.

Although it does not reconcile that conflict, *The Cannibal Galaxy* augurs the mode of consciousness necessary to effecting such a resolution. The novel delineates three modalities of the imagination as Ozick apprehends them: its inclination toward system-making, its proclivity to aestheticism, its highest potential for redemption. At the novel's nub are the issues central to achieving a consonance of artistic endeavor and moral substance—how the artist is to be educated, how the artist is to live. Those are the problems that sparked the storyteller's dialectic with the writers whose artistic consciousnesses Ozick explores, controverts, and then swerves from. Hers is the revisionism Bloom ascribes to genius.

Never one to render the complex simple, the conflicting harmonious, the striated solid, Ozick concludes *The Cannibal Galaxy* with the issues that clash throughout it still in collision. Though Joseph Brill's high muse of fusion has delivered up the ideal alternative to the "conditions of modernism," the Dual Curriculum founders in the principal's belief that it is possible to foretell who will prosper (M&M 234). One of the novel's epigraphs, two lines from a poem by Emily Dickinson, articulate Brill's desire: "The rest of Life to *see!* / Past Midnight! Past the Morning Star!" But the last lines of the poem gainsay the realization of that desire: "Ah, What leagues there *were!* / Between our feet, and Day!" Awareness comes to the schoolmaster, but only after a "lethargy had settled over him," when a "new fright" stirs him as he vacates his office before retirement, leaving the *Ta'anit* behind (156). Relinquishing his pursuit of the stars for the redemption of his life—"late, late"—he reflected how "saucy" Iris "had ravished him. . . . How the wormlet mockery swells to become the strangling serpent" (157). Having once seen his wife-to-be as "Something luminous. Shining," Brill, now an old man, finds that "nothing she said interested him," that her dyed hair "was a river of gleaming pitch" that matched the blackness of the Phlegethon (106, 142). His redeemed life, his recognition of error, his ability to change—these are modulated by the imagery which limns the end of his career.

If Iris's "sorcery" has become the serpent in his garden, his contact with Hades, the Brills' move to the "gates of Eden"—"Florida, with its hot winds"—foreshadows the loss of paradise, not its reattainment. Once the principal of a school which seemed to have a "horror of coasts and margins; of edges and extremes of any sort," Brill as an old man lives on the eastern edge of the continent, where he fears "he would never have the power to raise" his chin from his chest (3, 161). His posture ironically recalls his namesake's success at interpreting dreams. The biblical Joseph's expression, "lift up your head," simultaneously predicts that one of Pharaoh's officials will be pardoned, the other beheaded (Gen. 40:13, 19). No longer beleaguered by the Middle, Joseph Brill is assailed by the end. His dream does not endure: under Gorchak's leadership, The Edmond Fleg Primary School becomes the Lakeside Grade School. Modernized and streamlined, the school retains the motto *Ad Astra* only as the title of an award chosen by the former principal "to be given . . . to the eighth grader with the most creative potential" (161). Fearing he cannot raise his head, he sees Beulah Lilt's "head lift on the screen like a sculptured apparition"; sometimes imagining her as "his dream's incubus," he "succumbed to the iron belief . . . that her mother had spoiled his life—had, in fact, waylaid him, plundered and robbed him" (162). The East has brought to Brill the burning east winds that in Scripture blight vegetation; the Eastern waters in which, as in the Dead Sea, no fish can exist—Divine judgment, not Divine restoration.

Though she does not attempt, as she charges Brill, to know every "twist" and "contingency" of fate, though she is the novel's advocate of transformation, its upholder of future redemption, a Hebraist and a commentator, Hester Lilt nurtures an aesthetician and "courts amnesia of history" (112). Though she can imagine the unimaginable while the principal stops short of it, neither Hester Lilt nor Joseph Brill rears a child who possesses the higher imagination or who embodies the solution to the novel's central conflict. If in Europe Hester Lilt's "fame (she *had* no fame) was terribly narrow," the Dual Curriculum is eradicated because Gorchak believes the "European experience is irrelevant to [the] new generation" (139, 160). The philosopher disappears from the novel save in Brill's intractable belief that she had ruined his life, or else in her daughter's immense achievements, which continue to besiege him. Envisioning Hester Lilt "swallowed" up in the "belly of Paris," Brill associates her with the "cannibal galaxies, those megalosaurian colonies of primordial gases that devour smaller brother-galaxies—and when the meal is made, the victim continues to rotate like a Jonah-dervish inside the cannibal, while the sated ogre-galaxy, its gaseous belly stretched, soporific, never spins at all—motionless as digesting Death" (69). A galactic phenomenon, the cannibal galaxies are a summarizing metaphor for the various kinds of cannibalism in the novel: schoolmaster devouring student, parent plundering child, one civilization engulfing another civilization.[21] Those are the cannibal galaxies pervading Ozick's fiction from *Trust* onward; they are akin to the storyteller's dread of the "cannibal touch of story-making," the worry over usurpation (*Bloodshed* 12).

Tugged in contrary directions, Cynthia Ozick considers the realm of the Middle, where no one flourishes. To remain there, wavering between two worlds, is to inhabit the unredeemed wilderness of Numbers without the Promised Land of Canaan. At the end of *Why I Am a Jew,* Edmond Fleg confesses his failure to bring together the two worlds which divided him. Seeking a higher post-Christian synthesis of the extremes of moralism and intellectualism and declaring that both "leave their mark on all the history of our race and its development," Matthew Arnold then insists on their dissimilarity: "Language may be abundantly quoted from both Hebraism and Hellenism to make it seem that one follows the same current as the other towards the same goal. They are, truly, borne towards the same goal; but the currents which bear them are infinitely different . . . [for] underneath the superficial agreement the fundamental divergence still subsists" (5:166–67). Joseph Brill seeks to redirect the diverging currents into a confluence. Like Enoch Vand, he fails to go high; like Stanislav Lushinski, he ends in desolation. Struggling to unify the aesthetic and moral sensibilities, Ozick contemplates a congruence of the two. Positing the means to a higher post-Enlightenment synthesis, *The Cannibal Galaxy* then explores the reasons for its failure. Instead of resolving the dialectic she began in *Trust,* Ozick advances it.

Longing for a *tertium quid* that would satisfy her leanings in both directions, she continues to reflect on them in "Bialik's Hint." The essay's publication in 1983, several months after *The Cannibal Galaxy,* which Ozick has revealed was actually written in 1977, calls into question the conclusion that the novel "holds a place of important summation and focus, if not of synthesis, in Ozick's oeuvre" (Sokoloff, *"Cannibal Galaxy"* 253). From *Trust* to *The Cannibal Galaxy* the storyteller concludes her fiction not with a concurrence of forces but with their continuing rivalry. Her imagination must be regarded as fluid, not fixed and unchanging. The Ozick who envisions the Dual Curriculum is the Ozick who envisions the obstacles to its success: "every notion owns a double face" (M&M 238). Arising in the aftermath of fictive discovery and irresolution, "Bialik's Hint" rekindles the issues firing *The Cannibal Galaxy,* extends them into a meditation on postmodern culture, acts as commentary on the novel, and serves as its coda. If Rabbi Pult declares the "new slogan: There is no God, and the Jews killed him" the "legacy of [the] Enlightenment" and Joseph Brill abandons that "side of the mind . . . a cave teeming with bestial forms," Ozick, in "Bialik's Hint," muses upon the "effects of the Enlightenment and its concomitant issue, Jewish Emancipation" (CG 16; M&M 225). Where "Innovation and Redemption" ends "on a darkling plain" with an ambivalent conclusion about the imagination—its freedom to create or to penetrate evil—"Bialik's Hint" posits the means to fuse the freedom of the imagination "with the Sinaitic challenge of distinctive restraint and responsibility" (227).

In her essay and in her novel, Ozick attempts to find in the imagination a means to combat the dark crisis confronting our culture—its impulse to aestheticism, its retreat from tradition, its recoil from the moral sense. Having embodied three sorts of imagination in Hester Lilt, Beulah Lilt, and Joseph Brill, the storyteller registers in "Bialik's Hint," albeit indirectly, the inadequacies of all three, rendering attempts to see finality in her novel or essay indefensible. With the instructive example of Jewish cultural history in mind, she reveals how the "conditions of modernism," which have touched all contemporary writers, evolved historically to produce a "time of empty bewilderment," a period which has subverted, even threatened with extinction, the redemptive power of the imagination. If Hester Lilt's "midrashic stance" is seen as "one possible antidote for mediocrity," or as the factor which "differentiates authentic from inauthentic Jewish response to history," or as an "obsession . . . with the Jewish quality of interpretation," Ozick declares the "dependence on a single form," midrashim included, "no foundation for an entire literature" (Sokoloff, *"Cannibal Galaxy"* 252, Berger 136; Lowin 86; M&M 238).

Confronting the "need for a literature," "Bialik's Hint" intimates, contrary to Sokoloff's view, that "Beulah's triumph" does suggest an "exaltation of art over Judaism, a return of the repressed religion of Art" (M&M 238; Sokoloff, *"Cannibal Galaxy"* 252). The essay not only implies that Beulah's paintings originate in the religion of Art, it makes clear what the artist has repressed. Throughout "Bialik's Hint," Ozick stresses that lacking the "brake of tradition or continuity," liberty, carried to its highest pitch, implies the will "to imagine everything, hence to do anything" (M&M 226). She urges again and again the imperatives of "responsibility," "judgment," and "duty"; she praises as "stunning" Bialik's conclusion that the " 'whole justification' for 'literature' and 'creation' is the sense of duty" (228). Beulah Lilt has escaped from that " 'through the narrow wicket-gate of a dubious aestheticism' " (228).

If Bialik has "seized on a post-Enlightenment choice . . . the fusion of secular aesthetic culture with Jewish sensibility," Ozick has imagined the Dual Curriculum. Of its inventor's biblical namesake she writes in her essay: "One of the vastest minds of Scripture is surely the brilliantly original Joseph, wily dreamer and inspired dream-interpreter, salvational economist, and, no doubt, scientist and architect. Surely Joseph is what we mean when we speak of genius" (M&M 236). Attributing that to the Joseph of Scripture, Ozick affirms that the destruction of the Temple was decisive in altering "Jews and Jewishness forever" (236). She seizes upon Zechariah's prophecy of the "turn to the Jewish text" just as Hester Lilt catches up Zechariah's prophecy of salvation (236). The philosopher cites the "hoax of pedagogy" as the flaw in Joseph Brill's plan; the storyteller offers the "nobility of pedagogy" as the Platonic "source of study-consciousness" in the Jewish mind (236). And so Ozick broadens the cause of Brill's failure: the principal's lethargy results from relinquishing the "Socratic primacy of the intellect" and "choosing the herd," tedium over originality, assimilation over fusion (236, 237).

Consorting with the Middle is Ozick's metaphor for assimilation, and it, the preference for the "swallowing-up" in the "aftermath of the Enlightenment," inhabits the core of "Bialik's Hint" and lends another meaning to the novel's title (M&M 237). But to relegate the issue of assimilation solely to Jews diminishes the inclusiveness of Ozick's metaphor, which by no means is limited to Jews. The "Jewish spirit," the "Jewish Idea," the "Jewish way," the "Jewish sensibility," the "Jewish language of restraint, sobriety, collective conscience, moral seriousness"—these are distinct concepts derived from the culture that conceived them (231, 237). To establish their provenance is not to proclaim them exclusive to it, a result of which is but another form of the parochialism Ozick condemns. To allege these ideas belong only to a Jewish reality is to mistake Ozick's high muse of fusion for a muse of division. The very title of her essay argues against that, for in transforming James's phrase the "aesthetic hint" into the hint handed down by the modern Hebrew poet Chaim Nahman Bialik, Ozick adds Jewish moral seriousness to the aesthetic sensibility.[22] She commends to us "lordly civilization enmeshed with lordly civilization, King David's heel caught in Victor Hugo's lyre, the metaphysicians Maimonides and Pascal, Bialik and Keats, Gemara hooked to the fires of algebra" (CG 57). The cultural destiny of Jewish writers stretches outward, taking in all postmodernist writers: "By now, for writers to throw themselves entirely into the arms of post-Enlightenment culture is no alternative at all. It is a laziness. It is the final shudder of spent thought: out of which no literature, Jewish or otherwise, can hope to spring" (M&M 234).

Against that eventuality Ozick holds out the "new alternative": the "fusion of the offerings of the Enlightenment . . . with Jewish primacy" (M&M 236–37). To realize Bialik's hint, the "dream delivered up in shadowy shapes," is to attain the "astonishments of the unexpected, the explosive hope of fresh form" (237). Still, having advanced this option, Ozick modulates its reality by calling it a "hint (and it *is* only a hint, a hunch; an imaginative construct; an invention; a fiction)" and by requiring for its success "genius," "several geniuses," even a "collective genius developed over generations" (236, 237). Dreaming of fusion, Ozick, "with the hindsight of two millennia," then predicts its "inevitability," and that in the unforeseeable future. If Joseph Brill's Dual Curriculum collapses at the end of *The Cannibal Galaxy,* the high muse of fusion has, in "Bialik's Hint," succeeded in delivering up a hint which remains just that, a hint.

But Ozick soars beyond the conclusions she reached in "Toward a New Yiddish" and "Innovation and Redemption" and unmasks the central issue in the contemporary dispute between Hebraism and Hellenism—the destiny of imaginative literature. Whether its fate is to exist only in the company of other texts separated from its audience, its authors, and the world depends upon the demands literature can make upon the will and upon the writer's ability to state enduring truths about humanity in language that both embodies and conveys moral seriousness. This belief in the efficacy of language, the "notion of inexhaustible revelation through words and their exegesis," is central to the Judaic tradition, of which some have even argued "that language itself is of divine origin and that the experience of revelation is linguistic" (Alter, *Defenses* 43; Biale 114). From that tradition springs Ozick's idea that any language possesses Hebrew's capacity "to carry a fresh or revolutionary idea," to acquire "moral seriousness," and to become a "vessel for the revolution in human conscience" (239). The concern for the redemptive power of language manifest in "Bialik's Hint" is matched in *The Cannibal Galaxy,* where language without consequence is inconceivable, where to be in exile from *parole* is to be bereft of its saving truths, or else without its collective conscience. The historical experience and the linguistic example of the Judaic tradition, its "momentous standards . . . of anti-idolatry and distinction-making," furnish Ozick with the means to formulate a new alternative to the postmodernist experience of privatization, fragmentation, and relativism—the will to universalize conscience (224).

And it is precisely because hers is an "imagination of arrival" that she can aspire to the ultimate commingling of the aesthetic and moral sensibilities, that she can offer a progressive option to what Lionel Trilling foresaw in 1973 as the "regressive impulse" of contemporary culture, which he feared was moving toward a "world where, indeed, the will is to be so thoroughly abrogated that life will virtually cease to have meaning except in its formal aspects" (M&M; "Art" 147). Cynthia Ozick's fiction invites its readers to enter into a complex transaction with it; Cynthia Ozick's essays take the fullest and most precise account of the doubleness, complexity, difficulty, and possibility each notion owns. That Ozick reaches no synthesis in *The Cannibal Galaxy* is owing to her efflorescent mind and her resplendent imagination, to her effort not to simplify the human condition, to allow conflicting impulses to vie with each other, to welcome the "unimaginable fusion," or to be challenged by its absence. Speculative and adventurous, her high muse turns upward toward the summit.

SIX

The Magic Shawl

A writer who resists finality is a writer whose imagination is given over to a habit of many sidedness and multiplicity. Having concluded *The Cannibal Galaxy* and "The Laughter of Akiva" in Miami, Florida, with Joseph Brill and Reuben Karpov inhabiting at the end of their lives a metaphoric hell of their own devising, Ozick begins "The Shawl" and "Rosa," which she wrote during the same period, with Rosa Lublin first in the demonic hell of the Nazi death camps and then in the continuing hell of their aftermath. Initially published separately—"The Shawl" in 1980 and "Rosa" in 1983—before they appeared in a single volume in 1989, the two stories are wed thematically, yoked by corresponding images, and unified by a commanding metaphor; the tales flow seamlessly together. Ozick duplicates their imagery, pairs their events, and then allows them to coalesce so as to see them with double sight. In its emphasis on the relationship between mother and daughter, in its engagement with the significance of silence, in its involvement with the idea of cannibalism, *The Shawl* bears marked resemblances to *The Cannibal Galaxy* and "The Laughter of Akiva." But *The Shawl* turns their concerns inside out: "every notion owns a double face." Manifesting the storyteller's practice of shaping related tales into fictions that unfold alternate positions, *The Shawl* opens a perspective unlike the one Cynthia Ozick developed in her second novel.

I

Hidden in the cellar of a convent, Joseph Brill escaped the butchery of the death camps; incarcerated in one of them, Rosa Lublin experienced its horrors and witnessed a demonic world of unparalleled proportions. In *The Shawl* Ozick not only instances with piercing intensity the brutality common to the German hell but reveals how it continued to torment its victims and perpetuated the work of the victimizers. For the first time in her fiction, she tells a tale directly from the consciousness of a Holocaust survivor, enshrining her as a spokeswoman for the truth. To Holocaust literature *The Shawl* is undeniably of huge importance: the events in the German abattoir become searingly real as their effects emerge in Rosa Lublin's thoughts, which record the torment the survivor endured and so "rescue the suffering . . . from dreadful anonymity" (Appelfeld 92). Ozick's achievement does not end there, however, for incorporating into the tales facts gleaned from history and events derived from memoirs, the storyteller lays bare the intricacies of the human mind. As she has from the very beginning of her career, Cynthia Ozick penetrates the individual psyche by apprehending the historical occurrences that shaped it. If "The Shawl" and "Rosa" expose the anguish inflicted by radical evil, they affirm the courage displayed by human beings in their efforts to vanquish the powers of darkness.

Interwoven in "The Shawl" are allusions to Elie Wiesel's *Night,* to which Ozick refers in "A Mercenary," and to Primo Levi's *Survival in Auschwitz.* What memoirs contain are facts; and facts, as Enoch Vand and Stanislav Lushinski avow, constitute "what really happened." Facts register the "Real." The unfathomable reality of the German hell, the harrowing events reported by Wiesel and Levi, are evoked in *The Shawl* and lend to it the configurations of biography. It is to the interrelatedness of biography and fiction that Ozick increasingly turns; yoking the two forms, she implies they yield a key to the world's design. But the linear time of biography is radically dislocated in "The Shawl" and replaced by the terrifying feeling of timelessness, the sense that for the victims of the death camps "history had stopped" (Levi 107). For that reason, the beginning of "The Shawl," which recounts events from Rosa's point of view, affords neither orientation in time nor clarification of place. Instead, the tale opens with the elliptical, "Stella, cold, cold, the coldness of hell." What follows unfolds the effects of that hell on the three people imprisoned in it. Not until the second paragraph, when she mentions the yellow Star of David sewn into Rosa's coat, does Ozick reveal that Rosa, Stella, and Magda are Jews on a march whose destination is a Nazi concentration camp.

The stars, which in *The Cannibal Galaxy* represent the heights to which Joseph Brill once aspired, have in "The Shawl" become ominous signs of exclusion and doom. And they are buttressed by Rosa's description of Stella: "Her knees were tumors on sticks, her elbows chicken bones" (3). In "Levitation" flight signals the direction toward which the Jews soar to recover Covenant; for Joseph Brill, height points to success. But in "The Shawl" the dichotomy between the air and the ground marks the distinction between the innocent and the evil: "Rosa did not feel hunger; she felt light, not like someone walking but like someone in a faint, in trance, arrested in a fit, someone who is already a floating angel, alert and seeing everything, but in the air, not there, not touching the road" (3–4). Of separating the victims of the Holocaust from its perpetrators Ozick has written:

> The Holocaust happened *to* its victims. It did not happen *in* them. The victims were not the participants. The event swept over them, but they were separate from it. That is why they are "sanctified"—because they did not perform evil. . . . And if there is one notion we need to understand more than any other, it is this principle of separation. The people for whom the Holocaust "happened" were the people who made it happen. The perpetrators *are* the Holocaust; the victims stand apart. ("Roundtable" 284)

The metaphor of flight in "The Shawl" does not link Rosa to Feingold in "Levitation," nor does it attribute to her the ability "to overcome history"

(Berger 53). Rosa is in the air because she does not partake of evil. She is divided from desecration.

That intensifies Rosa's struggle to conceal Magda from the Nazis, which in turn increases the conflicts with a fourteen-year-old's jealousy and makes more fierce the battle Rosa must wage to stay alive. She judges her niece—Stella's relationship to Rosa is divulged in the following story—the epitome of coldness, her envy the prelude to cannibalism. Wanting "to be wrapped in a shawl, hidden away, asleep, rocked by the march, a baby, a round infant in arms," Stella, Rosa thinks, is "waiting for Magda to die" (3, 5). But it is Stella who studies the blueness of the baby's eyes, gazes at the roundness of its face, stares at the yellowness of its hair, and declares Magda an Aryan. In fact, Magda appears to be "one of *their* babies," the child, Ozick intimates, born of an S.S. officer in a concentration camp (4).

The implied connection between Rosa and a German recalls "The Suitcase" and "A Mercenary"—the relationship between Genevieve Lewin and Gottfried Hencke and the one between Stanislav Lushinski and his mistress Lulu. Imagery from those stories, as well as from *Trust*, reappears in "The Shawl." At first associating yellow with Europe and then with Tilbeck, Ozick ultimately joins the aestheticism that produced the Final Solution to paganism. Yellow is the color to which Mr. Hencke is "susceptible": buttercups remind him of his past in Germany, and the color suffuses the dream he has of his niece lying dead on a turntable in the nave, her body covered only by her yellow hair (PR 105). In *Trust*, however, a baby plays with a spool of yellow thread, an emblem of what is to come. Catching up those implications, Magda's yellow hair connects the infant to the color of Germany and to the baby in *Trust* who, like Magda, is an augury of the future. To the paganism conjured up by yellow in "The Shawl" Ozick adds roundness, a reminder of Lushinski's adopted and pagan country. That mourning is associated with roundness in "A Mercenary" suggests the "round infant" in "The Shawl," its tooth an "elfin tombstone of white marble," will be the reason for her mother's grief (4). Although Rosa shares with Lushinski's parents the impulse to give their child away, she can neither save her infant nor spare herself the horror of being a witness to her daughter's death. That is the event toward which "The Shawl" inexorably moves.

It is the event the shawl delays. To the main metaphor of "The Shawl" and "Rosa," Ozick attaches antithetical pairs of images—sound and silence, darkness and light. Wrapped in the shawl in the "place without pity," Magda is safe because quiet. The substitute for her mother's teat, its "duct crevice extinct, a dead volcano, blind eye, chill hole," the shawl is "guarded" by Magda: "No one could touch it; only Rosa could touch it. Stella was not allowed. The shawl was Magda's own baby, her pet, her little sister" (4, 6). Robbed of the shawl, Magda breaks the long silence that enabled Rosa to hide the baby in the barracks or to disguise the infant as the "shivering mound" of her mother's breasts. Because of its capacity to nourish an "infant for three days and three nights," Rosa believes the shawl is magic; because Stella took the shawl away, Rosa thinks her niece "made Magda die." But the reason Magda died had little to do with her lost shawl and less to do with her cries; Magda died because "the historical necessity of killing the children of Jews was self-demonstrative to the Germans" (Levi 16).

Even magic could not have saved Magda from those murderers. Bereft of her shawl, she toddles into the "roll-call arena" where her mouth spills a "long viscous rope of clamor," forcing her mother to decide whether to rush into the arena and grab the "howling" baby or to run back to the barracks, recover the shawl, and silence her grieving daughter (8). Having fetched the magical object she believes will preserve her infant's life, Rosa emerges from the dark barracks into the "perilous sunlight of the arena" only to glimpse her baby far away, "high up, elevated, riding someone's shoulder" (8, 9). It is the shoulder from which Magda is hurled against the electrified fence. If the absence of the shawl contributes to Magda's death, the shawl helps keep Stella and Rosa alive. Hidden under the shawl after she steals it from Magda, Stella sleeps safely in the barracks while Magda is being murdered. Juxtaposing those events, Ozick doubles Magda's milking the shawl at the beginning of the story with Rosa's stuffing the shawl into her mouth at the end of the story. Forced to watch Magda fall "from her flight against the electrified fence," Rosa knows that to cry out or to dash to her dead child is to be shot: the shawl, which once nourished the infant, now stifles its mother's screams—the "wolf's screech" that will bring instant death. The antithesis between sound and silence, between speech and muteness, pervades the story, recalls the role accorded to silence in *The Cannibal Galaxy,* and reinforces the shawl's significance. "The Shawl" begins with Magda's scream on the road to the camp and ends with Rosa's suppressed cry. Throughout the tale, it is silence that saves: "Everyday Magda was silent, and so she did not die" (7). But it is her infant's quietness that induces Rosa to believe that "Magda was defective, without a voice; perhaps she was deaf; there might be something amiss with her intelligence" (7).

Rosa's anxieties about Magda revive Brill's conclusions about Beulah Lilt: the principal regards her reticence as evidence of her stupidity, the sign of failure. In Ozick's second novel, the absence of language signals potential, the kind of silence André Neher accords to the "boundary event in the human history of silence"—Auschwitz (137). That silence—the stilling of "human sound," the muteness before the incomprehensibility of madness—counters the "curt, barbaric barking of Germans in command" in the description Levi provides of his journey to Auschwitz (15). In his memoir Wiesel tells of the silence of God, the "nocturnal silence" that robbed him "of the desire to live"; but in "The Shawl," it is silence and darkness which offer a chance for survival (Wiesel 31–32). The "grainy sad voices," which Rosa hears in the fence and which Stella says are "only an imagining," at first direct the mother to "hold up the shawl, high" to lure her child back and then turning "mad in their growling," the voices urge Rosa to rush to Magda. To obey the "lamenting voices," the voices she has internalized, would invite certain death and so Rosa "took Magda's shawl, and filled her mouth with it." Stifling her screams, she remains alive while her child dies in the sunlit arena.[1] In the pitiless world of the death camps, the sun's ordinary benefits were transformed into omens of danger: "it seemed," Primo Levi writes, "as though the new sun rose as an ally of our enemies to assist in our destruction" (12). It is the dark gloom of the barracks that conceals and protects in "The Shawl"; "in the perilous sunlight of the arena" Magda is detected and murdered (4).

Against the innocent "sunheat" which "murmured of another life, of butterflies in summer" Ozick juxtaposes the sunlit roll-call arena (8). Above the arena, separate from the evil perpetrated in it, or beyond the fence, where "green meadows speckled with dandelions and deep-colored violets" thrive, the light "was placid, mellow" (8). That light promotes bloom. But in the roll-call arena the harsh sunlight exposes Magda's murderer, his glinting helmet "tapped" by the light that "sparkled" the helmet "into a goblet" (9). To the opposing kinds of light, Ozick adds the competing round heads—the helmeted murderer's head, reminiscent of Morris Ngambe's "forehead, perfectly rounded, like a goblet," and the round, vulnerable infant's head. The contrasting images divide good from evil; but Magda's eyes, innocent of evil, are "horribly alive, like blue tigers." Magda's eyes reflect the fierceness born of deprivation. Outside the fence, nourished by nature's plenitude, grow "innocent tiger lilies, tall, lifting their orange bonnets" (8). Emblems of the life struggled for inside the fence and the life flourishing outside it, the tiger eyes and the tiger lilies divide the world of the death camp from the world that surrounds it.

Images of life vie with images of death as Ozick evokes the chilling events common to the death camps in almost unbearably moving terms. Because of its perfect narrative art, "The Shawl" manages to celebrate the power to imagine another life, the human endeavor to survive. The voices in the fence and the magic of the shawl are imaginings; when they direct Rosa to unfurl the shawl to attract Magda, the voices represent the saving power of the imagination. But the power to preserve coexists in the imagination alongside the power to destroy, as the "electrified voices" demonstrate when they begin "to chatter wildly" and command Rosa to die (9). The magic she attributes to the shawl is for the narrator of "Usurpation" forbidden, but in "The Shawl" Rosa owes her life to the shawl's magic. And Magda, her saliva redolent of cinnamon and almond—part of the sacred anointing oil in Scripture and a biblical symbol of divine approval—becomes for Rosa a holy babe capable of being sustained for three days and three nights as if by magic.

Indeed, Rosa's belief in the magic forbidden by Judaism is more accurately linked to paganism. More importantly, the three days and three nights the magic shawl keeps Magda alive conjure in her mother the infant Jesus Christ; and the allusion to Christ in context of the Holocaust recalls Lucy Feingold equating it with the Crucifixion. That alive the baby "flopped onward with her little pencil legs scribbling this way and that," that the child "swimming through the air" resembles a "butterfly touching a silver vine"—these are images which sever Magda from the evildoers in the camp, it is true. But the images are not evidence of Rosa's covenantal belief; they foreshadow the miraculous realm of the imagination to which Rosa will be forced to consign her beloved dead child and its magical shawl.[2] Although the child journeys "through loftiness," her flight ends in a fall against the electrified fence (9). Magda's fate is not Sheindel's. In employing the image of the butterfly by placing it first in the context of life and then in the context of death, Ozick summons up the doubleness with which she has endowed her image. Present at the conclusion of *The Cannibal Galaxy* as a sign of Beulah Lilt's aestheticism, the butterfly is a pagan emblem, one appropriate to the pagan act from which Magda was born. Seeing her fall to her death, Rosa envisions her child as Psyche's emblem. Yet at the end of "The Shawl," despite the imaginary voices urging her like sirens to follow them to the fence where she will be shot, Rosa contravenes what she imagines. Her will to live triumphs over her imagination, over rushing to her infant's remains, over her maternal instincts. The insupportable pain arising in the wake of such an experience constitutes part of the terrible cost of surviving the German hell.

II

What follows in its aftermath becomes achingly apparent in "Rosa," which takes place, though Ozick does not immediately divulge it, over thirty years after "The Shawl." Instead of presenting the events of Rosa's life directly, Ozick begins her novella evocatively: "Rosa Lublin, a madwoman and a scavenger, gave up her store—she smashed it up herself—and moved to Miami." The reasons she was driven to destroy her store emerge later in the tale, not in the chronology of biography but in the associations made by the psyche. In the sequel to "The Shawl" Ozick continues to disclose the linear past the way it appears in the consciousness of her character, but in "Rosa" the storyteller also employs the epistolary form to set forth the events in Rosa's life. Like Allegra Vand, Rosa Lublin recounts her history in the letters she writes. Whether imaginary or real, letters illuminate the workings of a mind, and letters occupy a prominent place in Ozick's fiction: they constitute chapters of people's lives. If in "The Shawl" the consequences of what Rosa has undergone are registered in her thoughts, in "Rosa" she refashions her history in the act of letter-writing. More than the portrayal of Rosa's psyche adjoins "The Shawl" to "Rosa," however. They are connected by common thematic concerns, unified by a mutual metaphor, linked by shared imagery; the tales are consanguineous. Doubling actions and images in "The Shawl" and "Rosa," Ozick penetrates the multiple significations inhering in all experience.

Not only are "The Shawl" and "Rosa" reflections of each other, they mirror the themes that obsess *The Cannibal Galaxy*. Haunting all three fictions is the idea of hell. At the beginning of Ozick's second novel, Joseph Brill envisions the Middle as a particular kind of hell; at the beginning of "The Shawl," Rosa Lublin ponders the coldness of hell in the death camp; but in "Rosa," under the blaze of Miami's sun, she "felt she was in hell" (14). In late middle age, the fifty-eight-year-old schoolmaster and the fifty-eight-year-old woman are melancholics, counters of losses, worshipers at altars of death. Bearing similarities to Joseph Brill, Rosa Lublin recalls Hester Lilt as well. Her relationship with Beulah, one the schoolmaster judges analogous to that between Madame de Sévigné and her daughter, is echoed and extended in the relationship between Rosa and Magda. If the kinship between mother and daughter provides, as it did for Madame de Sévigné, a muse for Hester Lilt and Rosa Lublin, the bond leaves Beulah Lilt an orphan of the future and turns Rosa Lublin into an idolator of the past. Sharing with *Trust* a concern for the relations between mothers and daughters, *The Cannibal Galaxy* and "The Shawl" are tied to Ozick's first novel by the issue of a mysterious paternity. But the puzzle of Beulah's paternity remains unresolved, that of Magda's only dimly perceived. Wholly disparate, the three tales are nonetheless harnessed by kindred themes and paired motifs. In fact, "Rosa," which is set in Miami and which begins where "The Laughter of Akiva" and *The Cannibal Galaxy* end, becomes a kind of sequel to them as well as to "The Shawl." Although the novella's three parts duplicate the number prominent in "The Shawl," they extend—they do not merely repeat—the significance of the number three. Matching images and related events occur throughout "Rosa," as Ozick doubles episodes within the novella and between it and the story to connect existence in the camp to life after it, to distinguish truth from illusion, to reflect emotional conflict, to measure psychic change. In evidence from the very beginning of "Rosa," doubling is the organizing principle of the novella.

In Miami Rosa lives "in a dark hole, a single room in a 'hotel' " that recalls the dark barracks of the camp (13). There she was starved; in her room she starves herself. She exists on "toast with a bit of sour cream and half a sardine, or a small can of peas heated in a Pyrex mug" or, like Zindel, on "two bites of a hard-boiled egg" (13, 14). Imagining the hot streets are a "furnace, the sun an executioner," she aligns them to the sunheat in the arena, to Moloch to whom children were sacrificed (14). In the darkness of her room, Rosa Lublin re-enacts the horrors she lived through in the past. But the scraps of food she eats—some fish, a bit of egg—augur fertility, betoken the renewal of life. On her writing board, Rosa composes letters to Magda in Polish and writes to Stella in English. Her letters set forth feelings about a daughter whose death Rosa often does not acknowledge and about her niece whom she addresses "Angel . . . for the sake of peace," but privately thinks is the "Angel of Death" (15). Rosa's description of Stella, "already nearly fifty years old," reveals that the novella takes place almost thirty-five years after "The Shawl," when Stella was only fourteen and when Rosa was convinced her niece made her daughter die (15). And Stella's "round . . . doll's eyes" and "buttercup lips" recall Magda as Rosa describes her in "The Shawl" (15). Attributing to them twin traits, Ozick implies that for Rosa Magda and Stella are opposing selves. In the death camp Rosa believed the fourteen-year-old girl had thoughts of cannibalizing the baby; in Miami Rosa has "cannibal dreams about Stella" (15). It is as if Rosa has revived the past in the present, for the "killing" sun in Florida—a "murdering sunball" which "fried" the elderly "scarecrows"—conjures up the perilous sunlight in the arena and its emaciated victims (15,

16). Over three decades later, even Florida is awash with reminders of the torment she endured in the German hell.

Ruminating over the past, Rosa gazes at her dirty sheets and knows she must wash them; at the laundromat an "old man sat cross-legged beside her, fingering a newspaper" (17). He speaks Yiddish, but she does not, and her mother's mockery of Yiddish explains why. Their mutual birthplaces in Warsaw, their inability to speak English fluently—these bring Rosa and Persky together, but she separates herself from him, lamenting her "lost and kidnapped Polish" the way Edelshtein mourns "in English the death of Yiddish" (*Shawl* 20; PR 43). The "Warsaw of her girlhood" is juxtaposed against the "thieves who took her life," and Warsaw survives "behind her eyes": a "bright field flashed; then a certain shadowy corridor. . . . Once, walking there, she was conscious of the coursing of her own ecstasy" (20). Of the "house of her girlhood" she recalls a "thousand books. Polish, German, French; her father's Latin books"; in that house she read the Polish poet Julian Tuwim (21). Hers was a family proud of its assimilation.

Born of middle-class Jewish parents, the Polish poet came from a background strikingly parallel to Rosa's. Not only do his allegiances clarify Rosa's, they signal the presence of another theme in the novella—the obsessions of the writer. Like Rosa Lublin's, Julian Tuwim's mother was an assimilationist who instilled in her son a devoted Polish spirit. The Polish poet's pervasive use of the word "blood," as Adam Gillon explains, "fits neatly into Tuwim's pantheistic view of the world, according to which everything can be deified, everything constitutes an element of God" (Gillon 10). Scorning the elderly in Florida for being bourgeois, preoccupied with fabrics, the "meals they used to cook," their hair, Rosa resembles Tuwim and his hatred of "Philistines . . . for their lack of imagination" (*Shawl* 20; Gömöri 51). In his poems he celebrated the sacredness of poetry, often alluding to Christ and even producing litanies.[3] An émigré in New York in 1944, Tuwim loved Poland ardently, but he was savaged by its antisemitic critics.[4] Out of his experience came "We the Jews of Poland," wherein Tuwim declared the "only binding ties those based on . . . the blood of martyrs, spilled by villains" (Markish 41). Tuwim's article became the manifesto of assimilated Jewry throughout Europe, and at the end of his life, the Polish poet gave his support to Israel. His path augurs Rosa's.

To her new acquaintance Simon Persky, a "third cousin to Shimon Peres, the Israeli politician," Rosa speaks of Warsaw, the model of "Cultivation, old civilization, beauty, history!" (22, 21). A "great light" illuminated Warsaw and its gardens; murderous sunlight burns the "perpetual garden of Florida" (21, 16). Doubling the gardens, Ozick dramatizes the way in which Rosa keeps the memory of Warsaw alive in Florida. That she calls herself "Lublin, Rosa" reveals her attachment to Poland; that Ozick chose the name Lublin stresses the fate of Rosa's assimilation. Originally planned as a reservation for the concentration of Jews by the Nazis, Lublin became one of the centers for mass extermination and was the site of a prisoner of war camp for Jews who had served in the Polish army. The Nazis made no distinction between Jews who abandoned their Jewishness and Jews who celebrated it: religious Jews were murdered alongside assimilated ones. Rosa's and Lushinski's histories accentuate the fundamental futility of the Jew in hiding.[5] Though they resemble each other in denying their identities, Rosa and Lushinski are opposites. Where Lushinski runs from the roil of Europe and masters the language of Africa, Rosa remains mainly ignorant of English and wants to return to her girlhood in Poland.

To gainsay any similarity to the Jew Persky, Rosa reiterates the distinction between her Warsaw and his. But Persky, "proud of being a flirt," is not easily discouraged. Instinctively sensing the reason she lives like a hermit, he admonishes her, " 'You can't live in the past.' " Before the window of the kosher cafeteria to which her new acquaintance leads her, Rosa descries a "ragged old bird with worn feathers, Skinny, a stork" (23). Of the reason the stork is deemed impure by Jewish law, Hester Lilt writes: "She hopes only for the distinction of the little one under her heart. She will not cherish the stranger's young" (CG 158). The window, like the mirrors in *Trust*, "Envy," and "The Doctor's Wife," throws back an image of the truth: Rosa cares only for Magda. Other facts emerge in the conversation Rosa and Persky have as they sit at a round table, a counterpart to the table in Rosa's room. His son, whom Persky supports, forced his father to sell the factory where he made buttons and accessories; Rosa, whom Stella supports, specialized in antique mirrors until she destroyed her own store. Their careers establish their differences: an unexceptional man, Persky wanted to make new and ordinary buttons. He sought to join things together, but treasuring a former time, Rosa detached herself from others. Without even a pocket mirror now—a reminder of her lost daughter's "pocket mirror of a face"—Rosa revived the past in her antique mirrors. But her missing button not only separates her from Persky, it is an emblem of the hell she crawled out of. Part of the hell of Auschwitz, Primo Levi observed, had to do with the "infinite and senseless" rites of the camp such as the "control of buttons on one's jacket, which had to be five" (29). And later in his memoir, the absence of buttons becomes a sign of the helplessness and vulnerability of those who were forced to leave the camp's infirmary, "naked and almost always insufficiently cured," and had to adapt to a new Block and a new *Kommando* (51). Finding herself in another hell three decades after the German one, Rosa, Ozick implies, is as ill-equipped for "human contact" as the partially healed man Levi describes in his memoirs (51).

Rosa's psychic wounds have not healed, for the "thieves" who wrested her life from her left Rosa no alternative save to retreat to a life "inside her eyes" (20–21). And so she toils away from a new human contact to withdraw to her room. On Miami's scalding streets, she thinks, "Summer without end, a mistake!" (28). Her reflection conjures up Joseph Brill's grim apprehension of perpetuity and alludes to E. B. White's essay, "Once More to the Lake." Revisiting the summer camp of his childhood with his son, the father witnessed the perdurability of nature, the "pattern of life indelible, the fade-proof lake, the woods unshatterable, the pasture with the sweetfern and the juniper forever and ever, summer without end" (200). The distinction between himself, his father, and his son blurred, White felt that "there had been no years," that the generations were linked "in a strong indestructible chain" (199, 202). But in the wake of that perception comes a more chilling one—his sudden awareness of the swift and inexorable passage of time, a glimpse of his own mortality. In Miami where her memories of the death camp are continually awakened, Rosa is racked not by her own mortality but by her daughter's death, not by the congruence of the generations but by their disjunction, not by the ravages of time but by "time at the fix."

The mirrored lobby yields up a reflection of the hotel's residents and Rosa sees they believe "in the seamless continuity of the body," in the eternal sameness of life, in permanence: "In these mirrors the guests appeared to themselves as they used to be" (28, 29). Forgetful of their children and their grandchildren, the aged grow "significant to themselves" (29). What is important to them is insignificant to Rosa, for she looks forward to finding her child's shawl delivered in the day's mail. Turning the box "round and round" in her room as if to mimic the shape of Magda's face, Rosa recollects her child's smell, the "holy fragrance of the lost babe. Murdered. Thrown against the fence, barbed, thorned, electrified; grid and griddle; a furnace; the child on fire!" (31). The bed covers "knotted together like an umbilical cord" link the mother's dreams in Miami to the infant who died in Germany. Of the ritual that accompanies Rosa's memories Stella writes:

> It's thirty years, forty, who knows, give it a rest. It isn't as if I don't know just exactly how you do it, what it's like. What a scene, disgusting! You'll open the box and take it out and cry, and you'll kiss it like a crazy person. Making holes in it with kisses. You're like those people in the Middle Ages who worshiped a piece of the True Cross, a splinter from some old outhouse as far as anybody knew, or else they fell down in front of a single hair supposed to be some saint's. (31–32)

And in Stella's comparison of Rosa's idolatry to the worship of the Cross, Ozick affirms what she implies in "The Shawl"—that the child who was kept alive for three days and three nights is for its mother an image of the infant Christ. It is an image that renders Rosa unable to relinquish the past and incapable of resuming her life. To face the truth of Stella's remarks is to sacrifice illusion and to suffer further loss. The Angel of Death who made Magda die wants to shatter Rosa's idol.

In a remarkably deft association, Ozick joins Stella's urging Rosa to live her life, her memory of the thieves who robbed her of her life, and her missing a pair of underpants. That loss, ostensibly a trivial one, symbolizes a loss of such magnitude that to confront it directly would be intolerable. Untangling a blue-striped dress, Stella's birthday present, from the bedsheets the way Persky had unwound her laundry, Rosa recalls the striped uniforms worn in the death camps: "Stripes, never again anything on her body with stripes!" (33). And she condemns Stella for buying the dress, denounces her for forgetting her past—

"As if innocent, as if ignorant, as if *not there*"—and for becoming "indistinguishable" from "ordinary" Americans who cannot "guess what hell she had crawled out of" (33). The memory of that hell prompts Rosa to remember Magda's shawl, which she means "to crush . . . in her mouth" the way she did when she witnessed her baby murdered (35). As if to receive communion, "She tidied all around. . . . She spread jelly on three crackers and deposited a Lipton's tea bag on the Welch's lid. It was grape jelly" (34). But the idea that Persky "had her underpants in his pocket" distracts her from her ritual and revives memories of a painful sexual experience: "The shame. Pain in the loins. Burning" (34). Ozick forges the links among the events indirectly, the way they appear in consciousness when ordinary sights and objects evoke deeper and more disturbing thoughts from which the mind turns in wincing pain.

Rather than remember the brute who violated her, Rosa makes Persky into the culprit: a "sex maniac, a wife among the insane, his parts starved" (34). That Stella believes her aunt belongs with the insane and has the power to put Rosa in a mental hospital, as Persky has his wife, induces Rosa to imagine herself with Mrs. Persky learning about "Persky's sexual habits" and telling her, a "woman with children," about Magda (35). In this manner, Ozick doubles the kinds of madness in order to distinguish them: she separates mental pathology from the madness brought about by war.[6] The intricacy of the consciousness Ozick has produced emerges in the letters Rosa writes and in her responses to the letters of others. Letters afford entry into Rosa's consciousness; they furnish the fragments of a history that must be fit together like the pieces of a puzzle. Vacillating between remembering her baby's death and denying it, Rosa bears testimony to the extent of her suffering. Of such agony Dr. James W. Tree from the "Department of Clinical Social Pathology at the University of Kansas-Iowa" knows little. His "university letter," which arrived along with Stella's letter, reduces Rosa's anguish to sociological jargon, conjuring up the mechanistic predictions of the psychologists against whom Hester Lilt inveighs and the pompous platitudes of the famous critic whom Ozick satirizes in "The Suitcase."

The recipient of funds from "the Minew Foundation of the Kansas-Iowa Institute for Humanitarian Context," Dr. James W. Tree finds "remarkable" the persistence in survivors' lives of "neurological residues" and "hormonal changes" (36). What "particularly engages" him is the " 'metaphysical' side of Repressed Animation (R.A.)," a theory he believes accounts for survivors' responses to the death camps: "It begins to be evident that prisoners gradually came to Buddhist positions. They gave up craving and began to function in terms of non-functioning, i.e., non-attachment. . . . Non-attachment is attained through the Eightfold Path, the highest stage of which is the cessation of human craving, the loftiest rapture, one might say, of consummated indifference" (37, 38). Rosa considers the "special word . . . *survivor*" the way Lushinski protests Lulu's exclusion of the Jews from mankind: "A name like a number—counted apart from the ordinary swarm. Blue digits on the arm, what difference?" (36). To Tree's request that she invite him to study her "survivor syndroming within the natural setting" Rosa cries, "Home. Where, where?" (38). Of his opinion that she is "ideally circumstanced to make a contribution to [the] R-S study" she thinks, "Drop in a hole! Disease! . . . this is the cure for the taking of a life" (38–39). And setting his letter afire, she throws it in the sink, consigning Tree to a dark void like her hotel room and submitting his letter to a fate like Magda's. But she revives Magda by writing to her, and imagining her daughter a "professor of Greek philosophy at Columbia University," Rosa invents a life for her child the way a storyteller brings a character into being.

Her letter—part biography, part fiction—chronicles the tale of three generations. The daughter of a father who "had the instincts of a natural nobleman" and "was never a Zionist," Rosa saved Stella from being "shipped . . . with a boatload of orphans to Palestine, to become God knows what, to live God knows how. A field worker jabbering Hebrew" (40). The scorn Rosa has for such a fate parallels her derision of Yiddish and bears the imprint of her family. Similarly, her belief, "like the Catholics, in mystery" stems from her mother's desire to convert: attracted to Christianity, her mother "let the maid keep a statue of the Virgin and the Child in the corner of the kitchen" (41). From motherhood, Rosa tells Magda, comes the ability "To pass on a whole genetic system"; from her mother, a poetess who "was not afraid to call herself a 'symbolist,' " comes Rosa's capacity to imagine other lives. Replicating traits of parents in their children, Ozick instances the continuity between generations.

If Rosa tells the truth about her own upbringing, she fabricates one for Magda. Claiming for her child parents who had "respectable, gentle, cultivated, lives," Rosa then reveals that she was not married to Andrzej but "engaged to be married" to him (43). Nonetheless, she denies "Stella's accusations," for they furnish a less than gentle account of Magda's father: "your father was not a German. I was forced by a German, it's true, and more than once, but I was too sick to conceive. Stella has a naturally pornographic mind, she can't resist dreaming up a dirty sire for you, an S.S. man! Stella was with me the whole time, she knows just what I know" (43). The suggestion in "The Shawl" that Magda could belong to a German and was born in a camp, the memory Rosa has of the degrading pain in her loins, the admission that she was raped by Germans several times—these revelations identify Magda's father as the S.S. man who raped Rosa. They are recollections too painful to face, they motivate the accusation that Stella "thieves all the truth"; they spur Rosa to create another history (43). Called a "parable-maker" by Stella, Rosa is one of Ozick's artists:

> What a curiosity it was to hold a pen—nothing but a small pointed stick, after all, oozing its hieroglyphic puddles: a pen that speaks, miraculously, Polish. A lock removed from the tongue. Otherwise the tongue is chained to the teeth and the

palate. An immersion into the living language: all at once this cleanliness, this capacity, this power to make a history, to tell, to explain. To retrieve, to reprieve!
To lie. (44)

That Magda will become her mother's muse is hinted at in "The Shawl" when Rosa considers her baby's "pencil legs" as they scribble into the arena and likens her daughter to a butterfly as she flutters through the air to her death. That Rosa calls Magda a "yellow lioness"—an allusion to the last three lines of Tuwim's poem, "Draw Blood with the Word"—attaches the child to writing: "O words! Sharp and Golden! / Pouncing words of prey, / Like lions! Like lions!" (Gillon 33). Oozing puddles, the pen recalls the volcanic typewriter in "Usurpation"; releasing lies, the pen is an instrument for mendacity as well as for veracity.

The "routine" Rosa practices after receiving "university letters" counters the ritual she engages in with Magda's shawl: in those acts she divides her rage from her grief. Dressed in "good shoes" and a "nice dress," Rosa mounts the "bed on her knees," as if kneeling before an altar (44). In that position she ruminates, like Joseph Brill, for hours on the "pitiless tableaux" of her past, worshiping like James's Stransom at an altar of loss (45). The word "pitiless" matches the triple repetition of the phrase, the "place without pity" in "The Shawl" and determines the provenance of the tableaux—the death camp where Magda was murdered. In the tableaux there are "Darkened cities, tombstones, colorless garlands, a black fire in a gray field, brutes forcing the innocent, women with their mouths stretched and their arms wild, her mother's voice calling" (44–45). In the newspaper after Rosa demolished her store there was a "big photograph, Stella standing near with her mouth stretched and her arms wild" (18). Bringing together the tombstones in the tableaux with Magda's "tombstone tooth," the violated women with the distraught Stella, Ozick links the rapists to the infant, a self-destructive act to a savage one, and makes Rosa's niece a witness to both. Absorbed by such recollections until late afternoon, Rosa becomes "certain that whoever put her underpants in his pocket was a criminal capable of every base act. Humiliation. Degradation. Stella's pornography!" (45). In those linked associations is the significance of the lost underpants: they symbolize Rosa's sexual organs which the rape violated and desecrated, dirtied like the "stains in the crotch [that] are nobody's business" (34).

Wanting "to retrieve, to reprieve," powers she accords to her pen, Rosa leaves the box she believes holds Magda's shawl on the table and goes in search of her underpants. Grieved by her loss of them, she is driven into the streets of Miami as once, bereft of her shawl, Magda toddled into the perilous roll-call arena, where she died. Like the arena, the streets are scalded by the "murdering sunball" during the day; toward dusk a "scarlet sun, round and brilliant as a blooded egg yolk" hangs in the sky. Reminiscent of Rosa's hard-boiled egg, the fertilized egg in "Puttermesser and Xanthippe," and the cosmic egg in

Trust, the egg alludes to the primordial egg from which Eros sprang, a symbol of the repetition of the primeval act. At the end of the long road, Ozick suggests, lies a new world, the possibility of a future. Oppressive by day, at night the streets "are clogged with wanderers and watchers; everyone in search, bedouins with no fixed paths" (45). Unlike the roll-call arena, the streets are an arena in which to reclaim life. Just as Puttermesser's "long introspective stride" up Lexington Avenue uncovers the lawyer's motives for creating a golem, Rosa's peregrination of Miami unearths the reasons the survivor must recover her underpants. And Rosa's impression of the sand is the first of several associations leading to the meaning of the "lost laundry": the "sand never at rest, always churning, always inhabited; copulation under blankets at night, beneath neon-radiant low horizons" (46). Her subsequent ideas of the underpants "smoldering in an ash heap" or in "conflagrations of old magazines" invoke the death camp and connect it to the underpants (46). To imagine "what a weight of sand would feel like in the crotch of her pants, wet heavy sand, still hot from the day" is to wonder what it would feel like to have the trunk of her body buried (47). Walking "unconnected to anything," seeing "everything, but as if out of invention, out of imagination," Rosa retreats to a landscape behind her eyes (47).

The one before them is littered with "so many double mounds," bodies in the sand which conjure up a photograph of Pompeii (48). Among the pictures taken of the fields of ash that preserved the shapes of corpses within a mold of a void, were casts of lovers "who fell together, side by side, mingling their last breath" (Brion 37). Ozick's reference to those photographs supplies the connection Rosa makes between her lost laundry and the fate of the buried lovers: "Her pants were under the sand; or else packed hard with sand, like a piece of torso, a broken statue, the human groin detached, the whole soul gone, only the loins left for kicking by strangers" (48). From that alliance emerges the reason she cares more for her underwear than for her store: it was only a "cave of junk" (21). But the theft of her pants left her broken like one of those shells Brill sees on the beach of the Phlegethon, the "life in them cleaned out, scooped, eaten, decomposed" (CG 86). Amid the "lovers plugged into a kiss," Rosa considers stepping "cleanly into the sea," a suicidal impulse like murdering "her business with her own hands" (48). As she does at the end of "The Shawl," Rosa rejects the pull toward death, the ease with which she could enter the "horizontal tunnel," for the "unpredictable"—for life (48). Double acts of self-preservation compete against double impulses to self-destruction: they manifest the way victimizers manage to perpetuate torment in their victims long after victimizing them. His oppressors drove Lushinski to murder his own soul, to appropriate another identity, to end in desolation. To overcome the desolation Rosa must repossess her soul.

On the beach she encounters a pair of homosexual lovers; their mockery elicits her hissing response, "Sodom," and Ozick establishes the chain of Rosa's associations—Pompeii, Sodom and Gomorrah, the death camps. In connecting those places, Rosa unites their history of sexual perversion, and the storyteller yokes the wicked biblical cities destroyed by the fire of heaven, the immoral pagan city buried by an eruption, and the modern country whose ferocious evil annihilated an entire civilization. Derided by the homosexuals' laughter and "locked behind" the "barbed wire" of the fence encircling the private beach, Rosa trembles in remembrance; but she is no longer in the place without pity, the place with the murderous fence (49). Although they conjure in her memories of sexual perversion and Nazi paganism, the homosexual lovers are not bent on killing her but on ignoring her: "They hated women. Or else they saw she was a Jew; they hated Jews; but no, she had noticed the circumcision, like a jonquil, in the dim sand. . . . No one knew who she was; what had happened to her; where she came from" (49). The jonquil parallels the buttercup to which she compares Stella's lips, the "harmless containers" in which the "bloodsucker comes," and both flowers bring back the innocent tiger lilies growing outside the fence at the end of "The Shawl" (15). Then Rosa could only gaze beyond the fence and dream of another life; in Miami the fence leads her to "light" and to freedom.

Free, she accosts the manager in the hotel lobby: " 'Only Nazis,' " she tells him, " 'catch innocent people behind barbed wire' " (51). Judging the way he runs his hotel evidence of Finkelstein's indifference to the Holocaust, Rosa is enraged. Whereas silence had been her savior in the camp, noise became her redeemer after she was liberated: "They had trapped her, nearly caught her; but she knew how to escape. Speak up, yell. The same way she saved Stella, when they were pressing to take her on the boat to Palestine" (52). Unlike the survivors in Ozick's other fiction—Sheindel in "The Pagan Rabbi," the rebbe in "Bloodshed," the refugee in "Levitation"—Rosa has inherited from her parents a "certain contempt" for Jews, whom she regards as "primitive" and common (52, 53). Finkelstein's red wig reminds her of Persky's red wig: "Florida was glutted with fake fire, burning false hair! Everyone a piece of imposter" (50). In Warsaw, she regarded the "swarm" of Jews as "shut off from the grandeur of the true world"; in Miami, she protests Tree's word, "survivor," because it excludes Jews from the "ordinary swarm" (52–53, 36). But she divides herself from both groups of Jews and leaves the Hotel Marie Louise "Irradiated, triumphant, cleansed" (52). To complete her victory, Rosa must find her underpants: she must reclaim her soul.

Like the trek to the laundromat, Rosa's walk culminates in a meeting with Persky. In her room, "miraculously ready: tidy, clarified," their differences become more apparent (55). Persky judges her room "cozy"; Rosa finds it "cramped." One seeks a good "way of describing," the other calls that a way of lying (56). Hugging the box she presumes contains Magda's shawl, Rosa feels as if "someone had cut out her life-organs and given them to her to hold," had removed her soul (56). Aware she has "to work things through," Persky advises her to " 'adjust,' " to become a " 'regular person,' " to forget the past so as " 'to get something out of life' " (57, 58). What Persky, an American Jew, cannot fathom and has no right to judge is her enduring memory of the Holocaust, and so Rosa shames him with her account of the survivor's three lives:

" 'The life after is now. The life before is our *real* life, at home, where we was born. . . . Before is a dream. After is a joke. Only during stays. And to call it a life is a lie' " (58). For the rebbe in "Bloodshed," a man who believes in "turnings," the life after holds possibility, potential, hope. On one thing, however, the rebbe and Rosa agree: the importance of remembering the past, and that conviction is fundamental to Ozick's thought, especially with regard to the Holocaust. In a discussion about writing and the Holocaust published in 1988, five years after "Rosa," Ozick anticipates the objections to her own "act of memorial," her steadfast refusal ever to visit Germany: "What can be done about it now? Let bygones be bygones. Choose erasure. Wipe out memory" ("Roundtable" 283). In Ozick's novella, it is Rosa who complains that Stella "wants to wipe out memory," but her aunt's "act of memorial" results in an obsession, in idolatrous worship of the dead—a pagan ritual.

To include Persky in that ritual is to yield to a stranger "what her own hands longed to do." It is "to prove herself pure: a madonna" (59). But the box shelters not Magda's shawl but houses Hidgeson's book, *Repressed Animation: A Theory of the Biological Ground of Survival,* the study of survivors Tree extolled in the letter Rosa burned in the sink. Enraged by Tree's note directing her to read Chapter Six, "Defensive Group Formation: The Way of the Baboons," Rosa hurls the book at the ceiling, the way she smashed up her store; and Ozick separates a melancholic self-destructive impulse from an angry and healthy one. Attempting to wreck Tree for his indifference to human suffering, Rosa adds to her first outburst of fury with Finkelstein a second eruption of rage against Tree and a third one against Persky. Connecting him to the researchers who have equated the human struggle to survive the inhuman conditions in the death camps with the habits of baboons, Rosa cries: " 'I'm not your button, Persky! I'm nobody's button, not even if they got barbed wire everywhere!' " (61). That she accuses him of being a "thief"—the name she calls the person who took her life—reveals she has projected onto Persky feelings about someone else. He has become in her mind the tormentor from her past. To her allegation Persky responds, " 'I can see I'm involved in a mistake,' " and Rosa discovers her mistake the next day when she finds the missing underpants "curled inside a towel" (61).

Unfolding from her character's consciousness the events that ultimately led to intense rage, Ozick instances the sorrows of Jewish history and brings them into sharp relief by depicting their grave effects on one woman's life. At the same time, the storyteller explores with acute and compassionate insight the way the human psyche can turn against itself, transforming rage into guilt and guilt into grief which, at its most extreme, can develop into the melancholia that abrogates interest in the outside world. That it is necessary for Rosa "to prove herself pure" attests to a deeper emotional demand: the need to deny the history of Magda's creation, to metamorphose her infant into a holy babe brought forth not from a violent rape but from an immaculate conception. The shawl's magical capacity to nurture a child for three days and three nights testifies to that psychic requirement. Three is a preponderant number in "Rosa." At first establishing an affinity in "The Shawl" between Magda and the infant Christ, the number three becomes in "Rosa" an insistent reminder of the death camps: under the Third Reich, one-third of the Jewish people were murdered. The three lives survivors possess, the three cups Rosa owns, the three crackers she prepares for her ritual, the three steps she takes to the bed, the three "bloodsuckers" she counts, and the three members of her family who she tells Persky remained alive after the Holocaust—these signal indelible memories of the German hell for which three is a symbol.

Nonetheless, Rosa delays writing to Magda and decides instead to reconnect her telephone. Ozick converts the electrified wire of the camp's fence from which Rosa heard "grainy sad voices" urging her to die into ordinary telephone wire empowering her to live. That she has begun to emerge from the landscape behind her eyes is suggested by her indifference to Magda's shawl. Once redolent of the holy fragrance of the murdered child, the shawl now "lay like an old bandage, a discarded sling," its "faint saliva smell . . . more nearly imagined than smelled" (62). Rather than engage in her ritual, Rosa telephones Stella who grimly tells her aunt to end her "morbidness," to recuperate, not to call "long *dis*tance" (64). On that phrase, "Magda sprang to life" and Rosa puts the shawl "over the knob of the receiver," transforming it into a "little doll's head," a reminder of Stella's round "doll's" eyes (64). But the shawl chokes off Rosa's conversation the way it once stifled Rosa's screams and revives the memory of the child lighting on the electrified fence like a butterfly on a silver vine.

The mother recoils from that memory and imagines her daughter at sixteen dressed in a "sky-colored dress," one of "Rosa's dresses from high school" (64). Beginning "to resemble Rosa's father," Magda begins to become Rosa, but she is bewildered by her daughter's "other strain": "The other strain was ghostly, even dangerous. It was as if the peril hummed out from the filaments of Magda's hair, those narrow bright wires" (65–66). In the imagery with which Rosa limns the girl is a clue to Magda's other strain. Reminiscent of the "lamenting voices" in the camp's fence, Magda's hair recalls the sirens' songs. If the daughter's "sky-filled" eyes are like the mother's blue dress, Magda's buttercup yellow hair is the color of the yellow badges issued in Nazi Germany. Inherited from "idolatrous Germans," Magda's "other strain" is the dangerous strain inhering in the imagination—the propensity for paganism (A&A 235). In calling Magda a butterfly and in choosing butterfly pins for Beulah Lilt's hair, Ozick makes the two girls, who are their mother's muses, symbols of the imagination in its capacity to invent idols. If Hester Lilt produces an aesthete who forgets her past, Rosa Lublin bears a daughter whose death anchors her mother in the past; if the painter escapes into a nimbus, the letter-writer retreats into her thoughts. Behind her eyes Rosa envisions various lives for Magda, fancies her a professor of Greek philosophy, pictures her a painter or a musician, conceives her history, writes her story.

The power of the imagination to remove a lock from the tongue, to impel the pen "to tell, to explain"—the imagination's crowning act of splendor—is illustrated in the second and imaginary letter Rosa writes to Magda. A kind of parable, the letter recounts the history of Rosa's family and doubles events from the past in each of Rosa's three lives. Despite their ability to enunciate "Polish . . . with the most precise articulation," despite their assimilation into Polish life, despite their denial of a Jewish identity, Rosa and her family were confined in a ghetto "with teeming Mockowiczes and Rabinowiczes and Perskys and Finkelsteins. . . . old Jew peasants worn out from their rituals and superstitions" (68, 66, 67). Including Persky and Finkelstein among the Warsaw Jews, Rosa renders them indistinguishable from American Jews. But all the Jews in Warsaw were separated from other Polish citizens by the wall built around the ghetto, and the memory of the tramcar that "came right through the middle of the ghetto" was one Rosa used to share with her customers as testimony to the evils she had witnessed. The bridge constructed to prevent the Jews from escaping into the "other side of the wall" kept them crowded together in a "terrible slum" while ordinary Poles traveled through the ghetto daily and witnessed the Jews' misery without protesting. In the death camp the wall of the ghetto was replaced by the fence, the overhead electric wire of the tramcar by the fence's electrified wires.

After she was liberated, Rosa remembered the woman she had seen with a head of lettuce protruding from her shopping sack: that plain, working-class woman was considered a Pole, better than Rosa and her well-educated family. That woman remained silent and unresponsive to the suffering around her. In New York Rosa "became like the woman with the lettuce": a witness, but one who spoke up "to the deaf" in her store (69). Impassive and indifferent like the Polish citizens the tramcar carried through the ghetto, Rosa's customers reignited the rage of abandonment Rosa experienced in the ghetto, the rage the tormented feels against the tormentor, the rage that later propelled Rosa to wreck her store. But in Miami Rosa met a former vegetable-store owner whose reminiscences of romaine lettuce revived the painful event she endured over thirty years ago in the Warsaw Ghetto. Her suffering there—the salivary glands that ached at the sight of the lettuce—became excitement for others: "They let their mouths water up. . . . Consider also the special word they used: survivor. . . . Even when your bones get melted into the grains of the earth, still they'll forget human being. Survivor and survivor and survivor; always and always. Who made up these words, parasites on the throat of suffering!" (36–37). Pairing events from the past and the present, Cynthia Ozick dramatizes their persistence.

If the witness who recounts the Nazis' atrocities to unconcerned Americans speaks English the way the uneducated woman in Warsaw spoke Polish, it is not because Rosa is uncultivated: "They, who couldn't read one line of Tuwim, never mind Virgil, and my father, who knew nearly the whole half of the Aeneid by heart" (69). Having lived in a house filled with art—"replicas of Greek vases" and "wonderful ink drawings"—Rosa has inherited a "whole genetic system," the legacy of classicism (68). To that tradition belong her ritual with Magda's shawl, her belief in mystery, her idolatry. But the imaginary letter, the ones she writes "inside a blazing flying current, a terrible beak of light bleeding out a kind of cuneiform on the underside of her brain," fatigues her and augurs change (69). In matching Magda's disappearance at the end of "Rosa"—the "blue of her dress" becoming "only a speck in Rosa's eye"—with Rosa's vision of the "speck of Magda" before she was thrown against the fence, Ozick doubles Rosa's losses (69, 9). The first is brought by Magda's death, the second by the collapse of Rosa's illusion. That is the illusion the imagination fashions: it can transform a telephone into a "little grimy silent god" akin to the "black baal" in *The Cannibal Galaxy*, an idol that founders before reality—"Voices, sounds, echoes, noise" (69). The silence that pervades "The Shawl" is broken in "Rosa" where the ringing phone heralds the arrival of Persky—the ordinary button, the shatterer of illusion, the harbinger of renewal. Accepting Persky, Rosa abandons her father's aversion for Jews.

In *Trust* Ozick alludes to the *Odyssey* as she charts the quest to recover a father; in "Rosa" the storyteller adverts to the *Aeneid* as she chronicles the need for separation from the father. To unlock the secret of her father's identity, the narrator of *Trust* must enter hell, the room where William apprises her of her illegitimacy. If "every story has its Charon," several of Ozick's tales have their hells. Referring to Edom in "A Mercenary," Ozick implies that Lushinski ends in a kind of hell; Joseph Brill and Rosa Lublin proclaim hell their habitations. Where Brill ends is where Rosa begins. Images from the *Aeneid* thread their way through "Rosa," but the parallels Ozick draws between Aeneas's journey to the underworld and Rosa's symbolic descent into the past broadens the meaning of the novella, lending to its revelations universal truth. From the very beginning of "Rosa," Ozick establishes resemblances between Rosa and Aeneas: survivors of wars which are moral tragedies and which result in exile, Rosa and Aeneas are aligned to Venus, Aeneas's mother, whose sacred flower, the rose, and whose emblem, the star, are alluded to in the names Rosa and Stella. In Ozick's novella and Virgil's poem, a slain daughter is a grim foreboding of a return, the sacrifice of Iphigenia to appease the gods a counterpart to the brutally irrational murder of Magda. Aeneas, whom Virgil likens to a wolf—the poet's symbol of "birth" and "violence"—must make his way into the particular hell of Troy's fall even as Rosa must stifle her "wolf's screech" and make her way into a private hell, the hell of the persistent "during" (Putnam 148; Virgil 2.383). Aeneas and Rosa both grieve over dead families, desire to die, and are forced to wander.

Ozick merges in "Rosa" episodes and motifs from several books of the *Aeneid*. Rosa's madness conjures up the madness which accompanies the fall of Troy in Virgil's poem, which like the novella possesses a "pattern of madness suppressed and released" (Putnam 16). The madness of the survivor is induced by the madness of war and is not madness at all. To have been forced to witness the murder of her own child is, as the dying Priam cries out angrily after watching the murder of his son Polites, the "worst pollution" (2.563). Small wonder, then, that Rosa in her grief must continue, like Andromache, to call Magda's "ghost to the place which she had hallowed / With double altars, a green and empty tomb" (3.304–5). The injustice, the horror, the madness of war—these point to the central question of the *Aeneid*: "What divinity can demand the righteous suffer and why?" (Medcalf 306). It is the question asked by Job; it is the question many raised in the aftermath of the Holocaust, and it is the unspoken question at the heart of "Rosa." Which is to say, the question has no answer. The triumphant experience Rosa has at the Hotel Marie Louise attests not to her discovery of saving truths in the Holocaust, for "no promise, no use, no restitution and no redemption can come out of the suffering and destruction of one-third of the Jewish people," but to her ultimate refusal to become someone's button, to surrender her soul, to die ("Roundtable" 279). Hers is a victory of the human spirit.

But it is a victory with its own demands. To possess a future Rosa and Aeneas must return to the past, liberate themselves from its shackles, master their grief. If Aeneas drives his fleet "To Cumae's coast-line" to begin his descent to the underworld, Rosa moves to the peninsula of Florida and writes to her niece, " 'Where I put myself is in hell' " (14). Throughout her novella, Ozick alludes to the first six books of the *Aeneid;* conflating episodes from it, invoking its imagery, rearranging its events, she summons up the Virgilian hell in Miami, Florida, to illuminate Rosa Lublin's harrowing experience in the German hell. At the beginning of her walk on the shore, the sun and the moon, "Two strange competing lamps. . . . hung simultaneously at either end of the long road"; they are reminders of Cumae, of Apollo's temple and Diana's grove, of the Sibyl's dwelling place (45). In the Sibyl's dusky cave the Trojan learns how to cross the Styx, to find his father, whom Aeneas carried out of Troy on his shoulders. Less loving shoulders dispatched Magda to her death. Driven like Aeneas and frenzied like the Sibyl in her cavern, Rosa resides in a "dark hole" in Miami, in a Sibylline cave.

In the *Aeneid* Apollo's temple stands near the priestess's cave, and its doors, carved by Daedalus, portray scenes akin to Rosa's experiences. "On a trip to Crete," Rosa's father discovered a Greek vase, a reminder of the urn on the temple doors, the urn from which lots were drawn to determine the children "For sacrifice each year" (*Shawl* 68; Virgil 6.23). The "land of Crete," to which Rosa's father traveled and from which Daedalus fled, rises out of the picture the artisan chiseled on the doors, which display "The mongrel Minotaur, half man, half monster, / The proof of lust unspeakable" (6.28–29). His overwhelming grief prevented Daedalus from including his son Icarus in the picture. The "souls of infants" who died "Before their share of living," the doomed youth Marcellus—these dead children, the children Aeneas sees in the underworld, are in "Rosa" versions of Magda, the murdered babe, proof of unspeakable lust (6.455, 457).

After that horror Rosa believed herself "used to everything"; thinking "no form of trouble . . . Is new, or unexpected," Aeneas begs the Sibyl to open the portals barring the way to his father. For Rosa as for Aeneas

> . . . the portals of dark Dis
> Stand open: it is easy, the descending
> Down to Avernus

> But to climb again,
> To trace the footsteps back to the air above,
> There lies the task, the toil. (6.144–148)

Entering the gates to the private beach of the Hotel Marie Louise, the "threshold of the wicked," Rosa sees "Vague forms in lonely darkness," unearths "matters buried deep in earth and darkness" (6.583,285,284). Just as Aeneas must confront his past in his descent, so Rosa must confront hers. But before Aeneas can see the Stygian kingdoms, he has to prepare Misenus for burial. Washing him from water in "Bronze caldrons," the men perform the rites required for admittance to Dis's portals; watching the "round porthole of the washing machine," where her underwear is "slapped . . . against the pane," her dress "against the caldron's metal sides," Rosa readies herself to conquer her furies (19). Then approaching their respective gates, Aeneas and Rosa brave their pasts.

On the beach, Rosa envisions her lost underpants "like a piece of torso" detached from the loins and Ozick summons up Priam's terrible death: "a nameless body, on the shore, / Dismembered, huge, the head torn from the shoulders" (2.581–82). Rending Priam's head from his shoulders, Pyrrhus leaves the proud ruler nameless, unidentifiable; forcibly desecrating her genitals, the Nazi wrested from his victim her very soul. To discharge her fury at Finkelstein is to force the deaf customers to hear what she witnessed, to redirect the rage that impelled her to a kind of suicide, to reclaim the "loins" the S.S. man "left for kicking" (48). It is "to trace the footsteps back to the air above." As Aeneas's two encounters with Palinurus and Dido precede the third and most important one with Anchises, so Rosa's conflicts with the homosexual couple and Finkelstein herald a vision of Magda.

And she is evoked by Stella's word "long *dis* stance." The god of the lower world, Dis is offered "An altar in the night," an altar such as the one Rosa prepares in her room (6.270). In its power to provide nourishment for three days and three nights, in its ability to save a mother from death, in its capacity to afford contact with the dead, Magda's shawl stands as a counterpart to the golden bough, which was sacred to Persephone, queen of the underworld. It is to that maiden Ozick alludes in Rosa's imaginary letter. Unlike the first letter, which Rosa begins, "Magda, My Soul's Blessing," the salutation of the second letter implies that Magda is a symbolic Persephone: "My Gold, my Wealth, My Treasure, my Hidden Sesame, my Paradise, my Yellow Flower, my Magda! Queen of Bloom and Blossom!" (39, 66). And Magda, in whom a ghostly, perilous strain runs has, like Persephone, "two aspects, girl-like daughter of the Corn Goddess and Mistress of the Dead" (Burkert 159). Attaching to Magda's hair "two barrettes, in the shape of cornets," emblems of Persephone's attribute, the cornucopia, Ozick joins Magda to Persephone as well as to Beulah Lilt, to whose hair the storyteller fastens symbols of the imagination.

The union of the three girls holds tightly together, their various strands of significance gathering in the fabric of Ozick's art into an intricate knot. If the imagination yields new bloom, it is bound to the world of the dead: as long as Demeter wanders through the world "fasting, with her hair untied, carrying flaming torches . . . propelled by pain and anger. . . . in mourning, a reversal of normal life takes place" (Burkert 160). The lost child halts germination, arrests growth; even as her return ushers in the cycle of vegetation, the revival of life, she introduces into it the presence of death. Yoked to Madame de Sévigné and Françoise Marguerite, to Allegra Vand and her daughter, to Hester and Beulah Lilt, Rosa Lublin and Magda raise the Demeter and Persephone myth into a parable about art, into historical truth. The motive force for the survivor's anguish and the pivot of Rosa's creativity, the death of Magda differs from the loss of Persephone.

Abducted and raped by Hades, Persephone returns periodically, and mother and daughter come together again. Only in Rosa's imagination can mother and child be reunited. If Persephone's marriage to Hades is a "common" metaphor "for death," if "[a]t bottom, the myth does not speak of a cycle either" but of how "things will never be the same as they were before the rape," Rosa's Hades speaks of history's reality, history's evil (Burkert 161). In Trust Ozick incorporates the myth of Demeter and Poseidon into the origins of the narrator's history; watching the intercourse between Stephanie and Tilbeck, the narrator of Trust, a symbolic Persephone, "witnessed the very style of [her] creation" and is initiated into the mysteries of her existence (Trust 598). In "Rosa" Ozick integrates the myth of Demeter and Persephone, the basis for the mysteries of Eleusis and its initiation rites, into the brutal events of Jewish history. A victim of them, Rosa Lublin becomes another kind of witness, a witness to the very style of destruction, and is initiated into the evils of existence. The narrator of Trust must recover her history to make a future; Rosa must overcome her history to have a future. Theirs are separate journeys.

Like Aeneas's final encounter with Anchises in the underworld, Rosa's imagined experience with Magda leads ultimately to an engagement not with death but with life. Although Magda "did not even stay to claim her letter" and runs from Persky, Rosa's unspoken words reveal her reluctance to sever her ties to Magda forever: "Butterfly, I am not ashamed of your presence: only come to me, come to me again, if no longer now, then later, always come" (69). It is a temporary farewell. Magda's "head as bright as a lantern" recalls the lamps at the beginning of Rosa's journey, conjures up Apollo, and aligns the brightness of Magda's head with the nimbus into which Beulah Lilt escapes (70). Present at the end of The Cannibal Galaxy and "Rosa" are signs of paganism along with emblems of the imagination. Yet the two hotels in which Rosa works through the anguish of the past, her own hotel a "parody of a real hotel . . . the Marie Louise," suggest her as a visitor, not an inhabitant, of hell—the way at Duneacres the narrator of Trust is a tourist, not a tenant, of the ruined abbey (70).

Doubling the hotels, Ozick doubles as well Rosa's experiences in those hotels. At seventeen the "future Marie Curie" felt the "coursing of her own ecstasy" as she walked to the "laboratory-supplies closet"; at fifty-eight, after forty-one years of wandering in the wilderness her life became, Rosa marches triumphantly "through the emerald glitter" at the Hotel Marie Louise and away from "its fountains, its golden thrones, its thorned wire, its burning Tree" (20, 52, 70). The "shadowy corridor" leading to the supply closet ultimately becomes the "hall of a palace," the hotel's lobby. There the "thorned wire" revives the "thorned" fence, the "burning Tree," the "child on fire"— the memories Rosa relives in her hotel room and which have placed an embargo on her life. But she prevails amidst the "golden babble" at the Marie Louise: she transforms the "frivolous" into the momentous, the trivializing term, "Repressed Animation," into healthy fury, the Tree of the Buddha's Awakening, which the narrator of *Trust* envisioned in the swamp at Dune-acres, into the tree of the sociologist's undoing (50). And Ozick, as she does in *Trust*, endows the tree in "Rosa" with multiple meanings. If Dr. Tree occasions Rosa's rage and elicits her mockery of his "Buddhist positions," the burning tree also conjures up the burning bush from which God spoke to Moses and the golden thrones in Ezekiel's description of God's appearance on His throne surrounded by fire. That her mind returns to the scene at the Marie Louise as Rosa awaits Persky's arrival implies that her liberation arises from her acceptance of the world of the Jews. The target of her catharsis, Finkelstein is the opposite of Persky, the dispeller of illusion, the agent of regeneration. But the journey toward renewal, the exit from hell, has persisted for over thirty years. Though she completes that journey, Rosa, in late middle age, faces a shrinking future. The thieves who took her life own most of it.

Invoking the Roman poet's hell in her novella, the storyteller becomes a kind of "Virgil of the German hell," a guide into the subterranean world of a survivor. In 1988, five years after the publication of "Rosa," Ozick wrote of Primo Levi, "He has been a Darwin of the death camps: not the Virgil of the German hell but its scientific investigator" (M&M 37). Her review of the last book Levi wrote, *The Drowned and the Saved*, before committing suicide revives the powerful electrical imagery in "The Shawl" and "Rosa," uncovers the consequence of Levi's famous and widely praised detachment, and affords a striking parallel to the psychic truths disclosed in Cynthia Ozick's own novella. Rather than merely accept the appearance of tranquility in Levi's books, Ozick exposes, in images that conjure up those in "The Shawl" and "Rosa," the "deadly anger" that saturates "Levi's final testimony": "Gradually, cumulatively, rumble by rumble, it ["the change of tone"] leads to disclosure, exposure—one can follow the sizzle flying along the fuse. . . . It may be cruel; but it is Levi's own hand that tears away the veil and sets the fuse. The fuse is ignited almost instantly, in the Preface" (M&M 41). Withholding his rage, Levi, Ozick reveals, achieved "not detachment" but the "slow accretion of an insurmountable pressure," a pressure that imploded in "a convulsion: self-destruction" (47). Conscious of the furies propelling Rosa to destroy her store, Ozick chronicles the catharsis that releases Rosa from the rage that led Primo Levi, more than forty years after Auschwitz, to commit suicide so as to escape the horrors of an endless "during." In her fiction and in her essay, Ozick probes the historical and psychic forces that drive human beings to turn rage into self-destruction. Hers is a vision that encompasses in its breadth historical veracity and emotional verity. To limit "Rosa" to "authentic Jewish response to catastrophe" or to "Holocaust melancholia," therefore, is to deny the painful truths of "Primo Levi's Suicide Note" (Berger 126, 127).

From the sadists who elicited the note from Levi, Rosa discovers a painful truth: their absolute idea of the Jew, traditional or assimilated. Disdainful of the Jewishness her father taught her to shun, Rosa Lublin ultimately comes to acknowledge as her own the identity he disavowed. In moving toward the Yiddish-speaking Persky, in welcoming him into her life, she separates herself from her father, from his Hellenism, and moves closer to Hebraism. That she removes the shawl from the phone, that its clamor, "animated at will, ardent with its cry," replaces Magda with Persky suggests Rosa's acceptance of the Jews she once resented being "billeted with" (70, 67). That Magda runs from Persky, that she is only "away" implies her eventual return. The ending of the tale bears its teller's elusive and inconclusive mark—the uncertain note on which Ozick closes her fiction from *Trust* onward.

Recurring to the concerns central to her first novel, Ozick inverts and augments them. What the narrator of *Trust* searches for, Rosa owns; what the girl celebrates, Rosa is forced to question. The one must discover her father's legacy, the other must repudiate it. And the storyteller's allusions to the *Odyssey* and to the *Aeneid* buttress Ozick's overarching concern with the father. The roles of the fathers in the two epics diverge, the fathers' fates part, the sons' paths fork. If Telemachos and the narrator of *Trust* must find their fathers, Aeneas and Rosa must detach themselves from theirs, must emerge from Virgil's hell, not encounter, as the girl does at Duneacres, the "Virgil of the Eclogues" (*Trust* 531). If the girl and Rosa have unlike quests, Tilbeck, Allegra Vand, and Rosa's parents are yoked by a reverence for Ancient Greece and Sacred Beauty, the idyllic vision of nature. In *Trust* the daughter compares her mother's idea of nature to an art object: a "vase with its dark dread hole kept secret and small . . . and the whole to be held to the light for an unimaginable and always absent flaw . . . as though nature had no bloody underside, and grief had no ugliness, and fact had no dirt in it" (*Trust* 422). Like the Greek jars Tilbeck collects, the Greek vase unearthed by Rosa's father testifies to a similar notion: the vase "was all pieced together, and the missing parts, which broke up the design of a warrior with a javelin, filled in with reddish clay" (68). In their veneration of Ancient Greece, the parents overlook the "tragic grain of nature," the savagery of war. Linked by their illegitimacy, the narrator of *Trust* and Magda are related to Beulah Lilt, whose father is unknown. The finding of the father, the fate of the fatherless, the farewell to the father—these evince an abiding interest in a figure to whom Ozick accords a further dimension in *The Messiah of Stockholm*, her third novel.

SEVEN

The Pulse of Ancestry

Evolving from *The Cannibal Galaxy* and *The Shawl*, *The Messiah of Stockholm* resonates with the concerns vital to *Trust*, to which Ozick's third novel is most closely joined. At the heart of Ozick's first novel is the quest for a father, the passion to uncover beginnings, and the desire to own an integral tradition with which the present may be connected and so ensure a future. If in *Trust* Ozick chronicles the narrator's successful discovery of the father the mother had attempted to hide from her daughter, in *The Messiah of Stockholm* the storyteller charts the fate of the fatherless, the life of one for whom the past has been irretrievably lost. What the narrator of *Trust* ultimately recovers is what the principle character of *The Messiah of Stockholm* must invent. The two novels explore the meaning of the father from a dual perspective. Though that crucial figure appears throughout the storyteller's fiction in various contexts and with multiple significations, the father occupies the vibrant center of Ozick's first and third novels. In *The Messiah of Stockholm* he is accorded a further dimension. An intricate reflection of her thriving preoccupations, Ozick's third novel reveals the new juncture at which the novelist has arrived, the threshold of her future art.

Although the germ of the novel came unexpectedly, it was an event that converged with a past interest. In 1984 on a trip to Stockholm for the publication there of *The Cannibal Galaxy*, Ozick heard an electrifying rumor—that Bruno Schulz's lost manuscript, *The Messiah*, had surfaced in Stockholm.[1] Her interest in Schulz was awakened in 1977 when his *Street of Crocodiles* was published in the series "Writers from the Other Europe." The editor of the series, Philip Roth, made Schulz accessible to her, provided her with letters and other Schulziana, and ultimately became the person to whom Ozick dedicated her novel.[2] Fathers loom large in Roth's fiction and in Ozick's, and the Polish writer whose father occupied the center of his son's consciousness fascinates the two American writers. Indeed, Roth pays homage to Schulz in *The Prague Orgy*, and Ozick transforms the events of his life and work into the fabric of *The Messiah of Stockholm*, reviving the relationship crucial to the Polish writer in the pages of her own tale. Schulz's father, an omnipresent figure in the two books Schulz published—*The Street of Crocodiles* and *Sanatorium under the Sign of the Hourglass*—haunted his son's imagination just as the Polish writer haunts Ozick's main character, Lars Andemening.

A Drohobycz merchant, Schulz's father slowly untied every knot that joined him to humanity, and his illness induced his ultimate retreat from reality. Schulz himself rarely left his native town, Drohobycz, never married, and made no attempt to escape Drohobycz even during the war when Polish writers and underground organizations provided him with false papers and a hiding place. His was a severely isolated and intensely inward life; transmogrifying his childhood memories into riddling images, Schulz registers a reality he found insubstantial—indeed, bankrupt. On Black Thursday, November 19, 1942, on the streets of Drohobycz, the very streets he had used for the intimate details of his myth, Bruno Schulz was gunned down by an S.S. man, carried to a Jewish cemetery in the safety of darkness by a friend, and buried. The manuscript of his masterpiece, *The Messiah*, is thought to have perished with the friend to whom it was given for safekeeping.

Such was the history of the writer who is pivotal to Cynthia Ozick's third novel. A decade before Ozick published it, she reviewed *The Street of Crocodiles*, a book which appeared in Poland in 1934 as *Cinnamon Shops* and which was not translated into English until 1963. Of the world of *The Street of Crocodiles*, Ozick writes:

> As in Kafka, the malevolent is deadpan; its loveliness of form is what we notice. At the heart of the malevolent—also the repugnant, the pitiless—crouches the father: Schulz's own father, since there is an inviolable autobiographical glaze that paints over every distortion. . . .
>
> . . .What is being invented in the very drone of our passive literary expectations is Religion—not the taming religion of theology and morality, but the brute splendors of rite, gesture, phantasmagoric transfiguration, sacrifice, elevation, degradation, mortification, repugnance, terror, cult. The religion of animism, in fact, where everything comes alive with an unpredictable and spiteful spirit-force, where even living tissue contains ghosts, where there is no pity. (A&A 225,227)

Where pity is absent, there idolatry reigns. His paralyzing obsessions, his fixation on his father, his cultivation of a supra-reality, his assimilation into Polish life, his paganism—these stand at the forefront of Ozick's initial reception of Schulz's world and they afford a foretaste of the "remarkable uses" Ozick would make of Schulz's "purposeful dark" when she wrote *The Messiah of Stockholm* years later (A&A 225).

The novel's principal character, Lars Andemening, believes himself to be Bruno Schulz's son, the son not yet born when the father was murdered. Unaware even of his mother's name, Lars worships his dead father in a ritual akin to Rosa Lublin's. Spared Magda's doom, Lars Andemening nonetheless has no history: his is the fate of one for whom there is no thread of genesis. But his obsession with Bruno Schulz governs Lars Andemening's life "from November to early in a certain bare and harrowing March, when he gave it up" (3). That he feels "he resembled his father" prompts Lars to mimic Schulz, to pattern his life on his dead father's, to become the Polish writer's double. Even Lars's apartment, which "was no bigger than a crack in the wall," recalls Drohobycz—a "cramped crevice of a place" Ozick called it in her review (*Messiah* 1; A&A 224). After the collapse of two marriages and the separation from his child whom his second wife has taken to America, Lars at age forty-two is without a wife, inhabiting an apartment where "any visitor [is] a biennial event" (3). He lives obscurely, shrinking himself "more and more into the phantasmagoria of the mind," imitating the men who people Schulz's tales (5). While his colleagues gossip at the *Morgontörn* (Morning watch), Stockholm's relatively young newspaper where he is a once-a-week reviewer, Lars naps under a "quilt, heaped on itself in large knots" (3). On that bed Lars has a visitation approximating the one Rosa Lublin has on the tangled bedclothes of her bed in a similarly cramped room.

Unmade beds abound in Schulz's books. The disordered bedclothes are a metaphor, for example, in "Mr. Charles," the story Ozick alludes to at the end of her first chapter. The captive of a "mountain of heavy, whitish dough" when he sleeps, Charles discovers an "island of safety" in the bedclothes where, like Lars and Rosa, Charles surrenders to "those hopeless musings" away from the "reality of the moment" (*Street* 82, 81, 83). A symbol of unconscious life in Schulz's tales—Father has his visitation as he hunches "among the enormous pillows" of his bed under an eiderdown—the bed in Cynthia Ozick's tales, well before the novelist read Bruno Schulz, is where imagining occurs, where writing takes place (*Street* 41). Near the "cocoon of his bed" on his night table Edelshtein keeps his pen for the "first luminous line of his new poem lying there waiting to be born"; atop her bed, a writing board on her knees, Rosa composes letters to Magda (PR 56). And it is Edith Wharton's bed, the "bed that was her workplace," that Ozick asks us "to visualize" in her restitution of justice to that author ("Justice (Again) to Edith Wharton," A&A 10, 11). The writer's workplace, the bed gives birth to the imagination's illusions: it is in her bed that Puttermesser discovers a golem. Lying in his bed "counting his omissions," Pincus Silver confronts himself with his destructive fantasies and resolves to "throw illusion away" (PR 188, 189). Constructing it out of a photograph in a biography of Chekhov, Pincus Silver, like Lars Andemening, clings to a notion that shrivels his future. For both Bruno Schulz and Cynthia Ozick, the bed—surely an allusion to those precincts approached in dreams—functions as a metaphor for the imaginative process.

At forty-two and the captive of his fantasies, Lars Andemening looks "much younger" than his actual age: his face "opened into unripeness—a tentativeness, an unfinished tone. The hand of an indifferent maker had smeared his mouth and chin and Adam's apple" (4). His physical appearance reflects his psychological state, prompting others to perceive him as more youthful than he is. "Often dealt with as if he were just starting out, heaving his greening masculine forces against life," Lars believes he is an "arrested soul: someone who has been pushed off a track" (4). Franz Joseph, Schulz writes in "Spring," "held [the world] within procedural bounds, and insured it against derailment into things unforeseen, adventurous, or simply unpredictable" (*Sanatorium* 55). Adrift in a world he cannot hold within any bounds, a world in which he is derailed, Lars is in a situation which corresponds to Schulz's, as Ozick described it in her review: an "assimilated, Polish-speaking Jew, not so much a Jew as a conscious Pole," Schulz felt the "homelessness and ultimate pariahship" in Drohobycz, the minute town where he was "digested" by his family (A&A 227, 224). Although Lars has no family to digest him, he is essentially homeless because he lacks a family. Choosing to identify with the ghost of Bruno Schulz, Lars mires himself in childhood, in an unresolved struggle for his origins. If he could arrive at them, he would more closely resemble the narrator of *Trust;* but in her account of him, Ozick invokes the golem Xanthippe and implies that Lars Andemening is Bruno Schulz's golem.

Lars's "unfinished tone" and youthful appearance not only recall the childlike Xanthippe but they shadow forth the views the Polish writer had of childhood. That period of life was decisive for Schulz, as he wrote the famous Polish writer Stanislaw Ignacy Witkiewicz: "I don't know how we manage to acquire certain images in childhood that carry decisive meanings for us. They function like those threads in the solution around which the significance of the world crystallizes for us" (*Letters* 110). If there are images which carry decisive meanings, there are also texts "lying in wait for us at the very entrance to life" (*Letters* 111). That is how Schulz describes his experience at age eight listening to his mother read Goethe's *Erlkönig.* So crucial to Schulz, who revealed in the same letter that *Erlkönig* shook him "to the bottom of [his] soul," Goethe's poem affects Ozick deeply for disparate reasons. It is evidence of the fancy's peril. But Goethe's line about the child carried by its father through the night—the line Puttermesser remembers right before she discovers Xanthippe—is for Schulz one of those images that "amount to an agenda, establish an iron capital of the spirit," and more importantly, "mark out to artists the boundaries of their creative powers" (*Letters* 111). Unconcerned with idolatry, Schulz could maintain, as he did in his essay for Witkiewicz, that the "migration of forms is the essence of life," that in *Cinnamon Shops* "this universal disillusioning reality" is "compensated for" by the "loosening of the web of reality," by "witnessing the bankruptcy of reality" (*Letters* 113). To recapture the limitless rich illusions of childhood, "that 'age of genius,' those 'messianic times' ", was to achieve an "ideal goal . . . to 'mature' into childhood" (126).

Lars's youthfulness reflects Schulz's ideal goal to be sure, but Ozick's commentary on that goal emerges obliquely in the kinship she envisions between Lars and a golem who runs amok and directly in the portrait she paints of a life ruled by an illusion. Like Pincus Silver's, Lars's life is bereft of a history, and as the doctor does, the orphan chooses an alternate life from a book. To posit an ancestry, Ruth Puttermesser and Lars Andemening invent one. Calling himself Andemening, the Swedish word for "inward meaning / consciousness" and Baruch, the Hebrew word for "blessed," Lars celebrates his and Bruno Schulz's journeys into the interior. But the name Lars resembles the Swedish word for embryo, "lares"; and Lazarus Baruch conflates the name of the man Christ raised from the dead with the name of Jeremiah's scribe.[3] To name himself Lazarus Baruch is to fancy himself the scribe who will resurrect the prophet Bruno Schulz. But he becomes Lars's "craze." The reviewer saves Central European writers from oblivion, but dooms himself to it; for in copying Bruno Schulz's life, or else the lives of the men in the Polish writer's tales, Lars comes to resemble Schulz's old-age pensioner, a "parasite" clinging to someone else's life (*Sanatorium* 163). Appropriating another identity, Lars conjures up Stanislav Lushinski, a similarity Ozick subliminally registered in 1977 when she joined Jerzy Kosinski to Bruno Schulz in their mutual fascination with birds. Schulz's birds, she commented then, were a "fore-echo of . . . another Pole obsessed by fearful birds" (A&A 226). Rescued from the Holocaust by strangers—Lars by a Swedish traveler, Lushinski by peasants—the two men share a common experience. Their passions divide them, however, for what fevers one man, the other seeks to disavow. At the heart of "A Mercenary" and *The Messiah of Stockholm* is the issue of Jewish identity.

To possess one, Lars Andemening becomes Bruno Schulz's double, but he is also his employer's double. A "relatively young newspaper of unsettled character," the *Morgontörn* has on its staff a Wednesday reviewer whose surname is a counterpart to the one the newspaper's Monday reviewer has picked for himself (3). In Swedish Hemlig means "secret, hidden, concealed, or private"; Gunnar Hemlig observes that Lars "exactly resembled the building that housed the *Morgontörn*," which in turn has the same name as the tavern located in the building one hundred fifty years ago (10). That Ozick establishes Lars's likeness to Bruno Schulz and the *Morgontörn* locates Lars in two worlds, the worlds that are at war within him. Placing the offices of the newspaper's cultural section on the topmost floor of the building where a "well-disciplined regiment of mice held their command post" and feasted on "prefaces for appetizers and indexes for dessert," Ozick juxtaposes the antics of the "literary stewpot," which Lars at first avoids, against the darkness of historical event to which he is obsessively drawn. The gossipy world of journalism Ozick depicts in her portrayal of the *Morgontörn's* cultural staff, though brilliantly witty, encapsulates a serious issue—the problem of parochialism.

For his commitment to Central European writers, his attention to the work of a culture other than Swedish, the Monday reviewer is ignored by his readers and derided by his associates. Lars's "trouble," according to Gunnar Hemlig, is " 'Central Europe. . . . all the crazies from the middle. . . . The more inscrutable the better' " (14). An advocate of Velveeta cheese, America's "fake cheese," Gunnar produces "velveetisms" and dismisses writers from Central Europe as an instance of parochialism (11). His is the charge critics, as ignorant of intellectual history as he is, often level against American Jewish writers. It is a position against which Ozick has often inveighed. "American Jewish literature," Ozick maintains, "is not an instance of 'regionalism,' 'parochialism,' or 'ethnicity.' . . . Jewish ideas and sensibility . . . are neither regional nor ethnic. They are the foundation and condition of the civilization we inhabit" ("Poetry" 9). But Gunnar eschews such serious ideas for the "comical" point, the "question of Lars and belles-lettres." His passion for that makes Lars an "exception" at the *Morgontörn:* " 'Not everyone,' " Gunnar reminds Lars, " 'has belles-lettres on the brain day and night. Some have water, and others wine' " (11). Though Gunnar refers to the bottle of vodka in Anders's desk, his quip alludes to the more melancholy truth Ozick articulates in her essay, "The Question of Our Speech: The Return to Aural Culture," which she wrote during the same period as her third novel and in which she observes: "The return to an aural culture is, obviously, not *all* a question of loss; only of the most significant loss of all: the widespread nurture by portable print; print as water, and sometimes wine" (M&M 167). The answer to the question of Lars and belles-lettres, which Gunnar says " 'leads to exaltation and other forms of decline,' " is Gunnar's "velveetisms," which lead to deflation and the most significant decline of all. But people listen to Gunnar rather than read Lars.

That those who lack talent in journalism are the ones who attain success in its world is an unfortunate fact in Balzac's *Lost Illusions,* a novel to which Ozick alludes and whose main character, Lucien de Rubempré, Gunnar links to Lars. The comparison is not fortuitous.[4] Indeed, *Lost Illusions* and *The Messiah of Stockholm* share, along with the mice in their printing houses, a common theme, the successive loss of illusions. Not only does Ozick allude to Balzac's biting portrait of journalism but she aligns Lars to Lucien. Their talent is of no avail in the world of journalism. As Etienne Lousteau advises Lucien about the literary world so Gunnar diagnoses Lars's troubles. To acquire fame, Lousteau tells Lucien, a writer must lack flair: "the more mediocre a man is, the sooner he arrives at success" (Balzac 249). And fathers, both dead and alive, are as important to *Lost Illusions* as they are to *The Messiah of Stockholm.* Their fathers' presence hinders the sons in Balzac's novel: avarice precludes Jérôme-Nicolas Séchard from helping his son, and his dead father's name shames Lucien into adopting his mother's name as the more respectable one. In Ozick's novel the absence of a real father sparks the illusion that grips Lars Andemening and arrests his life. All of the sons suffer the painful loss of their illusions: in Paris as in Stockholm, mediocrity triumphs.

That the absence of talent guarantees a reviewer's popularity emerges in the responses Lars unwittingly elicits from the *Morgontörn's* other reviewers. Gunnar reads aloud, "in a liturgical voice the first sentence of Lars's typescript: *Here is a universe as confined as a trap, where the sole heroes are victims, where muteness is for the intrepid only*" (13). The sentence might have come from one of Bruno Schulz's own reviews. About Witold Gombrowicz's novel *Ferdydurke* Schulz writes, "Here is a reservoir of powerful emotional tensions that these subcultural contents have the ability to concentrate and gather" (*Letters* 159). The very style of the Monday reviewer's writing as well as the nature of Lars's interests duplicate Bruno Schulz's; as the narrator of "Usurpation" pilfers from Bernard Malamud so Lars steals from Bruno Schulz.

Called the "Prince of the indecipherable" or a "Monday Faust" by Gunnar, derided by Anders Fiskyngel (fish-spawn) for reviving unknown, esoteric writers, published on a day when people yawn past the cultural pages, "Lars was unread, unmolested, unharassed; he was free" (14, 7). His situation conjures up Edelshtein's. Unknown and unrecognized, the Yiddish poet—he calls himself "Prince of Rationality"—laments his obscurity and suffers from the derision of someone more renowned (PR 81). And Lars has much in common with Elia Gatoff in "Virility": the two orphans pick names for themselves and share the same motto, "Even Leonardo da Vinci had only twenty-four hours in a day" (*Messiah* 7; PR 235). Unlike Gatoff, the Monday reviewer is "swept away" by the text. Whatever he reads utterly consumes him: he becomes the "man in the bedclothes," the man in Schulz's "Mr. Charles." To witness Lars read is to watch a swimmer "being filmed in slow motion." It is to recollect a passage from *Trust:* "I have an underwater sense of it, a flailing against veils and weight . . . we let ourselves be turned this way, that way, our heavy legs in their heavy motions seem both to swim and to be retarded . . . with the dumb violations of some disbelieving slow-motion camera, unreeling strangeness and remorse" (581). But the narrator of *Trust* uncovers her ancestry; Lars can only imagine one "under the wilderness of his quilt." He shares with Rosa Lublin the dead as a source of inspiration.

And he comes upon his review the way Puttermesser comes upon her golem. If the attorney possesses a "mind superfetate with Idea," the reviewer is "sated with his idea"; if Xanthippe suddenly appears in the golem-maker's bed, Lars's completed review materializes the moment the reviewer ceases to nap. One "knew what she knew," the other "understood what he thought": creation wells up "out of lightning insubstantialities" (*Levitation* 90, 122; *Messiah* 8; "Young Self" 166). Merging her imagery with Schulz's, Ozick instances the mind imagining. Lars's visitation invokes Father's: crouched in bed, Father perceives "sheaves of eyes and ears which swarmed out from the night . . . from the womb of darkness." His visions in "Tailor's Dummies" produce a "spiral of wrinkles" in his face, "at the bottom of which there flared the terrible eye of a prophet" (*Street* 39, 65). Those flights of fancy ultimately remove Father from his family and convince his son that his father has been transformed into a stuffed condor, the one remaining specimen from Father's "bird estate." Alive, the bird has stood "on one foot, in the pose of a Buddhist sage"; inert, "Only the pale-blue, horny, Egyptian protuberances on the powerful beak and the bald neck gave that senile head a solemnly hieratic air" (*Street* 111).

Ozick transmutes these riveting images into the elements of Lars's ruling illusion. Upon awakening from a sleep without "refreshment or restoration" and somewhat frightened from what he knows, Lars visualizes his completed review: "A greased beak tore him off his accustomed ledge and brought him to a high place beyond his control." There, before formulating even a word of his review, Lars envisions it "as a kind of vessel, curved, polished, hollowed out. In its cup lay an alabaster egg with a single glittering spot; no, not an egg; a globe marvelously round. An eye. A human eye: his own; and then not his own. His father's murdered eye" (8). Penetrating the images which characterize Father—"that incorrigible improviser, that fencing master of imagination," that defender of "the lost cause of poetry"—Ozick then demonstrates the process of artistic influence, the translation and permutation of another artist's materials (*Street* 51).

But Lars not only interprets them, he worships them: "more sacred" to him "than any cathedral" is the Academy in Stockholm (15). His walk around it in the snow, like all the introspective strides in Ozick's fiction, unfolds his consciousness, his conviction that Schulz, had he lived, would have won the Nobel Prize. The Library of the Academy, its records, it encyclopedias, the plenitude packed into the briefcases of the scholars at the worktables—these remind Lars of Thor's hammer, of the enemy of the giants, of the god whom Gustave Nicholas Tilbeck invokes. As if to bridge her first novel to her third, Ozick, at the beginning of *The Messiah of Stockholm*, portrays Stockholm's autumn sky as "an eggshell shielding a blue-black yolk," an image reminiscent of one near the end of *Trust*. There, in that novel's climactic scenes, Ozick renders the memories of her narrator's birth in egg imagery.

Egg imagery continues to be present in *The Pagan Rabbi*. A "yolk-colored sky" backs the final scene in "The Dock-Witch," as if to suggest that the two men standing before the figurehead, into which Sylvia-Undine has been transformed, must begin their lives anew (PR 169). To Zindel and Rosa, both of whom eat hard-boiled eggs, Ozick attaches emblems of the cosmic egg in *Trust* from which a new world springs. Her poignant "Washington Square, 1946," an essay about her first day at New York University, includes a memory of Thomas Wolfe's phrase, the "smoke-ochre of the morning," a phrase that "rises out of the old pavements of Washington Square as delicately colored as an eggshell" (M&M 118). But in *The Messiah of Stockholm*, the egg—an emblem of Schulz's reverence for childhood and an image for Lars's finished review—signals Lars's immaturity, the inability to envision a future. For that reason, to intimate his "circumstances" and his "predicaments," Ozick equips Lars with the "face of a foetus." "It was as if," she writes, "he was waiting for his dead father to find him, and was determined to remain recognizable" (6). The entire mien of the reviewer, especially his face, contrasts with his gray hair and his imminent need for reading glasses. Disparate from Lars's chronological age, Lars's appearance reflects an undeveloped psychology; like Schulz's "immobile . . . old-age pensioner" living in his old nursery, Lars is a "parasite of metaphors" (*Sanatorium*, 172).

His father's metaphors, writing itself, totally absorb Lars; out of love for writers, he shrugs away Gunnar and Anders's ridicule. Even as the Monday reviewer walks in the snow on his way to Heidi Eklund's bookstore in search of books by the Central European writers his fellow reviewers scorn, he hears their voices. Having established an affinity between Lars and his employer, Ozick then links the cubicle at the *Morgontörn*, where Lars works, to the "skimpy vestibule of [Heidi's] shop," where he reads, and both places to his apartment. If Gunnar announces Lars's similarity to Lucien de Rubempré, Heidi has filled her bookstore with Balzac. If Lars cherishes the scribblers at the newspaper, he has thought of marrying a woman like Heidi Eklund. To her Lars reveals what he knows of his history: how he was smuggled from Poland to Stockholm, where he was to be cared for by an elderly cousin, a refugee; how at sixteen, he came to live in a stranger's attic room, supporting himself by taking a job as a messenger boy on a newspaper.

Lars's early life corresponds to Elia Gatoff's and Joseph Brill's. Gatoff, too, was sent to his aunt in Liverpool by means of a forged passport and got a job as an office boy for a newspaper. Like Lars, Elia renames himself, and as Edmund Gate he begins to make writing his career, to become the parasite of someone else's metaphors, an impersonator who claims as his own the poems his aunt has written. And Joseph Brill finds himself housed in haylofts, places akin to attics. A man who shares with Lars the desire to maintain the "thread of genesis," who believes in "nature's prank of duplication" the way Lars believes in the "power of genes," the principal of The Edmond Fleg School is as much a "scholar of loss" as Lars believes his daughter Karin could become (47). To regard her name "commonplace" is to partake of Joseph Brill's aversion for the ordinary. Important in Lars's life, attics are significant locations in Schulz's fiction as well. In the cluttered attics of "The Gale," "darkness began to degenerate and ferment wildly" until the old pots and discarded empty bottles come to life and march "against the city" (*Street* 117). Freed of their litter, the attics shake noisily in the wind, but their clamor is taken for "prophecies" (*Street* 124). That as a young boy Lars lives alone in an attic room, that he gets a job on a newspaper, that he knows "his future was print"—these events indicate the prophecies he might have heard in the attic, a place where he could have imagined a father like Bruno Schulz.

It was in Heidi's bookshop, however, that Lars found a copy of Bruno Schulz's *Cinnamon Shops* in Polish. Though Heidi regards Lars "as her discovery," it is Lars to whom it came "instantly that he would tell this old woman what he knew about himself" (22, 23). For Gunnar and Anders, Lars feels a "tenderness"; with Heidi Eklund he feels an affinity (68). He makes her his confidante; to her he reveals his most intimate secret—his relationship with Bruno Schulz. In turn, she falls into "his condition alongside him, a companion, a fellow collector of his father's fate, a kind of partner" (32). Other likenesses yoke them. A "little hole-in-the-wall bookseller," Heidi, like Gunnar and Anders, like Lars himself, is "among the nighttime wakeful" (93, 18). Not only does her bookshop conjure up the image of his flat but, in essential ways, Heidi resembles Lars. If he has an "infantile graying head," she, at age sixty-five, has bangs that are curly like a girl's but white like an old woman's; if Lars rarely has visitors, she lives in "self-appointed exile" (40, 18). His name reflects his inwardness, hers a "bitingly private" disposition (22). But as is true of Johanna Spyri's heroine, after whom she is named, Heidi Eklund transforms the lives of the people around her. The young Heidi mitigates Uncle Alp's reclusiveness, Peter's aggressiveness, Clara's invalidism; the older Heidi, Lars's obsession.[5] Immersing herself in it, Mrs. Eklund "had more or less kidnapped him and locked him in with her" (27). As it becomes increasingly impossible to separate Xanthippe from Puttermesser, so with Lars and Heidi, it becomes "difficult to gauge . . . who was whose captive" (27).

If their similarities make them doubles, their differences sunder them into opposing selves. Together they gaze at photographs of Lars's father surrounded by women; separately Lars and Heidi speculate who might have been Bruno Schulz's lover. And they argue about the longing Schulz expressed, in a letter written to Tadeusz Breza, for a companion to acknowledge his inner world. What Lars envisages is himself as the "kindred spirit" his father wanted; what Heidi detects is Schulz's desire for a wife.[6] Tracing every tendril of Schulz's life in Drohobycz the way the daughter of *Trust* gathers information about her father, the reviewer and the bookseller accumulate speculations, collect the scattered pieces of a puzzle. Of Drohobycz itself there remains nothing at all, only the certainty that between it and Bruno Schulz "there had occurred a mutual digestion," which "paralyzed" Lars's father and rendered him incapable, save for a few trips, of ever leaving Drohobycz (35). As reclusive as Bruno Schulz, as immured as Pincus Silver in the "private side of his eyelids," as preoccupied as Rosa Lublin is with the landscape behind her eyes, Lars Andemening understands why Schulz lived "on correspondence. . . . The mitigation of solitude without the bother of human flesh" (37). Lars can imagine that because he utterly identifies with his imagined father: " 'We look alike, two peas in a pod. . . . And it isn't even a matter of looks. There's an affinity. His voice. His mind' " (25).

But Heidi disdains Lars for being "a master of the insubstantial: a fantasist." She is enmeshed, along with Enoch Vand and Stanislav Lushinski, in the "catastrophe of fact": it is to the shooting she is drawn, to what Lushinski extols—the "accretion of data" (32, 44; *Bloodshed* 38). Every route in her conversation leads to the shooting, every link she forges belongs to the wild action on Black Thursday. She scolds Lars "for turning his father into some sort of ceremonial mystification; there was a smoldering cultishness in all of it. His father's tales—animism, sacrifice, mortification, repugnance! Everything abnormal, everything wild" (33). She accuses the Monday reviewer of " 'expecting what isn't there to *be* there' " (32). And she tells him, as Stella tells Rosa: " 'You want to resurrect him. You want to *be* him. . . . You throw out your life' " (41). When Lars protests that Heidi causes him to " 'lose the thread,' " she denounces his notion of continuity (39).

For Heidi an identity does not come from " 'Nouns and verbs! . . . *Sentences!* Subjects! Predicates! Pieces of paper' " (40). Nor does she believe an identity can be achieved out of " 'Mimicry. Posing in a mirror!' " (41). By constantly returning to Black Thursday, to the fact of Bruno Schulz's death, Heidi Eklund repeatedly confronts Lars with reality, with deeds and their consequences, which she and Enoch Vand insist are inextricable from history where a real identity arises, not, as Lars Andemening believes, from a piece of paper. Of her own history, Heidi yields little, only a glimpse into "the life before Dr. Eklund" (42). Echoing Rosa Lublin's description of the survivors' three lives, Ozick implies, though the bookseller resolutely refuses to admit it to Lars, that Heidi Eklund survived incarceration in a death camp. As she summons up her memories, "strangely intimate views," of the sounds behind the fence, Lars surmises "she was one of them, but hidden—one of the shadows inside" (43).

Unlike Rosa Lublin, however, Heidi entered "the life after": leaving Germany behind, taking only her "daffodil lamp" and a "few old books," she married Dr. Eklund (43). If the reality of their survival links Heidi to Rosa, the intensity of their imaginative lives yokes Rosa and Lars. He proudly announces his father " 'turned everything into a piece of paper' " and proceeds to repeat, as if it is his motto, Schulz's view of reality: "Reality is as thin as paper and betrays with all its cracks its imitative character" (*Messiah* 37; *Street* 105). But Heidi finishes the sentence for Lars, emending "imitative" to "intuitive," and spits out her opinion of Schulz's idea: " 'Nincompoopery. Standing things on their head. What's real is real' " (37). Her alteration sets forth the conviction that reality is determinable rather than, as Schulz and Lars claim, contrived out of language by the imagination.

That dichotomy, the one between the imagination and the reason, courses through the world of Ozick's fiction. In *Trust* poets vie with attorneys, word-manipulators with lovers of language, rationalists with fantasts. Inaugurated in *Trust,* the clash between reality and illusion is wed to the dispute between Hebraism and Hellenism. Attorneys who fall prey to the fancy, or the rabbi and professor of Mishnaic history who yearns after nature, embody that age-old contest. George, the lawyer in "The Dock-Witch," relinquishes "rationality, responsibility; light" when he falls under the spell of Sylvia-Undine (PR 164). The self-declared rationalist and realist, the attorney Ruth Puttermesser believes "in the uses of fantasy"; "summoning reason," she endeavors to account for the golem in her bed, the product of powerful imagining (*Levitation* 91, 92). The narrator of "Shots" as well as the refugee of "Freud's Room" embrace the "literal," not the metaphoric (*Levitation* 42). In tale after tale, Ozick depicts the dark consequences of sustaining an illusion and the ambivalent rewards of returning to ordinary reality: the competing forces are locked in an enduring battle.

Employing Bruno Schulz's life and work as the subject of *The Messiah of Stockholm* and attaching to it an epigraph from Pär Lagerkvist's *Aftonland* as well as one from Schulz's *Street of Crocodiles,* Ozick signals the compelling significance these writers, who concerned themselves with reality's fragmentary nature, have for her novel. His letters and his stories constantly reveal the belief Schulz had in the primacy of the imagination over the tenuousness of reality; eschewing the "chaff of time" for his "own private mythology," the Polish writer contrives a world in which fact means little (*Letters* 114). The very title of his essay "The Mythologizing of Reality" proclaims his desire to reconstruct reality out of language: "We usually regard the word as the shadow of reality, its symbol. The reverse of this statement would be correct: reality is the shadow of the word" (*Letters* 116–17). That Schulz would have arrived at this conclusion is implicit in his desire to retain what for him were the perpetually meaningful illusions of childhood, in his sense that the "role of art is to be a probe stuck into the nameless" (*Letters* 113). Of *Cinnamon Shops*, the book he called an "autobiographical narrative" or a "spiritual genealogy," he writes: "Here the author feels close to the sensibility of classical antiquity; he regards his creative imagination and its phantasmagoric inclination as derived from a 'pagan' concept of life." That concept enabled Schulz to mine the "misty region of early childhood fantasies," which he championed as the "true spawning ground of mythical thinking" (*Letters* 114, 154). Such a conviction was prompted by the decisive influence of *Erlkönig*.

Definitive for the Polish writer, *Erlkönig* means something else to Ozick, who alludes to it in connection with Undine, the sirenlike figure in "The Dock-Witch." Lured by the strains from her lyre and beguiled by the lines she sings from *Erlkönig*, the lawyer in "The Dock-Witch" forfeits all rationality; wasted and ruined at the end of the story, he conjures up the vision of the dead boy in Goethe's poem. A similar misfortune awaits Puttermesser, another attorney moved by Goethe's poem. What befalls the two attorneys is what happens when reality is renounced for the imagination. The perilous magic inhering in the imagination, its potential for idolatry, excite Ozick's apprehensions, and they run counter to Schulz's celebration of a pagan concept of life. Her essay "S. Y. Agnon and the First Religion" unmasks the dangers of paganism. Commenting on the passage she has quoted from Pär Lagerkvist's fable *The Sibyl*, Ozick writes: "The Siren and the sibyl, potent representatives of the First Religion, swallow up all things—every achievement, every desire, every idea—into the poetry of ecstatic obliteration, Eros joined with degradation and death" (M&M 220). Whether it is a siren or a sibyl or an erlking, the song it chants is deathly; it is the loud song of annihilation. That is the song Ozick hears in Schulz's Drohobycz, the town Schulz transformed into myth. Inspired by paganism, unafraid "of the irrational," of the "dark places of alien myth," he could imagine discovering Pan in a "large, overgrown garden" near one of Drohobycz's courtyards (*Street* 78). The poet Tchernikhovsky would have been a more likely predecessor for the Polish writer than the "old writer of Jerusalem."

Implicit in Lars Andemening's obsession, a usurpation of Schulz's view of life, is Ozick's commentary on the Polish writer's paganism, a repudiation of Schulz's idolatry. Fatherless himself, Lars has fathered a daughter; once bitter against his second wife Ulrika for severing his relationship with Karin, he recognizes that "his little daughter had begun to fade" from his thoughts. Believing himself to be his father's "partner in discovery," wanting to receive "a signal through the genes," Lars nonetheless takes Karin's paint set to Ulrika's mother (37). He symbolically gives his daughter away to his former mother-in-law just the way he was once handed over to a relative. To be an orphan is, as Ulrika's mother observes, not to " 'know what it means to inherit anything' "(46). Considering how deprived a childhood Lars has had, his decision to abandon his daughter comes as no surprise. The compulsion to pass down a traumatic past to the next generation—the only signal Lars can send through the genes—is a tragic psychological fact.[7] Robbed of a real father,

Lars clings to a fantasized one—a kind of forefather—and remains undeveloped, immature, incomplete. However, his obsession, the exact opposite of Beulah Lilt's indifference, yields not moral enrichment but emotional impoverishment. Whereas Beulah becomes an idolator because she eschews responsibility and forgets her Judaic heritage, Lars becomes an idolator because that heritage has been denied him. He assumes a literary patriarch's identity and shrinks his own life.

The stinging realization that Heidi is entangled not with him but with the shooting, with his "father's skeleton," constitutes a turning point in the novel (44). It is the confrontation with Heidi, her revelation of the horrors behind the fence, that begins to shatter Lars's *idée fixe*. And in the vision Lars has on a Thursday night as he walks to the *Morgontörn* to type his review, Ozick intimates the ensuing dissolution of his obsession and adumbrates the theme of the second half of the novel—lost illusions. Envisaging his father's body "not at all a skeleton," Lars at first denies the reality of Heidi's perception; then he sees, in the dark night sky over the Academy, "an incandescent apparition billowing with light," a "balloon-father shedding luminosity." But the light fades, drifts "into the white flux" and merges with it: "First a blur, then a smudge, then a blankness" (49).

To imagine his father receding into "blankness" on a Thursday night, an allusion to Black Thursday when he was killed, is to begin symbolically to bury him. To judge the first sentence—the sentence that reveals Schulz's influence on Lars—of his review "trite, portentous, posturing. All gesture" is to identify not with Bruno Schulz but with Witold Gombrowicz, whom Schulz accused of siding with "inferiority" (*Letters* 124). Once impervious to the mockery of his fellow reviewers, Lars is now ashamed to hear a sentence of his review read aloud: "he felt himself without weight in the world, a molecule bobbing along in a sluice" (50). His metaphor recalls Joseph Brill's, the schoolmaster's characterization of himself as the "grub on Freud's shoe." Having willingly thrown himself on the altar of literature, as Joseph Brill had aimed for the heights, Lars Andemening now subliminally retreats, even as Brill settled for the middle.

That retreat diminishes Lars's sense of self. It is attenuated further when the reviewer receives a note from Heidi and returns to her shop to learn Schulz's lost manuscript, *The Messiah,* has appeared in Stockholm and is in the possession of a woman professing to be Bruno Schulz's daughter Adela— the name of the formidable servant girl in Schulz's stories. Disallowing the possibility of the manuscript's existence, Lars lays fierce claim to Schulz's paternity: " 'There's no room in the story for another child. It's not feasible. It can't be. . . . There's only me' " (53). But the two would-be children have heralded their arrival with a "biblical annunciation." Referring to the biblical responses of those summoned by God, like Abraham and Moses, or of those called by their fathers, like Isaac or Jacob, Ozick suggests Lars and Adela as competitors eager to answer God, the father's command. It is a command accompanied by bright light, which is associated not only with the God of the

Hebrew Bible but with Apollo, the Greek god of light. "Exaggerated white-ness," which "seemed to be crowding into the narrow vestibule of the shop," fills the shop when Adela enters it carrying the manuscript, and the light is linked to her "white beret" and to *The Messiah*. Before Lars meets Adela, he thinks of her as an "angel" or else a "lie"; God's messenger or his counterpart vying for Bruno Schulz's paternity. At stake is the coveted lost manuscript; but the existence of a rival for his father threatens to strip Lars of his very identity, one forged in desperation. When Heidi gives him the key to the shop and tells him Dr. Eklund is on his way, Lars calls Dr. Eklund a "phantom," a reminder of the apparition of Bruno Schulz seen billowing over the Academy, and Ozick augurs the novel's resolution.

A series of matching chapters, which move steadily toward the tale's res-olution, alternately depict the events in Lars's two worlds. Paralleling the in-cidents at the *Morgontörn* with those in Heidi's shop, Ozick establishes a congruence between the stewpot and the bookshop and deploys the forces bat-tling for ascendancy over Lars Andemening. Inspirited by the ghost of Bruno Schulz, Lars formed the "habit of the quilt"; he forgoes it when he heads for the *Morgontörn*, as he had when he envisioned his father's apparition over the Academy, and exchanges inspiration for gossip. What has brought the stewpot to "full boil" is the exposure of a plagiarism (63). Bubbling over with rumor, scandal, feuds—the "ultimate ironic burlesque of Swedish parochialism"—the literary world is a "stewpot of bad habits, all of it—so that imaginative writers wind up, by and large, a shifty crew, sunk in distortion, misrepresentation, il-lusion, imposture, fakery" (M&M 100). To catch "sight of his father's eye," Lars secluded himself in his flat, "shunned the stewpot," eluded its antics and the "bad characters" engaged in them. From her portrait of the artist as a bad character, Ozick excludes Bruno Schulz; never entangled with the stewpot, he was one in a "handful of mainly guileless writers who eat themselves alive. . . . Such creatures neither observe nor invent. They never impersonate. Instead, they use themselves up in their fables, sinew by sinew" ("Portrait of the Artist as a Bad Character," M&M 100). The opposite obtains at the *Morgontörn*: Gunnar and Anders are "a pair of desperate vaudevillians," the plagiarist Flodcrantz an "actor. The greatest Thespian of them all" (62). In that theat-rical imagery is a foretaste of the imagery Ozick employs to limn the final scenes in Heidi's shop and to connect it to the literary world. It is the link Balzac forges in *Lost Illusions*. To Lucien's perception of the theater, Lousteau responds: " 'It's the same . . . as the bookshop in the Wooden Galleries and any literary periodical: It's all cooked up' " (280). The "littleness of the life of letters in decrepit old Stockholm" replicates that in fashionable nineteenth-century Paris where " 'intrigue is superior to talent' " and " 'arouses less hos-tile passions' " (*Messiah* 63; Balzac 410).

The stewpot's intrigue involves speculation on the plagiarist's fate and a decision about the "fool in the case," Sven Strömberg who, as Lars Andemen-ing will, showed "up the imposter, even at the price of his own dignity." Thus the stewpot inadvertently predicts the verdict of Lars's case. On his afternoon with "the whole three-o'clock crew" at the *Morgontörn,* the Monday reviewer muses, "how weak they were before the altar of Lars's father's unmoving eye" (64). But Lars cannot forbear, though he denied it when Heidi told him, proclaiming the discovery of Bruno Schulz's lost manuscript from the "top of the stairwell," as Jeremiah's own scribe might have. As if aware of the Hebrew name Lars has given himself, Anders comments from "halfway down" the staircase: " 'All that resurrecting you do. All those unknowns and esoterics raised from the grave.' " To which Sven Strömberg's lover adds wittily, " 'Lars Andemening, the Messiah of Stockholm.' " (65). Like Baruch of the pseude-pigrapha, Lars Andemening heralds the coming of the Messiah. Yelling " 'Crocodiles' " up from the bottom of the staircase, Nilsson invokes Schulz's metaphoric Street of Crocodiles. On that street, from which an "odor of corruption" emanates, a "half-baked and undecided reality" obtains, producing the "misfortune of that area" and transforming it into a place where "nothing ever succeeds," where "nothing can ever reach a definite conclusion" (*Street* 108, 109). In the final paragraphs of "The Street of Crocodiles," Schulz writes:

> We shall wander along shelves upon shelves of books. . . .
> We shall get involved in misunderstandings until all our fever and excitement have spent themselves in unnecessary effort, in futile pursuit. . . .
> The Street of Crocodiles was a concession of our city to modernity and met-ropolitan corruption. Obviously, we were unable to afford anything better than a paper imitation, a montage of illustrations cut out from last year's moldering newspapers. (109–10)

Lars might have discovered the destiny of his obsession at the end of "The Street of Crocodiles," in the very tale from which he has chosen his idea of reality.

On the streets of Stockholm, in Gamla Stan, the Old Town, Cynthia Ozick has transformed and resurrected the "illusory and imitative character" of the Street of Crocodiles. On the pages of the *New York Times* six months later, she revived Nilsson's metaphor to characterize the contemporary state of letters: "professions isolated by crocodiled moats."[8] The situation she describes in her essay characterizes the offices of the *Morgontörn:* "The so-called mainstream judges which writers are acceptably universal and which are to be exiled as 'parochial.' The so-called parochial, stung or cowardly or both, fear all par-ticularity and attempt impersonation of the acceptable" (M&M 95). Judged by the reviewers at the *Morgontörn* and smelling the "odor of corruption" arising from the stewpot, Lars Andemening adds a fresh ingredient to it when he announces the "risen Messiah" (67). Although he believes Schulz's manu-script is lost, Lars is "threatened by possibilities, shaken by the nearness of ful-fillment"; but on the Street of Crocodiles, "possibilities fade and decline into a void, the crazy gray poppies of excitement scatter into ashes" (*Street* 109). His exultation begins to wane when he wonders whether Nilsson will throw him out "For the sins of unwholesomeness, theology, surrealism, existential dread," whether Nilsson's advice to give these sins up and become popular, was really a warning. Jubilation diminishes further when Lars meets the woman who claims to be Bruno Schulz's daughter and who calls herself Adela.

If she has picked her name from Bruno Schulz's stories, Lars has chosen his from a dictionary. And they share bodily features: "she was graying, like himself. . . . She looked to be his own age, or near it, but when . . . he caught the plane of her flat cheek, a momentary child flashed out. . . . Between her eyes—blackish-brown like his own—there were two well-established vertical trenches," like his (71). Lars sees in Adela a reflection of himself, a kind of twin—a rival for Bruno Schulz's patrimony. When she places the manuscript on his bed, the bed she calls "an act of God," and he "the bed of rebirth," Lars's exultation intensifies (73). Schulz's handwriting elates Lars, excites his primitive, animal-like self: "A beast—a sort of ape—began to jump inside his frame, from rib to rib. . . . An inward ape heaving itself about" (73). Like the doubleness informing Ozick's novel, the metaphor captures two meanings of the word "ape," the verb that means to copy or to imitate and the noun that is the name for the manlike primate intermediate between monkeys and man. Without an identity, Lars is unable to develop into manhood; he apes Schulz's life, acquiring a spurious self, and can evolve only halfway to manhood. And the metaphor captures Lars's shifting emotions about Adela's story. The inward ape heaves, becomes "blind and berserk" when Adela recounts the story of the "man in a long black coat" to whom the manuscript was given for safe-keeping; the ape calms itself, is "foreign," as Lars's skepticism increases (73, 75). But at the mention of the wild action, the "ape was hurled" (79). When at last Lars snatches the bag with the manuscript from Adela and demands it as his birthright, the "foetal ape was awake, unfurled, raging; huge" (82).

The scene foreshadows the climactic one in Heidi's bookshop and weaves together events from Bruno Schulz's life with images from the Polish writer's work. Ozick not only converts Schulz's disheveled beds and fearful birds into the elements of Lars's visitation but she transmutes Schulz's biography into fiction: the friend to whom Schulz entrusted the manuscript of *The Messiah* becomes in *The Messiah of Stockholm* a man in a long black coat, a hasid. That the man in Adela's story never returns for the manuscript, that it was stuffed into shoes, mistaken for "Jew-prayers . . . Hexes and curses," and deemed worthless by the Poles who discovered it in their house—these are Cynthia Ozick's additions to what is known of Schulz's life. They are commentary on the fate of a Jew who refused baptism when his Catholic fiancée requested it of him but who "offered a concession: he would forsake the world of the Jews." In her description of Schulz's family, Ozick conjures up Rosa Lublin's, repeating Rosa's exact word for the Jews with whom Rosa felt billeted: "His family had anyhow always kept their distance from the *teeming* outlandish hasidim in their long black coats. He was a Pole: he had already thrown himself on the unyielding breast of Mother Poland, and nestled into the underside of her tongue. If he had ever sipped a word or two of Yiddish out of the air, it did not ride his spittle or his pen" (*Messiah* 35; *Shawl* 67; emph. added).

To the man, Kazimierz Truchanowski, who was his follower and one of the group during the war, who urged Schulz to leave Drohobycz for a secure hiding place in the Kielec country, Schulz wrote: "*Messiah* grows, little by little; it will be the continuation of *Cinn. Shops*" (*Letters* 103). Of that same follower, Schulz later wrote: "This person's faculty of self-criticism seems to be paralyzed. He doesn't notice, or else doesn't care, that he repeats my turns of speech, statements, and formulations in a bungled and trivialized form. . . . In this way his counterfeit prose may set itself up in the reader's mind in the place mine belongs" (*Letters* 129). Schulz's opinion of Truchanowski's usurpation affords an interesting perspective on Lars's. Obsessed with Schulz's stories, Lars Andemening imagines his father in imagery drawn from his own stories. In the "Age of Genius" when first the Messiah glimpses the earth, he sees something "white, silent, surrounded by azure and contemplation" (*Sanatorium* 21). On a map, the Street of Crocodiles shines "with the empty whiteness that usually marks polar regions or unexplored countries of which almost nothing is known," like Drohobycz itself (*Street* 100). That whiteness at first signifies plenitude: "his father's eye, lit, steady, unmoving, strong and blatant, a violent white ray, was spilling out the wilderness of God" (*Messiah* 68).

Next, the whiteness represents *The Messiah*. When Heidi tells Lars that Schulz's daughter has appeared in Stockholm wearing a "white beret" and carrying her father's lost manuscript in a "little white plastic bag," the bookshop seems filled with a "wild morning brightness: snow-dazzle freakishly shot through with slashes of early sunlight, too sharp to bear" (54). The "empty whiteness" on Schulz's map that designates unknown countries, where the "grade of reality" is "undecided," is for Lars Andemening the "white light of plenitude," the light brought by the risen Messiah (69). Joseph Brill has a similar view: of Rabbi Pult's idea of the future Brill thinks, "it was the white space into which messianic redemption would intervene" (CG 23). But the "north light"—a light "too cold, too sharp"—knifes through his window as Adela continues her story, "contriving a cloud over his father's words," severing Lars from his father (74).[9] At the mention of Black Thursday, the "brilliant" light becomes an "unholy glare." It affects Lars like an "electric jolt," the "vivid thwack of restoration" Rosa feels when Magda is conjured (*Messiah* 79; TS 62).

The restoration of Bruno Schulz, however, brings the "morning's brilliance" that blocks Lars's sight of Adela's eyes. The fabricated story, the "ape, exhausted at last," diminished vision—these augur Lars's failure ever to summon the inspiring eye of his father again. When Adela hurls the last piece of her story at Lars—that her then fifteen-year-old mother was Schulz's model—the inward ape awakens, provoking Lars to snatch the bag containing the manuscript, to disavow the "daughter business," to claim as his own *The Messiah* as well as its author. In the ensuing battle, his rage ignited by Adela's attempt to rob him of the only father he has known, Lars cradles *The Messiah* "against his chest" and knocks Adela to the floor. It is a gesture so uncharacteristic of Father, whom Adela cows and intimidates in Schulz's books, that it signals not the reviewer's resemblance to the Polish writer but an essential difference from him, one that forecasts the imminent collapse of Lars's obsession. Even though he has not read it, Lars bemoans the sacrifice of *The Messiah*, but he forfeits more than an unread manuscript. He loses even imaginary access to a father: "how he had crumpled his father's brain. That cradling of *The Messiah*: good God, hadn't he held it in his arms. It had possessed, for one holy hour, his house; his bed; his quilt. He ought to have been on his knees to it. . . . He might have knelt there—gazing—before the caves and grottoes of his quilt" (82). Driven outside to find Adela, who has disappeared, he imagines her as a "churning angel" (83). The violence of the scene, his despair at her escape, his poignant memory of his brief contact with the manuscript, and his fantasy of Adela reveal the significance of his intense attachment to Bruno Schulz. What Lars fancies is that the author of the *The Messiah* is a god who has sent Adela as his messenger from heaven. Fatherlessness brings in its train the need for such a fantasy, and in it Ozick intermingles the writer's fixation on a literary predecessor.

With Lars's loss of *The Messiah* comes further loss—his priesthood on the altar of literature, which Ozick suggests when Lars leaves his apartment after the fight with Adela and decides to go to the *Morgontörn*, the way he did after his confrontation with Heidi. That he walks toward the newspaper after such experiences indicates the progressive diminishment of his craze and the increasing attraction to the ordinary world of journalism. Arriving at the *Morgontörn*, he goes to the book department and selects *Illusion* as the subject of his next review. The latest novel by the popular and celebrated Ann-Charlott Almgren proves proleptic, for in the novel a young man agrees to marry an elderly spinster in return for the right to claim her "paintings as his own and give them to the world" (85). *Illusion* is reminiscent of Ozick's "Virility," and with good reason: "The 'prolific Ann-Charlott Almgren,' author of *Illusion*, is an invention. Her names come out of the marriage columns of a Stockholm newspaper found abandoned at the airport, so they are 'authentic' names."[10] An instance of the storyteller's wit, the invention testifies to Ozick's delight in fabrication, the stuff of fiction.[11]

To review Ann-Charlott Almgren is to join the mainstream at the *Morgontörn*; it is to rid oneself, as Nilsson believes Lars has done, of Central Europe. Unsure of whether he has heard Nilsson mutter "crocodiles" or "cormorants," Lars gravitates toward his flat and his bed "in order to wake to his father's eye." But he wakes to "absence," empty darkness, the biblical desolation signaled by cormorants, the birds with which Lushinski finally aligns himself. The disappearance of Lars's father's eye, the lack of the "greased beak," the want of the "alabaster egg"—these foreshadow the ultimate separation of Lars from his literary patriarch Bruno Schulz. The eye through which Lars had seen the world vanishes during the fight with Adela, "his father's daughter. His sister, his sister." To have written his review without the visitation is to discover "The author of *The Messiah* had withdrawn" (86). It is to experience, as Lushinski does, the devastation in a land abandoned by God and unilluminated by His presence (86). Discovering Adela's white beret on the floor instead of a page from the unread manuscript, Lars falls "into the night toward Heidi's shop" (87). His journey recalls Rosa's: in search of her white underpants, Rosa, too, falls into the night, into the dark hell of her past. She emerges from the Marie Louise the way Lars will leave the bookshop— free to face the future.

But Ozick links the drama enacted in Heidi's shop with the stewpot's theatrics and both to the "greater theater of illusion" described in Schulz's "Spring" and remembered by Lars after announcing the appearance of *The Messiah*. He associates the wax figure exhibition of Drohobycz with the *Morgontörn*, the waxwork men with Gunnar Hemlig and Anders Fiskyngel; for Lars they embody Schulz's "real madmen, caught red-handed at the precise moment a brilliant *idée fixe* had entered their heads. . . . Ever since then, that one idea remained in their heads like an exclamation mark, and they clung to it, standing on one foot, suspended in midair" (*Sanatorium* 60; quoted in *Messiah* 68). And alluding to *Lost Illusions,* Ozick joins to the "theater of illusion" at the newspaper the drama of forgery at the bookshop, intimating that like Lucien de Rubempré's departure from Paris, Lars will emerge from Heidi's shop stripped of his illusions.

That eventuality is adumbrated by Lars's walk and by the bookshop itself; "shut up and black," it signals the final eclipse of the light that for a certain time had illuminated Lars's universe. A disparate light, one connected neither to redemption nor to inspiration, accompanies the pending drama enacted at the bookseller's where other eyes begin to supplant and at last supersede the "saving chimerical eye" of Lars's father (94). When Lars reaches the darkened shop, it is brightened only by the lamp in the back room. The "lit daffodil" has replaced Lars's father's "lit" eye, a "yellow mist" the "violent white ray" (68, 88, 68). If the white ray discharges plenitude, the yellow haze augurs emptiness. Like the "yellow and dull horizon" present on the evening the theater of illusion comes to Drohobycz, Heidi's lamp spreads a "foredoomed glare," the "dim light" into which Lars's brilliant *idée fixe* will fade (*Sanatorium* 69). Arriving at Duneacres where Tilbeck calls her a "tourist," the narrator of *Trust* ultimately deciphers the enigma of her paternity; provided with a key to Heidi's bookshop, Lars "wasn't a visitor, he wasn't anyone's guest" (88). He, too, solves a mystery, but it utterly annihilates his claim to a paternity.

The similarities of *The Messiah of Stockholm* to *Trust* increase when Lars meets Dr. Olle Eklund, who looks "like an oversize sleek startled horse" and whose "eyeglasses splashed light" (89). They bring to mind Thoreau Purse's "eyeglasses twinkling light like semaphores," and Ozick intimates, in the connection between Heidi's mysterious husband and the young Purse, that Dr. Eklund, who Heidi sometimes indicates is a psychoanalyst, is to be Lars's Charon the way Thoreau Purse is the girl's in *Trust* (*Trust* 483). As the narrator of that novel observes, "Charon the ferryman is part of every story" (550). He is accompanied in *The Messiah of Stockholm* by Heidi, whose "doglike" voice suggests Mrs. Eklund as a kind of Cerberus.[12] If the girl's Charon ferries her across to her "father's yellow beach," the beach of her "initiation into daughterness," Dr. Eklund, whom Ozick aligns with Tilbeck and the sea, completes Lars's acceptance of fatherlessness (*Trust* 25, 504). As if to hint at that eventuality, Ozick transfers the light from Bruno Schulz to Dr. Eklund. His bald head is "bright," his coat and vest are decorated "with glinting silver buttons," his "well-shaved" chin has a "shine of its own"; Dr. Eklund, whom Lars believed Heidi "made up," becomes Lars's new source of light (89). When he discovers that Dr. Eklund "got things out—people and things," the way Morris Rappoport in "Puttermesser and Xanthippe" does, Lars suspects Olle Eklund must be a fabricated name like Adela's, like Lars's.

Lars declared himself and Bruno Schulz as alike as "two peas in a pod," but Heidi insists on the likenesses between Lars and her husband. Their footsteps "sound exactly" the same—"Light as smoke" (28). They share an "interest in original behavior," "curiosities," "tangled lives," and "bizarre histories." Dr. Eklund, Heidi believes, is Lars's "psychological twin" (27, 95). The orphan is her psychological opposite. Unaffected by the " 'attraction—the seduction, the magnetism—of a sublime text,' " Heidi is compelled by the catastrophe of fact that drives Lars to the disaster of illusion (95). When it begins to crumble Lars hears, instead of "his father's own voice," a voice reminiscent of Adela's—Dr. Eklund's "actor's voice" (33, 89). The theatrical imagery and light imagery limn the theater of illusion in Heidi's shop, connecting it to the *Morgontörn*. Its actors are matched by Dr. and Mrs. Eklund; "Two old troupers in rehearsal," they are "theatrical," "operatic" (92). And the three chapters concerning the fate of *The Messiah* are like three acts of a play that move swiftly and inexorably toward the solution of a mystery. When Heidi reaches up "to switch on the lights," Adela enters the stage and Lars feels he is "in a theater" (99). As in a play relationships shift; they are "willed, directed, cued" (100). Although Dr. Eklund claims to understand Lars, Heidi becomes his "advocate," as imagery associated with the theater begins to compete with that of the law. Fact makes Lars conscious of being an "onlooker" before the "unintelligible drama" raging before him. To have "surrendered to the false daughter's tale" is to have given up "the author of *The Messiah*," to have "chopped" off an "old certainty," to be "stripped of verisimilitude," left without knowledge of "what . . . to be henceforth." Lars Andemening is, as Heidi says, "one of the century's casualties, in his own way a victim" (99, 100, 98).

And Ozick renders the wrenching emotional effects of such victimization—the desperate need to invent a father, an illusion which provides relief from the fear of nothingness but which exacts as its price the individual's own identity.[13] Small wonder, then, that Lars, after the undoing of his delusion, feels "How hard it was to breathe, to breathe in and out, without illumination! Everything quenched, snuffed, suffocated. Surrendered." If Bruno Schulz is "nobody's father," Lars Andemening is "nobody's son" (99, 100). Somebody's son, William's son is never addressed by his own name, nor is the narrator of *Trust:* neither has secured an identity. Lars, "who had named himself in secret," has an "orphan's terrifying freedom to choose" a name and an identity, the freedom being unread brings (102). Now the foetal ape lurches after "the truth," and the next act of the play begins.

In the role of a specialist in forgery, Dr. Eklund scrutinizes *The Messiah* to determine its authenticity. Out of "Ali Baba's jar," the "round brass jug; a sort of amphora. . . . or an urn," in which Adela has stuffed the manuscript, comes "a shower of ragged white wings, a jumbled armada of white sails" (96, 101). The implied connection of the manuscript to magic and "sorcery" recalls the narrator's repudiation of the stasis and monomania of magic near the end of *Trust*. But Dr. Eklund judges the handwriting of *The Messiah* real, "a scrimshaw of the nervous system," and impossible to "impersonate" (104). To relinquish his father's eye is one thing, *The Messiah,* quite another: "The original! Recovered; resurrected; redeemed. Lars, looking with all his strength, felt his own ordinary pupil consumed by a conflagration in the socket. As if copulating with an angel whose wings were on fire" (104). The passage, which revives Adela's story of the child whom she claims Bruno Schulz impregnated, is complex psychologically. The pupil of Lars's own eye refers to his father's, but Ozick puns on the word "pupil" and joins to Schulz's eye the pupil Adela claims as her mother. Leaving his room after that revelation, Adela seems to him like a "churning angel"; later that day in Heidi's shop, Lars bemoans—he rejects—the idea that "such a man . . . would copulate with a child" (83, 102). Still, gazing at the manuscript, Lars identifies with Schulz as Adela described him; and the text—art itself—takes on religious and sexual fervor when Lars imagines himself and Bruno Schulz, as if God's priests, consumed by their fiery feelings about art. For that Schulz refused to leave Drohobycz, where he died; for Bruno Schulz's patrimony, Lars lost "not one but two wives! And a child, lost, stolen! Himself now without even that paintbox. The last trace expunged. Erased" (101).

And he expunges *The Messiah*. Before she divulges its contents, Ozick reveals Lars has set fire to the manuscript: Lazarus Baruch, the prophet Jeremiah's scribe, becomes King Jehoiakim who burned the scroll containing the prophet's oracles as it was read to him (Jer. 36:23). But Lars Andemening "fell into the text with the force of a man who throws himself against a glass wall" (105). Once a meticulous reader swept away by the text, which depleted and exhausted him like the "strokes of a drowning man," he becomes the shatterer of the "glass retort" from which Schulz could not "escape" and in which Lars has confined himself, fancying its beak the "greased beak" of inspiration (*Letters* 37). The process reverses the significance of the description Schulz offered of his "walled up" room about which Jerzy Ficowski comments, "On one side of that door lies life and its restricted freedom, on the other—art" (*Street* 19). Impelled by the "terrible speed of his hunger" to chew "through hook and blade, tongue and voice of the true *Messiah*," Lars discovers its "incised" and "*bleeding*" language, a language that conjures up Rosa's imaginary letter written inside a "terrible beak of light bleeding out a kind of cuneiform on the underside of her brain" (*Messiah* 104; *Shawl* 69). Like Rosa Lublin, Bruno Schulz was a letter writer; from his letters to Deborah Vogel, *The Street of Crocodiles* "came into being" (*Street* 16).[14] His cannibalism of *The Messiah* and the amnesia overtaking Lars after he reads the manuscript suggest its significance for his psyche. And her version of *The Messiah* uncovers Cynthia Ozick's assessment of Bruno Schulz's art.

Little is known of Schulz's unfinished and lost *Messiah*. Schulz himself described it as a continuation of *Cinnamon Shops,* and Jerzy Ficowski infers from Schulz's brief remark that in *The Messiah,* the "myth of the coming of the Messiah would symbolize a return to the happy perfection that existed at the beginning—in Schulzian terms, the return to childhood" (*Street* 18). But in her account of Schulz's manuscript, Ozick depicts that return as a new beginning "because *The Messiah,* insofar as it could be determined to be 'about' anything . . . was about creation and redemption. It was a work of cosmogony and entelechy" (106–7). Into the fabric of that fable, Ozick weaves strands from Bruno Schulz's stories and images from the Polish writer's drawings; the result is her new meditation on art and idolatry. Indifferent to the injunction against idolatry, the source of Cynthia Ozick's conflict, Bruno Schulz declared a pagan concept of life the provenance of his art. In her rendition of Schulz's *Messiah,* Ozick removes all traces of the Polish writer's paganism, but retains in her text the essentials of Schulz's art. Even the manuscript's pages, the order of which Adela claims does not matter, follows Schulz's description of the "horoscope of spring"; "The text can be read forward or backward, lose its sense and find it again in many versions, in a thousand alternatives" (*Sanatorium* 25). Of *The Messiah* Ozick writes: "So it was with the intelligence of *The Messiah*'s order and number and scheme of succession: everything voluminously overlapping, everything simultaneous and multiform" (106). And the comment Schulz makes about his own story applies to Ozick's as well, for like Schulz's texts, Ozick's present a "thousand alternatives" and "follow many different tracks" (*Sanatorium* 25).[15] One of them leads to Drohobycz which Ozick imagines as deserted, except by the idols who, for want of worshipers, begin to worship each other.

Such a situation obtains in "The Book" where, upon the departure of "their splendid patriarchs," Schulz predicts "the village will fall into doubt and apostasy" (*Sanatorium* 11). But the consequences in Ozick's Drohobycz differ. That Ozick fills it with idols who result from the "inspired toil or armies of ingenious artisans" intimates the reason apostasy has taken over the abandoned town: to spurn the patriarch is to embrace idolatry. Unable to leave his native town, Schulz turned its very inhabitants, streets, and shops into myth: he peopled Drohobycz with idols. If she follows Schulz in imagining a forsaken town, Ozick pursues another track when she removes Adela from the pages of the manuscript and fancies her the bringer of *The Messiah*. In reading it, Lars discovers that although Adela was nowhere called Adela in the text,

"She was there, but not alive, and unnamed. . . . she had turned, with full purity of intent, into an idol. Her eyes were conventional green jewels" (107). To metamorphose Schulz's servant girl into an idol "made of some artificial dead matter" and to endow her with green jewels for eyes is to conjure up Beulah Lilt's polished green stones, to reinterpret Adela's significance in Schulz's text, to attribute to the work of artisans the creation of idols. Indeed, the Polish writer and artist compiled his own *Book of Idolatry,* a series of drawings in which men bend or cringe or else crawl in front of women, the way in Schulz's stories Father cowers before Adela: "In many pictures, the male figure multiplies into a whole tribe of idolatrous admirers of varying ages and degrees of ugliness" (Baranczak 29). The drawings unmask Schulz's "acute sense of inadequacy, unfulfillment," which Stanislaw Baranczak attributes in part to Bruno Schulz's divided background: "Writing in Polish made [Schulz] an outcast among the Jews. Being Jewish made him a stranger in Polish culture" (30, 31). Caught between two worlds, the Polish writer is reminiscent of the schoolmaster Joseph Brill, with whom Ozick aligns Lars Andemening.

Not only did Schulz's assimilation bring incompleteness and homelessness, it compelled the writer to invent a religion without theology or morality. For that reason "it was as if the former inhabitants of Drohobycz had converted to atheism and fled": the Drohobycz of *The Messiah* is a place where "religion had dried up," where idolatry reigns among idols. In their worship of each other's beauty, the idols of Drohobycz engage in a "religion of Art," the paganism from which Schulz drew inspiration (A&A 163). Carving their idols out of stone, the artisans have replaced the Tablets of Law with the beautiful objects to which the Law forbids devotion; like the planet Acirema, the stone idols crowd Drohobycz, setting it afire, "idols burning up idols in a frenzy of mutual adoration" (*Messiah* 109). Of the empty world they leave Schulz writes:

> On such a day the Messiah advances to the edge of the horizon and looks down on the earth. . . . and, not knowing what He is doing, He may descend upon earth. And in its reverie the earth won't even notice Him, who has descended onto its roads, and people will wake up from their afternoon nap remembering nothing. The whole event will be rubbed out, and everything will be as it has been for centuries, as it was before history began. (*Sanatorium* 21)

For her version of the Messiah's arrival, Ozick revives, in Lars Andemening's response, Schulz's vision of the people who not only ignore the Messiah but who forget Him, and she adds to that vision traditional Jewish ideas of messianism.[16] If for Schulz the coming of the Messiah goes unnoticed, His advent in the Drohobycz of Ozick's *Messiah* occurs in the midst of destruction and portends the imminent end of idolatry. The scene captures an antithetical notion in Jewish messianism: "These two aspects, which in fact are based on the words of the prophets themselves and are more or less visible there, concern the catastrophic and destructive nature of the redemption on the one hand and the utopianism of the content of the realized Messianism on the other" (Scholem, MIJ 7). Turning up in Drohobycz unexpected and unheralded, Ozick's Messiah—a kind of book with an "unreadable text" composed of drawings, the "characters of an unknown alphabet"—itself encompasses traditional Judaic notions of the Messiah's arrival and the apocalyptist's inaccessible vision, the riddling, allegorical, and mysterious words which must be "deciphered" (Scholem, MIJ 6). In that tradition the Messiah "comes suddenly, unannounced, and precisely when he is least expected or when hope has long been abandoned"; the messianic redemption, to which the idea of "birth pangs" is attached, is spontaneous and cannot be prepared for (Scholem, MIJ 11, 10). Ozick's Messiah, though "it" has seemed to some critics to adhere to Schulz's idea—that the Messiah "arrives only when he is no longer necessary, appearing in a world no longer capable of further transformation, for there is no one left to either remember or forget"—in fact diverges from it.[17] If idols presently populate the town, "their sojourn in Drohobycz" is short-lived, perhaps lasting only until the people return from their "journeys" or can "be rounded up" (109, 108). Ozick accents the temporary situation in Drohobycz—her words underscore the transitory—and she intimates that in Drohobycz, and by implication elsewhere, change can occur, that redemption is possible.

And that redemptive potential inheres in a book. Even though upon arrival the Messiah "almost immediately fell to pieces," He gives "birth to a bird." It carries "in its beak a single strand of dried hay," the "tiny wand" that dissolves the idols of Drohobycz. That the Messiah's genesis was the "cellar of . . . the Drohobycz synagogue" where the saintly "Moses the Righteous one" used to sleep on a "bundle of hay"; that Ozick depicts, in Schulz's precise words, the crumbling of the Messiah indicate her view of Schulz's "authentic Book."[18] In Schulz's tale, the book's pages free "flocks of swallows and larks," and when Father attempts to substitute the Bible for The Book, the son cries, " 'Why do you give me that fake copy, that reproduction, a clumsy falsification?' " (*Sanatorium* 1, 3). The "book of truth and splendor," which "at the moment of inspiration" returns to its ancient source, is a replacement of God by Demiurge (*Sanatorium* 34, 10). Engrossed in The Book, the son forgets mealtimes, ordinary daily existence—what for Ozick amounts to the "handiwork of the Creator" (A&A 206). What is authentic for one writer is idolatrous for the other. In envisioning Schulz's uncompleted manuscript as a "degraded and humiliated" book which gives birth to a bird, Ozick revives Schulz's tale; in reconceiving the purpose of the birds the pages of The Book release, she imagines a destiny for Schulz different from the one he pursued. The bird arising from her Messiah holds in its beak a remnant of Moses the Righteous one which destroys the idols of Drohobycz: the "tiny wand," a kind of covenantal rod, promises the return of the "Book, the holy original" and restores Drohobycz and Bruno Schulz to monotheism (109–11).[19]

The "sound of lamentation and elegy," which rises up at the idols' disintegration and which leaves Drohobycz empty save for the "small beating bird," becomes the lamentation belonging to Lars. His grief adverts to the verses in the Book of Lamentations mourning the destruction of Jerusalem:

> Mute imprint of noise—a city falling, crumbling, his own moans, relentless lamentation. Sound of shooting. Amnesia. Lost. Nothing remained.
> Lamentation remained. Elegy after great pain. (115)

And that allusion coupled with the one to Emily Dickinson's poem, "After great pain, a formal feeling comes," underscore the meaning of Bruno Schulz to Lars Andemening and glimpse the end of the novel. To refer to the Book of Lamentations is to suggest the nature of Lars's sorrow, for in that biblical book individual experience mirrors a major historical catastrophe: "The solution undertaken by the authors of Lamentations was to transfer to the collective the attributes of individual experience and to view the nation as a whole in the aspect of a single individual; simply put: personification" (Mintz 23). The fate of Bruno Schulz personifies for Lars Andemening the fate of the Six Million; and for that reason, he has chosen as his namesake the scribe in the Apocalypse of Baruch whom God elected to witness the burning of the Second Temple. As in Lamentations the pain endures; elegy replaces "formal feeling."[20] Retaining none of the text of *The Messiah,* Lars will ultimately recollect "the letting go."

He lets go of the author of *The Messiah* and his last manuscript with great pain. That his obsession with Schulz is destined for such an end is intimated in Lars's first meeting with Adela when she jumps up from where he has knocked her down "in a sudden spiraling of pure flight, as elastic as the rising up of a bird" and escapes with *The Messiah* (82). Her departure recalls Schulz's description of "ordinary books" which at first soar "like the phoenix, all its pages aflame"; but then consumed, rather than renewed, by the fire their pages crumble into a heap of ash (*Sanatorium* 10). The fate of Schulz's ordinary books becomes *The Messiah*'s. To "flood his eyes with that text" had been Lars's "great wish"; minutes after reading the manuscript he forgets it— "the thing itself, the words, the syllables, the letters!" (114). And then he apprehends the "lie in the room" (112). The "lie of illusion" that in *Trust* "falls like a damp pervading smoke" becomes in *The Messiah of Stockholm* a "made lie" which, as the narrator of *Trust* observes, "can be contradicted by the exposure of its contrary . . . and can be cut down" (*Trust* 317). The steady accumulation of the lie's elements, the painful exposure of the truth, the final cutting down of the falsehood—these quicken the final act of the play in Heidi's shop. Through the prism of Lars Andemening's consciousness can be glimpsed the plangent strength of illusion, the wrench of parting with illusion.

As if to join *The Messiah of Stockholm* to *Trust,* Ozick imparts Lars's experience and the girl's in the swamp at Duneacres in matching images. Awaiting her father's arrival, the narrator of *Trust* contemplates a blazing tree whose light seems to view her like an eye, an eye like the one belonging to Lars's father. Having conjured him, Lars "had penetrated into the entrails, the inmost anatomy, of that eye," had in effect penetrated the world with his father's eyes. The source of his vision appropriated by disparate eyes and other lights, Lars sees instead of "that sufficing eye" Dr. Eklund's "big glowing face with its bright lenses" (115). But now Dr. Eklund, his rings aglow, illumines Heidi's shop. "Darting in and out of the blocks of shelves like an over-sized rat in a tunnel," Dr. Eklund resurrects McGovern's rat in *Trust* and the mice at the Morgontörn—all of which feast on print, cannibalize text. Emblems of devouring time and a decaying paradise in *Trust,* the cannibalistic rodents in *The Messiah of Stockholm* foreshadow the destruction of the forged manuscript, the manuscript Heidi Eklund implores Lars to review.

But he has surrendered its author, and without him Lars feels powerless, "empty." Nor can he remember *The Messiah:* he had read it "too hotly—like a man half-blinded, who can descry only the flat light, not the character on a page" (117). Uncertain whether he had taken in the "true" *Messiah,* unsure of what he has seen of its text, Lars slowly begins to see "exactly" how *he* has been taken in: "He had fallen among players; among plotters." They have invented their names: the "fradulent daughter," Adela; the " 'Refugee imposter,' " an "ordinary Alter Eckstein," Olle Eklund (119, 120). They awaken the ape in Lars's chest which again brings the travail of breathing and his aching recognition: " 'Fakery. I've lived for fakery.' " His throat clutched by the ape, his fingers "like the staves of a fence on fire," Lars utters a truth worthy of Heidi Eklund: " 'The Messiah was burned up in those places. Behind those fences, in those ovens' " (121). In turn, she reverses her original role and urges him to believe in the authenticity of *The Messiah.* But the "ape" for which he has lived, the ape which threatens to choke him, dies at last; "its carcass was a dead weight on his lung." Free of the beast's grip and driven by the "blast of his own force" rather than by "his greening masculine forces," Lars ascertains Dr. Eklund, not Bruno Schulz, is the author of *The Messiah* and the father of Adela. That discovery severs the "ape's sprawling carcass" from Lars, and he presses Heidi to admit to forgery.

He turns, however, on Adela: "how she had toyed with him, how she had blotted out his father's eye, how she had orphaned him, how she had mocked and nullified the author of *The Messiah*" (126). When she enters Heidi's shop carrying the manuscript in a brass amphora, Adela seems like "Hebe the cupbearer, messenger, deliverer"—the "goddess as child" or "she who removes from sight" (101).[21] Like Joseph Brill's messenger, Iris Garson, Adela removes from Lars's sight the vision of the extraordinary. Her resemblance to the tiny bird which rises from the Messiah to eradicate the idols of Drohobycz establishes her as the destroyer of Lars's idol. Its loss cannot help but kindle the violent desire "to knock her down" and "pluck" her eyes out. The messenger's enlightenment, though it dissipates illusion, ends in a confrontation with reality too dark to bear and in a desecration of the man in whose ghost Lars sees the Six Million.

And he subjects the manuscript to their fate. That moment is carefully prepared for beginning with his arrival at Heidi's shop: "caught in the left sole" of Lars's boots is a "matchstick," one of the matches "designed to light a re-calcitrant fire" in Dr. Eklund's pipe (88, 118). Diving for the "tiny stick" Dr. Eklund has dropped, a reminder of the "tiny wand" with which the idols in Drohobycz are "dissolved into sparks," Lars throws a lit match down the brass amphora and sets fire to the inauthentic manuscript. Along with it the flames consume the ape—the "unholy beast rocking" in the jar "howling out its dying" (126). The last creation of his literary patriarch reduced to a mound of ash in a brass amphora, Lars Andemening is shut of his "theory of patri-mony." If, as Harold Bloom argues, Lars burns the manuscript as "a final sac-rifice after the Six Million," he also ignites the manuscript as a final "movement of self-purgation . . . so as to separate himself from . . . the pre-cursor" ("Book" 36; *Anxiety* 15). And so the fabric of Lars's fantasy is parted and the orphan enters the welter of reality, accepts its "intuitive" character, and arrives at the truth.

His illusory relationship with Bruno Schulz, Lars's drive to determine the "pulse of ancestry" amidst the "conspiratorial illusion" in Heidi's shop, the novel's pervasive images—eyes, lights, voices—these invoke the tragedy of *Oedipus the King*. What Oedipus ultimately penetrates—the "secret of his birth"—is what history has made impenetrable to Lars (1. 1335). But the two men begin with the knowledge that purification is imperative to their lives: Oedipus so as to end the plague in Thebes and Lars in order to cast "off his old married ways" (*Messiah* 6). Sophocles' play and Ozick's novel have in common imagery associating the gods with truth, as the Leader of the chorus of *Oedipus the King* discloses when he links Teiresias to Apollo: "Teiresias sees what the god Apollo sees. / Truth, truth" (11. 388–89). Equally crucial to *Oedipus the King* and to *The Messiah of Stockholm* are the gods Apollo and Zeus; if "Apollo . . . hurls light," the "glorious voice of Zeus" is the "voice who knows everything" (30). For these reasons the chorus calls to Apollo, to the "bright divinities" and their "saving light," and to Zeus, "handler of the fire," the "father" who can "make the god of [their] sickness ashes" (11. 213, 214, 259–61). As the father of Hebe, Dr. Eklund plays the role of Zeus in *The Messiah of Stockholm;* lighting his matches, voicing his opinion of the manu-script's legitimacy, Dr. Eklund possesses an all-knowing voice. Afraid that Apollo's prediction will prove true, Oedipus compares it to a "god's sunlight," which like the light filling his flat after Lars naps, "grows brighter on a man's face at dawn when he's in bed, still sleeping, and reaches into his eyes and wakes him" (68). Each man is accused of not being his "father's son." When Oedipus discovers the secret of his birth and realizes he has murdered his fa-ther, "no shining statues of the gods" remain. The king is left with "nothing" (1. 1791). The "ashes of burnt offerings" at the shrine of Apollo Ismenios re-veal the future, and the prophecy of the god of light comes true: Oedipus con-signs himself to a darkened universe.[22]

In interlacing allusions to *Oedipus the King* with elements in her novel, Ozick deepens the intricacies of Lars Andemening's illusion and widens the significance of his loss. That Lars endows Bruno Schulz with the powers possessed by the Greek god of light, prophecy, and inspiration; that the Monday reviewer attributes to the Polish writer imagery belonging to Apollo suggest the god's meaning to the orphan who has made a life of print. Even the mice at the *Morgontörn* refer to one of Apollo's attributes, as does the window of Lars's flat. An "archer's slit," the window recalls the god's sacred bow and arrow and implies that the light knifing through the flat belongs to the Greek god of inspiration (74). It vanishes along with the divinity's bright words when the flames in the brass amphora engulf the manuscript and *The Messiah* fades into dull ash. Marking the place where Oedipus killed his father is a "cluster of oaks." Standing near the brass amphora Olle Eklund—his name, oak grove, a reminder of those ancient trees—watches helplessly as the last vestiges of the manuscript, and Lars's fabricated father, recede into a specter of thought. Had he had a father, Lars would not have had to surrender to the idol he is eventually driven to destroy; he "might have thrown [his father] over, as one *does* throw over father and regents, saws and scepters and all" (*Trust* 244). When the narrator of *Trust* has that insight into her relationship with Enoch Vand, she has not yet come together with Gustave Nicholas Tilbeck. For Lars, however, such a meeting can never take place. The "darkness over his quilt" obliterates "his father's eye with [Adela's] outstretched arms," as Adela dooms Lars to the terrible freedom an orphan must own, to a future as devoid of illumination as the one Oedipus chooses.

Adela chooses as a container for *The Messiah* an amphora which shelters and then entombs the manuscript. Cynthia Ozick's abiding emblem of Hellenism from *Trust* onward, the burial place of *The Messiah* alludes to Keats's Grecian urn, that imperishable object of art on which the figures remain frozen in timelessness. Man's "terror of the urn" is decisive for Joseph Brill, and in Ozick's poem "Urn-burial" determines God to experiment with "human immortality," to punish humanity with "Life Permanent." As the drama in the bookshop progresses toward a "verdict," Lars comes to a conclusion about Adela and Dr. Eklund which affects the manuscript's survival. "Two urns of the same ancestry," the daughter and her father revive the two urns Athenian jurors used as receptacles in which to cast their lots for conviction or acquittal (124). Finally, the lots in Heidi's shop are tallied, but each juror has a different "version." "Drenched in smoke," in the reality of death, Lars reaches his own verdict—the "family business" wants "to be in competition with God" (128). To ascertain the relationship between the drama's actors and to expose the writer of the fraudulent manuscript is to come face to face with illusion, to accept as reality an irredeemable past, the unremitting fact of orphanhood.

Lar's conflict, the one between the illusion created by the imagination of an orphan and the reality upheld by his reason, is at the nub of *The Messiah of Stockholm* and is embodied in the novel's competing images, whose clash reaches a crescendo in the final scenes performed in the bookshop. At odds about the nature of reality, Lars and Heidi see it in different lights. Secluded under his quilt, Lars awakens to the "violent white ray" of light irradiating his flat. But Heidi's old German lamp—"the necessary daffodil"—illuminates her shop, casting a "yellow arc." Falling back into her chair under the lamp, Heidi insists, " 'What's real is real' " (37). And what is real to Heidi is not the white light from Lars's father's eye. Bruno Schulz's skeleton, the shooting, the horror of the Holocaust—these are the realities to which Heidi clings. After Lars relinquishes the illusion of Schulz's paternity, the "lit" daffodil lights his universe. The yellow lamp Heidi took with her from Germany is an enduring reminder of that country, of the yellow badges it forced on Jews prior to their slaughter. Included in the genera *Asphodelus,* the daffodil is a flower of death, one belonging to those flowers that fill the Asphodel Fields, Homer's meadow of the dead. Of significance, then, is Heidi's position "behind the fence of books" under the lit daffodil. Before the curtain rises on the drama in her shop, Heidi cannot engage Lars in the shooting; when the curtain rises on the last act, Lars is enmeshed in the "catastrophe of fact," the murdered Six Million (88). The fence of books, the fence of the death camp, and the fence of the Law reach an accord.

To renounce idolatry is to assume a position behind that fence. To rival God is to repudiate the Second Commandment, to dwell beyond the fence of Hebraism in the wildness of Hellenism, the region Dr. Eklund's face, a "worn old landscape lost to any habitation," mirrors when the curtain falls at last in the bookseller's theater (128). The "wild . . . look" on Dr. Eklund's and Adela's faces belongs to the frenzy of inspiration whose "genesis," Ozick tells us in an essay she wrote during the same period as *The Messiah of Stockholm,* "is in natural religion, or, rather, in the religion of nature" (*Messiah* 128; M&M 170). In "Metaphor and Memory," the storyteller recounts the history of inspiration, chronicles the events at the shrine of Apollo at Delphi, and differentiates inspiration, which gushed forth from the fount at Delphi, from memory, which is "history as judgment" (M&M 270, 276).

If she dramatizes the perils of inspiration to the writer in *The Messiah of Stockholm,* she establishes in "Metaphor and Memory" the preponderant importance of metaphor—"one of the chief agents of our moral nature" and the means "to convert the imagination into a serious moral instrument" (278). To metaphor Ozick ascribes the ability to imagine another's heart; to metaphor she attributes the power to transform the "strange into the particular," the capacity to turn "memory into a principle of continuity" (282). Of the dead writers she writes: they "have turned metaphoric; they contain our experience, and they alter both our being and our becoming" (282–83). About homage to the dead writers she admonishes: "To be any sort of competent writer one must keep one's psychological distance from the supreme artists" (A&A 297). His proximity to them subjugates Lars to their influence, hinders his becoming. Through metaphor, through the "drama of fiction," Ozick transforms his "experience into idea"; she empowers us to imagine his dilemma (273, 282).

What metaphor accomplishes is advanced in "Metaphor and Memory"; what results from metaphor becomes translucent in *The Messiah of Stockholm* in which idea and emotion come together in a moving and vivid tale. Moving, because it dramatizes the hidden psychological underpinnings of childhood deprivation and depicts its devastating effects on the adult's capacity to mature; vivid, because the novel's metaphors bridge the gulf lying between expression and thought. The predominant metaphor in *The Messiah of Stockholm* brilliantly instances how the novelist's metaphors work. Harnessing biblical and mythological beliefs in the power of the eye—its capacity to bestow as well as to take life, its use by "figures in authority to guide, punish, and reward those in a dependent position"—Ozick constructs a metaphor that incarnates the plight of her main character, connects the emotional shock of parental deprivation to his mental need for artistic domination, and completes her portrait of a writer's psyche (Riess 407).[23] Never content with a single view of a subject Ozick allows both views of the subject to coalesce in order to see them with double sight.

Thus Lars Andemening seven months after the play's finale: Now a man of unmistakable "middling years," "reformed . . . recovered from his old ailment" and "taking the reviewing business seriously," Lars Andemening, like Joseph Brill, settles for the ordinary (132). The Monday reviewer has moved from his minuscule apartment to a "large apartment" with furniture, an "automatic answering machine," a computer. He has exchanged his "cramped" flat where a greased beak once seized him and delivered him to a high place for a "bare" cubicle of his own at the *Morgontörn*, the white ray of light for the greenish glow of a computer screen, his father's voice for a recorded one of his own, "purification" for recognition. Instead of incurring the derision of the other reviewers, Lars insults them "by slamming himself like a beam in their eyes." If he once heralded a risen Messiah, it is now he who "had risen." Shut of "those indecipherables that steam up from the stomach-hole of Europe" and writing reviews of detective novels and autobiographies of film stars, he takes "on a touch of fame" (131). Lost illusions foster success; but it lands Lars where Bruno Schulz said Witold Gombrowicz landed—"on the side of inferiority against superiority" (*Messiah* 130, 132; *Letters* 124).

Visiting Lars at his cubicle, as she had at his flat, the woman who pretended to be Schulz's daughter proclaims him "just like the others," an "ordinary reviewer" (134). And Ozick continues to double and then divide the events in Lars's life before the orphan cast off his illusion from those occurring after he ignited the fire in the brass amphora. The cupbearer called herself Adela, the bringer of the little boy, Elsa Vaz. To her comment that the sick child on her lap was well an hour before they arrived at the *Morgontörn*, Lars replies, " 'Stage fright' " and questions her readiness, over seven months later, to "unscramble . . . the whole cast of characters" (137, 138). The theater's lights dim once more at the *Morgontörn;* in vain he tries to recapture his vision, the "magical eye" Dr. Eklund accused Lars of thinking "drops from heaven to inspire" (127). What Lars visualizes instead is a "very small mound of ash" whose "gray cinders might have passed for a "little heap of Elsa Vaz's hair" (139). Fakery, a "heap of ash"—for these Lars "had exchanged his daughter's hot life." But Elsa insists " 'Dr. Eklund's facsimile,' " the " 'last brainchild of Drohobycz,' " has " 'gone up in smoke' " (141). To the amphora, which made Lars, when he first saw it, "think of a mummy in a case, or else a round baby," Ozick joins the little boy in Elsa's lap and Lars's daughter Karin, renewing at the end of the tale the conflict coursing through the novel—the rift between reality and the imagination, the choice between life and art.

The last meeting between Lars and Elsa concludes as their first one had—with an abrupt exit. Snatching the manuscript from Lars in his tiny apartment, Adela left behind a reminder of *The Messiah,* her white beret. The bringer of the Messiah, Schulz's servant girl, becomes at the end of the novel Elsa Vaz, Schulz's "Elsa—the Liquid with a Swan" who brings in her vase a "balm that worked wonders" (*Sanatorium* 5). Upon her departure, Lars runs to the "top of the stairwell" where he had announced the risen Messiah and throws the last remnant of it, the white beret, down to the landing (142). If Elsa's balm is ameliorative, a "miraculous nostrum for all illnesses and infirmities," her wonders do not alleviate his "hallucination—it was a sort of hallucination"— of the ever present roasting smell in Stockholm. Puzzling to Lars at first, the origin of the odor finally becomes inescapably associated with the smoke rising from the chimneys of the death camps, with the man who Adela claimed rescued Bruno Schulz's lost manuscript but who, before he could reclaim it, perished like "All the Jews, all the hasidim in their long black coats" in Drohobycz (74). And it is that man, when Lars catches sight of him "inside the narrow hallway of his skull . . . hurrying with a metal garter box squeezed under his arm, hurrying and hurrying toward the chimneys," for whom Lars grieves at the end of *The Messiah of Stockholm.* That man replaces the ghost of Bruno Schulz in Lars's mind as a metaphor for the Six Million—what is, tragically, all of Lars's chosen history. In possession of the "linking meant to be carried forward into the horizons of the farthest future," Joseph Brill cannot bear to think of Beulah Lilt as "fatherless and motherless. An orphan of the future" (CG 22, 92). But no one carried that linking forward to Lars Andemening; he can discover neither his origins, as the narrator of *Trust* could, nor can he escape and ascend into the nimbus, as Beulah Lilt does. His is an orphanhood of the future as well as one of the past.

Lars Andemening's experience bears a remarkable resemblance to an episode in Cynthia Ozick's life, which Ozick recounts in "The Lesson of the Master," an essay she published three years before completing *The Messiah of Stockholm.* Describing herself when she was half Lars Andemening's age and under the spell of Henry James, she discloses, in imagery echoed in her novel, the effects of his influence:

> I had become Henry James, and for years and years I remained Henry James. . . .
> I carried the Jamesian idea, I was of his cult, I was a worshiper of literature, literature was my single altar; I was, like the elderly bald-headed James, a priest at that altar; and that altar was all of my life. Like John Marcher in "The Beast in

the Jungle," I let everything pass me by for the sake of waiting for the Beast to spring—but unlike John Marcher, I knew what the Beast was . . . the Beast was literature itself. (A&A 294–95)

In her novel Lars Andemening serves as her counterpart, but her Beast has become his ape, the "beam that flies out from the stupendous Jamesian lantern" becomes Bruno Schulz's white ray of plenitude (A&A 293). Of her experience Ozick concludes: "Rapture and homage are not the way. Influence is perdition"—a truth achingly apparent in her chronicle of Lars Andemening's life (297). If in Lars Andemening she dramatizes the toils of influence, the dangers besetting a life dedicated to the imagination, in Heidi Eklund Ozick depicts the obverse: a life given over to the reason, which regards as wild and repugnant— Heidi's opinion of Bruno Schulz's tales—the illusions constructed by the fancy. Together her two characters represent the novelist's "unholy conflict"; they are her opposing selves. One falls prey to idolatry, the other to forgery. Neither triumphs.

But idolatry of a literary predecessor is not the same as regard for his tutelage. To descry, as some critics have, the likeness *The Messiah of Stockholm* bears to James's novella, "The Aspern Papers" is to stop too soon; it is on their disparities the critic should concentrate. What James's and Ozick's characters have in common is an obsession with a dead literary figure, a consuming interest in his artistic remains. What Lars Andemening chooses from a dictionary James's nameless narrator seems not to possess. Neither man owns a resolute identity. In the revelatory fourth chapter of "The Aspern Papers," James unfolds the narrator's thoughts and feelings; in them can be seen a reflection of Lars Andemening's. Like Bruno Schulz, Jeffrey Aspern is the "spirit," the "prompter" who perpetually accompanies the narrator and who hovers before him like a "bright ghost" (28). Lars Andemening imagines a filial bond to Schulz, the narrator of James's tale "even a mystic companionship, a moral fraternity with all those who in the past had been in the service of art" (28). Hanging "high in the heaven of our literature," the god the narrator of "The Aspern Papers" worships is, like Lars's god, "part of the light by which we walk." Their devotion to those gods prompts Schulz's disciple and Aspern's admirer to regard themselves as "ministers" of their artists' temples (AP 3).

Because the *Morgontörn*'s reviewer and Aspern's devotee "deal with phantoms and dust, the mere echoes of echoes," they can only discover the fount of inspiration outside themselves, in the imaginative powers of another. In the grip of *idées fixes*, the narrator of "The Aspern Papers" and Lars Andemening become victims of their own obsessions; but Lars is betrayed and James's narrator betrays, convinced that he must use "hypocrisy" and "duplicity" to "arrive at" his "spoils" (7). His role in the "rich dim Shelley drama" is the duplicitous one the Eklunds play. Foiled by the fire Lars ignites in the amphora, their plan to legitimate a forged manuscript evaporates after Lars reads *The Messiah* and then burns it; but the "publishing scoundrel" has no opportunity to peruse the papers he covets before Miss Tina sets them aflame (xxxi).

If at the end of his experience, James's narrator can "scarcely bear [his] loss . . . of the precious papers," Lars Andemening grieves not for the lost *Messiah* but for a larger loss, one brought about by a catastrophe of history. James expresses in the preface to "The Aspern Papers" his "delight in a palpable imaginable *visitable* past," but Ozick attests in her novel to the necessity of the past leading to "forward continuity," to a future.

The complexities that entail are signaled in the epigraphs from Bruno Schulz and Pär Lagerkvist Ozick has appended to *The Messiah of Stockholm*. Her reasons for choosing the passage from Father's "most heretical doctrine" are two. The first is that the epigraph exemplifies Schulz's "religion of animism," the religion of art; for "Demiurge, that great master and artist," that author of the "second Genesis of creatures which was to stand in open opposition to the present era" is a rival of God, an artist and an idolator (*Street* 58, 61). The second reason for her choice is that it represents Father's theories of cosmogony, the principles Father espouses and the beliefs he transmits. Father's are lessons in idol-making, lessons Ozick seeks to remedy in her version of Schulz's last manuscript. If the epigraph from Schulz's *Street of Crocodiles* suggests the idolatry resulting from adherence to a father's convictions, the epigraph from Lagerkvist's *Aftonland* intimates the sorrow following the abandonment of those convictions. A constant theme of Lagerkvist's poetry as well as his fiction is the anguished "turning away from the conventional beliefs of his forefathers" (Spector 137). For Lagerkvist that meant becoming a wanderer, an outsider, a stranger. Recalling his childhood, the speaker of "With old eyes I look back" announces, "My soul has been chosen to search far away / for hidden things, to wander under stars" (Lagerkvist 110–111). Such a person might have been "a stranger born," one who "should like to be someone else," one who, like Lars Andemening, became someone else (*Aftonland* IV). Two lines from *Aftonland,* the lines quoted in the epigraph to *The Messiah of Stockholm,* epitomize Lars's feelings about Schulz: "I am the star that mirrors itself in you. . . . Your soul is my home. I have no other" (VIII). But the chasm separating the son from his father is painfully evident in "Father and I" and "Guest of Reality," Lagerkvist's autobiographical tales, one of whose characters is called Anders, the first name of Ozick's reviewer. An outsider and a stranger himself, Schulz placed his father at the center of his consciousness and could never leave his family. Diametrically opposed and placed at the beginning of *The Messiah of Stockholm* like beacons illuminating two diverging roads, Schulz's and Lagerkvist's experiences summon up an issue essential to Ozick's third novel—the meaning of tradition to the artist.

That is the reason the novel has three fathers in it. Of those one is illusory, the others real. A symbol of inherited values, the father transmits to his offspring the psychic heritage that governs a child's destiny. Owning only the specter of a father's presence, Lars Andemening proves ineffectual as a father. If an illusion fires Lars's imagination, that same illusion desiccates the reviewer's life. Her fascination with these intertwinings emerges in Cynthia Ozick's scrupulous attention to the interrelationship between biographies and novels throughout her career: recreating biographies of other writers in her fiction, she appraises the biographies written about them as well. This kinship between biography and fiction—she called it the "two ways of imagining True Being" in "The Apprentice's Pillar," an essay she published during the same year as her novel—becomes an integral part of *The Messiah of Stockholm*. An anguished conflict in her fiction, the relationship between an artist's life and work is of huge importance for Ozick.[24]

In "Usurpation" she furnishes as competing examples the lives of Tchernikhovsky and Agnon. She continues to probe the idea of usurpation in *The Messiah of Stockholm*, not the plunderage of a writer's stories, but the appropriation of a writer's life. Akin in their preoccupation with art and idolatry, the novella and the novel reach disparate conclusions. Usurping Schulz's tales, Ozick becomes what she imagined for her narrator in "Usurpation"; but in the very act of resurrecting the Polish writer's stories on the pages of *The Messiah of Stockholm*, Ozick preserves as well as usurps. If she censures Tchernikhovsky's displacement of the patriarch's stance in the conclusion of "Usurpation," she depicts at the end of her third novel the results of too strong an identification with a patriarch. If she aligns storywriting with idolatry in "Usurpation," she envisions a book—The Book—as the source of redemption in *The Messiah of Stockholm*. For Ozick the saving text springs from the matrix of tradition like the unfettered bird rising from the Messiah.

In *The Messiah of Stockholm* Ozick appears, as Harold Bloom avers, to have modulated "our apprehension of her ancient enemies, the idols"; yet that modulation emerges not in her third novel but from the concluding essay in her second volume of essays, *Metaphor & Memory* (36). Out of her "meditation on language," "explicitly the work of metaphor," comes the "hope of regeneration," the way to mitigate idolatry. To be a "priest of the original" or else a "priest at the altar of literature" is to become a "priest of some passionate sect, for whom scripture is subordinate to the hour of sacral access" (*Messiah* 117). The tragedy of those priests is the "tragedy of the Delphic priests": "Their system is not organized toward the universalizing formulation. The tragedy of the priests is that, cut off from the uses of history, experience, and memory, they are helpless to make the future. . . . they cannot construct a heritage. They have nothing to pass on. They cannot give birth to metaphor." Calling metaphor a "priest of interpretation," Ozick proclaims it the "enemy of abstraction," the interpreter of memory; and it is through the "transforming effect of memory" that she arrives at a means to battle the incursions of idolatry, lessening her fears of it (M&M 281–82). Never a writer to rest in rigid absolutes or to accept fixed certainties, Cynthia Ozick does not offer an answer in her third novel to the vexing problem of art's relationship to reality and illusion, nor does she resolve the debate between Hebraism and Hellenism. Rather, she deepens those perplexities: *The Messiah of Stockholm* intensifies the dilemmas fundamental to her fiction.

Afterword

God's exchange of human immortality for "Life Permanent" can have rather startling consequences for humanity, as "Urn-Burial," a poem Ozick published in 1982, reveals; for as soon as life becomes permanent, "The hinge of generation would not move" and the world grows static. Those "hinges of life"— the mysteries of transition, the evanescence of transformation—are what Ozick declares writers are drawn to. In a commencement address, an occasion she called an instant of "germination," she defined that moment as the one when human beings cease being "receivers" and become "transmitters."[1] And that idea of transmittal, the capacity to inherit a culture, which she deems critical to the energy to send a culture on and to nurture the inventive force necessary to supplement and adorn culture, informs her art. Again and again she returns to the power of historical understanding, the nurturings of a heritage; for without them, the past, as well as the present, is forfeited. For Cynthia Ozick, not to receive the achievements of a tradition is tantamount to rejecting continuity: it is to renounce the claim to culture and influence.

A cultural patrimony, the "hinge of generation"—these are convictions vital to her texts and they are embodied in that complex and multiform figure, the father who threads his way through all of Ozick's fiction. In *Trust*, the novel to which *The Messiah of Stockholm* is so closely tied, the narrator's search for a father yields up the "secrets of inheritance" the mother has denied her daughter by attempting to re-father her. To the figure of the father in her first novel Ozick attaches cosmic knowledge, comprehension of the shaping cultural forces of history, the tradition necessary for "being and becoming." The strife against that tradition obsesses the tales she published five years after *Trust*. The generations are embattled in *The Pagan Rabbi*; fathers disapprove of their children and they, in turn, endeavor either to divest themselves of their fathers' heritage or to quiet the inner roil such a desire arouses. In Ozick's first collection of stories, the lure of a pagan world challenges the demands of Mosaic law. The abandonment of it lies at the heart of *Bloodshed*. To become a secularist or an impersonator, a person who desires a father other than the natural one, is to abdicate one's cultural roots and to usurp another's identity. The "dread of imagination," of "fantasy and fancy," of idolatry is the idea toward which the tales in Ozick's second collection of stories drive. That the Supreme Patriarch must not be disobeyed; that the father's gift of transmission is crucial, a link in the unbroken chain of tradition; that discontinuity brings on competition with God—these ideas inhere in "Usurpation," a tale that adds a further dimension to the figure of the patriarch, that of literary predecessor.

If the last tale in *Bloodshed* upholds continuity, the one with which Ozick's third collection commences involves rupture; but "Levitation" is countered by "Puttermesser and Xanthippe," the volume's concluding tale in which rivalry with the Supreme Patriarch dismantles the attorney. Throughout Cynthia Ozick's fiction, the father symbolizes the bond between parent and child and the link between tradition and art. In such relationships, however, there are always "significant disjunctions," losses of idealization (Bloom, *Agon* 16–51). Artistic forefathers and the struggle against them constitute the central thematic concerns of Ozick's second novel, in which the absence of an identifiable patrimony signals not artistic freedom but moral deprivation. Ozick matched that conviction two years later in the novella "Rosa," wherein a woman must finally reject the heritage her father has bequeathed in order to accept her real identity, the identity he repudiated. The significance of the father and the meaning of tradition reach a climax in Lars Andemening's obsession with Bruno Schulz, the literary figure whom the reviewer chooses as her own father. Intermeshing the various meanings attached to the father in her third novel, Ozick arrives at a cognition of art's relationship to the past, a meditation on writing itself.

At the heart of that meditation is the relationship of fiction and biography, a persistent presence in Ozick's fiction, one inextricable from her belief in continuity. Inventing lives for her tales, the storyteller also writes lives, for she is concerned to revivify the dead, to recreate them for the living, to forge a link in the chain of tradition, to "increase and broaden and generate culture." That she conceives of fiction and biography as twin forms emerges throughout her fiction and her essays. Of Leon Edel's biography of Henry James, Ozick wrote in 1982: "Nowadays we give this sort of work a special name: we call it a nonfiction novel. I am referring, of course, to Leon Edel's ingenious and beautiful biography of Henry James, which is as much the possession of Edel's imagination as it is of the exhilaratingly reported facts of James's life" (A&A 295). Of *The Way of All Flesh,* she observed in 1987: "we are being asked to pretend it is a novel. If it is a novel, we are being asked to pretend it is an autobiography. The motivation is the same: to evoke believability in a story about the perilous span between birth and death" (M&M 133). And that span, described by novelist and biographer alike, is intertwined with the discoveries of history. To the powers of history Cynthia Ozick accords judgment of facts; to biography she attributes the capacity to recreate facts in order to judge a life.

Keenly sensitive to the intrinsic interrelatedness of biography and fiction, she maintains it is the "free imagination" that biographers and novelists must own; to come to life, a biography must have the "blood-force of a novel" (M&M ix, 66). In her essays "The Apprentice's Pillar" and "Emerging Dreiser," published in the late eighties, Ozick explains the meaning of biography to our time. Against the lost convention of the novel with "its chronological representations and its claim to imitation-of-life," our Zeitgeist, Ozick alleges, has inflamed an "unslakable infatuation with the rich-blooded old novel's royal cousin" (M&M 134). Reviewing the first volume of Richard Lingeman's two-part biography of Theodore Dreiser, Ozick not only distinguishes a "biography of information" from a "biography of psychological re-creation" but she penetrates into what Lingeman leaves unexplained, Dreiser's "human predicament" (M&M 67). And more: in her observations about *Sister Carrie*, a deep understanding of literary history is revealed. Her power to solve perplexing psychic conundrums is brilliantly instanced in "Henry James's Unborn Child." There she works from the inchoate rather than from the completed, as she does with Primo Levi's *The Drowned and the Saved*. To follow her as she deciphers such enigmas is rather like watching someone gather the shards of a broken crystal object and, as if aware of invisible boundaries, restore the pieces to their original structure.

Where modern biographies are written "as if they were psychological novels, historically grounded equivalents of books written by, say, John Updike or Iris Murdoch," Ozick simultaneously renders the individual person and the general culture to which that individual is connected (Mendelson 21). If modern biographers focus on the intricacies of interior being at the expense of the exterior cultural and historical backgrounds, Ozick associates her subject with an inherited ancestry. The fashionable emphasis on the self, whether in fiction or in biography, as divided from a heritage is for Cynthia Ozick like a heap of disparate events lacking connection and organization; amassed without direction or judgment, facts yield partial truths, only intimations of insights. Whirling up from all her reflections on biography are multiple revelations about the uses of imaginative writing and the nature of literary culture itself.

We live in a time when few are engaged with such large questions. Nowadays an aloof intellectuality predominates, yielding not insight into the meaning of a literary text, not comprehension of feeling and thought, not discovery of moral values, not disclosure of human existence, but a proliferation of literary-critical schools and *isms* which undertake to decontextualize literature and to enshrine method. What they have brought about is disconnection and isolation—amnesia of literary culture in its largest sense, nihilism. What Cynthia Ozick presses toward is something else. Writing about Sholem Aleichem, for example, she ushers us into the center of a writer's culture.[2] We discover the history of that writer's language; she recreates his life, and with the full knowledge of the writer's context we arrive at the mainspring of the writer's art. At the center of the universe, Ozick sees not the isolated self but the self as a product of its civilization. Writing lives, she interweaves the authenticating power of facts, the decoding power of psychology, and the shaping power of fiction; like a historian she judges deeds and their consequences. Virginia Woolf's notion of biography as "betwixt and between" art and fact is challenged by Ozick's conception of biography, for facts have a different significance for Cynthia Ozick than they had for Virginia Woolf (Woolf 196). Granite can be wed to rainbow.

From that wedding comes restoration. And it is to the restoration of artists' lives Ozick is drawn: they are what she judges, their lives are what she interprets. Hers is an unfashionable position. If she has argued against the "biographical fallacy" in penetrating Eliot's life to elucidate his poems, she addresses herself to what are now commonplaces of academic criticism, which hews to the ideology of relativism, cultural and interpretive, and which has thrown the very idea of the author into question. For Ozick as for T. S. Eliot, the death of the author has a very different meaning from what is has come to signify nowadays: "Nor am I ready to relinquish Eliot's stunning declaration that the reason we know so much more than the dead writers knew is that 'they are that which we know' " (TSE 124–25). She strives, in other words, to uphold tradition in art and to connect the individual talent, as a life and a personality, to that tradition. In her refusal to divide the author from the text, Ozick reaffirms the writer's creative and communicative power and makes the texts that writers construct their own rather than autonomous products of readers. To those who would deny the meaning in a text save in the context of interpretation, Ozick responds: books are "not simply . . . the instruments of knowing, but also of feeling, of doing, of being, of remembering, of empowering. Books are extra lives; they read us and translate us from the condition of receivers or inheritors to the condition of transmitters or teachers or nourishers or endowers or endurers.—Or masters" (Commencement Speech).

Suffused with the values Ozick accords to tradition—its capacity to endow and to empower—the statement urges new perceptions, intimates a distinction between tradition and invention, even a contradiction. Closely related and deeply dependent, the two terms shape the dialectical nature of Ozick's work. The storyteller's complex attitude toward tradition is illuminated in Harold Bloom's observation on the "facticity of tradition":

> The authority of so immense and so somber a history must compel awe and at least some recognition in every sensitive consciousness exposed to that tradition. This awe tends to obscure a curious truth about Jewish identity, or perhaps of any people's identity; always changing, such identity conceals its changes under the masks of the normative. The authority of identity is not constancy-in-change, but the originality that usurps tradition and becomes a fresh authority, strangely in the name of continuity. (Poetics 353)

Usurpation and continuity collide throughout Ozick's texts. They are the opposing forces in all of the characters the storyteller creates; for those forces fuel and ignite her own "unholy conflict," which endeavors on the one hand to maintain the nourishing ties to tradition and on the other, to aspire to the condition of Inventor. The boldness of her originality lies in her intricate transformation of tradition, in her dialectical apprehension of it, in her strong writing in the Bloomian sense. Her essays and stories balance two meanings and are frequently irreconcilable. Individual stories are double-natured within the same tale and often assume shifting implications, for she is concerned to show the doubling involved in all identity. Hers is a consciousness that apprehends ideas through a prism of its own, which splits into many colors the rather austere light others glimpse. To view her art in that light is to miss her lavishing imagination, to misconstrue the laws that govern her fiction; it is to be blind to what is uniquely and supremely Cynthia Ozick.

Notes

PREFACE

1. The words are Leon Edel's (WL 27).
2. For a recent articulation of this viewpoint, see Friedman (59).
3. See, for example, the full-length studies of Ozick's work by Pinsker and Lowin, published in the late eighties, in which Ozick is either proclaimed an "uncompromising" Jewish writer or enshrined as a titan of Jewish literature.
4. The words are Ozick's and are quoted in Kremer (219).
5. Cynthia Ozick made these remarks at a farewell tribute to Abraham Atik of the National Foundation for Jewish Culture, 11 June 1989.
6. For a related and important statement on this issue, see Ruth Wisse's essay, "The Hebrew Imperative." That many critics continue to use Ozick's art the way "some Jews have tried to use American Jewish literature" namely, "as a means of shoring up their own and their community's sense of identity" is evident in their choice of which of Ozick's stories to discuss and which to avoid (Wisse 36).

ONE. THE STRUGGLE FOR EXACTITUDE

1. In an essay "We Are the Crazy Lady and Other Feisty Feminist Fables" and in two interviews—one with Catherine Rainwater and William Scheick, the other with Tom Teicholz—Ozick describes the years of apprenticeship that preceded the writing of *Trust*. Before she wrote it, Ozick had completed two other novels, *Mercy, Pity, Peace, and Love* and *The Conversion of John Andersmall*, neither of which has been published.
2. Ozick's honor's thesis, "Lyricism and the Oversoul: Conscience and Mysticism in the Poetry of Blake, Coleridge, Wordsworth, and Shelley," which she wrote as an undergraduate at New York University, reveals her early and strong interest in philosophy.
3. Victor Strandberg's reading of *Trust* differs completely from the one offered here, both in its focus and conclusion.
4. Elisa New reviews the current critical books on Cynthia Ozick's fiction and provides commentary on the novelist's stature. Two of the books New discusses—one by Pinsker, the other by Lowin—either regard *Trust* as a novel with "thickly textured 'meditations' . . . longer on ideas than . . . on dramatically realized characters" or as an "exquisitely artful" novel but one whose "superabundance of language often . . . takes on the characteristics of a luxury, and like a fine champagne imbibed in doses too large by someone not accustomed to it, it can cause a relentlessly painful sensation" (Pinsker 24; Lowin 32–33). S. Lillian Kremer argues that "it is through Holocaust subject matter and the character of Enoch Vand, the only Jew in the novel and the only character who undergoes a major intellectual and moral transformation, that Cynthia Ozick emerges as a Jewish writer" (219).
5. F. R. Leavis, quoted in *The Portrait of a Lady*, ed. Leon Edel (xvii).
6. Ozick redefines innovation and redemption in her essay, "Innovation and Redemption: What Literature Means" (A&A 238–48).
7. See Boose and Flowers, for example.
8. In "We Are the Crazy Lady and Other Feisty Feminist Fables," Ozick writes that parts 3 and 4 were originally titled "Birth" and "Death" (681).
9. Compare this process with Ozick's discussion of Updike's *Bech* (A&A 122).
10. Strandberg comments on James's reaction to the "outbreak of World War I" and on the distinction between Ozick's comparison of Europe and America and James's (87).

11. Although Strandberg observes this Jamesian juxtaposition of Europe and America, he overlooks Enoch Vand's echoing the preface to *The Portrait* and claims that Tilbeck "is a singular example of Europe at its best," a questionable view since Tilbeck was untroubled by Germany in 1938 (89).

12. Ozick revealed the significance of Enoch's last name to Kremer (235).

13. Compare Enoch 43:3 and the "storehouse of beings."

14. Michael Meyer's collection contains examples of the Jewish idea of history.

15. Compare the statement Ozick makes in "On Living in the Gentile World" (173) with Enoch's declaration in *Trust* (172).

16. On the symbolism of the Inverted Tree, see Scholem (*Kabbalah* 105–16).

17. Eliade, *Rites and Symbols,* discusses the significance of trees in initiation rites (5, 6, 17–18, 67, 77–78, 89, 90, 93–94, 100, 119, 130). See Lewin (28–32), for the sun as an image of the father.

18. See, for example 1.216, and compare 1.103, 120, 255 where Odysseus stands in doorways. In 1.344–45, the double doors "fitted together with two halves."

19. For information on *Navapatrika* and an extensive analysis of the role vegetation plays in regeneration rites, see Eliade (*Patterns* 265–330).

20. For a discussion of Arcady, see Panofsky (295–320).

21. In the Second Letter (*Structure* 195) of Graetz's "Correspondence on Judaism and Semitism," the historian writes, "An idyll can survive only in a quiet corner; how can it possibly assert itself in the raucous, strident life of the present?"

22. Strandberg (94–96) argues that Nick's island "harbors like an Eleusinian mystery, nature's deeply immanent Life Force." Given the ambivalence of these gods, the events on the island must be seen in a dual light: the girl's initiation has as well as life-giving elements certain sinister ones.

23. See Kerényi (232) and Eliade (*Rites* 109), on the Curetes and the names associated with Persephone.

24. Eliade (*History* 1:300) identifies the time of year the Mysteries took place.

25. My discussion of the Mystery religions and the Gnostic tradition is derived from Eliade (*History* 2:280, 380–84).

26. Strandberg points to the "teachings of Gnosticism" as the "ideology which undergirds" this scene (98).

27. On this see Eliade (*Rites* 129).

28. Compare Eliade (*Cosmos and History* 12–17).

29. Compare Eliade (*Rites* 108–9). And see Eisler (346), on the labyrinth and birth in dreams.

30. Brower elucidates the metaphor of change in *The Tempest*.

31. Strandberg (98) explains the Christian symbolism in this scene.

32. In *History* (2:188), Eliade writes, "Zeus swallows Phanes [Eros] and the whole creation and produces a new world."

33. Strandberg (100) interprets this scene as one evoking Zeus and the swan.

34. For the "picture" of Poseidon in "myth," see Eliade (*Patterns* 206).

35. Strandberg points out that "in *Trust,*" Ozick has "framed her own . . . parable of the artist" (101). But exactly what that involves, it seems to me, is more complicated than the narrator's "transfiguring experience of Sacred Beauty."

36. The translation of *Et in Arcadia Ego* as well as the discussion of the imagery of time and decay in *Trust* derives from Panofsky's essay, "*Et in Arcadia Ego*."

37. The allusion is to the most famous story in all of rabbinic literature: "It happened that a certain heathen came before Shammai and said to him, 'Convert me on condition that you teach me the entire Torah while I am standing on one foot.' Shammai drove him away with the builder's measuring stick that was in his hand. He then came before Hillel who converted him. Hillel said to him, 'That which is hateful to you, do not do to your neighbor. This is the entire Torah; the rest is commentary—go and learn it'" (Babylonian Talmud, Shabbat 31a).

38. This description is based on Seltzer (283–84) and Plaut, "General Introduction to the Torah" (xviii-xxv).

39. William W. Halo (Plaut 1014–23) assesses Numbers as a literary unit in the Bible.

40. Quoted in Hertz (9).

41. Scholem (K&S 132) includes the tale in which Enoch was said to have been a cobbler.

42. Perl observes: "Half a lifetime's odyssey has been required for Odysseus to discover that life's signal adventure is the discovery of home" (19).

43. Strandberg believes the narrator chooses the legacy of self-trust, signifying that she has left "her mother's domain for her father's" (102). However, the author of the epigraph is Enoch Vand; in following him, the choice the girl makes once again reflects her divided loyalties.

44. Strandberg discusses the Purses as typical of "middle America," complete with "American characteristics" (96–97).

45. Quoted in Strandberg (82).

46. Ozick revealed this influence on her thinking in an interview with Bill Moyers in 1986.

47. On the sermon as a type of discourse embodying the difference between Hellenism and Judaism, see Baeck, "Greek and Jewish Preaching" (*Pharisees* 109–22).

48. See Baker (226, 240–41) on Shelley's use of Venus.

49. An interesting example of this is evident in the way in which the historian Heinrich Graetz's antipathy for paganism became decisive. Disparate and frequently conflicting ideas gleaned from his avid reading excited such confusion in Graetz that he underwent a crisis in his religious faith. The tumultuous experience is recorded in his diary entry for November 1835 (*History* 6:10).

TWO. THE INSISTENT SENSE OF RECOGNITION

1. Pinsker writes of Isaac's name that it hints "at the story's wider themes of father/son tension and of Oedipal sacrifice, while the Kornfield [*sic*] points toward nature" (33).

2. Eliade (*Patterns* 291), and compare the tree in *Trust* and its "burly" roots (481).

3. Jeffrey Rush claims that the rabbi's letter is a "denial of history," a "form of address which effaces the past" (51). While his point about the "four discrete units of narration" in the tale is suggestive, the letter does not efface the past; rather it returns to the past to explain the present (43).

4. This discussion is based on Urbach (214–54), Bostock (21–42, 197–214), and Guthrie (327–59).

5. In "Reflections on Jewish Theology" Scholem comments on the "three different stages in which the religious world of Judaism has unfolded" (OJJ 263–65).

6. In this connection, for example, consider Matthew Arnold's attempt to bring the Hebraic and Hellenic streams into confluence.

7. Walking is an important motif in Ozick's fiction: Edelshtein, Puttermesser, and Brill take walks, all of which lead to discoveries that are frequently painful and sometimes clarifying. Of walking Ozick remarked in an interview: "Walking is very hard for me unless I do it with a companion and we're chatting away about literature . . . I'm left with that inner hum and I hate it. It goes pounding away and everything rises up and all the *drek* . . . and all the inner, oh, what's the word? Dross, I think, and I'm left alone with that when I walk, and I dislike it. I'm frightened by it, the solitude (Interview with Kauvar 398–99).

8. In their anthology of Yiddish poetry, Irving Howe, Ruth R. Wisse, and Khone Shmeruk include an introduction on the major movements in Yiddish poetry. The *In Zikh* are discussed on pages 37–39. See also the introduction to *American Yiddish Poetry*.

9. Irving Howe, "Journey" (76).

10. On this theme in Glatstein's early poetry, see Novershtern (137). For a different reading of the Glatstein-Edelshtein issue, see Lowin (21–24).

11. In a telephone conversation on 7 July 1990 Ozick maintained she had not seen Glatstein's essay on Singer until after she had completed "Envy" and so her description of the process of translation becomes especially apt.

12. See Howe et al. for Bloch's translations.

13. Howe modifies this view by adding "that in other ways he [Singer] remains profoundly subject to the Jewish tradition. And if the Yiddish reader is inclined to slight the 'modernist' side of his work, any other reader is likely to underestimate the traditional side" ("Singer" 116). Jacob Sloan, one of Singer's translators, discusses Singer's "Yiddish detractors" and argues against Glatstein's assessment.

14. Of her fascination with the idea of "usurpation" Ozick remarked that one of her "first short stories, written for a creative writing class in college, was about plagiarism" and that using real writer's lives in fiction is for her "an act of homage" (Interview with Teicholz 178).

15. Ozick's description of the "vast brouhaha over this story" may be found in Teicholz's interview (179).

16. These comments on Schopenhauer are based on White (237–43). Interestingly enough, White's analysis of Schopenhauer's views in which "any impulse to act out of any motives whatsoever" is undermined approximates Leo Baeck's idea of romantic religion, a religion whose dictates Mr. Hencke seems to follow (238).

17. Knopp believes that "Genevieve is cast here in the familiar role of the Jew as prophet, as moral *nudnick,* chosen, perhaps choosing, to spread the gospel of truth and *mentshlekhkayt,* humaneness and compassion among the Gentiles" (25). But the name Ozick gives to her as well as her actions in the story would indicate the Jewish woman cannot be so clearly defined.

18. Strandberg claims Mr. Hencke's opening the suitcase at the end of the story is a "paradigm of his much larger and unanswerable need for innocence, brought to exposure by his remark that tomorrow he sails abroad" (107). It seems to me that Ozick exposes and answers that need in his dreams.

19. In his discussion of romantic religion, Leo Baeck explains that its adherents place their faith in the gift of divine grace that repudiates the necessity of deed and so ends in regression into the ineffectuality of yearning.

20. In "Mrs. Virginia Woolf: A Madwoman and Her Nurse," Ozick argues against the "latter-day choice of Virginia Woolf . . . as a current women's-movement avatar" on the grounds that Woolf's feminism was "classical" (A&A 51).

21. In "Torah as Feminism, Feminism as Torah," she argues that the "source for this uncompromising exclusion of the biological" is in Genesis (5:1). Her argument, like that in "Innovation and Redemption: What Literature Means" (A&A 238–48), returns to the traditional as the source for the inventive.

THREE. THE DREAD OF MOLOCH

1. Rosenfeld points out that Lushinski is a "character who will seem to many readers suspiciously like Henry Kissinger crossed with an adult version of the boy" in Kosinski's novel (77).

2. On this legend, see Ginzburg, 1, 321, 336.

3. Cf. *Trust* 421–22.

4. For legends of Esau, see Ginzberg (1:313–39).

5. Quoted in Plaut (173, n. 26).

6. Berger discusses the various theological responses to the Covenant after the Holocaust as well as its meaning in Ozick's fiction (1–35; 49–59, 120–37).

7. Strandberg comments that the "word *Jew*—abetted by the memory-evoking colors of his surroundings" leads "to a closing revelation: the name in the last two lines, of the man Lushinski had killed and buried in Warsaw" (113).

8. D'Avanzo points out that the map of Africa is analogous to Kurtz (289).

9. For a full discussion of this theme, see O'Connor (*The Lonely Voice* 78–98).

10. O'Connor (*The Lonely Voice* 91), illuminates these themes.

11. Shengold discusses the results of Chekhov's experiences with his sadistic father in "Sanity and Paranoia" (209–32).

12. Berger speculates that Bleilip's trip is a "pilgrimage," an "initiatory process," and that his visit implies "that even the most apparently acculturated of Jews is unable to resist the magnetic bond of peoplehood" (50).

13. Pinsker notices that "halves" govern the "major movements in 'Bloodshed,' " but dismissing *Trust*, he overlooks the origin of Ozick's use of halves (56).

14. Both Ruth Wisse (44) and Alan Berger (157) observe the resemblances between "Bloodshed" and Philip Roth's "Eli, the Fanatic."

15. General information on the hasidic movement may be found in Scholem (*Major Trends*, "Ninth Lecture" 325–50), and in Holtz (361–401).

16. On Judaic ideas of this era, see A. Cohen (346–89), Schechter (101–15) and Urbach (308–14).

17. For a history of the word see Schauss (300–301). In her essay "The Riddle of the Ordinary," published in 1975 (A&A 200–209), Ozick uses "instead of" to define an idol: "What is an idol? Anything that is allowed to come between ourselves and God. Anything that is instead of God. . . . There is no Instead Of. There is only the Creator" (207–8). Her notion of an idol is directly related to the modern definition of a scapegoat, as the Holocaust revealed.

18. See Roskies, "The Liturgy of Destruction" (14–52) for traditional Jewish responses to catastrophe.

19. The two positions approximate those of Emil L. Fackenheim and Richard Rubenstein. Fackenheim declared the will to live an act of defiance against the Nazis and despair a confirmation of them. For Rubenstein the death camps are a confirmation of the death of God which makes further loss impossible; he urges Jews, therefore, to substitute for traditional Judaism a pagan, nature religion.

20. Of the goats Chill explains: "This pair of identical goats was meant to remind the Jew of Jacob and Esau, who were identical twins. The goat that was dedicated to God was meant to recall Jacob who lived a life of godliness. The other goat, which was sent into the wilderness, represented Esau, who lived far away from his people. The casting of lots to decide which of the two goats was to be offered up to God and which allowed to go off into the desert was to remind the Jew of his opportunity to make his own choice between the two opposing ways of life represented by the two animals" (203).

21. For a discussion of this custom as the "essence of the Nazi system," see Fackenheim (170–71).

22. See Schechter (205ff), A. Cohen (98–99), and Urbach for a discussion of the talmudic injunctions against bloodshed.

23. In the preface to *Bloodshed*, Ozick explains why she was attracted to O'Connor's stories after completing *Trust* (4).

24. Young-Bruehl records Arendt's criticism of Heidegger (218).

25. That Clement supports the Greek way as Baeck describes it and chooses Paul Tillich to study allude to an interesting historical disagreement between the two men: the criticism Tillich leveled at Baeck for not releasing all his information about concentration camps (Young-Bruehl 364).

26. Strandberg comments that "Edelshtein himself exhibits telltale signs of cultural betrayal" (108). Clement's inability to produce, Ozick implies, results from his "cul-

tural betrayal" and is another instance of the storyteller exploring an issue from two perspectives.

27. My general observations are based on the essays in Colie and Flahiff.

28. This theme, the familial aspects in *The Princess,* has been discussed by many of James's critics. The Master's definitive biographer, Leon Edel, analyzes the biographical reasons for the many parental surrogates in *The Middle Years* (179–92). Lionel Trilling's well-known essay in *The Liberal Imagination* on *The Princess* contains a superb and detailed discussion of Hyacinth's parents and their psychological effects.

29. Trilling discusses the "elements of the legendary" in *The Princess Casamassima* as well as Hyacinth's ultimate incapacity for entering the adult world.

30. Lowin argues against this interpretation: "The major difference between the Chimeses and Una is that Una does *not* remain intact from start to finish. She undergoes an educational process" (56). Una's history, the repetitiveness of the events in her life, would suggest such a reading is untenable.

31. Maimonides, for example, was a champion of reason over the imagination.

32. Strandberg (109) links the stories through the issue of language.

33. See Montefiore and Loewe, *A Rabbinic Anthology* (298) for an example.

34. This summary is based on Band (1–29).

35. Quoted in Montefiore and Loewe (165), and compare note 1 on the use of the word "burned," where the suggestion is made that burned should be read as "derives benefit."

36. This discussion is based on the commentaries in Goldin (68–69) and in Hertz (23). Bloom sees in the crown image a reflection of the Keter (CO 3).

37. For a discussion of Ibn Gabirol's philosophy, see Husik.

38. Lowin comments on the frames in "Usurpation" and attributes to them the "commenting mode" in the tale (99). Though a frame narrative is undeniably an integral part of the tale's structure, doubling is the mode crucial to the novella.

39. In fact, she refers to the Talmud and to its several allusions to the magical power of letters. For a concise history of *gematria* and its use in the Talmud and the Kabbalah, see Scholem (K 337–43), on which this discussion is based.

40. Band (24) provides the details of the tragedy.

41. For a discussion of these issues from various points of view, see *Writing and the Holocaust,* ed. Berel Lang.

42. See, for example, Isa. 27:1 and Ps. 74:14.

43. For Strandberg this scene is important to the question of Jewish identity and to the inability to belong to an "alien culture" (110). However, the case of Tchernikhovsky seems to me not as simple as Strandberg believes, nor is Ozick's interpretation of the Hebrew poet without conflict, as the closing pages of the novella reveal. Contrary to Strandberg, "Usurpation" does not "portray the least blameworthy betrayal of the Jewish heritage"; the novella portrays the most significant betrayal—idolatry (111).

44. For the "Chain of Tradition," see Hertz, *Sayings of the Fathers,* chap. 1; for the meaning of the "Chain of Tradition" to Jewish history, see Yerushalmi (31, 66).

FOUR. THE USES OF FANTASY

1. Strandberg comments that the four tales in *Bloodshed* "make a convenient bridge from this title story of *Bloodshed* to the title story of *Levitation,* where Jewish history again transforms bloodshed into a singular mark of Jewish identity" (115).

2. Berger discusses Ozick's strategy for revealing the "difference between authentic and inauthentic Jews" in "Levitation" (54).

3. On this period of Jewish history see Ben-Sasson (388–488).

4. The story of Menachem ben Zerach is told by Graetz (*History* 4:77–78, 144–45).

5. See Schorsch's introduction to Graetz's *The Structure of Jewish History and Other Essays* for further explanation of this idea.

6. For this summary I am indebted to Kettle and to Schorer.

7. Schorer discusses the "wholly secularized life" in *Emma* (111).

8. Compare Ozick's comments on the Jew's indifference to aesthetics in "Toward a New Yiddish" (A&A 165).

9. This discussion is based on Williams's reading of book 5 of *The Faerie Queene*.

10. For the relationship of May Day and Minerva, see Graves, (WG 174).

11. This discussion and the one that follows are derived from Burkert (152–56).

12. Berger argues that at the end of "Levitation" Ozick uses a "contemporary variant of the *Luftmensch* as religious ideal" as a method to demonstrate that "authentic Jews must actually leave the world" (58).

13. Ginzberg includes in his legends one concerning the response of the dove after plucking the olive leaf: as she plucked it, she said to God: " 'O lord of the world, let my food be as bitter as the olive, but do Thou give it to me from Thy hand, rather than it should be sweet, and I be delivered into the power of men' " (1:164).

14. Joseph Cohen conceives of this story as one concerning relativity as opposed to the Newtonian absolute.

15. See Strandberg (280) for Ozick's use of Frazer's *The Golden Bough* in *Trust*. This juxtaposition of human and tree into a revelation of larger import is seen elsewhere in Ozick's fiction and is used symbolically in each context. Compare, for example, the narrator's realization in front of a blazing tree in *Trust* (480) and Isaac Kornfeld's suicide on the branches of a tree.

16. About the closing scene in "Shots," Joseph Cohen (103) comments: "the narrator picks up her camera, which Ozick describes in vaginal terms to remind us that relativity remains a seductively potent creative force, and takes a picture of the reflection of Sam and Verity in their daughter's mirror. This concluding act acknowledges the primacy of the marriage between humankind and Newton's laws."

17. In his biography of Freud, Gay explains that Freud elevated Hannibal into a symbol of " 'the contrast between the tenacity of Jewry and the origin of the Catholic Church' " (FLOT 12).

18. An example of Ozick's classical feminism, "The Sewing Harems" has been regarded as antifeminist by Sanford Pinsker, for example (90). E. M. Broner declares "Shots" antifeminist as well.

19. For a detailed discussion of Dreyfus's life and the Dreyfus affair, see Jean-Denis Bredin. Ben-Sasson (878–79) traces the relationship of antisemitism in France and the Dreyfus Affair, and Hertzberg discusses the Affair's influence on Zionism in the introduction to his book, *The Zionist Idea*.

20. This explanation is based on A. Cohen's discussion, "The Hereafter" (383–89).

21. Theodor H. Gaster explains the significance of Passover and the symbols associated with it (31–58).

22. Klein writes of the *Theaetetus* that it belongs together with the *Sophist* and the *Statesman* and that the three dialogues "are meant to be a 'trilogy,' regardless of when they were written" (3). For my reader's convenience, all my quotations from the *Theaetetus* are taken from the edition published by the Loeb Classical Library.

23. See Scholem (K&S 158–204; chap. 5, "The Idea of the Golem") and Goldsmith for discussions of the golem and the arts.

24. Harold Bloom's *Kabbalah and Criticism* (22–35) contains an illuminating explanation of the concept of the *Sefirot*.

25. On the Rite of Leah in the Lurianic Kabbalah, see Scholem (K&S 151–52).

26. These are contained in Graves (GM 1:58) and Burkert (152).

27. See, for example, Graves (WG 395) and Burkert (153).

28. See Benardete (1:189, n76) for the translation of "ringdove" as a species of wild pigeon.

29. See Scholem (K&S 150) for a discussion of the Rite of Leah.

FIVE. THE HIGH MUSE OF FUSION

1. Lowin (83) compares the roundabout way to the two ways taken by the "little Marcel of Proust's *Remembrance of Things Past*," but the word "roundabout" is a favorite of Henry James.

2. The biographical reasons for Ozick's transformation of "The Laughter of Akiva" into *The Cannibal Galaxy* are explained by a threatened lawsuit; for the history of this see Lowin (9).

3. Sokoloff discusses how Brill becomes the Other later in his life when Beulah Lilt refuses to acknowledge his Dual Curriculum ("*Cannibal Galaxy*" 246).

4. On the artists Paul Brill and Claude Lorrain, see Spencer (240–66).

5. Berger separates Brill from Fleg, claiming "Brill wanders through forty years of turbulent Jewish existence. . . . he neither enters the promised land nor does he deepen his covenant faith" (128).

6. In his introduction to *This People Israel*, Albert H. Friedlander quotes from a conversation he had with Leo Baeck: "There is a special obligation for that generation [German-Jewish children who had found refuge in America] to transmit the greatness of European Jewry's culture to America" (xxii). Baeck's statement is important to the idea of the Dual Curriculum.

7. Lowin claims that Hester Lilt is an interpreter, "not a writer of fiction. . . . She interprets Jewish fiction—midrash—and in doing so rewrites it" (86). Lowin denies to Hester Lilt what Ozick clearly accords her: an imagination such as the kind possessed by the artist.

8. See Baym (269–70) for a discussion of Hester Prynne as an artist.

9. For an analysis of the midrash upon which Hester Lilt draws and a comparison of it to the choice "post-Holocaust Jews" face, see Berger 131–32.

10. In fact, Ozick wrote an honor's thesis on the Romantics.

11. The quotations are from the well-known letter Keats wrote to George and Georgiana Keats from 14 February to 3 May 1819.

12. On the *kellipot* as "the realm of darkness," see Scholem (*Major Trends* 297; MIJ 96ff).

13. For a discussion of the shells in Jewish mysticism, see Altmann, "The Motif of Shells" (172–79).

14. It is curious that the history of Brill's fruitless pursuits has escaped comment. Pinsker, for example, never mentions the marriage, and it seems to have little relevance to Berger. Lowin (86) relegates Brill's marriage to an incident revealing "how Jewish Hester Lilt is (in Auerbach's terms)."

15. Kerényi (60–63) links Iris to the Harpies.

16. Talmon (44) discusses the night hag in the wilderness; Moses Gaster (130–62) and Barb comment on Lilith's role as water nymph, and Schwartz (4–11) traces the evolution of the legend of Lilith.

17. On the rabbis' negative ideas of women see, for example, Schwartz (18, n19).

18. Kerényi (61) points out that in Hesiod's *Theogony* Iris is a messenger to the underworld.

19. I am indebted to Hoffman for this interpretation of *The Scarlet Letter* as well as for the origin of Pearl's name—the "passage in Matthew which signifies truth and grace" (344).

20. Perkins comments "that because the poet worships Psyche in an unbelieving world, the worship must be private. It can exist only in the mind, and even in 'some untrodden region' of the mind, a place set apart and secluded where other processes of cognition will not intrude" (227). Perkins's explanation illuminates the reasons for the storyteller's divergence from the poet: the visionary imagination leads to idolatry.

21. Berger comments that the title "refers also to history; Europe's cannibalizing of the Jews" (131). Pinsker narrows the title to the issue of assimilation, calling his chapter on *The Cannibal Galaxy,* the "Astrophysics of Assimilation" (100).

22. For an interesting use of the term "aesthetic hint," see *A Small Boy and Others* in which James wonders where Couture "picked up the aesthetic hint for the beautiful Page with a Falcon" (*Auto.* 193). A form of that phrase appears in Ozick's essay on Capote, whom she criticizes for evading the "great moral hint . . . that lurks in *In Cold Blood"* (A&A 88). The phrase is refined further in the title "Bialik's Hint," which encompasses James's meaning and Ozick's.

SIX. THE MAGIC SHAWL

1. Berger remarks that "the dialectical movement between silence and speech as authentic responses to the catastrophe" is "curiously absent from Ozick's literary interpretation" of the Holocaust (58–59).

2. See Berger (53) and Lowin (109) for interpretations that attempt to join Rosa to Covenant.

3. This is a summary taken from Gillon (10–11).

4. Conflated from Gillon (10–11) and Markish (41–42).

5. Berger comments that Ozick uses Lublin and Warsaw to link the "fate of religious and assimilationist Jews" and claims that despite her religious attitudes, Rosa "exemplifies a specifically Jewish determination to survive and testify" (121).

6. To limit, as Berger does, Rosa's madness to "Wieselian moral madness," which is "anchored in the prophetic strain of Judaism," is to deny the significance of the Christian imagery in the story (122).

SEVEN. THE PULSE OF ANCESTRY

1. This experience was reported in the *New York Times* (25 March 1987), section C, 25.

2. About the reason for the dedication, Ozick (*New York Times,* 25 March 1987) said: "the reason I dedicated the book to [Roth] is very practical. I would not have known about Bruno Schulz if not for the series on Eastern European writers that Roth edited. And he also made accessible to me some of Schulz's letters that haven't been published in English."

3. Lowin believes the name "is an allusion to both the resurrected New Testament figure Lazarus and to the seventeenth-century Dutch-Jewish philosopher and theologian Baruch Spinoza, excommunicated for religious heresy by the Jewish community of Amsterdam" (146).

4. On the front page of the *New York Times Book Review* (22 March 1987)—the day *The Messiah of Stockholm* was reviewed—is a photograph of Ozick, one arm around a tree, the other holding three books, one of which she identified as *Lost Illusions* (Telephone conversation with E. Kauvar, 17 March 1987). Lowin (176, n8) quotes a sentence of a letter from Ozick in which she wrote to him upon her return from Stockholm: "The literary community lives at a high competitive pitch: a stewpot out of Balzac's *Lost Illusions"* (November 1984).

5. Lowin claims inaccurately, it seems to me, that Heidi is like Hester Lilt, a "writer of parables, of stories with hidden but necessary meanings," the "writer of *The Messiah"* (152).

6. Tadeusz Breza is not identified as the receiver of the letter in *The Messiah of Stockholm,* but the full letter has been published in Schulz's *Letters* (53).

7. A vast literature exists on the effects of childhood deprivation. For a recent study that chronicles the compulsion to repeat, see Shengold, especially 4–6, 28–29, 71–72.

8. Ozick's essay originally appeared in the *New York Times* (27 September 1987) under the title "Science and Letters—God's Work and Ours"; it was included in M&M as "Crocodiled Moats in the Kingdom of Letters."

9. Compare "North" (M&M 141) and the "time-before" that lurks in the north and the light that transfixes the imagination of a "Stockholm-bound traveler."

10. Letter from Ozick to Kauvar, 13 August 1989.

11. Naomi Sokoloff argues that *The Messiah of Stockholm* "conveys skepticism about the capacities of fiction," is "preoccupied . . . with the valuation and, especially, the devaluation of art," and "ends with a renunciation of art" (Sokoloff, "Reinventing" 183, 172, 178). I would argue that rather than devalue and renounce art, *The Messiah of Stockholm* explores the perplexities of art, the struggles of the writer who possesses particular interests, ones regarded out of the mainstream.

12. See, for example, 90, 95.

13. Shengold explains that for a deprived or abused child, "Interpretations of 'objective' reality threaten to effect the loss of the mental image of the 'good' parent, thereby restoring the danger of annihilation and its attendant traumatic anxiety" (26).

14. This and other biographical information about Schulz is from Jerzy Ficowski's introduction to *The Street of Crocodiles*.

15. Lowin's reading of Ozick's text as "not so much a rewriting of Schulz as . . . an allusion to Heidi's ability to begin anywhere and yet to wind up at the point of Schulz's murder," neglects Ozick's transformation of Schulz's Hellenism into Hebraism (160).

16. My argument against Finkelstein's view is based on Gershom Scholem's discussion of Jewish messianism.

17. Finkelstein argues that Ozick's Messiah is "true to Kafka and Schulz himself" (248).

18. Based on an interview with Ozick, Kremer identifies Moses the Righteous One as Moishe the *zaddik*, a figure of Drohobycz legend, and claims the "*tzaddik*'s bird implies the spiritual survival of Judaism after the false idols have been destroyed" (276–77).

19. Finkelstein comments that the "intensity of its [the passage's] writing indicates that Ozick herself wishes . . . that Schulz, in his masterpiece, transformed himself at last from idolater to iconoclast, from Terach to Abraham" (249). The significance of flight—a return to Covenant in Ozick's stories—would indicate otherwise.

20. See Mintz on the progress of "immediate pain" to "deeper and more abiding" pain in Lamentations (32).

21. Ozick's interest in Graves may have fired the idea of Hebe, for it is Grave's idea of Hebe to which the novelist refers.

22. See the note to line 27 in Berg and Clay (100) on the oracular shrine of Apollo Ismenios (Ashen Apollo), where the past, present, or future was revealed in Apollo's altar of ash.

23. A discussion of the ancient meanings of the eye may be found in Potts.

24. Compare that essay to her recent one, "T. S. Eliot at 101," in which Ozick concludes: "Knowledge of the life interprets—decodes—the poems: exactly what Eliot's theory of the objective correlative was designed to prevent" (144).

AFTERWORD

1. Commencement address given at Bryn Mawr College, 14 May 1988.

2. "Sholem Aleichem's Revolution" (M&M 173–98).

Works Cited

Ackerman, James S. "Jonah." *The Literary Guide to the Bible*. Ed. Robert Alter and Frank Kermode. Cambridge, Mass.: Harvard UP, 1987. 234–44.

Alter, Robert. "Defenders of the Faith." *Commentary* (July 1987): 52–55.

——. *Defenses of the Imagination: Jewish Writers and Modern Historical Crisis*. Philadelphia: Jewish Publication Society of America, 1977.

——. *The Pleasures of Reading in an Ideological Age*. New York: Simon and Schuster, 1989.

Altmann, Alexander. *Studies in Religious Philosophy and Mysticism*. Ithaca: Cornell UP, 1969.

Appelfeld, Aharon. "After the Holocaust." In Lang, *Writing* 83–92.

Arlow, Jacob. "Metaphor and the Psychoanalytic Situation." *Psychoanalytic Quarterly* 48 (1979): 363–85.

Arnheim, Rudolf. "On the Nature of Photography." *Critical Inquiry* 1 (1974): 149–61.

Arnold, Matthew. *The Complete Prose Works of Matthew Arnold*. Ann Arbor: U of Michigan P, 1965. Ed. R. H. Super. Vol. 5 of 11 vols. 1960–77.

Baeck, Leo. *The Essence of Judaism*. New York: Schocken, 1976.

——. *Judaism and Christianity*. Trans. Walter Kaufmann. New York: Atheneum, 1981.

——. *The Pharisees and Other Essays*. New York: Schocken, 1947.

——. *This People Israel*. Trans. Albert H. Friedlander. New York: Holt, Rinehart and Winston, 1964.

Baker, Carlos. *Shelley's Major Poetry: The Fabric of a Vision*. New York: Russell & Russell, 1961.

Balzac, Honoré de. *Lost Illusions*. Trans. Herbert J. Hunt. New York: Penguin, 1971.

Band, Arnold J. *Nostalgia and Nightmare*. Los Angeles: U of California P, 1968.

Baranczak, Stanislaw. "The Faces of Mastery." *The New Republic* (2 Jan. 1989): 28–34.

Barb, A. A. "The Mermaid and the Devil's Grandmother." *Journal of the Warburg and Courtauld Institute* 29 (1966): 1–23.

Baym, Nina. "The Romantic *Malgré Lui*: Hawthorne in 'The Custom House.'" *ESQ: A Journal of the American Renaissance* 19 (1973): 14–25. Rpt. in *The Scarlet Letter*. Ed. Seymour Gross. New York: Norton, 1988. 265–72.

Benardete, Seth, trans. *Plato's Theaetetus*. Chicago: U of Chicago P, 1986.

Ben-Sasson, H. H., ed. *A History of the Jewish People*. Cambridge, Mass.: Harvard UP, 1976.

Berger, Alan L. *Crisis and Covenant: The Holocaust in American Jewish Fiction*. Albany: State U of New York P, 1985.

Berger, John, and Jean Moher. *Another Way of Telling*. New York: Pantheon, 1982.

Biale, David. *Gershom Scholem: Kabbalah and Counter-History*. Cambridge, Mass.: Harvard UP, 1982.

Blissett, W. F. "Recognition in *King Lear*." In Colie and Flahiff, *Some Facets*. 103–16.

Bloom, Harold. *Agon: Towards a Theory of Revisionism*. New York: Oxford UP, 1982.

——. *The Anxiety of Influence*. New York: Oxford UP, 1973.

——. "The Book of the Father." Rev. of *The Messiah of Stockholm*, by Cynthia Ozick. *The New York Times Book Review* (22 March 1987): 1, 36.

——. *Kabbalah and Criticism*. New York: Continuum, 1975.

——. *Poetics of Influence*. New Haven: Schwab, 1988.

——, ed. *Cynthia Ozick: Modern Critical Views*. New York: Chelsea, 1986.

Boose, Lynda E., and Betty S. Flowers, eds. *Fathers and Daughters*. Baltimore: Johns Hopkins UP, 1988.

Bostock, David. *Plato's Phaedo*. New York: Oxford UP, 1986.

Bredin, Jean-Denis. *The Affair: The Case of Alfred Dreyfus*. Trans. Jeffrey Mehlman. New York: Braziller, 1986.

Brion, Marcel. *Pompeii and Herculaneum: The Glory and the Grief*. New York: Crown, 1960.

Broner, E. M. "The Five Fictions of Cynthia Ozick: 'Dazzling but Worrisome.' " Rev. of *Levitation: Five Fictions*, by Cynthia Ozick. *Ms.* (April 1982): 94, 96.

Brower, Reuben A. "The Mirror of Analogy": "*The Tempest*." *Fields of Light*. New York: Oxford UP, 1951. Rpt. in *The Tempest*. Ed. Robert Langbaum. New York: New American Library, 1964. 182–205.

Burkert, Walter. *Greek Religion*. Trans. John Raffan. Cambridge, Mass.: Harvard UP, 1985.

Carmi, T., ed. and trans. *The Penguin Book of Hebrew Verse*. New York: Penguin, 1981.

Charlesworth, James H. *The Old Testament Pseudepigrapha*. 2 vols. New York: Doubleday, 1983.

Chekhov, Anton. *Ward Number Six and Other Stories*. Trans. Ronald Hingley. New York: Oxford UP, 1988.

Chill, Abraham. *The Mitzvot: The Commandments and Their Rationale*. New York: Bloch, 1974.

Cohen, A. *Everyman's Talmud*. New York: Schocken, 1975.

Cohen, Joseph. " 'Shots': A Case History of the Conflict between Relativity Theory and the Newtonian Absolutes." In Walden, *World*. 96–104.

Cohen, Sarah Blacher. "Ozick and Her New Yiddish Golem." In Walden, *World*. 105–10.

Colie, Rosalie L., and F. T. Flahiff, eds. *Some Facets of King Lear*. Toronto: U of Toronto P, 1974.

Crane, Hart. *The Complete Poems*. New York: Doubleday, 1958.

D'Avanzo, Mario. "Conrad's Motley as an Organizing Metaphor." *College Language Association Journal* 9 (1966): 289–91. Rpt. in *Heart of Darkness*. Ed. Robert Kimbrough. New York: Norton, 1971.

Edel, Leon. *The Middle Years*. Philadelphia: Lippincott, 1962.

——. *Writing Lives: Principia Biographica*. New York: Norton, 1987.

Eiland, Howard. "Heidegger's Political Engagement." *Salmagundi* 70–71 (Spring–Summer 1986): 267–84.

Eisler, Joseph. "The Labyrinth." *The Psychoanalytic Reader*. Ed. Robert Fliess. New York: International UP, 1948. 346–47.

Eliade, Mircea. *Cosmos and History*. Trans. Willard R. Trask. New York: Harper & Row, 1959.

——. *A History of Religious Ideas*. 3 vols. Trans. Willard R. Trask. Chicago: U of Chicago P, 1978–85.

——. *Patterns in Contemporary Religion*. Trans. Rosemary Sheed. New York: New American Library, 1958.

——. *Rites and Symbols of Initiation: The Mysteries of Birth and Rebirth*. Trans. Willard R. Trask. New York: Harper & Row, 1958.

Erdman, David E., ed. *The Poetry and Prose of William Blake*. New York: Doubleday, 1968.

Fackenheim, Emil L. "The Human Condition after Auschwitz." *Understanding Jewish Theology*. Ed. Jacob Neusner. New York: KTAV, 1973. 165–75.

Feidelson, Charles. *Symbolism and American Literature*. Chicago: U of Chicago P, 1953.

Fein, Richard J., ed. *Selected Poems of Yankev Glatshteyn*. Philadelphia: Jewish Publication Society, 1988.

Finkelstein, Norman. "From Drohobycz to Stockholm." *Salmagundi* 76–77 (1987–1988): 245–49.

Fleg, Edmond. *Why I Am a Jew.* Trans. Louise Waterman Wise. New York: Bloch, 1945.

Freidman, Lawrence S. *Understanding Cynthia Ozick.* Columbia: U of South Carolina P, 1991.

Freud, Sigmund. "Family Romances." Trans. James Strachey. Rpt. in *The Sexual Enlightenment of Children.* New York: Collier, 1978.

——. *Introductory Lectures on Psychoanalysis.* Trans. and ed. James Strachey. New York: Norton, 1977.

Gaster, Moses. "Two Thousand Years of a Charm against the Child-Stealing Witch." *Studies and Texts in Folklore, Magic, Mediaeval Romance, Hebrew Apocrypha, and Samaritan Archaeology.* Vol. 2. New York: KTAV, 1971.

Gaster, Theodor H. *Festivals of the Jewish Year.* New York: Morrow, 1978.

Gay, Peter. *Freud: A Life for Our Time.* New York: Norton, 1988.

——. *Freud, Jews and Other Germans.* New York: Oxford UP, 1978.

Gillon, Adam, ed. *The Dancing Socrates and Other Poems,* by Julian Tuwim. New York: Twayne, 1968.

Ginzberg, Louis. *The Legends of the Jews.* 7 vols. Philadelphia: Jewish Publication Society of America, 1909–38.

Glatstein, Jacob. "The Fame of Bashevis Singer." *Congress Bi-Weekly* (27 Dec. 1965): 17–19.

Goethe, Johann Wolfgang. *Goethe: Selected Verse.* Ed. David Luke. New York: Penguin, 1964.

Goldin, Judah, ed. and trans. *The Living Talmud: The Wisdom of the Fathers.* New York: Mentor, 1957.

Goldsmith, Arnold L. *The Golem Remembered, 1909–1980.* Detroit: Wayne State UP, 1981.

Gömöri, George. *Polish and Hungarian Poetry, 1945–1956.* London: Oxford UP, 1966.

Goodheart, Eugene. "*Trust.*" In Bloom, CO. 11–14.

Graetz, Heinrich. *History of the Jews.* 6 vols. Philadelphia: Jewish Publication Society of America, 1895.

——. *The Structure of Jewish History and Other Essays.* Trans. and ed. Ismar Schorsch. New York: Jewish Theological Seminary of America, 1975.

Graves, Robert. *The Greek Myths.* 2 vols. New York: Penguin, 1960.

——. *The White Goddess.* New York: Noonday, 1988.

Guthrie, W. K. C. *A History of Greek Philosophy.* Vol. 4. Cambridge: Cambridge UP, 1975.

Hallo, William W. "Numbers and Ancient Near Eastern Literature." In Plaut, *The Torah: A Modern Commentary.* 1014–23.

Harshav, Benjamin, and Barbara Harshav, eds. *American Yiddish Poetry.* Berkeley: U of California P, 1988.

Hawthorne, Nathaniel. *The Scarlet Letter.* Ed. Seymour Gross et al. New York: Norton, 1988.

Hertz, Joseph H., ed. and trans. *Sayings of the Fathers.* New York: Behrman, 1945.

Hertzberg, Arthur, ed. *The Zionist Idea.* New York: Atheneum, 1986.

Hoffman, Daniel G. *Form and Fable in American Fiction.* New York: Oxford UP, 1961. Rpt. as "Hester's Double Providence" in *The Scarlet Letter.* Ed. Seymour Gross. New York: Norton, 1988. 343–49.

Holtz, Barry, ed. *Back to the Sources: Reading the Classic Jewish Texts.* New York: Summit, 1984.

Homer. *The Odyssey.* Trans. Richard Lattimore. New York: Harper & Row, 1965.

Howe, Irving, "I. B. Singer." *Critical Views of Isaac Bashevis Singer.* Ed. Irving Malin. New York: New York UP, 1969. 100–19.

——. "Journey of a Poet." *Commentary* (Jan. 1972): 75–77.

Howe, Irving, Ruth R. Wisse, and Khone Shmeruk, eds. *The Penguin Book of Modern Yiddish Verse*. New York: Viking, 1987.

Husik, Isaac. *A History of Mediaeval Jewish Philosophy*. New York and Philadelphia: Meridian and Jewish Publication Society, 1960.

Ibn Gabirol, Solomon. *Selected Religious Poems of Solomon Ibn Gabirol*. Ed. Israel Zangwill. Philadelphia: Jewish Publication Society of America, 1932.

James, Henry. *The Ambassadors*. Ed. S. P. Rosenbaum. New York: Norton, 1964.

——. *The Art of the Novel*. Boston: Northeastern UP, 1984.

——. *The Aspern Papers*. Ed. Adrian Poole. New York: Oxford UP, 1983.

——. *Autobiography*. Ed. Frederick W. Dupee. Princeton: Princeton UP, 1983.

——. *Eight Tales from the Major Phase*. Ed. Morton Dauwen Zabel. New York: Norton, 1958.

——. *The Portrait of a Lady*. Ed. Leon Edel. Boston: Houghton Mifflin, 1963.

——. *The Portrait of a Lady*. Ed. Robert D. Bamberg. New York: Norton, 1975.

——. *The Princess Casamassima*. Ed. Derek Brewer. New York: Penguin, 1987.

——. *Tales of Art and Life*. Ed. Henry Terrie. New York: Union College P, 1984.

Jameson, Fredric. "Postmodernism and Consumer Society." *The Anti-Aesthetic: Essays on Postmodern Culture*. Ed. Hal Foster. Washington: Bay, 1983. 111–25.

Katz, Steven T. *Post-Holocaust Dialogues: Critical Studies in Modern Jewish Thought*. New York: New York UP, 1983.

Kaufmann, Yehezkiel. "The Biblical Age." *Great Ages and Ideas of the Jewish People*. Ed. Leo Schwarz. New York: Modern Library, 1956.

——. *The Religion of Israel*. Trans. Moshe Greenberg. New York: Schocken, 1972.

Keats, John. *Letters*. 2 vols. Ed. Hyder Edward Rollins. Cambridge, Mass.: Harvard UP, 1958.

Kerényi, C. *The Gods of the Greeks*. Trans. Norman Cameron. New York: Thames and Hudson, 1979.

Kettle, Arnold. "*Emma*." (Originally entitled "Jane Austen: *Emma* (1816).") *An Introduction to the English Novel*, vol. 1. Rpt. in Watt, *Jane Austen*. 112–23.

Klein, Jacob. *Plato's Trilogy*. Chicago: U of Chicago P, 1977.

Knopp, Josephine Z. "Ozick's Jewish Stories." In Bloom, CO. 21–29.

Kosinski, Jerzy. *The Painted Bird*. New York: Bantam, 1972.

Kremer, S. Lillian. *Witness through the Imagination: Jewish American Holocaust Literature*. Detroit: Wayne State UP, 1989.

Lagerkvist, Pär. *Evening Land*. Trans. W. H. Auden and Leif Sjöberg. Detroit: Wayne State UP, 1975.

Lang, Berel, ed. *Writing and the Holocaust*. New York: Holmes & Meier, 1988.

Levi, Primo. *Survival in Auschwitz*. New York: Macmillan, 1961.

Lewin, Bertram D. *The Image and the Past*. New York: International UP, 1968.

Louÿs, Pierre. *Aphrodite*. Trans. Lewis Galantière. New York: Modern Library, 1933.

Lowin, Joseph. *Cynthia Ozick*. Boston: Twayne, 1988.

Mack, Maynard. "The World of Hamlet." *The Yale Review* 41 (1952): 502–23. Rpt. in *Shakespeare: Modern Essays in Criticism*. Ed. Leonard F. Dean. New York: Oxford UP, 1957. 237–57.

Malamud, Bernard. *Rembrandt's Hat*. New York: Farrar Straus Giroux, 1973.

Markish, Simon. "A Russian Writer's Jewish Fate." *Commentary* (April 1986): 41–42.

Medcalf, Stephen. "Virgil's 'Aeneid.' " *The Classical World*. Ed. David Daiches and Anthony Thorlby. London: Aldus, 1972. 297–326.

Mendelson, Edward. "Authorized Biography and Its Discontents." *Studies in Biography*. Ed. Daniel Aaron. Cambridge, Mass.: Harvard UP, 1978. 9–26.

Mendelssohn, Moses. *Jerusalem*. Trans. Allan Arkush. Hanover: UP of New England, 1983.

Meyer, Michael A., ed. *Ideas of Jewish History*. New York: Behrman, 1974.

Mintz, Alan. *Hurban: Responses to Catastrophe in Hebrew Literature*. New York: Columbia UP, 1984.

Miron, Dan. "Domesticating a Foreign Genre: Agnon's Transactions with the Novel." *Prooftexts* 7.1 (1987): 1–28.

Montefiore, C. G., and H. Loewe. *A Rabbinic Anthology*. New York: Schocken, 1974.

Murphy, Francis, ed. *Walt Whitman: The Complete Poems*. New York: Penguin, 1987.

Neher, André. *The Exile of the Word: From the Silence of the Bible to the Silence of Auschwitz*. Trans. David Maisel. Philadelphia: Jewish Publication Society of America, 1981.

New, Elisa. "Cynthia Ozick's Timing." *Prooftexts* 9.3 (1989): 288–94.

Novershtern, Abraham. "The Young Glatstein and the Structure of His First Book of Poems." *Prooftexts* 6.2 (1986): 131–46.

O'Connor, Frank. *Collected Stories*. New York: Vintage, 1982.

——. *The Lonely Voice*. New York: World, 1965.

Onians, Richard B. *The Origins of European Thought about the Body, the Mind, the Soul, the World, Time, and Fate*. Cambridge: Cambridge UP, 1951.

Ozick, Cynthia. *Art &Ardor*. 1983. Reprint. New York: Dutton, 1984.

——. "A Bintel Brief for Jacob Glatstein," *Jewish Heritage* 14 (Sept. 1972): 58–60.

——. *Bloodshed and Three Novellas*. 1976. Reprint. New York: Dutton, 1983.

——. *The Cannibal Galaxy*. New York: Knopf, 1983.

——. "Caryatid." *New Mexico Quarterly* (Winter 1963–64): 426.

——. Commencement address. Bryn Mawr College, Pennsylvania, 14 May 1988.

——. Farewell Tribute to Abraham Atik. Jewish Theological Seminary, New York City, 11 June 1989.

——. Interview. *Contemporary Literature*. With Elaine M. Kauvar. 26.4 (1985): 375–401.

——. Interview. *Heritage Conversations*. With Bill Moyers. WNET-TV, New York. 3 April 1986.

——. Interview. *The Paris Review*. With Tom Teicholz. 102 (1987): 154–90.

——. Interview. *Texas Studies in Language and Literature*. With Catherine Rainwater and William J. Scheick. 25.2 (1983): 255–65.

——. "The Jamesian Parable: The Sacred Fount." *Bucknell Review* 11 (1963): 55–70.

——. *Levitation: Five Fictions*. 1982. Reprint. New York: Dutton, 1983.

——. *The Messiah of Stockholm*. New York: Knopf, 1985.

——. *Metaphor & Memory*. New York: Knopf, 1989.

——. "On Living in a Gentile World." *Modern Jewish Thought*. Ed. Nahum N. Glatzer. New York: Schocken, 1977.

——. *The Pagan Rabbi and Other Stories*. 1971. Reprint. New York: Dutton, 1983.

——. "Parable in the Later Novels of Henry James." M.A. thesis, Ohio State University, 1950.

——. "Poetry and the Parochial." *Congress Monthly* (Nov.–Dec. 1986): 7–10.

——. "Roundtable Discussion." *Writing and the Holocaust*. Ed. Berel Lang. New York: Holmes & Meier, 1988. 277–84.

——. *The Shawl*. New York: Knopf, 1989.

——. "Stone." *Botteghe Oscure* 20 (1957): 388–414.

——. "Torah as Feminism, Feminism as Torah." *Congress Monthly* (Sept.–Oct. 1984): 7–10.

——. "T. S. Eliot at 101." *The New Yorker* (20 Nov. 1989): 119–54.

——. *Trust*. 1966. Reprint. New York: Dutton, 1983.

——. "Urn-Burial." *The Literary Review* 25 (Summer 1982): 613–16.

——. "We Are the Crazy Lady and Other Feisty Feminist Fables." *Ms.* 1 (Spring 1972): 40–44. Rpt. in *The Dolphin Reader*. Ed. Douglas Hunt. Boston: Houghton Mifflin, 1990. 672–83.

——. "The Young Self and the Old Writer." In Walden, *World*. 164–67.

Panofsky, Erwin. "*Et in Arcadia Ego:* Poussin and the Elegiac Tradition." *Meaning in the Visual Arts.* New York: Doubleday, 1957. 295–320.

Perkins, David. *The Quest for Permanence.* Cambridge, Mass.: Harvard UP, 1965.

Perl, Jeffrey M. *The Tradition of Return: The Implicit History of Modern Literature.* New Jersey: Princeton UP, 1984.

Pinsker, Sanford. *The Uncompromising Fictions of Cynthia Ozick.* Columbia: U of Missouri P, 1987.

Plato, *Phaedo.* Trans. G. M. A. Grube. Indianapolis: Hackett, 1977.

——. *Theaetetus. Sophist.* Loeb Classical Library. Vol. 7. Trans. H. N. Fowler. Cambridge, Mass.: Harvard UP, 1977. 7–257.

Plaut, W. Gunther, ed. *The Torah: A Modern Commentary.* New York: Union of American Hebrew Congregations, 1981.

Potts. A. M. *The World's Eye.* Lexington: U of Kentucky P, 1981.

Putnam, Michael C. J. *The Poetry of the Aeneid.* Ithaca: Cornell UP, 1988.

Riess, Anneliese. "The Power of the Eye in Nature, Nurture, and Culture." *The Psychoanalytic Study of the Child.* Vol. 43. New Haven: Yale UP, 1988. 399–421.

Rosenfeld, Alvin H. "Cynthia Ozick: Fiction and the Jewish Idea." *Midstream* 23 (1977): 76–81.

Roskies, David G. *Against the Apocalypse: Responses to Catastrophe in Modern Jewish Culture.* Cambridge, Mass.: Harvard UP, 1984.

Rush, Jeffrey. "Talking to Trees: Address as Metaphor in 'The Pagan Rabbi.' " In *Walden, World.* 46–52.

Sabiston, Elizabeth. "Isabel Archer: The Architecture of Consciousness and the International Theme." *The Henry James Review: New Essays on The Portrait of a Lady.* Ed. Daniel Mark Fogel. 7 (1986): 29–47.

Schauss, Hayyim. *The Jewish Festivals, History and Observance.* Trans. Samuel Jaffe. New York: Schocken, 1938.

Schechter, Solomon. *Aspects of Rabbinic Theology.* New York: Schocken Press, 1961.

Scholem, Gershom. *Kabbalah.* New York: New American Library, 1978.

——. *Major Trends in Jewish Mysticism.* New York: Schocken, 1961.

——. *The Messianic Idea in Judaism.* New York: Schocken, 1971.

——. *On Jews and Judaism in Crisis.* Ed. Werner J. Dannhauser. New York: Schocken, 1978.

——. *On the Kabbalah and Its Symbolism.* Trans. Ralph Manheim. 1969.

——, ed. *Zohar.* New York: Schocken, 1963.

Schorer, Mark. "The Humiliation of Emma Woodhouse." *The Literary Review* 2.4 (1959): 547–63. Rpt. in Watt, *Jane Austen.* 98–111.

Schulz, Bruno. *Letters and Drawings of Bruno Schulz.* Ed. Jerzy Ficowski. New York: Harper & Row, 1988.

——. *Sanatorium under the Sign of the Hourglass.* Trans. Celina Wieniewska. New York: Penguin, 1979.

——. *The Street of Crocodiles.* Trans. Celina Wieniewska. New York: Penguin, 1977.

Schwartz, Howard. *Lilith's Cave.* New York: Harper & Row, 1988.

Seltzer, Robert M. *Jewish People, Jewish Thought: The Jewish Experience in History.* New York: Macmillan, 1980.

Shakespeare, William. *King Lear.* Ed. Russell Fraser. New York: New American Library, 1987.

Shengold, Leonard. *Soul Murder: The Effects of Childhood Abuse and Deprivation.* New Haven: Yale UP, 1989.

Silberschlag, Eisig. *Saul Tschernichowsky: Poet of Revolt.* Ithaca: Cornell UP, 1968.

Simmons, Ernest J. *Chekhov: A Biography.* Boston: Little, Brown, 1962.

Sloan, Jacob. "I. B. Singer and His Yiddish Critics." *Congress Bi-Weekly* (7 Mar. 1966): 4–5.

Sokoloff, Naomi. "Cynthia Ozick's *Cannibal Galaxy.*" *Prooftexts* 6.3 (1986): 239–57.

——. "Reinventing Bruno Schulz: Cynthia Ozick's *The Messiah of Stockholm* and David Grossman's *See Under: Love.*" *The Journal of the Association for Jewish Studies* 13 (Spring and Fall 1988): 171–99.

Sophocles. *Oedipus the King.* Trans. Stephen Berg and Diskin Clay. New York: Oxford UP, 1978.

Spector, Robert D. *Pär Lagerkvist.* New York: Twayne, 1973.

Spencer, Jeffrey B. *Heroic Nature.* Evanston: Northwestern UP, 1973.

Stanley, Henry. *Through the Dark Continent.* Vol. 1. New York: Harper, 1878.

Steiner, George. *Language and Silence.* New York: Atheneum, 1982.

Stevenson, David L. "Daughter's Reprieve." In Bloom, CO. 9–10.

Strandberg, Victor. "The Art of Cynthia Ozick." In Bloom, CO. 79–120.

Talmon, Shemaryahu. "The 'Desert Motif' in the Bible and in Qumran Literature." *Biblical Motifs: Origins and Transformations.* Ed. Alexander Altmann. Cambridge, Mass.: Harvard UP, 1966. 31–63.

Tillich, Paul. *The Courage to Be.* New Haven: Yale UP, 1952.

Trilling, Lionel. "Art, Will, and Necessity." *The Last Decade.* New York: Harcourt Brace Jovanovich, 1977. 129–47.

——. "*The Princess Casamassima.*" *The Liberal Imagination.* New York: Harcourt Brace Jovanovich, 1979.

Urbach, Ephraim E. *The Sages.* Trans. Israel Abrahams. Cambridge, Mass.: Harvard UP, 1987.

Van Ghent, Dorothy. "On *The Portrait of a Lady.*" *The English Novel: Form and Function.* New York: Holt, Rinehart & Winston, 1953. Rpt. in *The Portrait of a Lady.* Ed. Robert D. Bamberg. New York: Norton, 1975. 698–703.

Virgil. *The Aeneid.* Trans. Rolfe Humphries. New York: Scribner's, 1951.

Walden, Daniel, ed. *The World of Cynthia Ozick.* Spec. issue of *Studies in American Jewish Literature* 6 (Fall 1987): 164–67.

Watt, Ian, ed. *Jane Austen: A Collection of Critical Essays.* New Jersey: Prentice–Hall, 1963.

Wegelin, Christof. *The Image of Europe in Henry James.* Southern Methodist UP, 1958.

White, E. B. *Essays of E. B. White.* New York: Harper, 1977.

White, Hayden. *Metahistory: The Historical Imagination in Nineteenth-Century Europe.* Baltimore: Johns Hopkins UP, 1975.

Whitman, Ruth, ed. and trans. *The Selected Poems of Jacob Glatstein.* New York: October House, 1972.

Wiesel, Elie. *Night.* New York: Bantam, 1982.

Williams, Kathleen. *Spenser's World of Glass.* Berkeley: U of California P, 1966.

Wisse, Ruth R. "The Hebrew Imperative." *Commentary* (June 1990): 34–39.

——. "Ozick as American Jewish Writer." In Bloom, CO. 35–46.

Wolfson, Harry Austryn. *The Philosophy of Spinoza.* Cambridge, Mass.: Harvard UP, 1962.

Woolf, Virginia. *The Death of the Moth.* New York: Harcourt Brace Jovanovich, 1974.

Young-Bruehl, Elisabeth. *Hannah Arendt: For Love of the World.* New Haven: Yale UP, 1982.

Yerushalmi, Yosef Hayim. *Zakhor: Jewish History and Jewish Memory.* Philadelphia: Jewish Publication Society of America, 1982.

Index

ELAINE M. KAUVAR, Associate Professor of English at Baruch College, City University of New York, has published articles on William Blake, Jane Austen, James Joyce, and Cynthia Ozick.